UN

L 7

This
be

Olympic Legacies: Intended and Unintended

For more than a century, the Olympics have been the modern world's most significant sporting event. Indeed, they deserve much credit for globalizing sport beyond the boundaries of the Anglo-American universe, where it originated, into broader global realms. By the 1930s, the Olympics had become a global mega-event that occupied the attention of the media, the interest of the public and the energies of nation-states. Since then, projected by television, funded by global capital and fattened by the desires of nations to garner international prestige, the Olympics have grown to gargantuan dimensions.

In the course of its epic history, the Olympics have left numerous legacies, from unforgettable feats to monumental stadiums, from shining triumphs to searing tragedies, from the dazzling debuts on the world's stage of new cities and nations to notorious campaigns of national propaganda. The Olympics represent an essential component of modern global history. The Olympic movement itself has, since the 1990s, recognized and sought to shape its numerous legacies with mixed success as this book makes clear. It offers ground-breaking analyses of the power of Olympic legacies, positive and negative, and surveys the subject from Athens in 1896 to Beijing in 2008, and indeed beyond.

J.A. Mangan is a Fellow of the Royal Historical Society, Emeritus Professor, University of Strathclyde, Founding and Executive Academic Editor of The International Journal of the History of Sport and Founding Editor of the journals Sport in Society and Soccer and Society and the series Sport in the Global Society. His latest monograph, *Soccer's Missing Men: Schoolteachers and the Spread of Association Football* (with Colm Hickey) will be published by Routledge in 2009. A collection, *Beijing 2008: Preparing for Glory - Chinese Challenge in the 'Chinese Century'* (edited with Dong Jinxia) was published by Routledge in 2008.

Mark Dyreson is an associate professor of kinesiology and an affiliate professor of history at Pennsylvania State University and a former president of the North American Society for the History of Sport. With Routledge, he has published *Crafting Patriotism for Global Dominance: America at the Olympics* (2008) as well as editing, with J.A. Mangan, *Sport and American Society: Insularity, Exceptionalism and 'Imperialism'* (2007).

Olympic Legacies: Intended and Unintended

Political, Cultural, Economic and Educational

Edited by J.A. Mangan and Mark Dyreson

Routledge
Taylor & Francis Group

LONDON AND NEW YORK

First published 2010 by Routledge
2 Park Square, Milton Park, Abingdon, Oxon, OX14 4RN

Simultaneously published in the USA and Canada
by Routledge
270 Madison Avenue, New York, NY 10016

Routledge is an imprint of the Taylor & Francis Group, an informa business

© 2010 Taylor & Francis

Typeset in Minion by Value Chain, India

British Library Cataloguing in Publication Data
A catalogue record for this book is available from the British Library

ISBN10: 0-415-55016-5
ISBN13: 978-0-415-55016-1

CONTENTS

SERIES EDITORS' FOREWORD

SPORT IN THE GLOBAL SOCIETY was launched in the late nineties. It now has over one hundred volumes. Until recently an odd myopia characterised academia with regard to sport. The global *groves of academe* remained essentially Cartesian in inclination. They favoured a mind/body dichotomy: thus the study of ideas was acceptable; the study of sport was not. All that has now changed. Sport is now incorporated, intelligently, within debate about *inter alia* ideologies, power, stratification, mobility and inequality. The reason is simple. In the modern world sport is everywhere: it is as ubiquitous as war. E.J. Hobsbawm, the Marxist historian, once called it the one of the most significant of the new manifestations of late nineteenth century Europe. Today it is one of the most significant manifestations of the twenty-first century world. Such is its power, politically, culturally, economically, spiritually and aesthetically, that sport beckons the academic more persuasively than ever – to borrow, and refocus, an expression of the radical historian Peter Gay – 'to explore its familiar terrain and to wrest new interpretations from its inexhaustible materials'. As a subject for inquiry, it is replete, as he remarked of history, with profound 'questions unanswered and for that matter questions unasked'.

Sport seduces the teeming 'global village'; it is the new opiate of the masses; it is one of the great modern experiences; its attraction astonishes only the recluse; its appeal spans the globe. Without exaggeration, sport is a mirror in which nations, communities, men and women now see themselves. That reflection is sometimes bright, sometimes dark, sometimes distorted, sometimes magnified. This metaphorical mirror is a source of mass exhilaration and depression, security and insecurity, pride and humiliation, bonding and alienation. Sport, for many, has replaced religion as a source of emotional catharsis and spiritual passion, and for many, since it is among the earliest of memorable childhood experiences, it infiltrates memory, shapes enthusiasms, serves fantasies. To co-opt Gay again: it blends memory and desire.

Sport, in addition, can be a lens through which to scrutinise major themes in the political and social sciences: democracy and despotism and the great associated movements of socialism, fascism, communism and capitalism as well as political cohesion and confrontation, social reform and social stability.

The story of modern sport is the story of the modern world – in microcosm; a modern global tapestry permanently being woven. Furthermore, nationalist and imperialist, philosopher and politician, radical and conservative have all sought in sport a manifestation of national identity, status and superiority.

Finally, for countless millions sport is the personal pursuit of ambition, assertion, well-being and enjoyment.

For all the above reasons, sport demands the attention of the academic. *Sport in the Global Society* is a response.

J.A.Mangan, Boria Majumdar
and Mark Dyreson – Series Editors

Sport in the Global Society

Sport in the Global Society

Series Editors: J.A. Mangan, Boria Majumdar and Mark Dyreson

Olympic Legacies: Intended and Unintended
Political, Cultural, Economic and Educational

Sport in the Global Society

Series Editors: J.A. Mangan, Boria Majumdar and Mark Dyreson

As Robert Hands in *The Times* recently observed the growth of sports studies in recent years has been considerable. This unique series with over one hundred volumes in the last decade has played its part. Politically, culturally, emotionally and aesthetically, sport is a major force in the modern world. Its impact will grow as the world embraces ever more tightly the contemporary secular trinity: the English language, technology and sport. *Sport in the Global Society* will continue to record sport's phenomenal progress across the world stage.

Other Titles in the Series

Sport, Culture and History
Region, Nation and Globe
Brian Stoddart

Sport in Asian Society
Past and Present
Edited by Fan Hong and J.A. Mangan

Sport in Australasian Society
Past and Present
Edited by J.A. Mangan and John Nauright

Sport in Europe
Politics, Class, Gender
Edited by J.A. Mangan

Sport in Films
Edited by Emma Poulton and Martin Roderick

Sport in Latin American Society
Past and Present
Edited by Lamartine DaCosta and J.A. Mangan

Sport in South Asian Society
Past and Present
Edited by Boria Majumdar and J.A. Mangan

Sport in the City
Cultural Connections
Edited by Michael Sam and John E. Hughson

Sport in the Cultures of the Ancient World
New Perspectives
Edited by Zinon Papakonstantinou

Sport in the Pacific
Colonial and Postcolonial Consequencies
Edited by C. Richard King

Sport, Media, Culture
Global and Local Dimensions
Edited by Alina Bernstein and Neil Blain

Sport, Nationalism and Orientalism
The Asian Games
Edited by Fan Hong

Sport Past and Present in South Africa
(Trans)forming the Nation
Edited by Scarlet Cornelissen and Albert Grundlingh

Sport Tourism
Edited by Heather J. Gibson

Sporting Cultures
Hispanic Perspectives on Sport, Text and the Body
Edited by David Wood and P. Louise Johnson

Sporting Nationalisms
Identity, Ethnicity, Immigration and Assimilation
Edited by Mike Cronin and David Mayall

Superman Supreme
Fascist Body as Political Icon – Global Fascism
Edited by J.A. Mangan

Terrace Heroes
The Life and Times of the 1930s Professional Footballer
Graham Kelly

The Balkan Games and Balkan Politics in the Interwar Years 1929-1939
Politicians in Pursuit of Peace
Penelope Kissoudi

The Changing Face of Cricket
From Imperial to Global Game
Edited by Dominic Malcolm, Jon Gemmell and Nalin Mehta

The Changing Face of the Football Business
Supporters Direct
Edited by Sean Hamil, Jonathan Michie, Christine Oughton and Steven Warby

The Commercialisation of Sport
Edited by Trevor Slack

The Cultural Bond
Sport, Empire, Society
Edited by J.A. Mangan

Prologue: Guarantees of Global Goodwill: Post-Olympic Legacies – Too Many Limping White Elephants?[1]

J. A. Mangan

"If you shut your door to all errors, truth will be shut out." [2]

What precisely is a legacy? There is virtue in the concision of this definition: 'a tangible or intangible thing handed down by a predecessor; a long-lasting effect of an event or process; the act of bequeathing.' [3] Legacies can be benign or malign, advantageous or disadvantageous, intended or unintended. Olympic legacies are no exception.

There are a large number of Olympic 'event legacies' which became the responsibility of governments, sports organisations and communities after the Games. These 'legacies' embrace a promiscuous assemblage of hope for outcomes covering:

> commonly recognised aspects (urban planning, sport infrastructure) to less recognised intangible legacies such as urban revival, enhanced international reputation, increased tourism, improved public welfare, additional employment, more local business opportunities, better corporate relocation, chances for city marketing, renewed community spirit, better inter-regional cooperation, production of ideas, production of cultural values, {affectionate} popular memory, education, experience and additional know-how. These positive legacies stand in contrast to negative legacies such as debts from construction, high opportunity costs, infrastructure that is not needed after the event, temporary crowding out, loss of tourists that would have visited the host city if the event was not taking place, property rental increases, and socially unjust displacement and re-distributions.' [4]

An acute concern of the International Olympic Committee (IOC) is positive Olympic legacies. Perhaps rather cynically it has been suggested that there are three reasons for this.

First, a positive legacy avoids the public in the host city/nation blaming the IOC and provides evidence that the event has been good for the host city/nation. Second, it justifies the use of scarce public resources for permanent or temporary event infrastructure. Third, it motivates other cities/nations to bid for future events and this increases the power of the IOC and secures the continuance of the Olympic Games. [5]

Regrettably some recent Olympic 'event legacies' however, have given birth to a not insubstantial herd of 'Limping White Elephants'.

These are given prominence below in a spirit of positive aspiration. This is not an analysis born not of perverse disposition, but of optimistic inclination rather than pessimistic proclivity. For reasons of space what follows is not a comprehensive scrutiny of the 'herd' but a short, selective inspection drawn mainly, but not entirely, from Olympic Legacies in the hope that from consideration comes change. [6]

Some 'event legacies' associated with both Summer and Winter Olympics over recent decades have left much to be desired. The IOC has shown a laudable concern with environmental and related issues, seeking to encourage responsible action, to promote sustainable development and to require that the Olympic Games lead by example. To bequeath positive legacies, therefore, has been a prominent intention of the Sydney, Athens and Beijing Games.

The impetus for change was in part the consequence of past failures associated mostly with the Winter Olympics. [7] In terms of their legacies the Winter Games, in particular, throw a metaphorical bucket of cold water over claims of economic advantage. There is precious little evidence that they have produced much in the way of major economic benefit. [8]

The IOC has confronted this and other problems. Its declarations and actions in the closing years of the twentieth century and the opening years of the twenty-first century have been commendable in intention and to an extent positive in outcome but legacy problems remain in both Winter and Summer Games and unrealised ambitions are still a reality. A green Olympics, for example, is a steadfast IOC objective: 'sustainable development ... is modern Olympism'. [9] But much remains to be done to achieve this and other ambitions as the following case studies make clear.

Both short term disappointments and long term deficiencies (some as yet unremedied) regarding desirable legacies characterise the aftermath of Sydney 2000. It has not helped that ambitions for post-Olympic legacies were improbably high. In the florid rhetoric of the then Prime Minister, John Howard, shortly after the Games:

> we should recommit ourselves to ensuring that the Australian spirit on display during the Olympics is not only maintained during our second century of Federation, but is extended so that we can achieve our full potential as a nation. [10]

A grandiose exhortation without the faintest hint of how it might be achieved. However, even the less grandiose ambitions fell short of this portentous aspiration, not least because inadequate attention was paid to 'legacy planning'; [11] There has to be a moment in the future when effective attention is given to these planning *lacunae*. It has not yet come.

One major problem for any Olympic legacy is that the Organising Committee of an Olympic Games (OCOG) disbands within two years of the Games' conclusion. In consequence, the IOC's Olympic Games Global Impact (OGGI) evaluation process is failing to provide a full and adequate, both positive and negative, assessment of the legacies of each of the Games. [12] Evaluation after two years does not allow this.

While the IOC's OGGI project can provide helpful immediate evidence of the extent of implementation, it has been argued that:

> it will take fifteen to twenty years to measure the true legacy of an event such as the Olympic Games and the OGGI project finishes two years after the event has been held. So far nobody has been prepared to commit the research resources required to carry out scientific study of net legacy benefits. [13]

In any evaluation of the impact of a legacy there is, of course, the matter of timing. [14] When should a realistic assessment of an Olympic legacy take place? Perfect appropriateness of the timing of an evaluation, however, does not mean that no evaluation should take place prior to that moment. 'Premature' evaluation can certainly overlook eventual successful action and produce error due to incomplete evidence. None the less, early evaluation can raise constructive concerns, alert the public to overlooked obligations and stimulate official action; 'present assessment might ensure future realism' at any time. [15] After the Sydney Olympics one regrettable legacy was immediate: the unfortunate description of the Sydney Olympic Park as a 'white elephant'. This was due to the additional and considerable cost to the New South Wales taxpayer of unanticipated post-Olympic adaptation and maintenance. For this and other reasons, Sydney's complacent sense of Olympic accomplishment was relatively short lived. Post Sydney 2000 concern about the under-utilisation of the venues, unease over the financial inheritance and anxieties for state health and education systems were summarised in this apocalyptic pronouncement in 2001:

> Future Olympic city hosts be warned. Despite the stunning sell-out success of the 2000 Games, Sydney's $200 million Olympic Stadium is shaping up as a white elephant of mammoth proportions. And the other sports venues and facilities at Olympic park are not doing much better. [16]

This media alert proved an effective early warning. Athens notably failed to take note. Will Beijing? With even more ample warning, will London?

A sense of perspective is of course essential in the discussion of Olympic legacies: there have been negative and positive legacies. One successful Sydney legacy was an improved general awareness of the Olympic Movement. In the assets column of the Sydney legacy cost sheet may also be found the creation of the Australian Youth Olympic Festival which has provided elite athletes with valuable competitive experience. In the debit column, however, is failure to stimulate grassroots participation. It seems that the most substantial sports participation-related impact of the Sydney 2000 Olympic Games was an increase in *passive* involvement, such as television spectating. Shortfall active grassroots activity went hand in hand with the under-utilisation of Games sports facilities, a consequence of disagreement over their use which inter alia led to the unexpected costs of adapting the facilities. This was particularly true of the Sydney Olympic Park project. Since the costly adaptation there has certainly been a steady increase in visits to the Park, but whether to watch or play is not clear. [17]

Regrettably elite sport has benefited at the expense of sport for all, at a time when obesity and associated ill-health is a national problem. [18] Can any warning of this nature be premature? And is there a warning here for London 2012? Grassroots deprivation as a result of the cost of the 2012 Games is already a fact in 2008, provoking severe criticism in some quarters. More of this later.

A further undelivered legacy of Sydney 2000 is an expected increase in tourism which has not materialized. Economic returns also appear to leave little scope for rejoicing:

> Now that the ongoing economic 'report cards' on the Games are beginning to be known, their Olympic rapture appears to have worn off. With the current troubles in NSW health, transport and other state government sectors, some are again questioning the longer term costs and benefits of the Games. [19]

With some justification, Australian politicians, like politicians elsewhere – Athens, Beijing and London come to mind – are sanguine when it comes to the beneficial influence of mega-sporting events on national image, patriotic fervour and international awareness, but global exposure can be a double-edged weapon. The world has applauded Beijing for the glitter and sparkle of its 'Fireworks' Olympics, a Glitzkrieg of impressive proportions, but the world censured, and still censures, China for failing to honour its promises on human rights. Sydney 2000 projected an image of Australia as a land of energetic Aussies, but international investment has been less then hoped for. [20]

In summary, the legacies of Sydney 2000 were a complex comixture: good and bad, pleasing and less pleasing. Assets were not as bountiful as expected: debts were greater than anticipated. The Games produced a foot dragging herd of 'Limping White Elephants' that with more careful attention to planning and more rigorous assessment of ambitions might not have appeared.

The legacies of Athens 2004 offer opportunities for both pessimism and optimism. The expectations of the host city were high: social, economic, environmental and sporting. Transport systems, buildings, sports facilities, low cost accommodation, were all to be improved: 'viable prospects for the post-Games exploitation of the Olympic legacy were considered imperative.' [21] Post-Olympic Athens 'aspired to present itself as a modern, socially, economically and culturally developed metropolis and thus an attractive tourist destination.' [22] In reality, after the Games the eventually admitted vast cost – hugely over the estimated budget – and the abandoned facilities resulted in ferocious political confrontation and recrimination. Plans were made gradually to utilise the facilities, but this has proved to be a lengthy, difficult and in some cases acrimonious process not yet completed. Indeed, to date, a number of

Athenian Limping White Elephants are only partially restored to health. In truth, to change the metaphor, the whole business of regeneration has been a blot on the Athenian landscape – not to mention a lesson for Beijing and London and by extension, a public relations humiliation for the International Olympic Committee, which raises the issue of its greater hands-on post-Olympic involvement in the future.

The tortuous process of the eventual utilisation of the Athenian facilities was stimulated by general public vexation: 'facilities ... remained unexploited ... [on] the first anniversary of Athens 2000 and the result was that the sight of abandoned facilities ... caused Greek agitation.' [23] The consequent unseemly political wrangling between government and opposition, each holding the other responsible for considerable delay, missed opportunities and lack of forward planning, did nothing to advance the ambition of the IOC to leave positive legacies in the wake of its Games.

Eventually, while there was a slow start to regeneration, disputes still occurred as late as the summer of 2008. The mayor of the municipal authority where the Olympic Complex was situated accused the government of commercial rather than social motives: 'instead of exploiting modern facilities for the benefit of local people. [it] allotted land to business interests.' Earlier criticism was more general, more pointed and savagely accusatory. Two years after the Olympics one influential newspaper, under the heading 'The Dowry was lost; the Debts are yet there!', stated that facilities remained unexploited despite the fact that 'the Greek people paid so much in anticipation of immediate exploitation.' It concluded, 'Greece's gamble on a successful Games was finally won but the gamble on the subsequent use of its assets was lost.' [24]

This was a damning condemnation and it had the virtue of shock therapy. Things gradually changed. By 2008 Goudi Hall had become a luxurious theatre, the largest in Greece. About the same time work began to transform the Galatsi Olympic Centre into a modern shopping and recreation centre. And there were positive moves too involving the Olympic Village and the International Broadcasting Centre. Plans were announced, also at broadly the same time for the Olympic Rowing Centre to be used by the International Rowing Association. The Press Centre was selected to become the Ministry of Health and the Nikea Weightlifting Centre was to be the new Piraeus University, while the Anno Liossia Olympic Centre was to be transformed into the Arts Academy and National Digital Museum. [25]

In summary, a number of hitherto white elephants no longer limped across the landscape. Public anxiety, frustration and exasperation and media exposure had played a large part in their restoration to health.

However, some members of the herd still limped badly. In the summer of 2008 some of the Olympic facilities were still neglected and in a state of disrepair and criticism of regeneration in some instances increased rather than diminished. The Olympic Sailing Centre, by 2008 a shopping and recreational complex, occasioned sharp criticism for insensitive environmental development – an unfortunate irony given the IOC's intentions and declarations. And frustrations remained acute four years after the Games over the delayed utilisation of the Pankritio Stadium in Heraklion. [26]

The world beyond Greece took note of this regrettable state of affairs. *The Daily Telegraph*, a leading London broadsheet, published an article entitled 'Ruined Athens Facilities – a Warning for London', in which attention was drawn to the fact that in the city,

> of the 22 venues ... 21 are in a state of disrepair and under guard to prevent vandalism ... The infrastructure which was installed in such haste has proven to be far too extravagant for the city ... A few miles outside the city centre, the sprawling Faliro complex ... is deserted ... elsewhere at Hellenikon piles of rubbish are mounting behind heavily padlocked gates and electric cables hang loose from the walls. [27]

This was all bad publicity for both Athens and the IOC – unpleasant umbrageous images. Whatever the future (and long delayed) plans for at least some of the sites and the action already taken at others, this balanced assessment cannot be contradicted:

> The common reality ... is that four years after the Games, the enduring benefits of the post-Olympic use of the facilities to the [Greek] economy, culture, sport and tourism ... still remain to be seen [28]

and, it should be added, the national image of Greece and the international image of the Olympic Movement remain tarnished.

What of Beijing? *Olympic Legacies* contains this sharp assertion with particular reference to the Beijing Games: 'the legacy of the modern games is consumption' with the result that the 'Celebrate Humanity' programme highlights the basic contradiction between the ideals of Olympism and the reality of the modern Olympics. [29] The mantra, in short, is less about celebrating humanity and more about celebrating market manipulation. [30] 'Celebrating Humanity', it has been forcefully asserted, is an exercise in enhancing brand equity for the benefit of the IOC and top sponsors. [31] The Olympics, like sport globally, is locked into the commodification of cultures. [32] Is this harsh accusation true, and if it is, what are the implications for future Olympics?

In his celebrated *Wealth of Nations*, Adam Smith wrote, 'People of the same trade seldom meet together for merriment and diversion but the conversation ends in a conspiracy against the public ...' [32] This cutting observation springs fittingly to mind when contemplating the marketing campaign associated with the Beijing Olympics. Despite its slogan, 'One World, One Dream', and the Chinese claim that this 'reflects the essence and universal values of the Olympic spirit – Unity, Friendship, Progress, Harmony, Participation', the Beijing Games, it has been claimed, has *de facto* utilised Olympic ideals for TOP partners to take advantage of a restrictive marketing opportunity. [33] Is it true that the IOC has utilised the slogan of 'Celebrating Humanity' to control commercialisation to its advantage through restrictive practice and is it true that this utilisation seems more about control of the brand and avoiding ambush advertising? Does the 'Celebrate Humanity' campaign

have more to do with the modern consumerism that characterises global sport
generally and less with celebrating the common ideals of humanity? Adam Smith
comes to mind once more when reflecting on the comment above:

> It is not from the beneficence of the butcher, the brewer or the baker that we expect
> our dinner, but from their regard to their own self-interest. We address ourselves
> not to their humanity, but to their self-love. [34]

If this is true, is the 'Celebrating Humanity' programme driven by commercial self-
interest rather than idealistic altruism? Does it follow then, that the key issue in the
future Olympic Movement will be the role of the multi-nationals, advertising
corporations and media empires? Again the question might usefully be asked: What
legacies would this bequeath to future hosts? Could the Olympic Games become
increasingly not only the unrestricted instrument of national political machination
but also the uncontrolled tool of commercial rapacity?

   Finally, was Beijing 2008, with its gargantuan spending probably never to be
exceeded, its razzmatazz Opening and Closing Ceremonies both with their 'casts of
thousands' and the dazzling plenitude of expense, ambition and effort, essentially
derivative rather than innovative, for the most part as has been claimed, the legatee of
both the Los Angeles Olympics, especially the second? [35] Was it mostly a neo-
American extravaganza that owed less to Chinese cultural heritage and more to
American Hollywood? Can it be true that despite the gargantuanism of Beijing 2008
it is Los Angeles 'that has left [a] more powerful legacy for the Olympic movement
than any other Olympic city'? [36] Is the New World bombast or American
perceptiveness? Whatever the truth of the matter the claim has the merit of
provocative assertion. Los Angeles established the modern bidding system, 'perfected'
the idea of the Olympic village and most pertinently successfully married the Games
to the modern entertainment industry. Has it bequeathed 'the California style
Americanization of the Olympics' to future Olympics? Was Beijing 2008 with its
American-style, glass and steel, glittering architecture, its Opening and Closing
Hollywood spectaculars, and its zealous embrace of American initiated consumerism
fundamentally an illustration of a Chinese California-style Game? Is a materialistic,
commercialistic legacy something the Olympic movement should welcome? Is the
future of the Olympics ever grander, gaudier, costlier? One negative legacy of Beijing
2008 that seems certain is the ending of a global Flame Relay:

> The Flame Relay, regrettably but understandably, [became] in its initial stages a
> symbol not of friendship but of friction, not of harmony but of disharmony, not of
> peace but of protest. Will it be the last in the present grandiose form? Have the
> claims of it as a token of amity, unity and concord been cruelly exposed as
> rhetorical conceits with the sadly anomalous and frankly farcical loading of the
> Flame on and off vehicles to rush it to empty places to avoid gestures of
> displeasure, uncomfortable media images and contradiction of purpose? If the
> Flame Relay in its present form becomes extinct what will have been the
> geopolitical contribution of Beijing 2008 to its expiry? One action, astounding in
> the crudity of its diplomatic public relations which will remain in the consciousness

of Londoners and other elsewhere in the world, was the sight of the allegedly Chinese Security Service on English soil manhandling its citizens including apparently Sebastian Coe, on the streets of the capital; unfortunate perdurable memories. Indiscriminating intolerance rather than universal tolerance was witnessed world-wide; dysphoric Olympic imagery. [37]

To pursue a sense of perspective again, for the Chinese the most important positive legacy is the elevation of Chinese confidence and pride. The powerful undercurrents of history have surfaced and the 'century of shame and humiliation' is buried beneath a tsunami of gold medals, a frenzy of fireworks, energetic zealotry and an outpouring of wealth. For the Chinese, Beijing 2008 announced China's arrival on the world stage as a coming global superpower. In a sentence Beijing 2008 is a political exercise in global international public relations. [38] The arts and sciences employed at astounding expense in the interests of the State. Does this reflect Olympic ideals or nationalistic aspirations? Are the Beijing Olympics going to give birth to yet even bigger White Elephants? What attentions will the IOC be paying to this possibility?

Of course if all the above is true, it is equally true that self-interest, concern for self-perpetuation, the instinct for self-survival and the desire for self-projection have the serendipitous consequence of bringing pleasure, excitement and joy to billions of people around the world. This remains a legacy of immense significance. The Olympic Games remain a positive global force of consequence; warts and all. If there is some contradiction there is also sweet paradox!

As for London there is already an anticipated Post-Olympic crisis of confidence regarding legacies and an immediate Pre-Olympic crisis of confidence regarding alleged inaccurate costings and political chicanery. The bonhomous Sebastian Coe and the sanguine Tessa Jowell exude irrefrangible self-belief and peddle meretricious messages exuding in tandem Panglossian expectations but it is an unfortunate fact that the initial period of planning has been something of a public relations debacle; the result of apparently official sophistic calculations. The consequence has been to say the least unfortunate:

> With many concluding that the costs outweigh the benefits of hosting the event. This hostile press and public criticism from politicians has gathered a considerable momentum in the UK over the past two years, despite the IOC's generally positive evaluations of London's preparations, evaluations informed by the IOC's own values of 'Olympism'. [39]

Costs have risen for one significant reason: the IOC insistence on

> a more advanced socially responsible commitment to economic development and urban renewal. Insistence is one thing; insurance is another! In response host cities incorporate these commitments into the bid without adequately undertaking the detailed tasks associated with evaluating such large scale projects. [40]

Aspiration does not pay adequate attention to practicality – the purpose of the bid is to win the Games. That done serious costing begins. As a consequence a '"technically polished" London bid was deeply flawed in relation to estimating clearly identifiable event related costs' [41] with the result that:

> The initial acclaim arising from the UK's successful bid was quickly replaced by articles critical of the uncertainties surrounding the budget, the continuous revisions of budget costs by government and the elaboration of more specific criticisms of the costs associated with the creation of the widely derided Olympic logo, the design and cost of the Olympic Park sporting arenas, the salary costs of LOCOG senior staff, and by early 2008, the revised estimates of land values emerging from the economic problems posed by the credit crunch. One journalist from the popular press summed up much of the media's perspective on the Games and 'money' in concluding that Olympic funding had gone from 'joke to scandal'. [42]

This is far from being the whole story. Much has been made of the part the Games will play in inspiring the young to play. Ironies with regard to this claim have been ruthlessly exposed. Money has been taken from grassroots sport for the Games' expenses. The British Prime Minister, increasingly an unconscious ironist, returned from Beijing exhorting the young to emulate the national performers at the same time as figures were published on the closure of school playing fields, a state of affairs neatly summarised in a letter to The Sunday Telegraph:

> Your description of the neglect of facilities for grassroots sport in Britain is depressing, especially on the very day that we received the flag for the 2012 Olympic Games (News, August 24). When London was chosen for 2012, both Tony Blair and Tessa Jowell, the Olympics Minister, promised a rejuvenation of sport and in particular a huge injection of funding into schools. What happened? Playing fields have been sold off, the allocation of PE time on the curriculum has been eroded, cheap access to school sports facilities is denied and extra legislation is discouraging volunteer recruitment. We must not forget that the junior members of sports clubs, many of which are suffering, are the very people we will rely on to maintain the legacy so well provided by our team in Beijing. [43]

And with regard to grassroots sports clubs another letter to the same newspaper on the same day reported that:

> A 15-year-old leisure centre in Somerset is being demolished – because the local council got its sums wrong – and youngsters will have a 50 mile round trip to the nearest public swimming pool. The council is opening new £4 million offices next month. It seems that plush chairs are far more important. [44]

There is much more available in the same vein. A wider view on this state of affairs points to the effect of siphoning off Lottery funding from grassroots sports provision to the Olympic 'war chest'.

Another aspect of the 2012 Olympics that has worried some observers is the amount of National Lottery money that will be diverted from good causes to help feed the Olympocrats' severe attack of spendicitis. In the original bid, it was expected that the Lottery would provide £1.5 billion. In the March 2007 Games budget, this was raised by £675 million to £2.175 billion. Of this £2.175 billion, about £515 million (24 per cent) was expected to come from new Lottery games associated with the Olympics and the other £1.66 billion (76 per cent) would have to be taken from revenue that should have gone to good causes. This loss of over £300 million a year for the next five years is likely to cause quite a degree of stress to many deserving charities around the country. However, not only would this raid on Lottery funds affect charities, perversely it would also mean almost £125 million being taken away from the sporting bodies that would be expected to produce the British athletes to compete in the 2012 Games: Sport England would lose £99.9 million, the Sports Council for Wales £7.3 million, Sport Scotland £13.1 million and the Sports Council for Northern Ireland £4.1 million.' [45]

One severe critic of political 'spin' associated with the London Olympics has stated scathingly:

> Some people reading newspaper headlines such as 'Olympic budget trebles to £9.3 billion' and 'London Olympics budget could pass £10 billion', and observing the various shenanigans that have gone on surrounding the cost of staging the London Olympics, may have the impression that this is yet another big government project spiralling hopelessly out of control – a bit like a couple of Millennium Domes, a few Wembley Stadiums and the NHS IT system all being thrown together in one huge mess of confusion, chaos and gut-busting profits for all the private companies lucky enough to get a piece of the action. However, those responsible for bringing us the Games deny that there is a problem. The Secretary of State at the Department for Culture, Media and Sport (DCMS), Tessa Jowell, claims that the organisers have everything under control: 'we are determined to keep an iron grip on costs'. [46]

This sententious iconoclast continued:

> Lord Coe, Chairman of the London Organising Committee of the Olympic Games and Paralympics (LOCOG), showed his confidence when he said:
>
> The core costs of the London Olympic Games have varied very little. The costs of the actual Olympic venues themselves are much as they ever were: a little higher but by no means out of control.
>
> Yet a member of the Public Accounts Committee (PAC) described the project as
>
> the most catastrophic piece of financial mismanagement in the history of the world. Clearly, there are rather different and conflicting views about whether a cause for national pride or an expensive shambles that will take years to live down and even longer to pay off. [47]

And the same relentless iconoclast produced with sequacious rigour details of initial and more recent estimates of expenditure. Initially, 'at the time of the original bid, taxpayers were going to pay about £1.8 billion (Table 1). [48] And in 2007, in the new 'budget', taxpayers would be paying over £7 billion (Table 2)'. [49]

Even these costings flatter to deceive. The inflated 2007 estimates still omitted significant future costs and was described tellingly as 'outline' budget as distinct from

Table 1 Original Cost!

Cost of the Games	£bn
'Core' Games	2.992
Infrastructure	1.044
Total Cost	4.036
Who pays for the Games?	**£bn**
National Lottery	1.500
Taxpayer	1.798
Private sector	0.738
Total funding	4.036

Table 2 Later Cost!

Cost of the Games	£bn
'Core' Games	4.905
Infrastructure	1.673
Contingency	2.747
Total Cost	9.325
Who pays for the Games?	**£bn**
National Lottery	2.175
Taxpayer	7.150
Total funding	9.325

a final budget: 'there were billions of pounds of Olympic costs that were still not included in the Government's new figures ... For example, the £9.325 billion only covered the costs of building the Olympic facilities but not the Olympic Village. Sponsorship, it was hoped, would cover that. [50] Meanwhile building costs are soaring following the 'credit crunch'.

Since it is a key feature of any Olympic bid that the government of the winning country must provide a guarantee that taxpayers will cover all costs of the Games and the final cost of the Games has been estimated at some 14 billion pounds, the taxpayer could pay a lot more than the 1.798 billion pounds originally estimated.

The same critic stated, 'costs for maintaining the Olympic venues and adapting them for public use after the Olympics were similarly left out of the budget ...' [51] Does this sound familiar? Little has been learnt, it appears, from the negative legacies of the Sydney and Athens Olympics. The jury is still out on Beijing. As an aside – it might be added, that some thirty years on Montreal has just finished paying off its legacy of Olympic debt.

It should be noted also that the London Development Agency (LDA), in effect underpinned by the taxpayer, has admitted that the land purchased for the Games had been undervalued to the tune of about one billion pounds and that the anticipated profits from the sale of the land after the Olympics may not materialise. [52]

In summary then, there are more than £4.3 billion of extra costs over and above the 15 March 2007 (£9.325 billion) 'budget' (Table 3). [53]

The transom of the Olympic financial edifice would appear to have been dangerously insubstantial.

Adam Smith's percipience again comes to mind:

> There is no art which one government sooner learns of another than that of draining money from the pockets of the people. [54]

Is it the case that London is about to give birth to its own large rampaging herd of Limping White Elephants; multiple births that could have been aborted by more careful planning, more accurate assessments, less apparent government distortion, more attention to the aftermaths of Sydney and Athens? [55] Whatever the reality of the costs, the fact remains that to date London 2012 has been a public relations calamity, most regrettably to the detriment of The British Government and the London Olympic Organising Committee, and the IOC. Need this have been so? Will White Elephants conceived well before the Games trample through and over the Games and leave a trail of negative legacies which need never have materialised? Has Macawberesque irrationality characterised Olympic optimists? Is the reflection of a distinguished historian of relevance?:

> '... humans in history, or anywhere else, are rarely rational.' [56]

Are there lessons to be learnt for the future, not only lessons of control, competence and efficiency, but also of the value of transparency, trustworthiness and honesty?

Finally, is there a case for the IOC to take on a stronger, longer commitment to ensuring that post-Olympic legacies do not tarnish the unquestionable shining (indeed golden) achievements of other aspects of a sports event that, whatever its shortcomings, as already remarked, brings pleasure, exhilaration and joy to billions? It would be a matter of some regret if the IOC was cast in the role of *Tantalus*. Should it be a matter of regret therefore that the IOC allows too many Limping White

Table 3 Latest Cost!

	£bn
Budget cost	9.325
LOCOG*	2.000
Olympic Village*	1.000
LDA land buying*	1.300
Adapting venues	not estimated
Total	13.625

*Estimates based on National Audit Office report.

Elephants to charge across its mostly pleasant and pleasurable pastures? Finally is criticism of the relative inactivity of the IOC justified and for one good reason:

'If you shut your doors to all errors, truth will be shut out.' [57]

Notes

[1] White Elephant … Troublesome possession or thing. *New Shorter Oxford English Dictionary*.

[2] Tagore, *Stray Birds*, quoted *in The International Thesaurus of Quotations*, 297.

[3] *New Shorter Oxford English Dictionary*, 3674.

[4] Gratton and Preuss, 'Maximising Olympic Impacts by Building up Legacies".

[5] Ibid.

[6] Mangan and Dyreson (eds.), Olympic Legacies: Intended and Unintended – Political, Cultural, Economic, Educational, Routledge, forthcoming.

[7] Chappelet, 'Olympic Environmental Concerns about a Legacy of The Winter Games'.

[8] Gratton and Preuss, 'Maximising Olympic Impacts …', See also Chappelet, 'Olympic Environmental Concerns …'.

[9] Toohey, 'The Sydney Olympics: striving for legacies …'.

[10] Chappelet, 'Olympic Environmental Concerns …', and at least as far as ecological issues are concerned.

[11] Ibid.

[12] Gratton and Preuss, 'Maximising Olympic Impacts by Building up Legacies'.

[13] Ibid.

[14] Toohey, 'The Sydney Olympics: striving for legacies – overcoming short term disappointments and long term deficiencies'.

[15] Ibid.

[16] Quoted in Ibid.

[17] Toohey, Ibid.

[18] Ibid.

[19] Ibid.

[20] Ibid.

[21] Kissoudi, 'The Athens Olympics: Optimistic Legacies, Post-Olympic Assets and the Struggle for their Realization'.

[22] Ibid.

[23] Ibid.

[24] Ibid.

[25] Ibid.

[26] Ibid.

[27] Ibid.

[28] Ibid.

[29] Maguire *et al.*, 'Olympic Legacies in the IOC's "Celebrate Humanity" campaign: Ancient or Modern?'.

[30] Ibid.

[31] Ibid.

[32] Ibid.

[33] Maguire *et al.*, 'Olympic Legacies in the IOC's "Celebrate Humanity" campaign: Ancient or Modern?'.

[34] Adam Smith, *The Wealth of Nations*, quoted in The Oxford Dictionary of Quotations, 650.

[35] Dyreson, 'Los Angeles is the Olympic City …', passim.

[36] Ibid.

[37] Mangan, 'Preface: Geopolitical Games: Beijing 2008', 753.
[38] Ibid., passim.
[39] Macrury and Poynter, 'The Regeneration Games: commodities, gifts and the economics of London 2012'.
[40] Ibid.
[41] Ibid.
[42] Ibid.
[43] Ibid.
[44] The Sunday Telegraph, 31.08.2008, 21.
[45] Ibid.
[46] Craig, *Squandered*.
[47] Ibid.
[48] Ibid.
[49] Ibid.
[50] Ibid.
[51] Ibid.
[52] Ibid.
[53] Ibid.
[54] Adam Smith, *The Wealth of Nations*, quoted in The Oxford Dictionary of Quotations, 651.
[55] For a recent pessimistic assessment of preparations for London 2012 see Kelso, 'The Honeymoon is nearly over', The Daily Telegraph, S12.
[56] Rowse, *Bosworth Field and the Wars of the Roses*, 25.
[57] Tagore, Stray Birds, quoted in The International Thesaurus of Quotations, 297.

References

Chappelet, Jean-Loup. 'Olympic Environmental Concerns about a Legacy of The Winter Games'. In *Olympic Legacies: Intended and Unintended – Political, Cultural, Economic, Educational*, edited by J.A. Mangan and Mark Dyreson. Abingdon: Routledge, forthcoming.

Craig, David. *Squandered*. London: Askews, 2008.

Dyreson, Mark and Mathew Llewellyn. 'Los Angeles is the Olympic City: Legacies of 1932 and Olympic Games'. In *Olympic Legacies: Intended and Unintended – Political, Cultural, Economic, Educational*, edited by J.A. Mangan and Mark Dyreson. Abingdon: Routledge, forthcoming.

Gratton, Chris and Holger Preuss. 'Maximising Olympic Impacts by Building up Legacies'. In *Olympic Legacies: Intended and Unintended – Political, Cultural, Economic, Educational*, edited by J.A. Mangan and Mark Dyreson. Abingdon: Routledge, forthcoming.

Kelso, Paul. 'The Honeymoon is nearly over – the next month is crunch time for 2012', *The Daily Telegraph*, 17 September 2008, S12.

Kissoudi, Penelope. 'The Athens Olympics: Optimistic Legacies, Post-Olympic Assets and the Struggle for their Realization'. In *Olympic Legacies: Intended and Unintended – Political, Cultural, Economic, Educational*, edited by J.A. Mangan and Mark Dyreson. Abingdon: Routledge, forthcoming.

'Letters to the Editor'. *The Sunday Telegraph*, 31 August 2008, p. 21.

Macrury, Iain and Gavin Poynter. 'The Regeneration Games: commodities, gifts and the economics of London 2012'. In *Olympic Legacies: Intended and Unintended – Political, Cultural, Economic, Educational*, edited by J.A. Mangan and Mark Dyreson. Abingdon: Routledge, forthcoming.

Maguire, Joseph, Sarah Barnard, Katie Butler and Peter Golding. 'Olympic Legacies in the IOC's "Celebrate Humanity" campaign: Ancient or Modern?'. In *Olympic Legacies: Intended and Unintended – Political, Cultural, Economic, Educational*, edited by J.A. Mangan and Mark Dyreson. Abingdon: Routledge, forthcoming.

Mangan, J.A. 'Preface: Geopolitical Games – Beijing 2008'. In *Beijing 2008: Preparing for Glory – Chinese Challenge in the 'Chinese Century'*, edited by J.A. Mangan and Dong Jinxia. Abingdon: Routledge, forthcoming.

Mangan, J.A. and Mark Dyreson, eds. *Olympic Legacies: Intended and Unintended – Political, Cultural, Economic, Educational*. Abingdon: Routledge, forthcoming.

Rowse, A.L. *Bosworth Field and the War of the Roses*. London: Panther Books, 1968.

Smith, Adam. *Wealth of Nations* quoted in The Oxford Dictionary of Quotations. Revised Fourth Edition edited by Angela Partington. Oxford: OUP, 1996.

The International Thesaurus of Quotations compiled by Rhoda Thomas Trip. New York: Thomas Y Crowell, 1970.

Toohey, Kristine. 'The Sydney Olympics: striving for legacies – overcoming short term disappointments and long term deficiencies'. In *Olympic Legacies: Intended and Unintended – Political, Cultural, Economic, Educational*, edited by J.A. Mangan and Mark Dyreson. Abingdon: Routledge, forthcoming.

Olympic Environmental Concerns as a Legacy of the Winter Games

Jean-Loup Chappelet

In 1994, exactly 100 years since its creation, the International Olympic Committee (IOC) adopted the environment as the 'third pillar' of Olympism. The Olympic ideology promoted by the IOC since its creation was henceforth no longer founded on the unity of sport and culture alone, as extolled by Baron Pierre de Coubertin at the beginning of the twentieth century, but was completed – for the twenty-first century – by ecological concerns. Five years later, the IOC adopted an Agenda 21 for the Olympic Movement, that is, a series of sustainable development principles to be respected by all the organizations it coordinates in order to stage Olympic summer or winter games every four years. On the same occasion, it added a thirteenth mission to the long list in the Olympic Charter of those it has taken upon itself. The new mission seeks 'to encourage and support a responsible concern for environmental issues, to promote sustainable development in sport and to require that the Olympic Games are held accordingly'. [1]

The IOC's thirteenth mission represents a major development within Olympic ideology. The new concern for the environment is not only a sign of the times but also a positive legacy of the Olympic Winter Games. In fact, although the principles of environmental protection are today applied at both the summer and winter games, they have progressively won recognition after initially being addressed in relation to the winter editions. After a brief definition of the concept of legacy, the gradual emergence of ecological ideas within the Olympic saga will be retraced via three periods, demonstrating the incontestable contribution of the winter games in this respect. The conclusion addresses the future of this legacy in the light of recent developments within Olympic history and the first winter games of the twenty-first century.

The Concept of Legacy

The concept of legacy is relatively new within Olympic circles: it appeared in the 1990s, during the organizational phase of the 1996 Atlanta games. The private organizers of these centennial games felt compelled to highlight what they would leave behind for the host city. For example, during the inauguration ceremony of the Georgia Tech Aquatic Centre – built for the Olympic swimming competitions in 1996 – the university's president evoked, in the presence of the president of the Atlanta Committee for the Olympic Games, the legacy that the games would leave for the campus: one that would be not only one of 'brick and mortar' but also one of experience and knowledge gained for the city's academic community. [2] A year after the Atlanta games, economist David Sjoquist published an edited collection entitled *The Olympic Legacy: Building on What Was Achieved*. [3] The concept of legacy was naturally adopted by Sydney for the organization of the Millennium Games, in a similar anglophone context. Those behind the candidacy of the Australian city had, moreover, already stressed this topic. [4] During its successful candidacy for the 2004 games, Athens presented its project under the title of 'A Legacy for Olympism'. [5] In its report in 2001, the IOC Evaluation Commission that was created to assess candidacies for the 2008 games – apparently inspired by Juan Antonio Samaranch, who during his last year as the IOC president fervently wished to see the games awarded to the world's most populous nation – stated: 'It is the Commission's belief that a Beijing Games would leave a unique legacy to China and to sport.' [6]

In 2002, the University of Barcelona Olympic Studies Centre organized an important symposium at the Olympic Museum in Lausanne under the title, 'The Legacy of the Olympic Games 1984–2000'. [7] The new IOC president, Jacques Rogge, attended some of the discussions. Rogge stressed: 'The recommendations formulated by this symposium should be considered as a starting point for a sustainable and useful legacy of the Olympic Games.' [8] A first overview regarding the legacy of the winter games was presented at the symposium by the author of this article. His work explicitly mentions the increasing awareness of the environmental dimension as a non-material legacy of the winter games. [9]

Drawing upon the 'Olympic buzz' and the concerns of the host cities, the IOC modified its charter in 2003 to include a fourteenth mission: 'to promote a positive legacy from the Olympic Games to the host cities and host countries'. [10] The concept of legacy thus took its place among the official concerns of the IOC. Several researchers have published works on the subject. [11]

In the wake of historian Richard Cashman's work on Olympic legacies, a distinction between hard and soft legacies emerged; that is, between material legacies such as sports facilities – relatively simple to identify – and non-material ones, such as socio-cultural development, which are harder to distinguish. More precisely, according to Cashman, legacies can be broken down into six categories: an economic legacy; a legacy of the built and physical environment; an information and education legacy; a legacy of public life, politics and culture; a legacy of sport; and a legacy of symbols, memory and history. The advent of ecological ideas within the world of Olympism can be seen as a legacy of public life, politics and culture. It could also be deemed an information and education legacy since it is, above all, a case of new knowledge being acquired by the organizers of an edition of the games and passed on to their successors, possibly with the IOC as an intermediary. [12]

According to the Olympic scholar John McAloon, a distinction should be made between legacy and heritage. The heritage of the games consists of those aspects that remain positive long after their organization and which therefore contribute – whether in economic, social, cultural or symbolic terms – to the Olympic capital that is acquired. Since the 1990s, sustainable development ideas have incontestably formed part of this capital that is handed down from one Olympics to the next. Little by little, this capital accrues and becomes part of Olympic tradition. [13] The ecological components of Olympic tradition can be traced back to the creation of the winter games more than to the revival of the summer games.

The First 40 Years of the Olympic Winter Games

The first winter games took place in Chamonix, France, in the form of an international winter sports week organized in January 1924 as a prelude to the Olympic Games held in Paris in the summer of the same year. It was only a year later that the IOC was officially to ratify the idea of a winter Olympic cycle. At the time, Chamonix was France's leading winter sports resort and promoted as such by the Paris–Lyon–Marseille Railway Company (PLM), a network that served south-eastern France with the terminus of one line in Chamonix. The resort built for the occasion an extremely large, outdoor ice-skating rink, the world's largest at the time, as well as a circular skijoring track, a nearby sports pavilion, a bobsleigh run and a ski jump. These first games enjoyed sporting and political success but proved to be a financial disaster. [14]

Chamonix marked the beginning of the rise in popularity of skiing and other winter sports in France, culminating in the organization of the 1968 winter games in Grenoble. This popularity also contributed to the progressive development of facilities in the French Alps in order to make them more accessible to city dwellers, mainly in the form of road building, mountain railways, cable cars, ski lifts, and the construction of hotels and holiday flats to house these new tourists. [15] The development took place without any real regard for ecological ideas, which until the 1960s were virtually non-existent in France. Within the context of international competition at a period when winter sports tourism was an emerging industry, the predominant considerations were of an economic nature; that is, how to develop the skiing areas.

It was without doubt not by chance that the second winter games took place in St Moritz, Switzerland, in 1928, in a country and a resort that since the nineteenth century had gained a reputation as the leading destination for winter sports tourism. This town in the canton of Graubünden was a logical choice for the IOC since the organizers of the 1928 games in Amsterdam could not host the winter games in the Netherlands although – according to the IOC rule at the time stating that such games were to take place in the same country as their summer counterparts – they would have been entitled to do so. Moreover, Switzerland constituted neutral territory in order for a German team to take part in the games once again after the First World War. For the occasion, St Moritz built a ski jump that at the time was the steepest in the world, and it is still in use today, a good example of sustainability. Bobsleigh and skeleton required no facilities to be built since the runs for these disciplines were traced on the snow and ice of the Celerina district, where they remain today, virtually without any negative impact on the local environment. The only dark shadow over the event was a lack of snow, which (already!) led certain journalists to predict impending doom for the winter games. [16]

The 1932 winter games took place in the United States at the resort of Lake Placid, New York, while the summer games were held in Los Angeles. Certain promoters would have preferred to keep that edition of the winter games in the western United States at Lake Tahoe, Yosemite Valley or Denver. The American West had to wait until the IOC awarded the 1960 winter games to Squaw Valley, California, a resort created specifically and completely for the event. The Lake Placid games were the first to raise environmental questions. the Lake Placid resort was in the Adirondack State Park, whose charter stressed it should remain 'forever wild'. New York state law forbade the felling of trees or any other changes in the 'natural' state of the landscape. The construction of the bobsleigh run, however, required the felling of 2,500 trees. [17] In March 1930, a local activist group (the Association for the Protection of the Adirondacks) lodged a successful objection to the construction of the run. [18] An alternative venue was found in South Meadows Mountains, later renamed Mount Van Hoevenberg. The site was redeveloped for the bobsleigh and luge runs for the 1980 winter games. The organizers nevertheless refused to build a skeleton run, so the discipline, which had taken place in St Moritz for the first time, only returned to the games in 2002 on the Utah combined bobsleigh and luge run. The Lake Placid organizers did, however, force the village authorities into debt as a result of building an indoor ice rink. The size of the rink was, according to the New York government, disproportionate to its post-Olympic use, so the state refused to subsidize it as it had the other facilities that were built. [19] The skating rink nevertheless permitted the resort to become a renowned training centre for skating after the Second World War, and was renovated to form part of the ice sports complex for the 1980 games. [20]

The grandiose backdrop of the Bavarian Alps served as the setting for the 1936 winter games, awarded to Garmisch-Partenkirchen. Nazi Germany spared no effort to make the event – a prelude to the Berlin games – a success. Arenas that were immense for the time were built, notably a stadium with a capacity of 60,000 for the ski jump and an artificial, outdoor skating rink for 10,000 spectators. [21] The monumental ski jump arena from 1936 was among the venues proposed in Munich's bid for the 2018 winter games. [22] These facilities and others that used pre-existing sites led to no protests, from an environmental point of view, within a regime sensitive to ecology, as French philosopher Luc Ferry stresses. [23]

The same phenomenon of reusing facilities occurred after the Second World War when the winter games cycle resumed. In 1948, St Moritz used its original sites from the 1928 Olympics, slightly extended and improved. [24] The winter games during the third quarter of the twentieth century were held at times in cities (Oslo in 1952, Innsbruck in 1964 and Grenoble in 1968) and also in mountain resorts (St Moritz in 1948, Cortina d'Ampezzo in 1956 and Squaw Valley in 1960). This move by some hosts to opt for a city was a result of the already significant size of the event, an aspect that, as of 1964, finally led the IOC – with a few exceptions – to select increasingly large cities. Winter resorts were no longer able to handle the large number of Olympic participants and spectators. During the 1950s and 1960s, controversies surrounding the construction of the various facilities that were required focused more on their cost and size than on environmental considerations, an issue that emerged only at the end of the period. [25]

The 1968 Grenoble games were the emblematic example of a failure to take environmental issues into account. The bobsleigh run on the Alpe d'Huez was too exposed to the sun, meaning that it proved necessary to hold the competitions at night. The ski jump at Saint-Nizier was too exposed to the wind, which disrupted the Olympic training sessions. The Chamrousse downhill ski runs were too much affected by mist, and at an altitude too low for snow cover to be guaranteed. The luge run at Villars-de-Lans (not yet an artificial one) was at an altitude too low to guarantee ice. In fact, most of the sports facilities for those games were to be abandoned a few years later, and the buildings for the Olympic and Press Villages in the 'new town' rapidly became derelict. [26] Some 40 years later, Grenoble is nevertheless preparing to submit its candidature for the 2018 games in order to celebrate the fiftieth anniversary of those in 1968, which turned the town into a regional metropolis thanks to the many non-sport infrastructures built for the games.

The Period from 1970 to 1980

Political ecology emerged at the end of the 1960s and during the 1970s, notably following the publication by the Club of Rome of a report entitled *The Limits to*

Growth, which was to become a best-seller. [27] The ideas therein rapidly found their way into Olympic circles, which were aware of the proportions that the games had taken on. Some thought that the games had already reached the limits of what was possible, and spoke openly of gigantism regarding the summer editions. The size of the games was not, however, seen as a threat to the environment at the time. Today, we can, of course, interpret the student demonstrations that preceded the 1968 Mexico City games and led to dozens of deaths, as a criticism of the lack of sustainability within the development policies adopted by the Mexican government. At the time, however, the demonstrations were considered more as a purely political confrontation. [28]

The first edition of the winter games to take the environment into account in a serious way was that of Sapporo in 1972. The election of this Japanese city in 1966 had been a surprise, since Banff, in the Canadian province of Alberta, was convinced it would be awarded the games because a joint bid with nearby Calgary had been narrowly defeated for those of 1968. Certain sources saw in the IOC's decision the key influence of environmentalists, since the Canadian Wildlife Association was actively opposed to a venue near Lake Louise in Banff National Park. IOC members mentioned the looming conflict with Canadian environmental groups shortly before they voted. Moreover, the main promoter of the Japanese candidacy was an engineer, a bobsledder and the head of the Hokkaido Comprehensive Development Institute. He promised to develop his region while protecting its natural environment. [29]

Like Grenoble, Sapporo derived considerable benefit from the overall infrastructures that were put in place for the winter games, including a metro, a railway station, new roads, and improved urban heating systems, water supplies, and sewage treatment facilities. On the other hand, Sapporo chose to organize all the sports competitions within a maximum radius of 35 km from the Olympic Village (shorter than the over 90 km in Grenoble), with most of them taking place in the city itself. This meant a reduced transport system and easy reuse of the facilities after the games. For environmental reasons, the smaller ski jump was relocated from the site initially proposed. The Mount Eniwa downhill run, the only one with a sufficient gradient in the region, had to be traced out on the slopes of Shikotsu National Park. It was removed after the games in order to replant the trees that had to be cut down in order to create it. [30]

Innsbruck, Austria, owed its opportunity to organize the winter games for a second time in 1976 to the withdrawal of Denver, United States, following referendums held at a city and state level and initiated by a group of activists under the name of 'Citizens for Colorado's future'. A massive turnout for these referendums of 93% led to more than 60% of votes going against the allocation of public subsidies for the Denver games. [31] Beyond the financial aspects, those opposing the organization of the games also feared their environmental impact on fragile mountain zones. The cross-country ski events, for instance, were to be held in Evergreen, a name that indicated the rarity of snow cover there. The resort of Aspen had already been eliminated from the candidate dossiers as a result of opposition by certain residents who were concerned by environmental issues. [32]

When it obtained the 1976 games after Denver's bid failed, Innsbruck stated that its aim was to hold 'simple games' and that it would recycle facilities from 1964. In fact, the winter games had grown considerably over 12 years, and therefore required more infrastructure. Innsbruck found it necessary, for example, to create – at enormous cost – an artificial bobsleigh and luge run. Innsbruck's challenge was thereafter to be repeated at every edition of the winter games that followed, with the exception of Lake Placid in 1980, where improvements were made in the 1932 courses. Indeed, bobsleigh and luge runs constitutes the main 'white elephants' among Olympic facilities. It is of course difficult to justify this type of facility given the small number of athletes competing in these disciplines and the quantities of ammonia necessary to refrigerate the runs, a potential danger to the environment if leaked. [33] This question was to be a particularly sensitive one for the 1992 Albertville games.

These problems, together with others that affected the summer games (gigantism, boycotts, terrorism) became more widely known and led to a dearth of bids for the Winter Olympics. Lake Placid was the only candidate for the 1980 games, since Vancouver (Canada) withdrew just a few days prior to the IOC's decision. Since 1932, this small village in the Adirondacks had grown at a far slower rate than the winter games, and many ecological associations had emerged. A Federal Environmental Impact Statement was issued after the IOC's decision to grant the games to Lake Placid. Several of the facilities proposed (the Mount Van Hoevenberg bobsleigh run, the new luge run, the cross-country and biathlon tracks, and the downhill runs) were located on land belonging to the Adirondack Park and under the administration of the New York State Department of Environmental Conservation (ENCON), which was to build and operate these venues for the games. Considerable opposition arose, notably to the height of the large and small ski jumps (brought together for the first time), which were considered to be too close to a historical site; the extension of the downhill runs on Whiteface Mountain; and the size of the new ice rink in the centre of the village. The opposition was finally withdrawn, but it considerably delayed building work to the point that the organization of the games was at risk. The journalist Jane Keller provided an extremely clear analysis of the environmental debates surrounding the 1980 Lake Placid games. [34] Moreover, major transport problems turned the beginning of the games into chaos. [35]

A few months after the Lake Placid games, a large majority of the citizens of the Swiss canton of Graubünden voted against the candidacies by Davos and St Moritz, and also those by Chur and Arosa for the 1988 games, based on ecological and cultural concerns. [36] The same fate had affected planned candidatures by Zürich-Hochybrig and Interlaken for the 1976 winter games.

After Lake Placid, the 1984 games in Sarajevo, Yugoslavia, and those in 1988 in Calgary, Canada, that rounded off the decade were less remarkable from an environmental point of view. In Yugoslavia, political ecology bore little weight in the face of the government's determination to become the first socialist state to organize the winter games. Most of the sites were completed over a year prior to the games without having suffered any delays due to opposition. In Calgary, the businesslike style of the organizing committee left little room for ecological considerations despite powerful local and national associations for the protection of nature. For 1988, the downhill skiing venue was relocated to Mount Allen, despite its well-known lack of snow, and the sport relied on artificial snow cannons. Bobsleigh, luge and ski jumping were organized in a wind-exposed park built for the occasion at the edge of the city rather than the more appropriate Bragg Creek site that was too far away from Calgary. For the first time, the speed-skating events took place in an indoor stadium. This arena then became the standard for future winter games and a heavy burden for the new Winter Olympic cities, which were frequently at a loss to know what to do with such a huge covered space once the games were over. [37]

The 1990s

The winter games returned to Europe at the beginning of the 1990s, those of Albertville in 1992 and Lillehammer in 1994 firmly bringing the concept of ecology into the minds of the organizing committees and above all of the IOC. Both of these editions were staged in small towns in the heart of the mountains, and they were separated by only two years, since the IOC decided to change the practice of holding the winter games in the same year as their summer counterparts. These were the games that initially led the Olympic movement to develop an awareness of the importance of environmental questions, and then to tackle the issue of sustainable development. The summer games in Barcelona and Atlanta, which took place during the same period, did not place the same emphasis on these questions, since they were held some distance away from natural surroundings. Nevertheless, Barcelona – and to a lesser extent Atlanta – took advantage of the games to rehabilitate certain industrial wastelands, but neither city stressed the ecological dimension of these urban development projects. Economic development took precedence over environmental and above all social aspects. Both editions of these summer games in fact led to numerous housing evictions in order to construct the Olympic sites. [38]

As soon at the games were awarded to Albertville in 1986, Michel Barnier, the co-president of the organizing committee and the future French Minister for the Environment, promised exemplary games with the lowest possible impact on the environment despite the spread of the competition venues over 13 Alpine communities. [39] These games were both the climax within the intensive period of developing tourist facilities in the Savoie Region and the prelude to the phase of improving the quality of tourism products there and advertising them internationally. [40]

The Albertville Olympic projects took environmental considerations into account. For instance, the cross-country tracks on the Les Saisies site were relocated in order to protect high-altitude turf beds. The route and the construction work on the motorway between Chambéry and Albertville were the subject of particular care with a view to protecting the fragile surroundings. The new Bellevarde downhill run included a so-called 'columbine' turn to avoid a field where this alpine flower grew. Nevertheless, the ski jumps and the bobsleigh and luge run were very controversial. The ecological organizations expressed numerous criticisms, which were taken up by the press as the games approached. An environmental group – Fédération Rhône-Alpes de la protection de la nature (FRAPNA) – raised many issues and organized a march before the opening ceremony, carrying coffins as a representation of the environmental damages caused by the games. [41] The IOC could not afford a repeat of Albertville environmental criticism in subsequent games.

In 1988, when the preparations in the Savoie Region were already well under way, the IOC awarded the 1994 winter games to Lillehammer (Norway) after an impressive presentation by the Norwegian Prime Minister, including a call for 'an ethic of solidarity with our current and future generations, a responsibility to the global balance of nature and an understanding of our role within it'. [42] After the unexpected victory, the Norwegian government decided to make the event a showcase for its environmental policy. In 1990, the country's parliament – which needed to vote on massive credits to finance the games – decided to expand the initial objectives of Lillehammer's bid to include five 'green goals'. The legislation required Norway's Olympic organizers to increase international awareness of ecological questions; to safeguard and develop the region's environmental qualities; to contribute to economic development and sustainable growth; to adapt the architecture and land use to the topology of the landscape; and to protect the quality of the environment and of life during the games. [43] Certain groups, however, strongly opposed the games, and not for ecological reasons alone. [44]

It should be recalled that the Norwegian Prime Minister at the time was Gro Harlem Bruntland, former president of the World Commission on Environment and Development, which popularized the phrase 'sustainable development' and organized the famous Earth Summit of June 1992 in Rio, at which an IOC representative took part within the framework of the forum for non-governmental organizations (NGOs). In January 1991, President Samaranch had also taken part in the Davos World Economic Forum that addressed the same topic, accompanied by Jean-Claude Killy, the co-president of the Albertville organizing committee (and by Sebastian Coe). In September 1991, the question of holding major events in mountainous zones and in particular the Alps was widely discussed in the presence of the IOC president during the First International Conference of Winter Olympic Games Host Cities and Regions in Chambéry, near Albertville. These conferences raised Samaranch's awareness of the environmental issue. [45]

That same year, the Olympic Charter was amended to state that the Olympic Games should be held under conditions that respected the environment. [46] The manual for cities wishing to host the games was modified accordingly. For the first time, candidates for 2002 were required to answer several questions on 'environmental protection', which formed Chapter 5 of the candidacy files to be submitted to the IOC. The city of Sion (Switzerland) accompanied its responses, which according to the IOC's instructions could not exceed six pages, by an additional document called the 'green paper'. [47]

Such a document was moreover demanded of candidates as of 2004. Those behind the 2002 Sion bid promoted it as a device for insuring a 'balanced games', based on existing facilities that respected the environment in a canton – the Valais – known at the time for taking liberties with legislation on land development and environmental protection. To seal this 'green' strategy, the promoters signed a 'nature contract' with the cantonal authorities and four ecological associations in January 1995. Sion was nevertheless easily beaten by Salt Lake City, which did not particularly highlight its ecological concerns but focused on lobbying among the IOC members. This exaggerated lobbying was to lead to a scandal in 1999 that forced the IOC to impose sanctions on around 20 of its members and to undertake major reforms. [48]

The scandal in question, provoked by a Swiss IOC member, was to a large extent responsible for the failure of Sion's bid for 2006. [49] Beyond environmental protection, the second consecutive Swiss candidacy highlighted sustainable development. The 'green paper' gave way to a 'rainbow paper' stating the intentions of the Valais regarding balanced development, via the games, in the economic, social, cultural political and environmental sectors. These ideas were also adopted by the Piedmont region for the city that would defeat Sion, Turin. [50]

The idea of a 'green' winter games, which had become commonplace in bids by the early twenty-first century, took root in 1994 in the Olympic movement in Norway. The Lillehammer games were a resounding success from many points of view. The small town covered in snow and in an idyllic setting was to some extent responsible for giving back some virginity to the Olympic movement. At the opening ceremony, Samaranch spoke of white and green games. All through the years of preparation, the organizing committee provided a great deal of communication on the subject, and the world's media drew upon it comprehensively. An environmental coordinator was appointed within the committee at a very early stage, to review all the Olympic projects. The Norwegian government even allocated US$100,000 per year in order for the ecological organizations to be associated with a group named Project Environment-Friendly Olympics and thus to cooperate with the organizing committee. One of the best-known results of their actions was the relocation of the speed skating arena in Håmår in order to protect a sanctuary for rare birds. Like its sponsors, the organizing committee made a commitment to operate their offices and activities in line with strict environmental standards (green office protocol): a protocol that was later adopted up by over one-quarter of Norway's municipal administrations. It should nevertheless be noted that vast sections of forests were cleared to make way for the ski runs and even to draw a giant on the mountainside that was visible from the town. [51]

Lillehammer went beyond the concept of environmental protection and towards that of sustainable development, as emphasized in 1992 by the IOC in a statement of principle that was adopted by its executive board and drawn up by Canadian member

Richard Pound. [52] In 1993, a special edition of the *Olympic Message*, an official IOC publication, was devoted to the same topic. [53] In 1994, the International Ski Federation adopted a green manifesto at its Rio congress. [54] In Lillehammer, the determination to promote sustainability took the form of reflection on the post-Olympic use of the facilities as sports centres but also as schools and congress centres. The wooden houses of the Olympic Village were dismantled after the games and sold throughout Norway. The organizers also wished to mark their solidarity with the city of Sarajevo, destroyed during the civil war, by creating the Olympic Aid programme. This programme, today run by an organization known as 'Right to Play', inspired the IOC to launch humanitarian programmes and those for development through sport in conjunction with several UN agencies. [55]

The 1994 winter games were also the first to benefit from the Olympic Truce following a resolution by the 1993 UN General Assembly, which also declared 1994 to be the International Year of Sport and the Olympic Ideal. [56] The year coincided with the IOC's centenary, and for the occasion the IOC organized an Olympic Congress in Paris, the city where it had been founded in 1894. IOC leaders chose sport and the environment as one of the subthemes of the congress. Among the 26 contributions under that heading, Jean-Loup Chappelet suggested modifying the motto 'citius, altius, fortius', since it served as a synonym for unrestricted growth and had become incompatible with the ideas of sustainable development. [57] The suggestion was not adopted, but, in 2005, Coubertin's chosen Latin motto quietly disappeared from the IOC's headed paper. In the final declaration of the Congress, the IOC also created a permanent Sport and Environment Commission and decided to organize conferences on the subject every two years, in cooperation with the United Nations Environment Programme (UNEP), with which it signed a special agreement. The first conference took place in Lausanne in 1995. In 1995, the UNEP co-signed a brochure with the Norwegian Minister for the Environment that highlighted the exceptional results of the Lillehammer games. [58] This intergovernmental organization has been since involved in Olympic environmental efforts. [59]

In 1998, the games in Nagano, Japan, continued along the path traced by Albertville and Lillehammer. Respect for nature was mentioned as one of the three aims of the organizing committee, along with the promotion and participation of children, and peace and friendship. [60] The sites proposed in the bid for downhill skiing and biathlon were changed, and existing runs were used. The start of the downhill run was nevertheless highly controversial right up to the eve of the games because of the sensitive ecologic zone in which it was located. Many young trees were planted at the Olympic sites. Particular attention was paid to recycling materials and the waste from the games. For example, the volunteers' uniforms were made from recyclable materials. Not everything was perfect, however, and after the games certain criticisms were made regarding the environmental policy adopted by the organizers and the government. [61]

At the very end of this decisive decade in terms of incorporating notions of sustainability through Olympism, the IOC adopted in June 1999 an Agenda 21 for the Olympic movement. Its new policy had three major directions. It sought to improve socio-economic conditions; to conserve and manage resources for sustainable development; and to strengthen the role of major groups (women, young people and indigenous populations) in Olympic decision-making. This fundamental document was, however, completely overshadowed by the 'Salt Lake crisis' that the IOC was undergoing at the time. [62] The IOC followed Agenda 21 six years later with a more practical manual, drawn up by the same authors, on the implementation of sustainable development by the various Olympic sports, notably the winter sports. [63] In 2000, the IOC launched the OGGI (Olympic Games Global Impact, later the Olympic Games Impact) programme, which urges organizing committees to use around 150 performance indicators in the three areas of sustainable development in order to measure their achievements. [64] The IOC has now made this tool, which is to be used over the 10 years spanning a candidacy and the organization of an edition of the games, mandatory for all host cities. [65]

The Future of the Environmental Legacy of the Olympic Games

The first winter games of the twenty-first century continued the pioneering environmental policies of those held during the 1990s. Naturally, the organizers of the summer games in Sydney (2000), Athens (2004) and Beijing (2008) also took the environmental concerns adopted in the 1990s very much into account. For example, in September 1993, Greenpeace drafted the concept of a 'Green Olympics' for the Sydney bid. [66] Sydney's organizers also needed to address many other concerns such as ensuring that the Olympic venues were ready in time and defending their plans for projecting images of their city and nation. The winter games of Salt Lake City (2002), Turin (2006) and Vancouver (2010) all constituted progress in terms of the ecological organization of the games and enhancing their environmental legacy.

Overshadowed by the corruption scandal linked to their bid and the security problems just before they were staged, the contribution of the Salt Lake City games to environmental issues did not receive a great deal of attention. The organizing committee (SLOC) nevertheless implemented, from the outset, an efficient environmental management system for all aspects of the games, including site construction, water and energy conservation measures, transport and accommodation systems, and educational programmes. SLOC's plan adopted four aggressive objectives. They insisted on zero waste, net zero emissions, urban forest advocacy, and zero tolerance for environmental and safety compliance errors. According to SLOC, Salt Lake City's plan met the first two goals, notably by recycling or composting 95% of the waste. Over 100,000 trees were planted in Utah by primary school classes under the 'Tree-cology' programme implemented in cooperation with the US Forest Service. The sponsors, suppliers and contractors to the games were involved in the various initiatives. The SLOC was certified as climate-neutral by Climate Neutral Network, an NGO that no longer exists but that listed companies and organizations whose products and services had a net zero impact on the environment. [67]

The 2006 Turin games went even further. In accordance with its intentions stated during the candidacy phase through a plan called 'pastille verde' (green card), the organizing committee (TOROC) adopted a Charter of Intents and carried out a strategic environmental assessment, as required by an Italian law of 9 October 2000 specific to the games. TOROC also adopted an environmental management system that permitted it to gain ISO 14001 certification in March 2004 and to be registered in accordance with the European Union EMAS (Eco-Management and Audit Scheme) six months later. It was the first major sports event to receive such certification. The organizers also launched the HECTOR (Heritage Climate Torino) programme that aimed to compensate for the production of 100,000 tonnes of greenhouse gas during the period of the games and to increase awareness regarding questions of climate change. Over 7 million euros was spent on these measures, intended for the recovery of alpine land in the province of Turin and thus create a long-term legacy, notably in the form of building waste water treatment plants and artificial freshwater basins in the mountain sites for the games. [68]

In addition, TOROC cooperated with the UNEP regarding the publication of annual sustainability reports, which are the main tools to verify that the principles of the Charter of Intents are respected and for communicating its commitments regarding the economic, social and environmental impact of the 2006 games. [69] TOROC was also the first organizing committee to publish a report on Olympic social responsibility within the framework of a European Commission project entitled 'Ethics and Social Values in Sport'. [70]

The organizing committee for the 2010 Vancouver games (VANOC) has yet to reveal fully its intentions but has clearly placed its candidacy and its organizational plans for the games in the category of sustainable development by defining six performance goals for itself, i.e.: accountability, environmental stewardship and impact reduction, social inclusion and responsibility, Aboriginal participation and collaboration, economic benefits from sustainable practices, and sport for sustainable living as basic goals. [71] These objectives combine the classical environmental themes with new ones such as governance (accountability), diversity and social responsibility. Paralleling VANOC's plan, the provincial government has created a company called Legacies Now! to put in place and support action aimed at ensuring that each region of British Columbia benefits from the games during the organizational phase and, of course, beyond it. [72] The idea of working towards an immediate legacy – to all appearances an oxymoron – has been made possible by the environmental practices of the winter games.

The IOC has awarded the 2014 winter games to the seaside resort of Sochi, Russia. The snow events are to take place in the resort of Krasnaya Polyana, located in the Caucasus Mountains around one hour from the host city. The Russian government's aim is to develop this small mountain village by means of massive cash injections into a resort that can rival even the most famous alpine winter sports towns. Several environmental organizations expressed concern at the time of the candidacy since several sites were planned in Sochi National Park, a pristine area of over 800 hectares.

The Olympic Village in Polyana and the bobsleigh and luge run were even planned for locations in the buffer zone of the Caucasus State Biosphere Reserve – a UNESCO World Heritage site where, due to the re-zoning of Sochi National Park, the construction of infrastructure for tourism and recreation has been permitted. [73] In September 2006, prior to the election of Sochi, Greenpeace Russia decided to file a complaint with the Russian Supreme Court against the organizers and the IOC regarding plans for Olympic development in the region. In 2008, this complaint has not yet been adjudicated. Greenpeace Russia's chances of success are considered to be low despite intense media coverage. The Sochi games could thus represent in the environmental history of Olympism a step backward. However, as IOC President Jacques Rogge declared in a commentary on the situation for the *Financial Times*, the 'Olympics must go for green as well as gold'. [74]

Conclusion

The emergence of concerns relating to environmental protection and sustainable development has been considerably more significant in relation to the Winter Olympic Games than to their summer counterparts. These concerns, which began to appear as early as the 1930s, have become fully integrated in Olympic rules and ideology. After a somewhat shaky start, notably on the occasion of the 1932 games in Lake Placid, which represented the first time that environmental questions were taken into account to any real extent by the organizers of winter games, environmental issues became increasingly important during the 1970s and 1980s, notably for Sapporo 1972 and Lake Placid 1980, albeit without the IOC taking any notable or direct action. During the 1990s, these questions became the focus of media attention and were taken into account to a significant degree by organizing committees: particularly by those of Albertville (1992) and Lillehammer (1994). On the occasion of its centenary in 1994, the IOC made the environment the 'third pillar' of Olympism. In a few years, the IOC had adopted an environmental policy fully integrated into its philosophy. [75] Almost simultaneously, the concepts of sustainable development were introduced in bids by several candidates for the winter games, notably that by Sion in 2006. These new concepts were integrated by the successive organizing committees of both summer and winter editions but also by the IOC. Olympic leaders adopted the Agenda 21 for the Olympic movement in 1999 and in 2007 made respect for both sustainable development and the environment one of the three core values of Olympism. [76]

This evolution, which has taken place over more than 70 years, has occurred in parallel to the progressive change whereby the winter games have moved away from mountain resorts (Chamonix, St Moritz, Lake Placid, Garmisch, Cortina) towards cities in alpine valleys (Innsbruck, Grenoble, Nagano), and then to metropolises on the plains (Calgary, Salt Lake City, Turin) or even seaside cities (Vancouver, Sochi) relatively far away from the mountains. This change has come about as a result of the ever-increasing size of the winter games, and could be perceived as a consequence of the very notion of durability, since larger towns are more easily able to guarantee sustainable post-Olympic use for the installations built for the games.

Olympism has progressively incorporated, thanks mainly to the winter games, the dominant ideas regarding sustainable development that appeared at the end of the twentieth century. Olympism adopted a similar approach, when it was formulated by Coubertin at the end of the nineteenth century, in that it became strongly associated with peace, as the Olympic scholar Dietrich Quanz has demonstrated. [77] Sustainable development has come to join peaceful coexistence in the syncretism that is modern Olympism. This is an intangible legacy that should help it to strive through another century, now that the impetus of the Cold War has disappeared.

Notes

[1] International Olympic Committee, *Olympic Charter*, 12.
[2] Clough, 'The Atlanta Olympics and Academia', 1.
[3] Sjoquist, *The Olympic Legacy*.
[4] McGeoch, with Korporal, *The Bid*.
[5] Athens Bid Committee, *A Legacy for Olympism*.
[6] International Olympic Committee, *2008 Evaluation Commission Report*, 95.
[7] De Moragas, Kennett, and Puig, eds, *The Legacy of the Olympic Games*.
[8] Rogge, 'Message from the President of the IOC', 13.
[9] Chappelet, 'The Legacy of the Winter Games', 63.
[10] See rule 1.14 in IOC, *Olympic Charter*, 12.
[11] See, for example, Cashman, *The Bitter-Sweet Awakening*; Ong, 'New Beijing, Great Olympics', 35–49; Ross, *Olympic Homecoming*.
[12] Cashman, 'What Is "Olympic Legacy"?', 35.
[13] McAloon, 'Cultural Legacy', 271–8.
[14] Arnaud and Terret, *Le Rêve blanc*.
[15] Ibid., 89–106.
[16] Simmons, 'St. Moritz 1928', 228–31.
[17] Fea, 'Lake Placid 1932', 232–6.
[18] Essex and Chalkey, 'The Winter Olympics', 48–58.
[19] Ortloff and Ortloff, *Lake Placid*.
[20] Fea, 295–301.
[21] Stauff, 'Garmisch-Partenkirchen 1936', 237–41.
[22] Available at http://www.gamesbids.com/forums/index.php?showtopic = 9303&st = 0, accessed 5 March 2008.
[23] Ferry, *Le Nouvel Ordre écologique*.
[24] Simmons, 'St. Moritz 1928', 228–31.
[25] Ashwell, 'Squaw Valley 1960', 263–9.
[26] Arnaud and Terret, *Le Rêve blanc*, 220–1.
[27] Meadows, *The Limits to Growth*.
[28] Arbena, 'Mexico City 1968: The Games of the XIXth Olympiad', 139–47.
[29] Addkinson-Simmons, 'Sapporo 1972', 284–5.
[30] Kagaya, 'Infrastructural Facilities Provision for Sapporo's Winter Olympic of 1972', 61.
[31] Essex and Chalkley, 'The Winter Olympics', 48–58.
[32] Kennedy, 'Innsbruck 1976', 289.
[33] Ibid., 289–94.

[34] Keller, 'Olympics Illuminate the Long War over the Future of the Adirondacks', 42–51.
[35] Fea, 'Lake Placid 1980', 298.
[36] Bridel, 'Les Candidatures suisses aux Jeux olympiques d'hiver', 37–44.
[37] Wamsley, 'Calgary 1988', 310–17.
[38] Centre on Housing Rights and Evictions, *Mega-Events, Olympic Games, and Housing Rights*, 97–113.
[39] Landry and Yerlès, *One Hundred Years*, 286.
[40] Ponson, 'Les XVIᵉ Jeux olympiques d'hiver d'Albertville et de la Savoie', 109–16.
[41] Lellouche, 'Albertville and Savoie 1992', 319.
[42] Mathisen, 'Are We Using This Golden Opportunity?', 15.
[43] OL'94, 'Olympic Games with a Green Profile', 2.
[44] Klausen, *Olympic Games as Performance and Public Event*, 34.
[45] Landry and Yerlès, *One Hundred Years*, 286.
[46] Rule 2.10 at the time.
[47] Chappelet, *Le Rêve inachevé ou les candidatures de Sion aux Jeux olympiques d'hiver*, 12.
[48] Chappelet, *The International Olympic Committee and the Olympic System*, 21.
[49] Chappelet, *Le Rêve inachevé ou les candidatures de Sion aux Jeux olympiques d'hiver*, 53–60.
[50] Chernushenko, 'Sion 2006 Olympic Bid Creates Sustainability "Rainbow Paper"'.
[51] United Nations Environmental Programme, *Olympic'94: A Showcase for Environmental Policy in Norway 1988–1994*.
[52] Landry and Yerlès, *One Hundred Years*, 288.
[53] *Olympic Message*, March 1993, 35.
[54] Available at www.fis-ski.com/uk/insidefis/fisandtheenvironment1.html, accessed 5 March 2008.
[55] Available at http://rtpca.convio.net/site/PageServer?pagename=rtp_History, accessed 5 March 2008.
[56] Resolution A/RES/48/10, adopted on 25 October 1993.
[57] Chappelet, 'Olympism, Culture and Nature', 39–40.
[58] United Nations Environmental Programme, *Olympic '94*.
[59] Available at www.unep.org/sport_env/Olympic_games/index.asp, accessed 5 March 2008.
[60] Nagano Olympic Committee, *Official Report of the XVIII Olympic Winter Games*, 11.
[61] Matsumura, 'Nagano Olympic Wastes'.
[62] International Olympic Committee, *Olympic Movement's Agenda*, 21.
[63] International Olympic Committee, *Guide on Sport, Environment and Sustainable Environment*, 142–60.
[64] Dubi *et al.*, 'Olympic Games Management', 403–13.
[65] International Olympic Committee, '2016 Candidature Procedure and Questionnaire', 11.
[66] Greenpeace Australia Pacific, *How Green Are the Games?*
[67] Salt Lake Olympic Committee, *Official Report*, 194–203.
[68] Torino Olympic Committee, *Sustainability Report – 2004/05*, 109–48.
[69] Torino Olympic Committee, *Sustainability Report, 2004/2005*, 6.
[70] Torino Olympic Committee, *Olympic Games and Social Responsibility in Sport*.
[71] Vancouver Olympic Committee, *Vancouver 2010 Sustainability Report 2005–06*, 4–9.
[72] Ibid., 119.
[73] International Olympic Committee, *2014 Evaluation Commission Report*, 14.
[74] Jacques Rogge, 'Olympics Must Go for Green as Well as Gold', *Financial Times*, 25 Oct. 2007.
[75] Cantelon and Letters, 'The Making of the IOC Environmental Policy as the Third Dimension of the Olympic Movement', 294–308.
[76] Maass, 'The Olympic Values', 30.
[77] Quanz, 'Civic Pacificism and Sports-Based Internationalism', 1–24.

References

Addkinson-Simmons, Donna. 'Sapporo 1972, XIth Olympic Winter Games'. In *Historical Dictionary of the Modern Olympic Movement*, edited by John E. Findling and Kimberly D. Pelle. Westport, CT: Greenwood Press, 1996: 284–8.

Arbena, Joseph L. 'Mexico City 1968: The Games of the XIXth Olympiad'. In *Historical Dictionary of the Modern Olympic Movement*, edited by John E. Findling and Kimberly D. Pelle. Westport, CT: Greenwood Press, 1996: 139–47; Pierre Arnaud and Thierry Terret, *Le Rêve blanc, Olympisme et sport d'hiver en France: Chamonix 1924, Grenoble 1968*. Bordeaux: Presses universitaire, 1993.

Ashwell, Tim. 'Squaw Valley 1960: VIIIth Olympic Winter Games'. In *Historical Dictionary of the Modern Olympic Movement*, edited by John E. Findling and Kimberly D. Pelle. Westport, CT: Greenwood Press, 1996: 263–9.

Athens Bid Committee. *A Legacy For Olympism*. Brochure published by the Athens 2004 Bid Committee, 1997.

Bridel, Laurent. 'Les Candidatures suisses aux Jeux olympiques d'hiver'. *Revue de Géographie Alpine* 79, no. 3, (1991): 37–44.

Cantelon, Hart and Michael Letters. 'The making of the IOC Environmental Policy as the Third Dimension of the Olympic Movement'. *International Review for the Sociology of Sport* 35, no. 3, (2000): 294–308.

Cashman, Richard. *The Bitter-Sweet Awakening: The Legacy of the Sydney 2000 Olympic Games*. Sydney: Walla Walla Press, 2006.

——. 'What Is "Olympic Legacy"?' In *The Legacy of the Olympic Games, 1984–2002*, edited by Miguel de Moragas, Christopher Kennett and Noria Puig. Documents of the Olympic Museum. Lausanne: International Olympic Committee, 2003: 31–42.

Chappelet, Jean-Loup. 'The Legacy of the Winter Games: An Overview'. In *The Legacy of the Olympic Games, 1984–2002*, edited by Miguel de Moragas, Christopher Kennett and Noria Puig. Documents of the Olympic Museum. Lausanne: International Olympic Committee, 2003: 54–66.

——. 'Olympism, Culture and Nature'. In *Centenary Olympic Congress, Texts and Abstracts*. Lausanne: International Olympic Committee, 1994: 39–40.

——. *Le Rêve inachevé ou les candidatures de Sion aux Jeux olympiques d'hiver*. Lausanne: IDHEAP, 2000.

——. *The International Olympic Committee and the Olympic System*. London: Routledge, 2008.

Chernushenko, David. 'Sion 2006 Olympic Bid Creates Sustainability "Rainbow Paper"'. *Sustainable Sports Sourceline*, available at www.greengold.on.ca/newsletter/nl1999_01.html, accessed 5 March 2008.

Clough, Wayne. 'The Atlanta Olympics and Academia'. *Georgia Tech Alumni Magazine*, (Fall 1995), 1.

Centre on Housing Rights and Evictions (COHRE). *Mega-Events, Olympic Games and Housing Rights: Opportunities for the Olympic Movement and Others*. Geneva: COHRE, 1997.

De Moragas, Miquel, Christopher Kennett and Nuria Puig, eds. *The Legacy of the Olympic Games 1984–2000*. Documents of the Olympic Museum. International Olympic Committee, Lausanne: 2003.

Dubi, C., Pascal Van Griethuysen and Pierre-Alain Hug. 'Olympic Games Management: From the Candidature to the Final Evaluation, an Integrated Management Approach'. In *The Legacy of the Olympic Games, 1984–2002*, edited by Miguel de Moragas, Christopher Kennett and Noria Puig. Documents of the Olympic Museum. Lausanne: International Olympic Committee, 2003: 403–13.

Essex, Stephen J. and Brian S. Chalkey. 'The Winter Olympics: Driving Urban Change, 1924–2002'. In *Olympic Cities*, edited by John R. Gold and Margaret M. Gold. London: Routledge, 2007: 48–58.

Fea, John. 'Lake Placid 1932: IIIrd Olympic Winter Games.' In *Historical Dictionary of the Modern Olympic Movement*, edited by John E. Findling and Kimberly D. Pelle. Westport, CT: Greenwood Press, 1996: 232–6.

Ferry, Luc. *Le Nouvel Ordre écologique: l'arbre, l'animal et l'homme.* Paris: Grasset, 1992.

Greenpeace Australia Pacific. *How Green Are the Games? Greenpeace Environmental Assessment of the Sydney 2000 Olympics.* Amsterdam: Greenpeace International, 2000.

International Olympic Committee (IOC). *Olympic Movement's Agenda 21: Sport for Sustainable Development.* Lausanne: International Olympic Committee, 1999.

——. *2008 Evaluation Commission Report: Games of the XXIX Olympiad in 2008.* Lausanne: International Olympic Committee, 2001.

——. *Olympic Charter: In Force as From 1 September 2004.* Lausanne: International Olympic Committee, 2004.

——. *Guide on Sport, Environment and Sustainable Development.* Lausanne: International Olympic Committee, 2006.

——. *2014 Evaluation Commission Report: XVII Olympic Winter Games in 2014.* Lausanne: International Olympic Committee, 2007.

——. *2016 Candidature Procedure and Questionnaire.* Lausanne: International Olympic Committee, 2008.

Kagaya, Seiichi. 'Infrastructural facilities provision for Sapporo's Winter Olympic of 1972'. *Revue de Géographie Alpine* 79, no. 3, (1991): 59–71.

Keller, Jane Eblen. 'Olympics Illuminate the Long War over the Future of the Adirondacks'. *Smithsonian* (10 Feb. 1980): 42–51.

Kennedy, John J. 'Innsbruck 1976'. In *Historical Dictionary of the Modern Olympic Movement*, edited by John E. Findling and Kimberly D. Pelle. Westport, CT: Greenwood Press, 1996: 289–94.

Klausen, Arne Martin. *Olympic Games as Performance and Public Event.* New York: Berghahn Books, 1999.

Landry, Fernand and Madeleine Yerlès. *One Hundred Years. The Idea, the Presidents, the Achievements.* Vol. III: *The Presidencies of Lord Killanin and Juan Antonio Samaranch.* Lausanne: International Olympic Committee, 1996.

Lellouche, Michele. 'Albertville and Savoie 1992'. In *Historical Dictionary of the Modern Olympic Movement*, edited by John E. Findling and Kimberly D. Pelle. Westport, CT: Greenwood Press, 1996: 318–25.

Maass, Steven. 'The Olympic Values'. *Olympic Review* 63 (April–June 2007): 28–33.

Mathisen, Ola Matti. 'Are We Using This Golden Opportunity?' Oslo: Norwegian Ministry of Foreign Affairs, 1993.

Matsumura, Kazunori. 'Nagano Olympic Wastes: Development Policy and Peasant Body Culture'. Paper presented at the Nationalism, Sport, and Body Culture in the 20th Century International Conference, Tsukuba University, 2000.

McAloon, John. 'Cultural Legacy: The Olympic Games as "World Cultural Property"'. In *The Legacy of the Olympic Games, 1984–2002*, edited by Miguel de Moragas, Christopher Kennett and Noria Puig. Documents of the Olympic Museum. Lausanne: International Olympic Committee, 2003: 271–8.

McGeoch, Rod, with Glenda Korporal. *The Bid: How Australia Won the 2000 Games.* Sydney: William Heinemann, 1994.

Meadows, Donella and Dennis Meadows. *The Limits to Growth.* New York: Universe Books, 1972.

Nagano Olympic Committee. *Official Report of the XVIII Olympic Winter Games.* Nagano: Nagano Olympic Organising Committee, 1999.

OL'94. 'Olympic Games with a Green profile'. In *Olympic Information.* Organising Committee of the XVII Olympic Winter Games, Lillehammer, 1994, May 1992.

Ong, Ryan. 'New Beijing, Great Olympics: Beijing and Its Unfolding Olympic Legacy'. *Stanford Journal of East Asian Affairs* 4, no. 2, (2004): 35–49.

Ortloff, George C. and Stephen C. Ortloff. *Lake Placid, The Olympic Years, 1932–1980: A Portrait of America's Premier Winter Resort.* Lake Placid, NY: Macromedia, 1976.

Ponson, Claude. 'Les XVIᵉ Jeux olympiques d'hiver d'Albertville et de la Savoie: les enjeux de l'aménagement'. *Revue de Géographie Alpine* 79, no. 3, (1991): 109–16.

Quanz, Dietrich. 'Civic Pacificism and Sports-Based Internationalism: Framework for the Founding of the International Olympic Committee'. *Olympika: The International Journal of Olympic Studies* 2 (1993): 1–24.

Rogge, Jacques. 'Message from the President of the IOC'. In *The Legacy of the Olympic Games, 1984–2002*, edited by Miguel de Moragas, Christopher Kennett and Noria Puig. Documents of the Olympic Museum. Lausanne: International Olympic Committee, 2003: 13–14.

Ross, John F. *Olympic Homecoming: Greece's Legacy and the 2004 Athens Games.* Athens: Explorer, 2004.

Salt Lake Olympic Committee. *Official Report of the XIX Olympic Winter Games.* Salt Lake City, UT: Salt Lake Olympic Committee, 2002.

Simmons, Donald C. 'St. Moritz 1928: IId Olympic Winter Games'. In *Historical Dictionary of the Modern Olympic Movement*, edited by John E. Findling and Kimberly D. Pelle. Westport, CT: Greenwood Press, 1996: 228–31.

Sjoquist, David L., ed. *The Olympic Legacy: Building on What Was Achieved.* Atlanta, GA: Research Atlanta, 1997.

Stauff, Jon W. 'Garmisch-Partenkirchen 1936: IVth Olympic Winter Games'. In *Historical Dictionary of the Modern Olympic Movement*, edited by John E. Findling and Kimberly D. Pelle. Westport, CT: Greenwood Press, 1996: 237–41.

Torino Olympic Committee. *Sustainability Report – 2003.* Turin: Organising Committee for the XX Olympic Winter Games, 2004.

——. *Sustainability Report – 2004/05.* Turin: Organising Committee for the XX Olympic Winter Games, 2005.

——. *Olympic Games and Social Responsibility in Sport.* Turin: Organising Committee for the XX Olympic Winter Games and European Commission General Directorate Employment and Social Affairs, 2006.

United Nations Environment Programme (UNEP). *Olympic'94: A Showcase for Environmental Policy in Norway 1988-1994, Planning, Results and Follow-Up.* Oslo/Nairobi: Miljoverndepartmentet, UNEP, 1995.

Vancouver Olympic Committee. *Vancouver 2010 Sustainability Report 2005–06.* Vancouver: Organizing Committee for the 2010 Olympic and Paralympic Winter Games 2006.

Wamsley, Kurt B. 'Calgary 1988'. In *Historical Dictionary of the Modern Olympic Movement*, edited by John E. Findling and Kimberly D. Pelle. Westport, CT: Greenwood Press, 1996: 310–17.

The Albertville Winter Olympics: Unexpected Legacies – Failed Expectations for Regional Economic Development

Thierry Terret

France has organized the Winter Olympics three times: at Chamonix in 1924, [1] Grenoble in 1968 and Albertville in 1992. Although the economic ramifications were considerable for those involved, [2] the first two events were mostly organized by the host country in a climate dominated by political and nationalist considerations. In the first case, the idea was to reposition France after the First World War, which had considerably modified the world power balance. The French authorities designed the 1924 Olympic Games to allow the country to impose itself as a European leader as well as to counterbalance the rising importance of the United States internationally. [3] As *Deputé* Noblemaire declared when the French candidature was presented to the IOC, 'It is absolutely vital that France does not lose in the eyes of the world of athletics, which is predominant in numerous countries such as America, Britain and the Scandinavian countries, the prestige which had been bestowed upon it by that supreme sport: war.' [4] More than 40 years later, the Grenoble games were conceived in the context of the Cold War. The aim of General De Gaulle was to turn France into a third political option located between East and West, while at the same time improving the country's image, which was then particularly low in the United States. [5] According to Georges Lagorce and Robert Parienté, 'Defeat in Grenoble would have meant the defeat of France as a whole.' [6]

In reality, the political benefits of Chamonix and Grenoble were minimal, just as their effects on the national economy were negligible and, indeed, negative at a local level. [7] The people of Grenoble were to pay for the cost overruns of the 1968 games until 1995! The 1992 Albertville games, however, were quite different from their predecessors. For one thing, the economic stakes and infrastructure development were emphasized more than the political stakes, even though the preparation phase was carried out during the Cold War. In addition, winter sports were themselves going through a major crisis in the 1970s, which eroded convictions concerning their inevitable profitability. [8] Finally, Savoie's candidature came at a moment when, under the influence of the new president, François Mitterrand, the implementation of the main laws of decentralization considerably reinforced the powers (and thus the expectations) of the regions. Nevertheless, comparison of political speeches with the observations of the media, together with economic analysis, highlights substantial differences that relativize the results of the Albertville games.

Political enthusiasm and scientific prudence

In December 1981, Jean-Claude Killy, the triple gold medallist of Grenoble turned businessman, and Michel Barnier, the young *deputé* for the party Rassemblement pour la République (RPR) and ally of Jacques Chirac, [9] got together to organize a candidature project, in the name of a region and not just a town, for the organization of the Winter Games of 1992. This was officially announced to the IOC two years later, on 26 January 1983, and a 'candidature committee' was formed on 27 April 1984 in order to prepare the defence of the candidature before the Olympic authorities; first during the 90th IOC session in West Berlin on 6 June 1985, and again in Lausanne on 17 October 1986. This time, Albertville came out ahead of Anchorage (United States), Berchtesgaden (Germany), Cortina d'Ampezzo (Italy), Lillehammer (Norway), Falun (Sweden) and Soria (Bulgaria).

An organizing committee for the Olympic Games (OCOG) was rapidly set up. Jean-Claude Killy was elected President on 13 January 1987, but Michel Barnier presided over the Council Executive Committee from 24 February. This coordination was designed to demonstrate the complete understanding that existed on a local level between the political, economic and sporting powers. The simultaneous nomination of Yves Cabana as *chargé de mission* (head of mission) for interministerial coordination completed the organization.

The originality of this candidature, as well as its limits, were to be found in the idea of having different locations. Around Albertville (OCOG logistics, ceremonies, ice-skating and ice hockey), 13 other communities, small villages or renowned ski resorts, all relatively far apart from each other, [10] would in fact benefit from the Olympic label and be host to competitions or services: Brides-les-Bains (Olympic village), Moûtiers (radio and television centre), La Léchère (press centre), La Plagne (bobsleigh and luge events), Pralognan (curling), Les Allues-Méribel (ice-skating, ice hockey and downhill skiing), Bourg-Saint-Maurice–Les Arcs (speed skiing), La Tania (Olympic village for ice-hockey players), Tignes (artistic skiing and Paralympics), Val d'Isère (downhill skiing), Saint-Bon–Courchevel (ski jumping and ice-hockey training facilities), Les Menuires (slalom) and Les Saisies (cross-country skiing and biathlon). This arrangement raised local expectations and made the initial negotiations so difficult that Jean-Claude Killy threw in the towel a few days after his nomination as the head of the OCOG. He resigned before taking up his functions one year later, in March 1988.

Nevertheless, one of the positive outcomes of having different locations was the acceleration of public works related to the games' installations, which were often completed more than a year ahead of schedule. The Tignes Olympic stadium, for example, was inaugurated as early as December 1990. The bobsleigh run at La Plagne, the ski jump in Courchevel and the speed ring in Albertville were also operational for the French team's preparations one year before the games began.

Between 1982 and 1992, the 11 years dedicated to designing and preparing the Albertville games also saw an increase in expectations and ambitions, mostly local and regional rather than national, which accelerated in 1985 and 1986 for three reasons. The first was linked to the decentralization laws (known as the 'Defferre laws') implemented by François Mitterrand in 1982 and 1983, but not truly effective before 1985. Thereafter, the departments and regions were no longer administrative entities charged with the implementation of government decisions. They had become collectivities controlled respectively by *conseils généraux* and *conseils régionaux* (county and regional councils) elected by universal suffrage and endowed with their own missions. This profound reorganization of French structures gave considerable free space to local, elected officials, who, in the case of the Savoie Department and the Rhône-Alpes Region, believed themselves able to develop their ambitions for the games without too much overbearing control from Paris. As Pierre Kukawa, Pierre Préau, François Servoin and Robert Vivian quite rightly pointed out, 'set up in 1986, at the time of the spectacular development of moves towards privatization and rejection of the State, [the OCOG] has decided to keep its distance vis-à-vis the powers that be.' [11] Not all aspects of such independence, however, were positive. In 1990, the Inspection Générale de l'Administration (civil service inspectorate) issued an accusatory report outlining 49 mountain communities in difficulty, including several Olympic sites, and denouncing management errors and risky investments. [12]

The second reason was similarly linked to political rupture. In March 1986, the RPR–UDF alliance came out ahead of the Socialist Party in legislative elections, obliging Mitterrand to install Jacques Chirac, newly appointed majority leader, as *premier ministre* (prime minister). It happened that Michel Barnier's Savoie was devoted to Chirac's cause, thus eliminating any risk of pressure from Paris on the games' local organizers. The last reason obviously resulted from the IOC's decision to award the XVIth Winter Games to the Savoie city in 1986: the dream was becoming a tangible reality.

In this context, local officials' key expectations focused primarily upon the economic aspects of the Olympic event. All other criteria became secondary. Could the games be an opportunity for teaching humanist values to the young? The question hardly came up. In France, the concept of 'Olympic education' itself was virtually unknown. Of course, a few initiatives were taken here and there, notably in Savoie, with a contest around the games being organized in primary schools throughout November and December 1987, but they remained localized with no lasting effect.

The primary expectations were pragmatic in nature, and a long way from being Olympic ideals: the games were designed to generate the necessary financial means to improve sewage management as well as domestic rubbish collection and treatment in the greatly under-equipped towns and ski resorts of Savoie. This argument proved difficult to sell to the IOC, and understandably was not subsequently publicized. Seen as more 'acceptable', the candidature project and preparation of the games were thus initially based on the idea of improving transport access to Savoie's ski resorts, [13] notably by opening up the Tarentaise valley. This geographical bottleneck was a converging point for all of the region's ski resorts, most of which had been built in the 1960s, when winter sports were not as popular, and it caused the systematic congestion of roads from the first winter weekends onwards. [14]

The Savoie Department was now faced with a serious problem. Firstly, with 70 winter sports resorts and 55,000 hectares of skiable area, a large proportion of its economy was reliant on winter tourism (40% of income). Secondly, access difficulties had been analysed, rightly or wrongly, as constituting a risk to the tourist economy, which was also under particular pressure from Swiss and Italian competition. Regional budgets proved insufficient for the necessary investment, but asking the state to help meant finding a pretext. Through their effect upon the national mindset, the Olympic Games could play a part by inducing the French government to take on a large part of the infrastructure costs not directly linked to sporting events. At the same time, the realization of these projects would inject dynamism into the building industry and, more generally, boost employment all over the region.

From this point of view, the results were positive and rapid. As early as 1983, thus even before the candidature committee was set up, an initial roads project, designed to free up the Tarentaise, was launched by the government. In 1985, the mayors of Savoie's ski resorts, and, ironically, the Fédération nationale des travaux publics (national federation for public works), signed a report-cum-petition, demanding that this action be carried even further. [15] A second project would soon follow, in January 1986, to extend the first. Moreover, on 25 January 1985, an outline agreement was signed by the government, offering financial guarantees to the organization project, and reassuring Savoyards and the IOC alike. Very astutely, this state participation was not included in the official games budget, not only in order to offer more reasonable and attractive figures when the Olympic officials were choosing the host city, but also, later, for the sake of the intermediary reports produced between 1986 and 1992.

The other side of winter tourism related to the production of sports equipment, a major industrial element at the regional level. This is why, even as late as 2000, the Rhône-Alpes Region played host to two-thirds of French sport article production, of which half was dedicated to winter sport articles alone, with world-leading producers, such as Rossignol and Salomon, involved. From the beginning of the 1980s, economists agreed that skiing equipment producers were in need of a new lease of life, [16] although public authorities and economic policymakers showed more optimism, and expressed resolute confidence in the future. In 1986, when the IOC awarded the XVIth Winter Games to Albertville and Savoie, many commercial players, faced with stagnant markets and excessive debt, had already given up hope.

The political authorities and members of the OCOG became progressively more worried, although they did their best to minimize the risks in public declarations. Nevertheless, Savoie's *conseil général* set up an agency to observe the economic changes in July 1987. A national conference of towns and villages involved in the organization of the winter games was also held in Chambéry, near Albertville, on 10–12 September 1991, and was attended by delegations from all 15 Olympic towns from Chamonix in 1924 to Nagano in 1998. The aim was to study and compare the various results of profitability and the reassignment of equipment and installations. With the games only one year away, fears could no longer be dissimulated. The press hinted at them more so than the official intermediary reports. 'Savoie is laughing, Savoie is crying. The post-games period begins in one year from now. There is no lack of local development projects. The same goes for serious worries,' wrote Francine Aizicovici, for example, in *Le Monde* on 30 January 1991. The journalist, Michel Delberghe, went even further when he spoke of 'lost illusions' and concluded, 'The people of Savoie no longer expect an economic miracle, and they are already thinking about post-92.' [17] The spectre of the financial difficulties which followed the 1968 Grenoble games was recalled. This history lesson had been sufficiently hard, moreover, for political authorities to begin worrying about the possible negative results of the Albertville games, and an independent team of university experts was assembled around a well-reputed economist, Wladimir Andreff, in order to study the probable socio-economic impact of the Savoie event. [18] The conclusions of the report by a panel of economists, sociologists and historians mainly emphasized the need for prudence, and even went against several points contained in the official line, by demonstrating that the Albertville games would have hardly any positive effects apart from those upon infrastructure. Analysis of the development of the national and regional winter sports market led, for example, to the idea that this Olympic event could not do much to counter the underlying trends that had been hardening since the beginning of the 1980s; that is, that what the French ski resorts had to offer no longer corresponded to the demands of a population that was becoming less and less attracted to traditional skiing, and that the likely spectators and television viewers of the Albertville games were not necessarily future skiing adepts. [19] The analysis of the Olympic host communities' budgets was the object of warnings about excessive debt. [20] Moreover, the panel's economists showed unambiguously that, apart from the building industry, the 1992 games would play no more than a minor role in the development of the national and regional sports equipment market, and would in no way prevent the disappearance of several companies. [21]

The rather pessimistic conclusions of this report went largely uncommented on by the authorities. When it was made public, *Figaro* journalists adopted an ironic tone and made fun of the researchers, who were, they said, incapable of producing a serious analysis. The idea of publishing some of the conclusions in the form of a book available to the general public resulted in political pressure that led to its publication being put off until 1993, one year after the games. In the absence of a veritable long-term study commissioned by the OCOG, Wladimir Andreff's report was the only perspectivist approach to the Albertville games. *Le Monde Diplomatique* printed a bold article, in February 1992, in which Christian De Brie considered some of the experts' warnings, quoting the 'voluminous and remarkable report written by a group of researchers [that] contributes points of view in contradiction with official optimism ... which no doubt explains why the study remained confidential'. [22] Nevertheless, the study in question turned out, in many respects, to be corroborated by the facts.

Self-satisfaction and budgetary criticism

The XVIth Winter Olympic Games were held from 8 to 23 February 1992, and contained several remarkable elements: the opening and closing ceremonies produced by the choreographer Philippe Decouflé, and unanimously praised for their artistic quality; 'unified' teams (Germany and some ex-Soviet countries) and teams standing alone (Croatia, Slovenia, Lithuania, Estonia and Latvia); new disciplines (artistic skiing, short-track speed skating, and female biathlon), which were all part of an enormous programme of 57 disciplines; brilliant performances resulting in new champions (Bjorn Daelie, Vegard Ulvang, Bonnie Blair, Gunda Niemenn, Mark Kirchner, Petra Kronberger, Kim Ki-hoon, etc.), continuing champions (Alberto Tomba, who kept his downhill Olympic title), and young champions, such as Toni Niemenen (16-year-old gold medallist high jumper).

But as far as the organizers were concerned, the most important thing was for the two weeks to go by smoothly. After the games, Jean-Claude Killy and Michel Barnier, co-presidents of the organizing committee, expressed their unmitigated and complete satisfaction. The IOC joined this chorus, concluding, through the voice of its spokeswoman, Michéle Verdier, that 'it was a challenge, and the challenge was met perfectly.' [23] Some newspapers in France echoed this sentiment, *Libération*, for example, which lauded the success of the games, and reiterated a clear endorsement of their organizers by promising those disappointed in the short term that all the investments would be beneficial to the region later. [24]

Beyond the French borders, however, opinions were more cautious. *The New York Times* expressed scepticism concerning both the legacy and the final cost of the games. [25] In Britain, Michael Calvin expressed multiple criticisms in *The Daily Telegraph* by heavily emphasizing the financial skids: 'The Albertville Olympics were a costly exercise in political expediency, undertaken, largely, for the benefit of CBS television. Small Alpine communities will be paying for them for generations.' [26] And he added: 'The story which sums up the distorted values of Albertville, 1992, concerns an aluminium ladder, of the type which costs £27.95 at a DIY superstore near you. It was needed by CBS, to reach a camera position on the downhill course at Val d'Isère. The Organising Committee who insisted the ladder be purchased through them, charged £550.'

Comment was hardly more favourable in Switzerland. 'This feeling of satisfaction will only be felt by convinced optimists,' wrote Fred Hirzel in *Le Nouveau Quotidien*. [27] He then turned his attention to the Albertville balance sheet: budget in deficit in spite of the organizers' declarations, a drastic fall in tourism during the two weeks of the games, and extensive damage to the environment, all of which hardly pleaded in favour, in his opinion, of Swiss candidature for the organization of such an event in the future. In fact, four years earlier, Lausanne had already given up the idea of trying its luck for the Olympic adventure of 1994 in view of the refusal of public opinion to accept the financial risk. It was, moreover, for this same reason, backed up by the unhappy experience of Albertville, that the inhabitants of Val-d'Aoste, in north-west Italy, massively rejected (85%, by referendum) their region's candidature for the winter games of 2002 in June 1992. [28]

The strongest criticism, in France as well as abroad, had begun to be expressed even before the games, and mainly concerned financial considerations. The official budget had announced expenses of around 4 billion francs (600 million euros), broken down into 1.4 billion for the organization (213 million euros), 950 million for sports installations (144 million euros), 1 billion for technology and the media (notably for the construction of a press centre) (152 million euros), 445 million for accommodation (68 million euros), and 150 million for various expenses (23 million euros). These amounts were to be covered by television rights (280 million dollars – 230 million euros – of which 242 million would be provided by the American network CBS), publicity rights paid by the 12 multinationals and French companies, respectively, under contract with the IOC and the OCOG (1 billion francs – 152 million euros), ticket sales, resale of equipment, and sale of games-related products.

In reality, the budget, which was presented a good many times, did not include all the expenses incurred by infrastructure (roads, railways, airport, environment), the cost of which came to around 7 billion francs (1.06 billion euros). In other words, although the official statements of Killy and Barnier had never stopped reminding everyone since 1986 that 'The Games must pay for themselves', and the organizers in Savoie had never stopped claiming to achieve the antithesis of what had been done in 1968, when the state supplied 75% of the total budget, representing a more or less similar level of investment to that observed during the Grenoble games. Moreover, despite this state participation, the final figures, presented in July 1992, showed a deficit of 280 million francs (43 million euros), or 6.6% of the games budget (4,210 million francs). Despite the protocol signed in November 1987 by the then 'premier minister' Jacques Chirac and the OCOG, which provided for payment parity in the event of deficit, the shortfall was eventually covered to the tune of 75% by the state and 25% by the department of Savoie. [29] It was therefore without a doubt French taxpayers, and, to an ever larger extent, taxpayers living in Savoie, who paid for the Albertville games.

As early as February 1992, an initial report by the Inspection Nationale des Finances (ministerial finance inspectorate) came to the conclusion that procedures open to criticism and 'financial dissimulation' were imputable to the OCOG. [30] Equipment and accommodation, referred to as 'a veritable disaster' by the report, were two very badly run elements, and the main reason for the deficit. Michel Barnier admitted to slight investment overruns on the bobsleigh track [31] and the ski-jump ramp, but merely attributed the results to the unfavourable slide in the dollar! [32] One year later, the figures got even worse after a report from the Cour des comptes (accounts inspectorate) put global costs at 12 billion francs (1.8 billion euros), broken down into 4.2 billion francs (640 million euros) for the OCOG's budget, and 7.8 billion for infrastructure costs (1.2 billion euros). They also heavily criticized the financial mishandlings. [33] Meanwhile, the mayor of Val-d'Isère, André Degouey, was taken to the Albertville Court by the Appeals Court of Chambery, 'for having, in Val-d'Isère during 1991 and 1992, as Mayor of the town openly or via the interposition of third parties, taken or received benefit from companies or action under his administration or supervision, notably certain development projects for the Olympic Games'. [34]

For some of the communities or small ski resorts involved in the games, the results were equally dramatic. Although Albertville and its 18,000 inhabitants got off relatively unscathed, things were different for the other sites. With populations ranging from a few hundred up to 6,000 at the most, several found themselves close to financial disaster six months after the games. At Pralognan, a village of 627 inhabitants, debt reached 50% of the communal budget, with 5 million francs owed to the OCOG. At Brides-les-Bains, the town council did not know which way to turn in the face of bank refusal and the withdrawal of regional and national authorities: debts reached 70 million francs for an annual budget of 18 million! [35] Even the renowned resort of Les Saisies still owed 34 million with no idea of where to find the money. [36] Reports from the Cour des comptes and newspaper investigations clearly contradicted the region's official declarations, which still wanted to appear reassuring in 1994: 'In spite of an unfavourable financial and economic conjuncture, the

Olympic communities and sites have not met with disaster as announced by certain commentators.' [37]

Economy and tourism legacy

Giving access to the Tarentaise was the principal objective of the 1992 winter games organizers. It was incontestably one of the successes. The Albertville games, thanks in particular to the substantial investment the state poured in for the occasion, accelerated work that would have taken much longer without them: improvements in the road and motorway network, modernization of the rail network, construction of bus stations, implementation of a new system of telecommunications and weather information, help with the construction of new tourist accommodation, and valorization of the local cultural heritage. [38] Without wanting to sum up the Olympic Games in terms of a sewage treatment plant, rubbish collectors and a disposal system for household waste, even the water clean-up programme was completed successfully thanks to national funding to develop water conveyance.

These many large projects had a large impact on the building sector during the years spent preparing for the games. Nevertheless, the sudden drying up of work in 1992 instantly left 5,000 people without a job, despite the aid programme set up in November 1991. [39] Moreover, apart from purely sporting equipment, 42% of the contracts (in value) were attributed to local companies. Given their size and imposed completion dates, most of the projects were handed over to national or international groups, thus reducing direct economic impact in Savoie. One year after the games, the local employment situation was, moreover, sufficiently serious to provoke demonstrations by the unemployed during the celebrations in Albertville of the first anniversary of the Winter Olympic Games. [40] Michel Barnier stated at the time to CGT trade union officials, 'If we had not had the Games, we would be in an even worse situation today. The Games have allowed us to update our infrastructure, and to improve the image of the valley.'

After the question of debt repayment came that of the future of the equipment installed for the Olympic Games that were meant to act as a catalyst for urban change. [41] This point had been largely anticipated, and, in 1989, the mayor of Albertville was able to make public the 'after-games' programme, which consisted, depending on each individual case, in either dismantling or reassigning the installations, or reusing fully logistical and sporting equipment. [42] Even though not all problems were resolved, a study carried out by public authorities two years after the games seems to indicate that local officials, generally, managed to limit the difficulties, albeit with some disparity depending once again on the individual cases. [43]

More specifically, the ceremonial theatre in Albertville was dismantled, apart from the central mast, which symbolizes the town's Olympic heritage to this day. The site was turned into outdoor games areas and sports fields. The capacity of the ice hall was reduced from 9,000 to 2,400 places to be more in keeping with its sports and events utilization (galas and concerts in 1992 and 1993). With operating costs of 3 million francs (450,000 euros), the facility is struggling, nevertheless, to reach its break-even point. The speed ring was converted into an athletics track. At Les Arcs, the speed-skiing run continued to be used for competitions as well as by the general public, thus contributing to the resort's improved offer. It was the same, in Courchevel, for the ice-skating rink and the ski-jump runs with, for the latter, a not-negligible financial bonus thanks to guided tours of the site (14,000 people in 1992, 10,000 in 1993). In Méribel, the ice hall underwent a seating reduction of 6,000 places, to 1,500, while opening the women's alpine skiing course to competitors and the general public ensured optimal use. The results were identical for the men's slalom course at Les Menuires, the downhill skiing course at Val D'Isère, the skating rink at Pralognan, the cross-country and biathlon courses at Les Saisies, and the artistic skiing course at Tignes. Following a few adaptations, these facilities remained true to their sporting vocation by continuing to host national and international events; they became quite attractive to tourists, apparently due to their Olympic image, and this helped them to break even.

According to initial estimates, the trickiest case was that of La Plagne, which had to manage the bobsleigh and toboggan runs, given that these two sports were almost unknown in France. With 12 high-level competitions in 1993 and 1994, their sporting viability was optimal. An association, 'Bob-Luge France La Plagne '95', was also set up to increase public interest in these facilities. Attractions known as 'Taxi bob' and 'Bob raft' were developed, with between 100 and 300 daily visitors during the winter season. These were good results, augmented by the money earned by tourist tours (10,000 in the summer of 1992, although only 4,000 in the summer of 1993). This was, however, far from being enough to cover the 4 million francs of annual operating costs.

Lastly, there were the logistical sites. In Albertville, as planned, the OCOG's headquarters made it possible to extend a high school and open a new boarding school. The press centre lost half of its surface area and was turned into an urban complex with flats, an events hall, a gymnasium, a media centre and other facilities. In Brides-les Bains, conversion of the Olympic village made it possible to offer new services or widen existing ones to tourists (a thermal complex, a casino, new housing, etc.); in Moûtiers, the radio and television centre underwent an identical conversion, but over a longer period.

Globally, this side of the Olympic heritage was quite successful. Moreover, it was part of a more generalized policy to change ski resorts in Savoie. The development errors of the 1970s, which had turned the area into an ecological and economic disaster zone, were finally addressed in the 1980s. Most of the resorts were counting on urban reorganization to make them more welcoming, and to offer more services to tourists than just traditional skiing facilities.

Did these changes result in an increase in tourism? For some resorts, the answer is unarguably positive. In Les Saisies, for example, which had hosted cross-country skiing and received the most media coverage of all the resorts during the games, awareness of the possibilities began as early as summer 1992, with excellent levels of reservation for its 10,000 places. It was a village of only 180 people, who became millionaires thanks to the property fever which hiked up the value of their property. However, compared to the level of debt incurred, this result must be considered cautiously. The Olympic legacy, if not constantly maintained, can quickly melt away. In June 1992, the dismissal of Jean-Claude Perez, general manager of the Maison des Saisies (centre for tourist information and promotion), and the disappearance of the resort's promotional services were ominous signs of a badly prepared future. [44] The political authorities could not be counted on either: 'We are in a period of decentralization, and each and everyone must assume their responsibilities,' announced Michel Barnier, then president of the *conseil général*, in reaction to the pleadings of the Olympic resorts. [45] Nor was there now any use in counting upon the OCOG, which had been dissolved on 15 July 1992. On a larger scale, as was stated by the journalist Claude Francillon, after observing the fate of the speed run in Val d'Isère, 'Ten months after the Albertville Games, Savoie is having problems running the large Olympic installations.' [46]

According to Roux and Camy, the increase in tourist capacity and affluence in the Olympic resorts had followed an average growth pattern during the years of preparation, without any particular effect from the Olympic Games, although the situation varied widely from one resort to another. [47] During the two weeks of the games, the resort revenues were even below usual levels, although official declarations during the following seasons were optimistic and announced 'highly satisfying' results and a renewal of the clientele. [48] Nevertheless, and with the advantage of hindsight, the figures given by the Institut national de la statistique et des études économiques (INSEE) (Institute for Statistics and Economic Studies), based on regular surveys, spoke for themselves and demonstrated much less enthusiasm. [49] The French took 164,000 days of winter holiday in 1999, compared to an almost identical figure (162,000) in 1984. Even though there was an increase in 1993, with 183,000 days, it was very short-lived. Moreover, in percentage terms, French mountain holidays remained more or less stable between 1975 and 1999, representing 17–20% of total holidays. To be even more specific, winter sports represented 25.2% of winter holidays (in terms of days), but this percentage fell to 22% in 1989 and 1992, and then to 7.5 and 6.9% in 1994 and 1999, respectively (with identical accommodation facilities). In other words, in conformity with the predictions contained in the Andreff report, and contrary to official political declarations, the Olympics had no long-term effect on winter tourism in Savoie.

As explained by Yves Lebas to the interministerial delegation for the 1992 winter games, as far as the public authorities were concerned, the Albertville games were to 'demonstrate the excellence of the French offer' via the economic development of Savoie and the scientific, tourist, industrial and human potential of the Rhône-Alpes Region. [50] What really happened to industry? Following three bad years from 1989 to 1991, the management of Dynastar, a French company specializing in skiing equipment, was counting on Albertville, and considered itself satisfied with the three gold medals that had been won by its sponsored skiers. In the short term, the company was also counting upon concrete results from foreign sales. [51] Rossignol, with a total of 22 medal winners (9 supplied with alpine skis, 13 with ski boots), was by far the biggest French company at the games, even though it lagged far behind the Austrian companies Fischer and Atomic, who, respectively, supplied the Nordic skiing equipment for 35 and 25 medal winners. Salomon, for fixations of ski, obtained 15 medals and was ranked first in the unofficial competition between ski industries. The large French producers obtained results which reflected their place in the economic hierarchy, and generally rejoiced in these achievements. [52] Local political authorities naturally and quickly referred to the formidable impact of the Albertville games on the economy of Savoie.

These games were, in fact, held one year before the opening up of the unified European market, and the consequences of the latter were contrary to the expectations of the former. Effectively, while the ambitions of Savoie were oriented specifically towards increasing the concentration of winter sports industries upon its territory, the new economic context led to an acceleration of industrial restructuring, in conformity with the sector's tendencies, [53] which continued to grow before finally peaking with the relocating of certain key players of French industry to Asia or their sale to foreign companies. Thus, the development of Salomon and Rossignol after the games was largely built upon the diversity of their products (golfing equipment, bicycles, etc.), until these strongly region-based companies were unable to resist much larger financial operations that resulted in relocation and substantial job losses in Savoie. Rossignol came under the control of the American company Quiksilver, with plans to relocate its snowboard production to China and its cross-country ski production to Spain in 2008. Salomon was bought in 1997 by the German company Adidas, who then sold it, in 2005, to the Finnish group Amer Sport, already the owner of its main competitor, Atomic. Early in 2008, Amer Sport announced the loss of 400 jobs worldwide, including 284 in its factories in Savoie (i.e. about 25% of its personnel). In Rumilly, the factory that produces Salomon skis was scheduled to shut down in 2008, cutting the number of employees by 50%. [54] Salomon and Atomic skis are to be produced in Austria and Bulgaria. The figures say it all. Between 1987 and 2005, skiing equipment companies in the Rhône-Alpes with 50 or more employees shed more than 1,500 jobs. [55] The Albertville games were not able to counteract much larger macroeconomic processes.

The media – image and recognition

This very mixed set of economic figures merits an explanation. Certainly, an underlying dynamic in the sports equipment sector and other areas has been hit by a general slowdown in winter tourism in Europe that nothing, not even the Olympics, can change. In Albertville, however, there are more specific reasons. The reputation of Olympic sites after the games depended upon the creation and diffusion of an image of quality and local welcome. The media were the first concerned.

A better image of Albertville and the resorts of Savoie, indeed of the French Alps in general, was expected. The first good news came from ticket sales for the competitions. With nearly a million spectators, the results were 20% above expectations, and led to expectations of substantial effects on tourism. A study of these ticket sales reveals a less rosy picture, however, as half of the tickets had been bought by people from the Rhône-Alpes Region – in other words, by a local or nearby population that was already won over by Alpine winter sports.

Then there was television and, to a lesser degree, radio, which could convey the desired image of Savoie all over the world. Here again, the broadcasting of the games was a great success. Fifty-five television channels obtained image diffusion rights for 2 billion television viewers in 82 countries. In the United States, the average audience for CBS was 18 million, while 28 million Japanese watched the men's biathlon on NHK. On a national scale, 148 hours of programmes, 112 live, created audience records with a peak of 16 million television viewers for the closing ceremony. [56] In spite of large variations (3.3% of audience for Nordic skiing versus 11.9% for skating, for example), the results were remarkable and much better than initial predictions. [57]

And yet, even for the American channel CBS, which, according to observers, had 'colonised the Games', [58] these good results should be treated relatively. As early as 1988, *The New York Times*, via the journalist Peter J Boyer, was questioning the economic benefits of the Albertville games for CBS: 'Will it ever see the gold?' [59] The answer came immediately after the games. Certainly, publicity revenues and audience figures were higher than expected. 'CBS spent a pile of money to buy the rights to the Winter Games, then ran into trouble selling commercial time at full prices. Advertisers were concerned because other big CBS sporting events, the Super Bowl and the late-March college basketball championship, are already stretching their resources. Moreover, since France is six hours ahead of Eastern Standard Time, American viewers could learn results of the events before they sit down to watch them. We were dubious', said John H. Bennett, senior vice-president for events marketing at VISA USA, an Olympic sponsor. 'But now, Visa and the network's other advertisers are believers. Ratings for the first four nights have run higher than most people expected – CBS scored an average 19.7 in ratings and 30 in audience share through Feb. 12, far above the 17 rating it guaranteed advertisers (one rating point equals 431 151 households).' [60] However, these good results did not cover the rights to be paid to the organizers and the IOC: 'CBS paid roughly $243 million for the Albertville Games. And there is no way the network can make back that much by selling advertising time,' reckoned Alan J. Gottesman, a media analyst at the time, 'so once again, CBS is losing money on sports, just as it has with Major League Baseball, the National Football League and college basketball.' [61] In fact, it is believed that CBS finished with a deficit of around 20 million dollars for the Albertville games. More generally, for all channels, the 1992 games enabled the books to be balanced, with no profit, the rights to pay only just being covered by advertising revenue. [62]

But the real problem lay elsewhere. It concerned the image of the games themselves. In France, it was rather positive, as shown by a poll carried out for the Savoie *conseil general* two years after the games. Of those polled, 87% considered that the organization and management of the games had been 'a good' or 'a rather good' success, with 61% remembering in particular the spectacular opening ceremony of Philippe Decouflé. [63] On an international level, however, the image of the games was tarnished by two aspects to which the organizers had not paid sufficient attention: the Olympic 'spirit' and the environment.

Concerning the first point, the lack of conviviality was systematically linked to the separation of the sites. In Britain, Michael Calvin remarked ironically in *The Daily Telegraph*: 'Juan Antonio Samaranch, President of the IOC, called the youth of the world to south-east France, and then scattered them over 650 square miles. The spirit he was supposed to nurture was lost on the wind. Competitors, from Switzerland to Senegal, complained about the lack of atmosphere. [...]. Athletes were made to feel that they were merely ratings fodder.' [64] It was the same in Switzerland, where Michel Busset denounced, in *Le Matin*, the lack of atmosphere of the games due to their diffusion, [65] and even in France, where journalists had to admit that, for spectators and participants alike, the spreading out of the games over 11 sites, combined with the length of the games, destroyed the Olympic spirit and the special feeling of everyone being in one place. [66] The British and Americans were, moreover, particularly upset by the excesses of commercialism and the economy-first attitude, which they denounced as contrary to the spirit of the games. [67]

To this can be added questions concerning the effects of all the development on regional ecology, a subject that probably interested France less than other countries in the 1980s. Effectively, the IOC and OCOG initially appeared relatively unconcerned by environmental questions during the games' preparation, even though an active campaign was developing locally to guarantee the protection of plant and animal life as well as of the Alps themselves. Posters were even to be seen in Albertville to increase public and media awareness of this issue. [68] And yet, the state did intervene in three areas. Firstly, an effort was made to limit the impact of large structures and new roads on the countryside and biotopes, thanks to the preliminary identification of risk zones and the consultations held with a landscape expert. Secondly, all the most remarkable areas, and notably the Vanoise National Park, near Olympic sites received systematic protection measures. Finally, local officials were made aware of environmental protection issues. [69] It must be admitted, however, that these efforts were limited. Images of the inhabitants of La Plagne being given gas masks because of the risk linked to the storage of the 40 tonnes of ammonia needed to freeze the bobsleigh run did not help either. In her retrospective appraisal of the Albertville games, the American author Ellen Galford went over the environmental question ruthlessly, recalling the predictions of ecologist groups.

> Outraged environmentalists declared construction work would devastate plant and animal habitats. And once the anticipated 800,000 spectators arrived, the fumes of

the inevitable traffic jams would poison the clear mountain air. The organizers made some efforts to limit the damage. Trees uprooted during the construction of new ski runs were replanted, and the course of the men's downhill was replotted to swerve around one particularly rare wildflower habitat. The green critics weren't placated. They pointed to the million cubic meters of earth hacked out of the mountainsides, to scarring above the tree line, especially at Val d'Isère and Méribel, that might take centuries to heal. At Courchevel, they lamented the decision to reject a proposal for a light metal ski jump tower – easily dismantled after the Winter Games – in favour of a bulky construction with concrete walls and prestressed pilings. Olympic development would only compound the damage done to the already-shrinking Alpine wilderness by 30 years of ski development. And virgin landscapes, like any other sort of virgin, could never, once violated, be restored to a pristine state. [70]

Conclusion

The Calgary games made a profit; Albertville did not and ended with a deficit of 43 million euros. The results were dramatic for some of the Olympic sites in which local resorts had strongly invested. In addition, a medium-term economic analysis highlighted the lack of the impact of the games on the flow of tourists. Their effect on the local economy was positive only for the building industry and was limited to the winter sport equipment industry. Even the main TV channels, which broadcast the event, admitted that they had made no money from the games, because the benefits generated by the advertisements had only covered the cost of the rights. The image of Albertville itself was not improved significantly after 1992 and was even damaged by the declarations of ecologist groups during the preparation phase of the games. Yet, the picture is not entirely negative and, to be fair, the relatively efficient rehabilitation of the Olympic installations after the event and the better accessibility of the Tarentaise thanks to the improvement of the road network in the region should be mentioned. This last issue was considered the most important by the local officials, who declared that they were relieved because things could have been even worse! However, as Claude Francillon of *Le Monde* ironically put it, 'The results of the Winter Olympic Games: everyone loses, everyone's happy.' [71] A few years later, this lesson would be remembered by observers. During the organization of the World Football Cup in France in 1998, unfavourable comparisons were made with Albertville. [72] And during the candidature of Lyon, the largest metropolis in the Rhône-Alpes Region, for the Olympic Games of 2004, the excesses and failures of 1992 were still present in people's minds. [73]

Never had the question of the legacy of the games been so present in so many minds. [74] Moreover, the issue of legacies was incorporated in the Olympic Charter in 2002. Ten years earlier, it had been on the 'back-burner' of the organizers of the Albertville games, but an analysis based on other criteria than political affirmation alone leads one to relativize the results. Nevertheless, it would be unfair to concentrate solely on the negative aspects, in particular because Savoie has resolved its infrastructure problems and, even if the Olympic Games did not pay for this investment, they clearly constituted the pretext needed for the region to obtain state funding. At the end of the day, was not that the most important ambition of the first initiators of this adventure, back in 1981?

Notes

[1] The 'International Winter Sport Week', which was organized between 25 January and 5 February 1924, was renamed 'First Winter Olympic Games' during the IOC congress in Prague in 1925. The decision was confirmed during the IOC's 24th session in Lisbon, 2–7 May 1926 (Archives IOC).

[2] This dimension is analysed in Arnaud and Terret, *Le Rêve blanc. Olympisme et sport d'hiver. Chamonix 1924 – Grenoble 1968.*

[3] Terret, *Les Paris des Jeux olympiques de 1924*, especially Chapter 2: 'Prendre ses repères? La Semaine internationale de sports d'hiver à Chamonix'.

[4] *Journal Officiel*, Débats Parlementaires, Chambre des députés, Document parlementaires, annexe no. 802, session 20 April 1920, p. 855.

[5] According to the Institute Gallup, just before the Olympic Games, France was one of the least popular countries for Americans. See *Le Monde*, 8 Feb. 1968.

[6] Lagorce and Pariente, *La Fabuleuse histoire des Jeux olympiques. Eté-hiver*, 761.

[7] Arnaud and Terret, *Le Rêve blanc. Olympisme et sport d'hiver. Chamonix 1924 – Grenoble 1968.*

[8] Di Ruzza and Gerbier, *Ski en crise. Le Cirque blanc: du profit … à la compétition.*

[9] Michel Barnier became the president of the Conseil Général de Savoie in March 1982, a position he held until 1999. Jacques Chirac, who had just failed in his attempt to become the President of the French Republic, was president of the RPR and the mayor of Paris.

[10] 118 km between Les Saisies and Val d'Isère.

[11] Kukawa *et al.*, *Albertville 1992. Les Enjeux olympiques*, 170.

[12] *Le Monde*, 2–3 Dec. 1990; C. Francillon, 'La Contre-Attaque des stations de sports d'hiver', *Le Monde*, 17 Nov. 1991.

[13] This argument was the most important in the Association du corps préfectoral et des hauts-fonctionnaires du ministère de l'Intérieur, *Administration. Revue d'étude et d'information*, 1989.

[14] Copin, 'La Savoie olympique. Quel impact pour les l'économie de la région?', *Le Dauphiné Libéré*, 30 April 1985; 'Après les Jeux olympiques, la Savoie attend la manne', *La Suisse*, 27 Feb. 1992.

[15] Association des maires de Tarentaise-Vanoise, le club des 11, l'Association des maires de la région d'Albertville et la Fédération Nationale des Travaux Publics, *80 maires poussent un cri d'alarme*. Archives of the Ministère de l'Ecologie, de Développement durable et de l'Amenagment du territoire, available at: http://www.ecologie.gouv.fr/Repertoire-detaille-AN-19880070.html

[16] Reydet and Robert, 'Les Industries d'équipement du skieur à la recherche d'un second souffle'; Sonois, 'Les Sports d'hiver: déclin ou maturité?'

[17] M. Delberghe, 'Les Illusions perdues de la Savoie olympique', *Le Monde*, 3 Feb 1991.

[18] The report was published two years later: Andreff, *Les Effets d'entraînement des Jeux olympiques d'Albertville*. At this time, Wladimir Andreff was an expert in economics for UNESCO and the president of the Scientific Council of the National Observatory of Sport Economy.

[19] Roux and Camy, 'Formes de pratiques et modes de consommation des sports d'hiver dans la Région Rhône-Alpes'.

[20] Roux, 'Les Enjeux des Jeux olympiques et l'évolution des pratiques et des consommations de sports d'hiver en Région Rhône-Alpes', 198–9.

[21] Andreff *et al.*, 'Les Effets d'entraînement des Jeux olympiques sur les industries de sports d'hiver en Rhône-Alpes'.

[22] C. De Brie, 'Affaires d'Etat, affaires 'argent, les J.O. d'Albertville. Les comptes de la Mascotte', *Le Monde diplomatique*, Feb. 1992. Taken from press book IOC, Lausanne.

[23] Quoted in *The Expositor*, 24 Feb. 1992.

[24] L. Le Vaillant, 'Dernières médailles à la boutonnière', *Libération*, 25 Feb. 1992.

[25] A. Riding, 'Albertville Concentrates on Big Picture', *New York Times*, 2 Feb. 1992.

[26] M. Calvin, 'Cold Comfort for Olympic Spirit', *Daily Telegraph*, 24 Feb. 1992.

[27] F. Hirzel, 'Au revoir, Jeux de la démesure', *Le Nouveau Quotidien*, 23 Feb. 1992.

[28] 'A l'occasion d'un référendum Le Val-d'Aoste dit 'non' aux Jeux olympiques', *Le Monde*, 18 June 1992.

[29] 'L'Etat épongera 75% du déficit des Jeux d'Albertville', *Le Monde*, 2 July 1992; C. Francillon, 'Longtemps minimisé par les organisateurs, le déficit des Jeux d'Albertville s'élève à plus de 280 millions de francs', *Le Monde*, 9 July 1992. See also A. Riding, 'Albertville Puts Loss at $56 Million', *New York Times*, 11 July 1992.

[30] 'Budget du COJO d'Albertville: un rapport critique de l'inspection des finances', *La Lettre de l'économie du sport*, 173 (1 July 1992), p. 3. See also Francillon, note 29.

[31] Its costs increased from 90 to 235 million francs! The cost of the springboard, in Courchevel, increased from 60 to 117 million francs.

[32] J.-N. Biré and J. De Miscault, 'Pas d'impôt en plus pour les JO d'Albertville', *Le Dauphiné Libéré*, 7 July 1992.

[33] C. Francillon, 'Les Jeux n'ont pas payé les Jeux. Le rapport annuel de la Cour des comptes', *Le Monde*, 4 July 1993.

[34] P. Revil, 'A la suite d'aménagements pour les Jeux olympiques de 1992, le maire de Val-d'Isère est renvoyé en correctionnelle pour ingérence', *Le Monde*, 15 June 1993.

[35] J. De Miscault, 'Brides-les-Bains: après les Jeux, l'ardoise', *Le Dauphine Libéré*, 28 April 1992.

[36] I. Doiseau, 'Les Communes olympiques en quête d'argent', *Libération*, no date, Press book IOC, Lausanne.

[37] 'XVIes Jeux olympiques d'hiver. Deux ans après, quel impact sur la Savoie?', *Rapport*, Feb. 1994 (Archives IOC, Lausanne), p. 13.

[38] Kukawa *et al.*, *Albertville 1992. Les Enjeux olympiques.*

[39] M. C. Betbeder, 'Le Bâtiment après les Jeux', *Le Monde*, 18 March 1992.

[40] 'A Albertville manifestation pour l'emploi en Savoie', *Le Monde*, 10 Feb. 1993.

[41] Essex and Chalkley, 'Olympic Games: Catalyst of Urban Change'.

[42] Henri Dujol, 'Les Communes sites et les Jeux olympiques'.

[43] 'XVIes Jeux olympiques d'hiver. Deux ans après, quel impact sur la Savoie?', *Rapport*, Feb. 1994 (Archives IOC, Lausanne).

[44] G. Px, 'Les Saisies: communication coupée', *24 heures*, 6–7 June 1992.

[45] De Miscault, see note 35 above.

[46] C. Francillon, 'Dix mois après les Jeux d'Albertville, la Savoie a du mal à gérer les grands équipements olympiques', *Le Monde*, 5 Dec. 1992.

[47] Roux and Camy, 'Formes de pratiques et modes de consommation des sports d'hiver dans la Région Rhône-Alpes'.

[48] 'XVIes Jeux olympiques d'hiver' (see note 37 above), 17.

[49] Rouquette and Taché, 'Les Vacances des Français', pp. 19 and 26. According to the standard definition, 'holiday' is here defined as at least four nights spent away from home.

[50] Lebas, 'La Valorisation économique', 91.

[51] M. H., 'Derrière les Jeux, la chance et … les gains', *Le Figaro*, 25 Feb. 1992.

[52] H. Pilichowski, 'JO: les médailles des fabricants', *Le Dauphiné Libéré*, 4 March 1992.

[53] Minquet, 'Les grandes tendances stratégiques dans l'industrie du sport'.

[54] B. Bissuel, 'Emotion en Haute-Savoie après la fermeture de l'usine Salomon', *Le Monde*, 11 Jan. 2008.

[55] P. Chantelat *et al.*, *Les Emplois du sport en Rhône-Alpes*.

[56] 'Les Jeux d'hiver: de l'or pour les chaines', *France soir*, 25 Feb. 1992.

[57] M. Dalinval, 'JO: le plein d'audience', *Le Figaro*, 25 Feb. 1992.

[58] M. Calvin, 'Cold Comfort for Olympic Spirit', *Daily Telegraph*, 24 Feb. 1992.

[59] P. J. Boyer, 'The Media Business: Television; CBS Wins the Olympics: Will It Ever See the Gold?', *New York Times*, 30 May 1988.

[60] 'Ah, Albertville: A Sweet Surprise for CBS. The Winter Games Are Drawing Unexpectedly High Ratings, If Not Profit', *International Business Week*, 24 Feb. 1992.

[61] Ibid.

[62] O. Benyahia-Kouider, 'Les JO pulvérisent les records d'audience', *Libération*, 25 Feb. 1992.

[63] P. Revil, 'La Bonne image des Jeux d'Albertville', *Le Monde*, 20 Feb. 1994.

[64] Calvin (see note 58 above).

[65] M. Busset, 'L'Heure des questions', *Le Matin*, 1 March 1992.

[66] A. Giraudo, 'L'Esprit olympique dilué', *Le Monde*, 25 Feb. 1992.

[67] See, for instance, I. Macleod, 'Ideal of Excellence Redundant in the Games with No Soul', *Daily Telegraph*, 25 Feb. 1992.

[68] K. Chujo, 'Sports and Environment', *Asahi Evening News* (Tokyo), 22 March 1992.

[69] Bastion, 'Les Jeux olympiques d'Albertville et l'environnement'.

[70] Galford, *The Olympic Century. XXIV Olympiad: Seoul 1988, Albertville 1992*.

[71] C. Francillon, 'Actualité le bilan des Jeux olympiques d'hiver J.O.: tous perdants, tous contents', *Le Monde*, 3 March 1992.

[72] 'En 1992, les Jeux n'avaient pas payé les Jeux?', *Le Monde*, 12 Jan. 1999.

[73] B. Causse, 'Lyon et la région Rhône-Alpes candidats pour les JO de 2004', *Le Monde*, 20 Sept. 1995; B. Causse, 'Les Lyonnais s'interrogent sur les raisons de leur échec', *Le Monde*, 9 Nov. 1995.

[74] Preuss, *Economics of the Olympic Games*.

References

Andreff, W. ed. *Les Effets d'entraînement des Jeux olympiques d'Albertville. Retombées socio-économiques et innovations dans le domaine du sport en Région Rhône-Alpes. PPSH* 15 (Jan. 1991).

Andreff, W., M. Andreff, J. Calvet and B. Gerbier. 'Les effets d'entraînement des Jeux olympiques sur les industries de sports d'hiver en Rhône-Alpes'. In *Les effets d'entraînement des Jeux olympiques d'Albertville. Retombées socio-économiques et innovations dans le domaine du sport en Région Rhône-Alpes*, edited by W. Andreff. *PPSH* 15 (Jan. 1991): 235–332.

Arnaud, P. and T. Terret. *Le Rêve blanc. Olympisme et sport d'hiver. Chamonix 1924–Grenoble 1968*. Bordeaux: Presses universitaires de Bordeaux, 1993.

Association des maires de Tarentaise-Vanoise, le club des 11, l'Association des maires de la région d'Albertville et la Fédération Nationale des Travaux Publics, *80 maires poussent un cri d'alarme,* typed document, 1985.

Bastion, J.C. 'Les Jeux olympiques d'Albertville et l'environnement'. *Administration. Revue d'étude et d'information* (1989): 92–3.

Chantelat, P., T. Terret, N. Chanavat and P.O. Schut. *Les emplois du sport en Rhône-Alpes. Etat des lieux général et perspectives pour l'industrie d'articles de sport*, Rapport à la Région Rhône-Alpes, 2006.

Di Ruzza, F. and B. Gerbier. *Ski en crise. Le Cirque blanc: du profit … à la compétition*. Grenoble: Presses universitaires de Grenoble, 1977.

Dujol, H. 'Les Communes sites et les Jeux olympiques'. In Association du corps préfectoral et des hauts-fonctionnaires du ministère de l'Intérieur, *Administration. Revue d'étude et d'information*, 1989: 46–50.

Essex, S. and B. Chalkley. 'Olympic Games: Catalyst of Urban Change'. *Leisure Studies* 17 (1998): 187–206.

Galford, E. *The Olympic Century. XXIV Olympiad: Seoul 1988, Albertville 1992*, vol. 22. Los Angeles: World Sport Research & Publications, 2000.

Kukawa, P., P. Préau, F. Servoin and R. Vivian. *Albertville 1992. Les Enjeux olympiques*. Grenoble: Presses universitaires de Grenoble, 1991.

Lagorce, G. and R. Pariente. *La Fabuleuse Histoire des Jeux olympiques. Eté-hiver*. Paris: ODIL, 1972, 1977.

Lebas, Y. 'La valorisation économique'. In Association du corps préfectoral et des hauts-fonctionnaires du ministère de l'Intérieur, *Administration. Revue d'étude et d'information* (1989): 88–91.

Minquet, J.P. 'Les grandes tendances stratégiques dans l'industrie du sport'. *Problèmes économiques* 2616 (June 1999): 15–20.

Preuss, H. *Economics of the Olympic Games. Hosting the Games 1972–2000*. Sydney: Walla Walla Press, 2000.

Reydet, P. and J. Robert. 'Les Industries d'équipement du skieur à la recherche d'un second souffle'. *Points d'appui pour l'économie Rhône-Alpes* 22 (Feb. 1983): 19–25.

Rouquette, C. and C. Taché. 'Les Vacances des Français. Résultats de l'enquête 'Vacances' 1999'. *INSEE Résultats, Sociétés* 4 (May 2002): 3–38.

Roux, C. and J. Camy. 'Formes de pratiques et modes de consommation des sports d'hiver dans la Région Rhône-Alpes'. In *Les Effets d'entraînement des Jeux olympiques d'Albertville. Retombées socio-économiques et innovations dans le domaine du sport en Région Rhône-Alpes*, edited by W. Andreff. *PPSH* 15 (Jan. 1991): 126–67.

Roux, F. 'Les Enjeux des Jeux olympiques et l'évolution des pratiques et des consommations de sports d'hiver en Région Rhône-Alpes'. In *Les Effets d'entraînement des Jeux olympiques d'Albertville. Retombées socio-économiques et innovations dans le domaine du sport en Région Rhône-Alpes*, edited by W. Andreff. *PPSH* 15 (Jan. 1991): 168–220.

Sonois, J.P. 'Les Sports d'hiver: déclin ou maturité?' *Espaces* 84 (Feb. 1987).

Terret, T. ed. *Les Paris des Jeux olympiques de 1924*. Biarritz: Atlantica, 2008.

Maximizing Olympic Impacts by Building Up Legacies

Chris Gratton and Holger Preuss

Introduction

The Olympic Games are expensive for host cities and cause substantial deficits for cities and countries (in particular the Olympics in Montreal in 1976 and in Athens in 2004). Today the International Olympic Committee (IOC) controls the finances of the operation of the event, but there is still the problem of how to finance the infrastructure needed for the event. Host cities often invest in new infrastructure that is oversized or not needed in the long term. Since 2004, many Olympic facilities built for the 2004 Olympics in Athens have remained unused.

One of the main interests of the IOC is a positive 'legacy' of the event. There are three reasons for this. First, a positive legacy avoids the public in the host city/nation blaming the IOC and provides evidence as to why the event has been good for the host city/nation. Second, it justifies the use of scarce public resources for permanent or temporary event infrastructure. Third, a positive legacy motivates other cities/ nations to bid for future events. High demand increases the power of the IOC and secures the continuance of the Olympic Games.

This contribution adds to the controversial discussion of the investment of scarce public resources in mega-sport events such as the Olympic Games. The positive, or negative, legacy of mega-sport events has to be considered when discussing the opportunity costs of resources committed to an event. This contribution provides a definition of legacy and then goes on to discuss how legacy might be measured and what are the key elements that make up a legacy.

Definition of 'Legacy' and Literature Review

In the literature, an immense variety of so-called legacies from sport events can be found. Surprisingly, there is no definition of 'legacy' available. 'Event legacy' – as used by the IOC – captures the value of sport facilities and public improvements that are turned over to communities or sports organizations after the Olympic Games. The legacy includes a 'legacy fund' for ongoing operations of sports facilities and venues. This legacy fund is an important feature because the required event facilities, for example the bobsleigh/luge tracks constructed for Winter Olympics, need ongoing operating subsidies. [1]

However, this definition seems to be narrow in comparison to the various characteristics of 'legacy' mentioned in the literature. Examples range from commonly recognized aspects (urban planning, sport infrastructure) to less recognized intangible legacies, such as urban revival, enhanced international reputation, increased tourism, improved public welfare, additional employment, more local business opportunities, better corporate relocation, chances for city marketing, renewed community spirit, better interregional cooperation, production of ideas, production of cultural values, popular memory, education, experience and additional know-how. These positive legacies stand in contrast to negative legacies such as debts from construction, high opportunity costs, infrastructure that is not needed after the event, temporary crowding out, loss of tourists that would have visited the host city if the event were not taking place, property rental increases, and socially unjust displacement and redistributions. [2]

In 2000, the IOC launched a project called the 'Olympic Games Global Impact' (OGGI). This project was initiated in order to improve the evaluation of the overall impacts of the Olympic Games on the host city, its environment and its citizens, as well as to propose a consistent methodology to capture the overall effects of hosting the games. The OGGI project covers an 11-year period, starting with the bidding stage right through the hosting of the event itself to 2 years after the event being held. There are three categories of indicators to measure these effects: economic, social and environmental. [3] The main problem, however, with the OGGI project is that it ends 2 years after the event, which is much too soon to measure the legacy of the event.

Aware of the variety and importance of legacy, the IOC initiated a congress on 'The Legacy of the Olympic Games: 1984–2000' in 2002. It attempted to define legacy, but the participants 'found that there are several meanings of the concept, and some of the contributions have highlighted the convenience of using other expressions and concepts that can mean different things in different languages and cultures'. [4] Cashman adds to this hesitancy by stating that the 'word legacy, however, is elusive, problematic and even a dangerous word for a number of reasons. [5] When the term is used by organising committees, it is assumed to be entirely positive, there being no such thing as negative legacy when used in this context. Secondly, it is usually believed that legacy benefits flow to a community at the end of the Games as a matter of course .... Thirdly, legacy is often assumed to be self-evident, so that there is no need to define precisely what it is' (p. 15). [6] Cashman collected a variety of evidence about legacies. [7] He identified six fields of legacies: economics; infrastructure; information and education; public life, politics and culture; sport; symbols, memory and history.

However, this rather qualitative definition needs a broader perspective. A general definition of legacy should be independent of qualitative examples or IOC suggestions. Three legacy dimensions can be identified: first, the degree of planned structure; second, the degree of positive structure; third, the degree of quantifiable structure. A definition considering these dimensions is as follows: 'Legacy is planned and unplanned, positive and negative, intangible and tangible structures created through a sport event that remain after the event.' In the following discussion, the word 'structure' is used in this context.

The three dimensions of legacy form a 'legacy cube' (Figure 1). The legacy cube has eight smaller cubes. A holistic evaluation of a mega-sport event would be necessary to identify all legacies. In reality, most pre-event studies and bid committees focus on only one subcube (planned, positive, tangible). [8] Many of the pre-event feasibility and impact studies that consider legacies are potentially biased, because the ambition of those commissioning the studies is to favour the hosting of the event, and therefore they emphasize only this particular subcube. This issue is constantly criticized by authors investigating the economic effects of hosting major sport events. [9] Kasimati analysed all impact studies of the Summer Olympics from 1984 to 2004 and found, in each case, that the studies were done prior to the games, were not based

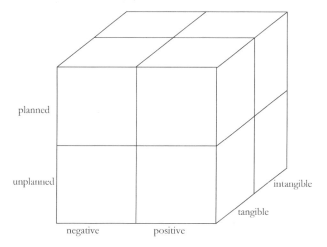

Figure 1 Legacy cube.

on primary data, and were, in general, commissioned by proponents of the games. [10] He found that the economic impacts were likely to be inflated, since the studies did not take into account supply-side constraints such as investment crowding out, price increases due to resource scarcity, and the displacement of tourists who would have been in the host city had the Olympics not been held there.

The Measurement of Event Legacies

The measurement of a legacy should start with the changes events create. An economic event impact is strong, but short-term and only on the demand side. Tourist and operational expenditures, investments in temporary structures, volunteer and management activity, etc., peak for a short time. [11] However, the induced consumption-based economic activity constantly decreases over time due to taxes, savings and imports. In the long run, both the event demands and the leakage of money influx most likely return to the equilibrium income of the pre-event level. In other words, the huge figures of economic impacts are not an event legacy.

Long-term economic growth requires a constant influx of autonomous money. In terms of economic growth related to events, this can better be reached if the event has changed the host city's structure – in other words, its supply side. It should be the aim of politicians to initiate structural changes that improve the 'location factors', which are the basis of new post-event impacts. Chalip emphasized the necessity to leverage the post-event impact to justify public investment in infrastructure. [12] Ritchie goes further and talks about the need to 'embed' an event in broader processes of the city development. [13] Both authors stress planning the legacy before an event is staged. Faber Maunsell suggests that there is a need to start earlier: 'Commitment and funding for legacy need to be in place when planning the event' (p. 55). [14]

Studies of mega-sport events often measure the economic impact or those impacts that are related to economics. These can be tourism, [15] employment [16] and infrastructure development. [17] Most studies also mention environmental impacts [18] and social impacts, [19] but in a qualitative and general way, often based on experiences of past events. This can be explained by the fact that the majority of studies are written prior to the event, and the legacies cannot be measured or be based on scientific evidence.

Event Structures and Their Effect on the Host City

Each mega-sport event requires specific structures. All event structures that exist after the event change the quality of the host city in a positive or negative way. Each city has different quality factors that make the city more or less attractive for living in, for tourists, for industry, or for hosting future sport events.

Today cities are in global competition to attract economic activity. [20] Where the event legacy in these terms is significant, the host city is in a better position to face this global competition. The possibility of this happening is enhanced by strategically embedding the event in the broader processes of development. [21]

The strategy of building up an event legacy starts with the decision to bid for a specific event (1) (Figure 2). Mega-sport events differ in the structures they require and cities differ in the structures they can provide. The strategy focuses on the additional structures an event creates and the long-term need for these structures. During the candidature process, (2) some required structures ('compulsory measures') as well as some 'optional measures' will be provided. By means of the 'optional measures', the city aims to be strategically best positioned in the bid competition. [22] Therefore, these measures may not be sustainable. During the preparation for the event (3) the compulsory structures are set up. 'Optional measures' can be embedded to improve the competitive position of the host city to attract more economic activity in the future. During the event (4), all 'event structures' are present. After the event (5), some 'event structures' disappear or are reduced in size, but others exist for a long time after the event. Six 'event structures' are usually preserved after an event.

Six 'Event Structures'

Infrastructure

Infrastructure obviously means the sport infrastructure for competition and training, but also the general infrastructure of a city such as airports, roads, telecommunication, hotels, housing (athletes, media and officials), entertainment facilities, fair grounds, parks, etc. All infrastructure left after an event should fit into the city's development. Today temporary constructions can avoid negative legacies such as oversized and extraneous facilities. Examples are a movable velodrome (Olympics, Atlanta 1996), a temporary 50-m indoor pool in a fair hall (FINA World Cup,

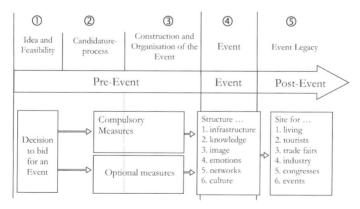

Figure 2 Process of building up planned event legacy.

Fukuoka 2001) or an athletic stadium transformed into a football stadium (Commonwealth Games, Manchester 2002). Szymanski supports this idea. He claims that all spending should be directed at the most productive activities (p. 3). [23]

The Commonwealth Games in Manchester 2002, for example, provided world-class sporting facilities, including the City of Manchester Stadium. Time pressure, however, accelerated investment in major transport links, a new rail station, ground interchange at the airport, quality bus corridors, etc. [24] Germany invested 1.5bn euros in stadiums for the FIFA-Football World Cup 2006. [25] The old arenas, most dating from the last German World Cup in 1974, did not meet the modern requirements for marketing and entertainment. Finally, the upgrade of the Athens infrastructure to stage the Olympic Games 2004 cost more than 5bn euros. While some facilities still remain unused and many are oversized, some general infrastructure (airport, airport link, metro, the revitalization of the coastal line and the old airport area) will provide great value for the further economic growth of Athens.

Knowledge, Skill-Development and Education

The host population gains knowledge and skills from staging a mega-sport event. Employees and volunteers achieve skills and knowledge in event organization, human resource management, security, hospitality, service, etc. Spectators and volunteers learn to use public transportation and are acquainted with environmental projects. They also gain greater knowledge about the history of their city and country, culture and other issues.

For example, almost 50% of 10,000 volunteers recruited for the Commonwealth Games in Manchester 2002 felt that they had acquired new skills and capabilities through their experience, 18% believed that being a volunteer had improved their chances of employment, and 46% agreed that being a volunteer had enhanced their personal development. [26] An example of a negative effect is the policy of global sponsors of mega-sport events who try to establish brand loyalty at the youngest age possible. [27] Events offer them opportunities for youth marketing. In regards to sponsors from Sydney 2000, Lenskyj wrote: 'Their cynical exploitation of "Olympic spirit" rhetoric and pseudo-educational initiatives were key components of the campaign to reach children and youth' (p. 126). [28] Corporations investing money in educational programmes certainly aim to promote the Olympic idea, but also the Olympic industry, thereby socializing children to become 'global consumers' of their goods.

Image

Mega-sport events have tremendous symbolic significance and form, and reposition or solidify the image of a city, region and country. Usually, events create a positive imagery, and the city and politicians can 'bask in [its] reflected glory'. [29] On the other hand, the worldwide exposure of the event, the host city and its culture depends on the media representatives and cannot be entirely controlled by the organizers. [30] Negative incidences such as a bomb attack, hooligans, organizational shortcomings or just bad weather also influence the image of the host. Not only negative incidents, but also general bad attributes can be transported through a mega-event to millions of potential visitors, customers or business partners. Exaggerated nationalism or unfair spectator behaviour spoils hospitality, and poverty and crime create doubts about a potential tourism destination.

For example, one of the aims of hosting the FIFA-Football World Cup 2006 was to reposition the stereotype of Germans as 'conformist, time-dominated, serious'. [31] The organizers and government launched a hospitality concept including service of government resorts, location marketing for Germany, a cultural programme, and a service and friendliness campaign. [32] Another example is Qatar's hosting of the 2006 Asian Games in Doha. Ultimately, the country was trying to reposition its image and infrastructure to become the Arabic sport and entertainment centre. Mega-sport events are often used as a catalyst to transform a location into a tourist destination. This corporate-centre strategy requires the building of convention centres, sport facilities, museums, shopping malls, and entertainment and gambling complexes to reach economic growth by consumption-oriented economic development. [33]

Emotions

Mega-sport events give politicians a common vision to gain international prestige, and citizens may become emotionally involved. The pride of hosting such an event creates local identification, vision and motivation. An example is the Olympic Games in Seoul 1988, which created a national perspective; a feeling of vitality, participation, and recognition; and an international perception of being modern and technologically up-to-date. [34] The Chinese were keen to demonstrate their increasing economic importance through the Olympics in 2008. [35]

Private industry is stimulated by the expected influx of money and a potentially positive post-event legacy. This may change the readiness to invest instead of saving funds. [36] 'The announcement of the event leads to a programme of anticipatory investment. Directly, or indirectly it is the catalyst for a number of 'piggy-back' events (which in turn promote further investment). And during the event itself, there is a boost to local demand. While all of these boost the local economy in the short term, the key to any long-term effects lies in whether and how these leave a permanent legacy in the infrastructure, or in industry competencies'. [37] There are several indications from Olympic Games that these anticipatory investments have taken place. Critically seen, some have created oversupply. [38]

Negative emotions may also be caused if new event facilities use the space of former workers' areas. Then citizens living there suffer from expropriation and relocation, but also from gentrification of their area, leading to a loss of their social environment. [39]

Networks

International sport federations, media, politics, etc., need to cooperate in order to stage an event successfully. Their interaction creates networks. In general, events improve political networks, such as close partnership with the central government. In particular, the greater knowledge of sport, networks between politicians and sport federations, and the image of being a sport city increase the affiliation to sport. Grass-roots coaching programmes, facilities for schools, sport for all, and additional sport events may be the result.

For example, through the Olympics in Athens 2004, an international security network was established, which gave Greece a new standard of security in general. Manchester used the Commonwealth Games 2002 to form a basis for providing new business opportunities, utilizing the games as a promotional asset for trade and investment. [40]

Culture

Mega-sport events produce cultural ideas, cultural identity and cultural products. Opening ceremonies especially include a cultural-artistic aspect that is a condensed display of the host country's culture. A positive cultural image, increased awareness, new infrastructure and additional tourist products, combined with the soft factor of better service quality, have a great potential to increase tourism in the long term. [41] Barcelona, for instance, used the Olympics to transform its infrastructure to become a 'cultural city'. [42] The cultural presentation educates the host population and forces them to address their history. For example, there was increased awareness of Aboriginal history in Australia during the 2000 Sydney Olympic Games, and increased understanding of Mormon traditions in the USA during the 2002 Salt Lake Olympic Winter Games. However, it is critical that the cultural awareness betters the situation of these minorities. Another example is 'the Spirit of Friendship Festival', which was launched for the Commonwealth Games 2002 and aimed to celebrate the Commonwealth, thus leaving a cultural legacy. 'It was a nationwide programme [and was ...] set out to communicate the visual and performing arts and cultural traditions of countries in the Commonwealth'. [43]

Case Study: Commonwealth Games Manchester 2002

Although the Commonwealth Games are not on the scale of the Olympics, they are a multi-sport event that requires substantial infrastucture investment similar to the Olympic Games. The Commonwealth Games held in Manchester in 2002 involved an investment of £200 million in sporting venues in the city and a further £470 million investment in transport and other infrastructure. This was by far the largest investment related to the hosting of a specific sports event ever to be undertaken in Britain prior to the investment for the London Olympics in 2012. It was also the first time in Britain that planning for the hosting of a major sports event was integrated within the strategic framework for the regeneration of the city, in particular East Manchester.

In 1999, 3 years before the games were held, the Commonwealth Games Opportunities and Legacy Partnership Board was established to manage the legacy of the games. Legacy activities were funded under the 2002 North West Economic and Social Single Regeneration Board Programme, which operated from 1999 to 2004. This was the first time in Britain that an ambitious legacy programme was designed around a major sports event. The objective was to ensure that the benefits of hosting the event would not disappear once the event was over, but rather that there would be a long-term permanent boost to the local economy of East Manchester.

Despite the long-term planning for the games and the legacy, there was one major omission: no economic impact study was carried out during the games in 2002, and so no primary data were available on the immediate economic benefit of the games. Cambridge Policy Consultants produced a pre-event estimate of the economic impact in April 2002 and then revised it in November 2003, [44] using secondary evidence available from the games period. They estimated that the games generated an additional 2,900 full-time equivalent (FTE) jobs in Manchester. However, without any visitor survey data available for the games themselves, there must be serious doubts as to the validity of such an estimate.

A further study of the benefits of the games was carried out for the North West Development Agency in 2004 by Faber Maunsell, in association with Vision Consulting and Roger Tym and Partners. [45] The study used secondary sources and interviews with key stakeholders. As part of the study, they measured employment change in East Manchester between 1999 and 2002, as revealed by the Annual Business Inquiry (ABI) data. This showed an increase of 1,450 jobs (including both part-time and full-time jobs) or a 4% increase over the 1999 level. However, these are annual data, and therefore it is difficult to isolate how much of this increase was due to the games. The distribution of the increase in construction (23% increase), distribution, hotels and restaurants (14% increase), and other services (24% increase) is consistent with the games having been the main generator of the increase in jobs. Moreover, out of the 210 new jobs in 'other services', 200 were in the 'recreational, cultural, and sporting' category, suggesting again a significant games effect. However, the gain of 1,450 new jobs, which included part-time jobs, is considerably lower than the 2,900 FTE jobs estimated by Cambridge Policy Consultants, although this figure relates to the effect on the whole of Manchester, not just East Manchester.

The net additional value of capital investment in the games was estimated by Faber Maunsell at £670m, of which £201m was for the sporting venues and £125m was for transport infrastructure. Other major investment included an Asda-Walmart superstore occupying 180,000 square feet and employing 760 FTE staff.

Since no visitor survey was carried out during the games, actual tourism indicators were difficult to obtain. Using annual tourism data from the UK Tourism Survey (UKTS) and the International Passenger Survey (IPS), Faber Maunsell indicated a

7.4% increase of overseas visitors to Greater Manchester in 2002 compared to 2000. [46] However, there was a 6.4% decrease in UK resident visitors to Greater Manchester over the same period and a 2.2% decrease in the number of nights overseas residents spent in Greater Manchester. Overall, though, there was a 21% increase in UK residents' expenditure and a 29% increase in overseas residents' expenditure in Greater Manchester in 2002 compared to 2000. Again, because these are annual figures, it is impossible to isolate the influence of the games on these figures, but it is reasonable to conclude that they were the most significant factor.

The Faber Maunsell study does not give a detailed media analysis of the games, indicating only that the opening and closing ceremonies had an 'estimated' worldwide audience of 1 billion. The Commonwealth Games are an unusual event in that they do get television coverage across most continents, but they are not a global event in the same way as the Olympics and the football World Cup are. There are key markets where there will be no coverage at all, such as the USA, the whole of the rest of Europe outside the British Isles, Japan and China. The event, therefore, is limited in the potential effect on the image and profile of the host city.

Some indication of the public profile benefits of the games is indicated by Manchester's moving up the European Cities Monitor from 19th in 2002 to 13th in 2003. The monitor, a measure of the best European cities in which to locate a business, is compiled by Cushman and Wakefield Healey and Baker. It is constructed from the views of Europe's 500 leading businesses on the top business locations in Europe and is used to indicate aspects affecting business location decisions. For Manchester, it is an indicator of an improvement in the city's image from a business perspective and an indicator of greater potential for inward investment.

Despite the lack of hard evidence on the economic impact of the Commonwealth Games on Manchester in 2002, there is enough evidence to indicate that East Manchester has benefited considerably. Manchester City now use the City of Manchester stadium as their home ground, and other sporting venues in East Manchester have become the English Institute of Sport and are used for the training of elite athletes. Since much of the funding for the new investment for the facilities came from the National Lottery or central government, this is a clear economic boost for the area. We will have to wait and see whether the legacy benefits are as great as were hoped for, but the indications are promising.

Longer-term benefits of hosting major sport events

Although it is too early to assess the urban regeneration legacy benefits of Manchester 2002, it should be possible to assess the long-term benefits of events held 10 or 20 years ago. Unfortunately, there are few research studies that attempt to measure systematically such long-term benefits. Spilling found he could identify no long-term economic benefits for Lillehammer from hosting the Winter Olympics in 1994. [47] He concluded: 'If the main argument for hosting a mega-event like the Winter

Olympics is the long-term economic impacts it will generate, the Lillehammer experience quite clearly points to the conclusion that it is a waste of money.'

Spilling seems to question whether there can be any long-term effect for an area the size of Lillehammer, a city of 24,000 inhabitants situated 180 km north of Oslo. The two Winter Olympics prior to the Lillehammer games, in Calgary in 1988 and in Albertville in 1992, had been in larger regions, and there was more evidence of a continuing benefit several years after the games. In the case of Albertville, this was partly due to massive transport infrastructure investment that made access to the region by car substantially easier, although at a severe cost to the alpine environment. Certainly, there is little evidence to support the argument that the Winter Olympics leave a substantial long-term benefit.

There is some evidence, however, that the Summer Olympics do generate a legacy benefit. One example that is often quoted to support the argument that there are long-term benefits of hosting major sports events is the case of the Barcelona Olympics in 1992.

R. Sanahuja provided evidence on the longer-term economic benefits of hosting the Olympics in Barcelona in 1992. [48] The paper analysed the benefits to Barcelona in 2002, 10 years after hosting the games. Table 1 shows an almost 100% increase in hotel capacity, number of tourists, and number of overnight stays in 2001 compared to the pre-games position in 1990. Average room occupancy had also increased from 71% to 84%. In addition, the average length of stay had increased from 2.84 days to 3.17 days. In 1990, the majority (51%) of tourists to Barcelona were from the rest of Spain, with 32% from the rest of Europe, and the remainder (17%) from outside Europe. By 2001, the absolute number of Spanish tourists had actually risen by 150,000, but given the near doubling in the number of tourists overall, this higher total only accounted for 31% of the total number of tourists. The proportion of tourists from the rest of Europe went up from 32% to 40% (representing an absolute increase of around 800,000) and from the rest of the world from 17% to 29% (representing an absolute increase of around 600,000).

Table 1 Legacy benefits of the Barcelona Olympic Games

	1990	2001
Hotel capacity (beds)	18,567	34,303
Number of tourists	1,732,902	3,378,636
Number overnights	3,795,522	7,969,496
Average room occupancy	71%	84%
Average stay	2.84	3.17
Tourist by origin		
Spain	51.2%	31.3%
Europe	32%	39.5%
Others (USA, Japan, Latin America)	16.8%	29.2%

Source: Turisme de Barcelona (BarcelonaTourist Board) and Sanahuja (2002).

Overall infrastructure investment prior to the games was $7.5bn compared to a budget of around $1.5bn for the Olympic Committee to stage the games. The Olympics in Barcelona were the most expensive ever staged prior to Beijing. However, Barcelona's use of the games as a city marketing factor is generally regarded as a huge success. This is evidenced by Barcelona's rise in ranking in the European Cities Monitor from 11th in 1990 to 6th in 2002.

Conclusions

This chapter has attempted to improve understanding of the concept of the legacy of hosting a major sport event and to describe its many dimensions. Despite some ad hoc evidence from the Manchester 2002 Commonwealth Games and the Barcelona 1992 Olympic Games, it remains the case that the scientific evidence needed to evaluate the economic importance of the legacy of hosting major sports events, such as the Olympic Games, simply does not exist. This situation will not be resolved by the IOC's new Olympic Games Global Impact (OGGI) project, although this will substantially improve the evidence base. The problem is that it will take 15–20 years to measure the true legacy of an event such as the Olympic Games and the OGGI project finishes 2 years after the event has been held. So far, nobody has been prepared to commit the research resources required to carry out a scientific study of net legacy benefits. There is also the political position that host governments may not welcome a truly scientific assessment of the true legacy benefits of hosting the Olympic Games.

Notes

[1] Fuller and Clinch, 'The Economic and Fiscal Impacts of Hosting the 2012 Olympic Games on the Washington–Baltimore Metropolitan Area'; Thorpe. *The Economic Impact of the Winter Olympic and Paralympic Games: Initial Estimates.*

[2] Ritchie and Aitken, 'Assessing the Impacts of the 1988 Olympic Winter Games: The Research Programme and Initial Results'; Haxton, 'Community Involvement and the Olympic Games – A Review of Related Research. International Olympic Academy'; Lenskyj, *Inside the Olympic Industry: Power, Politics and Activism* and *The Best Olympics Ever? Social Impacts of Sydney 2000*; Moragas *et al., The Legacy of the Olympic Games: 1984–2000*; Kasimati, 'Economic Aspects and the Summer Olympics: A Review of Related Research'; Preuss, *The Economics of Staging the Olympics: A Comparison of the Games 1972–2008*; Cashman, *The Bitter-Sweet Awakening: The Legacy of the Sydney 2000 Olympic Games*; Vigor *et al., After the Gold Rush. A Sustainable Olympics for London*; Kesenne 'Do We Need an Economic Impact Study or a Cost-Benefit Analysis of a Sport Event?'

[3] Furrer, 'Sustainable Olympic Games: A Dream or a Reality?'; IOC, 'What is the Olympic Games Global Impact Study?'

[4] Ritchie & Aitken, 'Assessing the Impacts of the 1988 Olympic Winter Games: The Research Programme and Initial Results'; Haxton, 'Community Involvement and the Olympic Games – A Review of Related Research. International Olympic Academy'; Lenskyj, *Inside the Olympic Industry: Power, Politics and Activism* and *The Best Olympics Ever? Social Impacts of Sydney 2000*; Moragas *et al., The Legacy of the Olympic Games: 1984–2000*; Kasimati, 'Economic Aspects and the Summer Olympics: A Review of Related Research'; Preuss, *The Economics of*

Staging the Olympics. A Comparison of the Games 1972–2008; Cashman, *The Bitter-Sweet Awakening: The Legacy of the Sydney 2000 Olympic Games.*; Vigor *et al.*, *After the Gold Rush. A Sustainable Olympics for London.*; Kesenne 'Miscalculations and Misinterpretations in Economic Impact Analysis').

[5]   Cashman *The Bitter-Sweet Awakening: The Legacy of the Sydney 2000 Olympic Games.*

[6]   Ibid., p. 15.

[7]   Ibid.

[8]   See Ibid., p. 15

[9]   Mills, 'The Misuse of Regional Economic Models'; Crompton, 'Economic Impact Analysis of Sports Facilities and Events: Eleven Sources of Misapplication'; Howard and Crompton, *Financing Sport*; Kesenne, 'Miscalculations and Misinterpretations in Economic Impact Analysis'; Porter, 'Mega-Sports Events as Municipal Investments: A Critique of Impact Analysis'; Preuss, 'Electing an Olympic City – a Multidimensional Decision'; Baade & Matheson, 'Bidding for the Olympics: Fool's Gold?'; Szymanski, 'The Economic Impact of the World Cup'; Kasimati, 'Economic Aspects and the Summer Olympics: A Review of Related Research'; Cashman, *The Bitter-Sweet Awakening: The Legacy of the Sydney 2000 Olympic Games.*

[10]   Kasimati 'Economic Aspects and the Summer Olympics: A Review of Related Research'.

[11]   Rahmann *et al. Sozioökonomische Analyse der Fußball-WM 2006 in Deutschland.*; Preuß & Weiss, *Torchholder Value Added, der ökonomische Nutzen Olympischer Spiele in Frankfurt Rhein/Main 2012).*

[12]   Chalip, *Leveraging the Sydney Olympics for Tourism.*

[13]   Ritchie, 'Turning 16 Days into 16 Years Through Olympic Legacies'.

[14]   Faber Maunsell, *Commonwealth Games Benefits Study.*

[15]   Getz, 'Special Events: Defining the Product' and *Festivals, Special Events, and Tourism*; Hall, *Hallmark Tourist Events: Impacts, Management and Planning*; Kang & Perdue, 'Long-Term Impact of a Mega Event on International Tourism to the Host Country: A Conceptual Model and the Case of the 1988 Seoul Olympics'; Dwyer *et al.* 'Evaluating Tourism's Economic Effects: New and Old Approaches'; Solberg & Preuss, 'Major Sporting Events and Long-Term Tourism Impacts'.

[16]   Burns *et al.*, *The Adelaide Grand Prix: The Impact of a Special Event*; Mules and Faulkner, 'An Economic Perspective on Special Events'; Ritchie, 'How Special Are Special Events? An Impact Study of the National Mutual New Zealand Masters Games on Dunedin's Economy'; Ritchie, 'Assessing the Impact of Hallmark Events: Conceptual and Research Issues'; Hotchkiss, Moore and Zobay, 2001 [missing].

[17]   Evans, The Role of the Festival in Urban Regeneration: Planning for the British Millennium Festival'; Hughes, 'Olympic Tourism and Urban Regeneration; 1996 Summer Olympics'; Meyer-Künzel, *Der planbare Nutzen. Stadtentwicklung durch Weltausstellungen und Olympische Spiele.*

[18]   May, 'Environmental Implications of the 1992 Winter Olympic Games'.

[19]   Shultis *et al.* 'Social Impacts of a Hallmark Event; Development and Description of a Case Study in Thunder Bay Ontario'; Hodges and Hall, 'The Housing and Social Impacts of Mega Events: Lessons for the Sydney 2000 Olympics'; Lenskyj *The Best Olympics Ever? Social Impacts of Sydney 2000*; Fredline *et al.* 'The Development of a Generic Scale to Measure the Social Impacts of Events'; Misener and Mason, 'Creating Community Networks: Can Sporting Events Offer Meaningful Sources of Social Capital?'

[20]   Sassen, *Metropolen des Weltmarktes. Die neue Rolle der Global Cities.*

[21]   Ritchie, 'Turning 16 Days into 16 Years Through Olympic Legacies'.

[22]   Preuss, 'Electing an Olympic City – a Multidimensional Decision'; McIntosh, 'The Olympic Bid Process as the Starting Point of Legacy Development'.

[23]   Szymanski 'The Economic Impact of the World Cup', p. 3.

[24]   Faber Maunsell, Commonwealth Games Benefits Study, p. 52.

[25] Süßmilch and Elter, *FC Euro AG – Fußball und Finanzen*, p. 148.

[26] Faber Maunsell, *Commonwealth Games Benefits Study*, p. 21, 51.

[27] Klein, No Logo! Der Kampf der Global Player um Marktmacht. Ein Spiel mit vielen Verlieren und wenigen Gewinnern, pp. 103–121.

[28] Lenskyj The Best Olympics Ever? Social Impacts of Sydney 2000, p. 126.

[29] Snyder *et al.* 'Distancing After Group Success and Failure: Basking in Reflected Glory and Cutting Off Reflected Failure', 1986.

[30] Preuß and Messing, 'Auslandstouristen bei den Olympischen Spielen in Sydney 2000'.

[31] Lewis, When Cultures Collide: Leading Across Cultures, p. 223.

[32] BMI, Die Welt zu Gast bei Freunden, p. 15.

[33] Burbank *et al.*, 2001, p. 35 [missing].

[34] Denis, Dischereit, Song, and Werning, *Südkorea. Kein Land für friedliche Spiele*, p. 229.

[35] Lin, 'Economic Impact of Beijing Olympic Games 2008'.

[36] Thurow, Die Zukunft der Weltwirtschaft.

[37] Swann, 'When Do Major Sports Events Leave a Lasting Economic Legacy?', pp. 2–3.

[38] Preuss, The Economics of Staging the Olympics. A Comparison of the Games 1972–2008; Teigland, Impacts on Tourism from Mega Events – The Case of Winter Olympic Games.

[39] Garcia, 'Barcelona und die Olympischen Spiele', p. 260; Cox *et al.*, The Olympics and Housing. A Study of Six International Events and Analysis of Potential Impacts of the Sydney 2000 Olympics, p. 75; Lenskyj, 'When Winners Are Losers. Toronto and Sydney Bids for the Summer Olympics', p. 395; Preuss, 'Winners and Losers of the Olympic Games'.

[40] Faber Maunsell, *Commonwealth Games Benefits Study*, p. 48.

[41] Solberg and Preuss, 'Major Sporting Events and Long-Term Tourism Impacts'.

[42] Garcia, 'Barcelona und die Olympischen Spiele'.

[43] Faber Maunsell, *Commonwealth Games Benefits Study*, p. 24.

[44] Cambridge Policy Consultants, 2003 [missing].

[45] Faber Maunsell, *Commonwealth Games Benefits Study*.

[46] Ibid.

[47] Spilling, 'Beyond Intermezzo? On the Long-Term Industrial Impacts of Mega Events: The Case of Lillehammer 1994'.

[48] R. Sanahuja, *Barcelona – An Olympic City – The City Strategy 10 Years After the Olympic Games in 1992*.

References

Baade, R.A. and V. Matheson. 'Bidding for the Olympics: Fool's Gold?' In *Transatlantic Sport: The Comparative Economics of North America and European Sports*, edited by C.P. Barros, M. Ibrahimo and S. Szymanski. London: Edward Elgar, 2002: 127–51.

BMI (Bundesministerium des Inneren). *Die Welt zu Gast bei Freunden*. Fünfter Fortschrittsbericht des Stabes WM 2006 zur Vorbereitung auf die FIFA Fußball-Weltmeisterschaft 2006, 2005.

Burns, J., J. Hatch and T. Mules. *The Adelaide Grand Prix: The Impact of a Special Event*. Adelaide: Centre for South Australian Economic Studies, 1986.

Cashman, R. *The Bitter-Sweet Awakening: The Legacy of the Sydney 2000 Olympic Games*. Sydney, Walla Walla Press, 2005.

Chalip, L.H. *Leveraging the Sydney Olympics for Tourism*. Barcelona, Centre d'Estudis Olímpics i de l'Esport (UAB), 2000, available at http://olympicstudies.uab.es/pdf/od008_eng.pdf, accessed 6 Feb. 2006.

———. *Using the Olympics to Optimise Tourism Benefits*. Barcelona, Centre d'Estudis Olímpics i de l'Esport (UAB), 2002, available at http://olympicstudies.uab.es/lectures/web/pdf/chalip.pdf, accessed 6 Feb. 2006.

Chang, W.-H. 'Variations in Multipliers and Related Economic Ratios for Recreation and Tourism Impact Analysis'. Dissertation, Michigan State University, 2001.

Cox, G., M. Darcy and M. Bounds. *The Olympics and Housing. A Study of Six International Events and Analysis of Potential Impacts of the Sydney 2000 Olympics.* Housing and Urban Studies Research Group, University of Western Sydney, 1994.

Crompton, J.L. 'Economic Impact Analysis of Sports Facilities and Events: Eleven Sources of Misapplication'. *Journal of Sport Management* 9, no. 1, (1995): 14–35.

Denis, M., E. Dischereit, D.-Y. Song and R. Werning. *Südkorea. Kein Land für friedliche Spiele.* Reinbeck: Rororo, 1988.

Dwyer, L., P. Forsyth and R. Spurr. 'Evaluating Tourism's Economic Effects: New and Old Approaches'. *Tourism Management* 25 (2004): 307–17.

Evans, G. 'The Role of the Festival in Urban Regeneration: Planning for the British Millennium Festival', Paper presented at International Festivals Association Second European Research Symposium, Edinburgh, 17 August 1995.

Faber Maunsell. *Commonwealth Games Benefits Study.* Final Report. Warrington, 2004.

Fredline, E., L.K. Jago and M. Deery. 'The Development of a Generic Scale to Measure the Social Impacts of Events'. *Event Management* 8, no. 1, (2003): 23–37.

Fuller, S.S. and R. Clinch. (2000). 'The Economic and Fiscal Impacts of Hosting the 2012 Olympic Games on the Washington–Baltimore Metropolitan Area'. Prepared for Washington/Baltimore Regional 2012 Coalition. Unpublished typescript.

Furrer, P. 'Sustainable Olympic Games: A Dream or a Reality?' *Bollettino dalla Societa Geografica Italiana* Serie XIII, 7 (4) (2002), available at http://www.omero.unito.it/web/Furrer%20 (eng.).pdf, 23 Oct. 2008.

Garcia, S. 'Barcelona und die Olympischen Spiele'. In *Festivalisierung der Stadtpolitik. Stadtentwicklung durch große Projekte*, edited by H. Häussermann and W. Siebel. *Zeitschrift für Sozialwissenschaft*, 13 edn., Opladen, 1993: 251–77.

Getz, D. 'Special Events: Defining the Product'. *Tourism Management* 10, no. 2, (1989): 125–37.

———. *Festivals, Special Events, and Tourism.* New York: Van Nostrand Reinhold, 1991.

Hall, C.M. *Hallmark Tourist Events: Impacts, Management and Planning.* London: Belhaven Press, 1992.

Harper, D. 'Legacy'. In *Online Etymological Dictionary*, 2001, available at www.etymonline.com, 23 Oct. 2008.

Haxton, P.A. 'Community Involvement and the Olympic Games – A Review of Related Research. International Olympic Academy'. *Report on the IOA's Special Sessions and Seminars 1999.* Athens, 2000: 142–64.

Hodges, J. and Hall, C. 'The Housing and Social Impacts of Mega Events: Lessons for the Sydney 2000 Olympics'. In *Tourism Down Under II; Towards a More Sustainable Tourism*, edited by G. Kearsley. Dunedin: Centre for Tourism, University of Otago, 1996: 152–66.

Howard, D.R. and J.L. Crompton. *Financing Sport.* Morgantown: Fitness Information Technology, 1995.

Hughes, H. 'Olympic Tourism and Urban Regeneration; 1996 Summer Olympics'. *Festival Management and Event Tourism* 1, no. 4, (1993): 137–84.

International Olympic Committee. 'What is the Olympic Games Global Impact Study?' *Focus Olympic Review* 6, June (2006): 1–2.

Jones, Lang LaSalle. *Reaching Beyond the Gold: The Impact of the Olympic Games on Real Estate Markets.* 2001, www.joneslanglasalle.com/publications/global_insights_0106/Reaching.pdf, accessed 2 Jan. 2006.

Kang, Y. and R. Perdue. 'Long-Term Impact of a Mega Event on International Tourism to the Host Country: A Conceptual Model and the Case of the 1988 Seoul Olympics'. In *Global Tourist Behaviour*, edited by M. Uysal. Now York: International Business Press, 1994: 205–25.

Kasimati, E. 'Economic Aspects and the Summer Olympics: A Review of Related Research'. *International Journal of Tourism Research* 5 (2003): 433–44.

Kesenne, S. 'Miscalculations and Misinterpretations in Economic Impact Analysis'. In *The Economic Impact of Sports*, edited by C. Jeanrenaud. Neuchâtel: CIES, 1999: 29–39.

——. 'Do We Need an Economic Impact Study or a Cost-Benefit Analysis of a Sport Event?' *European Sport Management Quarterly* 5, no. 2, (2005): 133–42.

Kim, J.-G., S.W. Rhee, J.-Ch. Yu, K.M. Koo and J.Ch. Hong. *Impact of the Seoul Olympic Games on National Development*. Seoul: Korea Development Institute, 1989.

Klein, N. *No Logo! Der Kampf der Global Player um Marktmacht. Ein Spiel mit vielen Verlieren und wenigen Gewinnern*. Leipzig: Goldmann Wilhelm, 2005.

Lenskyj, H.J. 'When Winners Are Losers. Toronto and Sydney Bids for the Summer Olympics'. *Journal of Sport and Social Issues* 20, no. 4, (1996): 392–410.

——. *Inside the Olympic Industry: Power, Politics and Activism*. Albany, NY: State University of New York Press, 2000.

——. *The Best Olympics Ever? Social Impacts of Sydney 2000*. Albany, NY: State University of New York Press, 2002.

Lewis, R.D. *When Cultures Collide. Leading Across Cultures*. Boston: Nicholas Brealey, 2006.

Lin, X. 'Economic Impact of Beijing Olympic Games 2008'. *Proceedings of the 2004 Pre-Olympic Congress, 6–11 August, Thessaloniki, Greece*. Athens: (2004): vol. 1, 100.

May, V. 'Environmental Implications of the 1992 Winter Olympic Games'. *Tourism Management* 16, no. 4, (1995): 269–75.

McIntosh, M. 'The Olympic Bid Process as the Starting Point of Legacy Development'. In *The Legacy of the Olympic Games: 1984–2000*, edited by M. Moragas, Ch. Kennett, and N. Puig. Lausanne: International Olympic Committee, 2003.

Misener, L. and D.S. Mason 'Creating Community Networks: Can Sporting Events Offer Meaningful Sources of Social Capital?' *Managing Leisure* 11, no. 1, (2006): 39–56.

Meyer-Künzel, M. *Der planbare Nutzen. Stadtentwicklung durch Weltausstellungen und Olympische Spiele*. Hamburg and München: Dölling und Galitz, 2001.

Mills, E.S. 'The Misuse of Regional Economic Models'. *CATO Journal* 13, no. 1, (1993): 29–39 (published in April 1994).

——. 'Sectoral Clustering and Metropolitan Development'. In *Sources of Economic Growth*, edited by E. Mills and J. McDonald. Brunswick, NJ: Centre for Urban Policy Research, 1992: 3–18.

Moragas, M. Ch. Kennett and N. Puig. eds. *The Legacy of the Olympic Games: 1984–2000*. Proceedings of the International Symposium 14–16 November 2002. Lausanne: International Olympic Committee, 2003.

Mules, T. and B. Faulkner. 'An Economic Perspective on Special Events'. *Tourism Economics* 2, no. 2, (1996): 107–17.

Porter, P.K. 'Mega-Sports Events as Municipal Investments: A Critique of Impact Analysis'. In *Sports Economics: Current Research*, edited by J. Fizel, E. Gustafson and L. Hadley. New York: Praeger Press, 1999: 61–73.

Preuss, H. 'Electing an Olympic City – a Multidimensional Decision'. In *Bridging Three Centuries: Intellectual Crossroads and the Modern Olympic Movement*, edited by K.B. Wamsley, S.G. Martyn, G.H. MacDonald, H. Gordon and R.K. Barney. London, ON: Centre for Olympic Studies, University of Western Ontario, 2000: 89–104.

——. *The Economics of Staging the Olympics. A Comparison of the Games 1972–2008*. Cheltenham: Edward Elgar, 2004.

——. 'The Economic Impact of Visitors at Major Multi-Sport-Events'. *European Sport Management Quarterly* 5, no. 3, (2005): 283–304.

——. 'Winners and Losers of the Olympic Games'. In *Sport and Society*, edited by B. Houlihan. London: Sage, 2nd edn, 2006.

—— and M. Messing. 'Auslandstouristen bei den Olympischen Spielen in Sydney 2000'. In *Tourismus im Sport*, edited by A. Dreyer. Wiesbaden: Deutscher Universitäts-Verlag, 2002: 223–41.

—— and H.-J. Weiss. *Torchholder Value Added, der ökonomische Nutzen Olympischer Spiele in Frankfurt Rhein/Main 2012*. Eschborn: AWV-Verlag, 2003.

PricewaterhouseCoopers. 'Business and Economic Benefits of the Sydney 2000 Olympics: A Collation of Evidence'. Unpublished document, 2002.

Rahmann, B., W. Weber, Y. Groening, M. Kurscheidt, H.-G. Napp and M. Pauli. *Sozioökonomische Analyse der Fußball-WM 2006 in Deutschland*. Köln: Sport und Buch Strauss, 1998.

Ritchie, B. 'How Special Are Special Events? An Impact Study of the National Mutual New Zealand Masters Games on Dunedin's Economy'. In *Tourism Down Under II; Towards a More Sustainable Tourism*, edited by G. Kearsley. Dunedin: Centre for Tourism, University of Otago, 1996: 73–9.

Ritchie, J.R. 'Assessing the Impact of Hallmark Events: Conceptual and Research Issues'. *Journal of Travel Research* 23, no. 1, (1984): 2–11.

——. 'Turning 16 Days into 16 Years Through Olympic Legacies'. *Event Management* 6, no. 1, (2000): 155–65.

—— and K. Aitken. 'Assessing the Impacts of the 1988 Olympic Winter Games: The Research Programme and Initial Results'. *Journal of Travel Research* 22 (3) (1984): 17–25.

Sananhuja, R. *Barcelona – An Olympic City – The City Strategy 10 Years After the Olympic Games in 1992*. International Conference on 'Sporting Events and Economic Impact', April, Copenhagen: Sport Foundation Denmark, 2002.

[...] *lobal Cities*. Frankfurt, New York: Campus,

[...] s of a Hallmark Event; Development and [...] tario'. In *Quality Management in Urban* [...] ted by P. Murphy. University of Canada,

[...] After Group Success and Failure: Basking [...] ailure'. *Journal of Personality and Social*

[...] tion of the Direct Economic Impacts from [...] *nt Management* 9, no. 3, (2002): 20–8.

[...] Term Tourism Impacts'. *Journal of Sport*

[...] cts'. *Journal of Sport Management*, 21, no.

[...] dustrial Impacts of Mega Events: The Case [...] *Scandinavian experiences*, edited by L.L. [...] s Corporation, 1998.

[...] *inanzen*. 4. Auflage. Studie der WGZ-Bank [...] d KPMG Deutsche Treuhand-Gesellschaft Aktiengesellschaft Wirtschaftsprüfungsgesellschaft. Düsseldorf und München: 2004.

Swann, G.M.P. (2001). 'When Do Major Sports Events Leave a Lasting Economic Legacy?' Draft (Working Paper), Manchester Business School, University of Manchester.

Szymanski, S. 'The Economic Impact of the World Cup'. *World Economics* 3, no. 1, (2002): 1–9.

Teigland, J. *Impacts on Tourism from Mega Events – The Case of Winter Olympic Games*. Report 13/96, Western Norway Research Institute, 1996.

Thorpe, R. *The Economic Impact of the Winter Olympic and Paralympic Games. Initial Estimates*. A Report Prepared for Honourable Ted Nebbeling, Minister of State for Community Charter and 2010 Olympic Bid, 2002.

Thurow, L. *Die Zukunft der Weltwirtschaft*. Frankfurt, New York: Campus, 2004.

Vigor, A., M. Mean and C. Tims. *After the Gold Rush. A Sustainable Olympics for London*. London: ippr & Demos, 2005.

The Seoul Olympics: Economic Miracle Meets the World

Brian Bridges

The Seoul Olympics of 1988 represented a hugely symbolic 'coming out party' for the Koreans. Some 160 nations and over 13,000 athletes competed at what was, at that time, the biggest ever Olympics. For Koreans, it was not just the scale but the national effort and pride that they put into achieving a successful hosting that was important. After a traumatic twentieth-century history in which colonialism, division, civil war, and authoritarian governments had all left their mark, the Olympics provided an opportunity for the South Koreans not just to unite in one gigantic task but also to transmit the cultural essence of 'Korean-ness' to the outside world.

In considering the various dimensions of the shorter-term impact on and the longer-term legacies for South Korea, it is necessary to remember that legacies (or to use the even more positive connotations of the French equivalent 'heritage') of mega-events, such as the Olympics, can be both tangible (or 'hard'), often with the implication of being monetary and subject to measurement, and intangible (or 'soft'), appearing more nebulous and less susceptible to quantification. This is not to imply that one may be more important than the other [1]. Certainly, in the case of South

Korea, it is possible to discern both tangible and intangible legacies; certainly, both were to be important for the government and people of Korea.

The Road to the Seoul Olympics

Since its formal foundation in 1948, the Republic of Korea (South Korea hereafter) has been involved in a highly competitive struggle with its northern neighbour, the Democratic People's Republic of Korea (North Korea hereafter), which has found expression not just through the military clashes of the Korean War but also through diplomatic, economic and cultural means in the subsequent years. In the Cold War environment, the South was recognized and supported by the United States and the West Europeans, while the North was similarly endorsed by the Soviet Union, China and the East Europeans. Both Koreas worked hard to achieve support and recognition among the emerging 'Third World' countries. Sport was no exception to this struggle for advantage, prestige and legitimacy. [2]

Ha Nam-Gil and J.A. Mangan have commented that post-1945 South Korean sport was 'closely linked to political priorities, purposes and personnel' and was 'politically-driven, resourced and endorsed and it was the direct product of ... ideological purpose'. [3] This assessment could with equal validly be applied to North Korean priorities as well. Sport represented a tangible means to showcase the proclaimed superiority of each political system in this intense bilateral rivalry for national and international legitimacy.

The South Korean National Olympic Committee (NOC) quickly and successfully applied for International Olympic Committee (IOC) recognition and even sent athletes to the 1948 London Olympics, but the North's attempts to gain IOC recognition for its own NOC were initially rebuffed on the grounds that there could not be more than one recognized NOC in any one country. In the late 1950s, however, pressure began to build up from the Soviet bloc, which, drawing on the experience of the two Germanies, argued for full recognition of the North Korean NOC, which was finally given in 1962. South Korea had made its first and abortive major international sporting event bid in the 1960s for the Asian Games, but once the government had decided on full commitment to bids for both the 1986 Asian Games and the 1988 Olympics, the South Korean NOC waged a campaign that, though initially confused, was effective enough and well-funded enough in the later stages to culminate in the 1981 IOC decision to award the 1988 Olympics to Seoul, which defeated the only other candidate, Nagoya, Japan, by a comfortable margin of votes. [4]

In fact, during the 1960s and 1970s, the South Korean government of President Park Chung-hee had used sports promotion as one of several means to create a national revival after the traumas of colonization, civil war and political instability. Labelled by some as the 'father of modern sport' in Korea, Park introduced a number of innovative sports policies at both the elite and mass level. Given his strong top-down style of government and his personal admiration for the Japanese model of economic development (and what he saw as the beneficial impact of the Tokyo Olympics on that national development process), it was not surprising that the idea of winning the right to host the Olympics originated during Park's period in power. [5]

It was the partial boycotts of the 1980 and 1984 Olympics, and the IOC's determination to secure a boycott-free Olympics in Seoul that made the 1988 Olympics a particular focus of political controversy. Two aspects in particular were of concern: the domestic stability of South Korea, given that President Chun Doo Hwan had seized power in a military coup in 1980 only the year before the IOC decision to award the games was made, and the ever tense relationship with North Korea. The North Koreans, with particularly vocal support from Cuba, criticized the choice of Seoul on safety grounds, but the IOC held firm and refused to change venue. Consequently, the North asked for a co-hosting arrangement. Both the South and the IOC rejected this proposal (not least because the Olympics are awarded to only one city), but the IOC at the same time showed some willingness to discuss the possibilities of some events being held in the North. There then followed during 1985–88 a series of convoluted discussions, which are described in impressive detail in Richard Pound's classic insider account. At one stage the two Korean NOCs and the IOC did come close to agreement over some preliminary rounds of a few sports being held in the North, but the offers were never sufficient to satisfy the North – nor were they intended to be by the IOC – and, despite IOC willingness to keep the door open until the very last minute, North Korean athletes did not participate in the Seoul Olympics, nor were the games broadcast to the North Korean people. [6]

In considering the impact and legacies of those Seoul Olympics on South Korea, it is possible to divide them into three broad categories: economic, socio-cultural, and political-diplomatic.

Economic Costs and Benefits

Since the Montreal Olympics (1976) incurred widely publicized debts, a number of studies have shown that there have generally been wide gaps between the economic costings – and optimistic forecasts of benefits – made prior to a mega-event such as the Olympics and the actual benefits for the local economies for the short and medium term. [7] The Korean government officials were aware of Montreal's financial problems, but that did not discourage them from arguing not just for the likely economic benefits from the Seoul games but also for investing in significant infrastructure development.

Unlike the 1984 Olympics in Los Angeles, which had used many existing facilities, the Koreans decided to build a completely new Olympic stadium, an Olympic Park, and many associated facilities. South Korea invested around US$3.6 billion in Olympics-related infrastructure developments, of which the central government and the city contributed roughly one-third each, with the remainder coming from private companies. Three new underground railway lines in Seoul were completed, additional capacity was added to Kimpo international airport, roadsides within Seoul were improved and 'beautified', parks and gardens within the city were expanded or renovated, and a massive project to clean up the Han river, which flows through the centre of Seoul, and make it more accessible to the public was carried out, as was the cleaning up of the polluted Suyong Bay, Pusan, where the sailing events were held. [8] All these urban reconstruction developments have remained as a very visible legacy of the Olympics. Although not all the sporting stadiums around the 1.7-km^2 Olympic Park are used regularly (the velodrome seems to be the one most in use), the whole area has become a popular place for Seoulites to walk, jog and picnic, and many see it as a 'green lung' in the centre of the city.

By the 1980s, particularly after the Los Angeles games, it was clear that two important sources of income for any Olympic host were the revenue from the global television rights and inflows from corporate sponsors. In the case of Seoul, there was significant competition to secure the television rights around the world, but as regards the key US television market, the Seoul Olympic Organising Committee (SLOOC) was unable to secure as good terms as they had expected, and the negotiations became extremely protracted. The US networks were concerned about the political instability on the peninsula and, no doubt more importantly, the 14-hour time zone difference between Seoul and New York, which led to demands to check – and potentially alter – the event schedule so as to allow prime-time viewing in the United States. NBC finally won with a bid of $300 million for the American rights, even though this was only about half of what the Koreans had originally been led to expect. Agreements with the Europeans and the Japanese, however, did bring in another $80 million. [9]

Corporate sponsorship by multi-national companies was also important to Seoul. At the suggestion of Horst Dassler, chief executive of Adidas, his marketing agency ISL cooperated with the IOC in establishing what became known as the TOP scheme. 'The Olympic Programme' (TOP) meant that a few select companies were allowed to claim worldwide partner status. It was first employed in the run-up to the Seoul Olympics. Firms were invited to bid in 43 product categories for the exclusive right to use the Olympic symbol: Coca-Cola paid $22 million to use the five rings on its cans, while Visa paid $15 million. Other companies involved in TOP-1 included Brother, Philips, 3M, Federal Express and Matsushita. [10] Altogether 23 companies each paid $2 million upwards to become official sponsors, while another 57 companies became official suppliers, providing cash, goods or services. [11]

For the Korean government, there were clearly the direct though often short-term benefits of increased production and employment, particularly in the construction and related industries. Another sector that benefited from increased employment was tourism, as the number of visitors did increase, but actually more potently in the year after the Olympics (one estimate has a benefit of $1.3 billion over the three years from the Olympics). [12] Over the longer term, however, the main beneficiary was to be the telecommunications industry, which not only rose to the challenge of creating a full-scale integration of computer and communications systems for providing results and other information but also gained a significant 'across-the-board impetus' in developing new hardware and software for the related information industries. By 1988, the electronics industry, both consumer and industrial electronics, had overtaken textiles as Korea's leading export industry; it was to go on to become a world-class element of South Korea's export machine. [13]

Overall, government economists pointed to heightened economic growth rates in the years surrounding the Olympics as representing the positive side of the economic balance sheet. Certainly, the construction and other activities related to the Olympics did contribute to the strong economic growth record prior to the Olympics for South Korea, which averaged just over 10% per annum in the 1986–88 period, one of the highest rates in the world, although there was a slowdown in 1989 to only 6% growth – a figure that was still the envy of many slow-growing Western economies at that time. [14]

But also there occurred a more indirect and longer-term legacy or 'soft' structural improvement (to use Olympic economist Holger Preuss's term) on economic policies in general, which underwent greater pressure for more openness. [15] The economic success of South Korea – the so-called 'miracle on the Han river' – had been predicated on a strong government role, especially in promoting key sectors of industry and underpinning the exporting machine, while at the same time being more restrictive of imports (apart from necessary raw materials and components) and inward foreign investment. The involvement of major foreign companies through the TOP scheme and other sponsorships in the Olympics inevitably increased the pressure on the Korean government to open up other aspects of the economy, or, to be more precise, to speed up the rather grudging pace of liberalization of the economy that had begun in the early 1980s. However, although liberalization did proceed, it was the much more traumatic effects of the Asian financial crisis in 1997–98 that finally saw a sea change in South Korean thinking about economic openness. [16]

Not everything was positive. South Koreans – or Seoulites at least – did grumble about having to pay heavier taxes or being encouraged to contribute to national fund-raising lotteries – and the traffic problems in areas near the Olympic Park were at the very least inconvenient. Yet, there do not seem to have been any major increases in the cost of living for Seoulites. [17] Some critics argued that the financial resources being poured into the Olympics were distorting what should be the economic priorities of the government, but the major South Korean economic think tanks generally emphasized that, considering the economy as a whole, the benefits outweighed the costs. What economists, however, have not agreed upon is the exact amount of these benefits. Different organizations and different scholars have come up with varying estimates, depending on the methodologies and definitions employed. Christophe Dubi, for example, by examining the size of both direct and created demand, argued that the Seoul Olympics had a total impact equivalent to US$9.3 billion. The SLOOC's own official report lists a 'cumulative total of surplus' worth $7.9 billion. On the other hand, other estimates put the 'surplus' or 'profit' in the order of only $349 million or $556 million. [18] Whatever the figure – and much depends on the methodology used – there seems to be basic agreement about the positive balance.

Socio-Cultural Legacies

The impact upon socio-cultural legacies is more intangible and therefore even more difficult to quantify, but two aspects seem to have been important to the Korean government in the run-up to the Olympics: the promotion of a national sporting culture and the promotion of traditional culture – both of which were intended to combine to create a raised sense of national pride. The first involved efforts by the government and the NOC to raise public awareness of sport in general, by which was meant both participation and watching, and the Olympic Games and Olympic sports in particular. In 1981, South Korea had no ministerial-level government body dealing with sports, so the government of President Chun tried hard to promote the concept of a 'sports republic'. A Ministry of Sports was established in 1982. Funding was poured into identifying promising athletes and training them by the best methods available. The successful hosting of the 1986 Asian Games became an important 'test-run' for the Olympics, not just in terms of Korean athletes doing well but also, and more importantly, in organizational and logistical management. Finally, the creation of a professional baseball league for the first time not only drew large numbers of people to sport but also acted as a kind of 'diversion' from the political troubles of the time. The amount of sports shown on Korean television increased significantly during the 1980s, and the increased 'professionalism' of sport was noticeable. [19]

These developments did have the effect of heightening consciousness among Koreans about participating in sports and taking exercise more regularly. However, at the actual games, there seem to have been some limitations to the extent of this new sporting culture, at least as far as spectators were concerned. Some observers commented on the lack of spectators at certain Olympic events (including even the athletics in the main stadium) and the excessive partisanship when Korean athletes were involved, typified most unfortunately by the verbal and physical attacks on a New Zealand boxing referee who gave a decision against a Korean boxer. The boxing match incident, indeed, became one of the most controversial aspects of the whole Olympics, not so much for the original behaviour by the Koreans (which many fellow Koreans found embarrassing), but because of the repeated coverage of the incident, especially by the US TV channel NBC, which was widely regarded by Koreans as being 'intrusive and arrogant to the host country'. [20]

At the same time, the government and the NOC wanted to use the Olympics to showcase traditional Korean culture, primarily through the opening and closing ceremonies, but also through 41 related exhibitions and performances during the months before and after the actual games. Nonetheless, the opening ceremony was regarded by the Korean organizers as the key moment, with a special planning committee devoted to deciding on the music, dances and other performances that would combine 'something Korean and something cosmopolitan' to demonstrate the

Olympic theme of 'harmony and progress', to use the words of the SLOOC President Park Seh-jik. The Olympic theme song, 'Hand in Hand', sung by the pop group Koreana, sold over 9 million copies worldwide and in part because of its references to 'breaking down the wall' was apparently picked up to become a theme song of pro-democracy demonstrators in Eastern Europe and China in 1989. [21]

The initial reticence of ordinary Koreans early in the 1980s, when many still saw the Olympics as being a 'military show', shifted as the event came nearer into a general feeling that for reasons of national pride the Olympics should be held successfully. Massive television coverage of the Olympic events undoubtedly contributed to the ordinary Koreans' sense of pride, even if their direct involvement as spectators had been more limited. According to surveys immediately after the Olympics, 55% of Koreans had actively watched the Olympic broadcasts and 86% had seen at least some of the broadcasts. [22] For ordinary Koreans, as opposed to foreign spectators or global television viewers, enthusiasm for the games was not to find spontaneous expression on the streets in the way that the later 2002 World Cup would. [23] Indeed, given that the country was only just coming out of an era in which governmental power had been used to discourage strongly street activities unless approved in advance, the 'festival' aspect of the Seoul Olympics was, perhaps not surprisingly, rather muted. [24]

International media coverage involved not just the two weeks of sporting activities but also the run-up to the Olympics and their aftermath, and also non-sporting stories, with inevitably some negative aspects as well as positive aspects highlighted (at least as far as the Koreans interpreted overseas media coverage). Yet, as James Larson and Park Seung-soo have suggested, 'There is good reason to believe that the overall impact of television surrounding the 1988 Olympics as an *event* not only helped to change South Korea's image around the world but also began to change it in a positive direction.' [25]

Political-Diplomatic Breakthroughs

At the time of the award of the Olympics to Seoul in 1981, 37 countries with NOCs did not have formal diplomatic relations with South Korea and there was concern in South Korea and within the IOC that, perhaps out of solidarity with North Korea, all or some of the NOCs of these countries might boycott the games. In the end, North Korea had few friends (only Cuba, Ethiopia, and Nicaragua) that joined them in refusing to compete in the Seoul games. The key North Korean allies that became the focus of pre-Olympic discussions and lobbying were undoubtedly the Soviet Union, China, and, because of its sporting prowess, East Germany.

From early 1986, informal contacts between the SLOOC and Soviet sports officials began, with the blessing of the IOC, while several East European states, whose athletes had missed out on the 1984 Olympics because of the boycott, also put pressure on the Soviet Union to agree to participate. By late 1987, the Soviet Union, while still quibbling over some small details on security, had basically agreed to participate.

In March 1987, East Germany sent its sports minister to Seoul. He promised that East German athletes would be competing in Seoul. China, however, had moved even faster towards South Korea, not only because it saw increasing economic advantages coming from closer links but also because Beijing wanted to be the host of the 1990 Asian Games, which required that all member countries of the Asian Olympic Council be allowed to send athletes to the games. As early as 1984, senior Chinese officials had committed Chinese athletes to competing not only in the 1986 Asian Games in Seoul but also in the Olympics. In June 1988, three months before the opening, China sent a senior Politburo leader to Pyongyang to tell Kim Il Sung politely but firmly that China wanted the games to run smoothly. So, although these communist states did encourage South Korea to make some concessions to North Korea over co-hosting, they also made it clear that such concessions were not a prerequisite but rather that such steps would make it easier for them to defend their decision to participate to North Korea. [26]

But for South Korea, the Olympics were crucial not just for securing global sporting participation but also for acting as a springboard to possible diplomatic recognition from socialist allies of North Korea. As the 'cultural politics' part of this strategy, the SLOOC had, for example, specifically invited East European sculptors to contribute to the outdoor Sculpture Park. Some sporting equipment from Eastern Europe was also utilized. Sporting officials from East European countries visiting Seoul in the run-up to the Olympics also suggested that exchanges could be widened to other forms of cultural, social and economic contacts. Diplomatic contacts followed soon after. The Soviet Union opened a temporary consular office in Seoul for the duration of the games. On the eve of the games, Hungary agreed to the establishment of permanent missions, which were a precursor to the formal recognition of South Korea a few months later; this was followed in subsequent months by recognition by most of the other East European states. [27]

Although it is less easy to link directly the Soviet recognition of South Korea in 1990 and the similar Chinese move in 1992 quite so specifically to the 1988 Olympics, the interactions before and during the Olympics certainly helped to develop greater trust and understanding between South Koreans and Chinese and Soviet officials. While Barry Gills has argued that the South Korean diplomatic breakthrough in Eastern Europe 'was more of an unexpected windfall than the result of a particular effort', primarily because of the sudden changes in political atmosphere in Eastern Europe as communist governments faltered and then collapsed, South Korean diplomats have claimed more foresight in South Korean policymaking and have been convinced that the Olympic Games were the 'decisive turning point' for improving relations with the communist governments. [28]

Crucially, the Olympics also helped to underpin a changing perception among South Koreans – both policymaking elites and the public – who had been brought up on strong anticommunist propaganda during the decades since the Korean War, that it was indeed possible to work with such countries with differing political systems. Paradoxically, the Olympics – or, at least the run-up to them – did not do anything either to improve North–South Korean relations or improve South Korean impressions of the North. The North had objected first to Seoul's being chosen as the host, describing it as 'an insecure city ... dominated by a warlike atmosphere', but after the special IOC meeting in 1984 had re-endorsed Seoul, the North turned to a campaign for co-hosting the games. [29] Over the course of three years of tortuous negotiations, the North made a series of demands, some more unrealistic than others, that angered and annoyed the South Korean NOC, government, media and public. The North received some support from a very small number of radicals within South Korea, but no sympathy from other South Koreans, particularly after North Korean complicity in the fatal bombing of a Korean Air Lines (KAL) airliner in November 1987 was revealed. [30]

Not long before the Olympics, in July 1988, President Roh Tae Woo had announced his 'northern diplomacy' (*nordpolitik*), indicating a renewed interest in dialogue and exchanges with the North and offering full diplomatic relations to other communist states. It was the latter part of the 'northern diplomacy' that bore fruit, while the North–South dialogue stuttered. [31] After the Olympics sports officials from North and South did meet again in 1989 to discuss, ultimately unsuccessfully, a joint team for the 1990 Beijing Asian Games, but serious negotiations between North and South on other issues were intermittent and frustrating at least until prime-ministerial talks began in late 1990. One step forward and one step backward remained a characteristic of the South–North dialogue throughout the 1990s. Despite more reconciliatory policies from successive South Korean governments and recent diplomatic interactions, including summit meetings in 2000 and 2007, the two Koreas remain far apart. The Olympics have continued to act as a forum to bring them together from time to time, but only in irregular and persistently inconclusive discussions before each Olympics about forming a joint team. The inter-Korean discussions about a joint team for the 2008 Beijing Olympics similarly have failed. [32]

In addition to the diplomatic kudos, the Seoul Olympics were to have an unexpected but beneficial impact on domestic politics and serve the cause of democratization. In the 1980s, the authoritarian government of President Chun, a general who had seized power through a *coup d'état* before shedding his uniform, came under increasing pressure from domestic advocates of constitutional and democratic reform. These conflicts reached a head in early 1987 with massive street demonstrations and clashes with police, particularly after Chun tried to use the Olympics as an excuse for delaying any democratic reforms until after the games had finished. Consequently, one of the ruling party leaders, Roh Tae Woo, reversed policy in June 1987 by declaring a raft of democratizing measures that met most of the demands of the demonstrators. [33] As the demonstrations began to subside, Chun no longer felt the need to consider the imposition of martial law, a step that would almost certainly have led to the IOC removing the games to elsewhere. Roh, who had previously served for three years as the president of the SLOOC, then won the next presidential election in December 1987 after the opposition movement could not decide on a single candidate, and in February 1988 the first peaceful transfer of power in South Korea's political history occurred. [34]

Roh himself had argued in a letter to IOC President Samaranch in June 1987 that there was a 'consensus of opinion in Korea that welcomes the Games'. [35] Public opinion polls did suggest that most Koreans across the political spectrum, even among the pro-democracy opposition, did want to make a success of the Olympics. The only opposition came from radicals who saw the Olympics both as the political project of a military dictatorship and as a diversion of resources that could be better used for social welfare. [36]

Consequently, there was widespread relief that Roh's compromises had removed any doubts that the IOC might move the games elsewhere. The words of two senior sports officials at the centre of the arrangements for the Seoul Olympics are worth quoting in this context. IOC Vice-President Pound reflected on the external pressures that the Koreans felt, writing that 'there can, in retrospect, be little doubt that the evolution of democracy was accelerated considerably as a result of the efforts of South Korea to respond to the expectations of the rest of the world', while SLOOC President Park was more concerned about internal political dynamics when he wrote, 'Under the influence of the Olympics, the extreme rightist camp turned somewhat more liberal and democratic in their political activities.' [37] The Olympic factor was not the only one at play in the dramatic months of the first half of 1987, but undoubtedly it was one of the most important ones. As such it contributed a significant legacy to South Korea.

Enduring Legacies

At the beginning of the 1980s, much of the world still knew little about Korea. Images of the Korean War (no doubt reinforced by the popularity of the *M*A*S*H* television series) and of more recent clashes between police and demonstrators obscured the changing realities of what was becoming a major economic power. Psychological distance compounded geographical remoteness for non-Asians, and despite the growing presence of Korean businessmen operating in North American, European, Middle Eastern and Southeast Asian markets, the Koreans – and their culture – were little known or understood outside north-east Asia. It was, therefore, not surprising that the Koreans saw in the Olympics a way not only to symbolize their leap from 'Third World' to 'First World' in economic terms but also to propagate a new image of their country around the world. The Seoul Olympic slogan, 'The World to Seoul, Seoul to the World', was designed to encapsulate these ideas.

The day after the closing ceremony, one of the leading English-language newspapers in South Korea ran the headline, 'We Did It!' This sentiment, which combined pride with a sense of relief that nothing major had gone wrong, was widely shared among Koreans. As Holger Preuss has argued, the Olympic Games create 'memories and associations for all people in the world'. [38] In that sense, the images of both Seoul and South Korea, as hosts, undoubtedly did improve, especially given their relatively unknown position in global thinking beforehand. South Korea came to be seen as a country with a colourful culture and a safe and pleasant place to visit. Yet, over time, it once again slipped slightly off the map – or, worse, suffered a downgrading in international status through its economic collapse in the Asian financial crisis – until the even more colourful and popular World Cup in 2002 're-invented' Korea and the Koreans again.

Olympic scholars Vassil Girginov and Jim Parry have argued that the Olympic ideal represents a 'political project' that can be assessed on two levels: national and international. [39] In the national context, this implies enhancing the economy through additional employment and urban regeneration, increasing the people's participation in healthy activities, promoting nation-building, and forging social integration. At the international level, this implies using sport to perform political functions, such as boosting prestige, developing diplomatic links, and outmanoeuvring rivals.

At both these levels, the Seoul Olympics provided definite and broadly positive legacies for South Korea. Indeed, for the Koreans, the combination of the economic, socio-cultural and political-diplomatic dimensions discussed above did result in what the Seoul Olympic Museum's own displays describe as the 'foundation of an advanced nation' and an 'upgraded international status' for South Korea. At the same time, the Seoul Olympics also bequeathed a legacy to the Olympic movement. After the ideological confrontations between the 'West' and the 'East' during the previous two Olympiads, the Seoul Olympics represented a different meaning of the terms 'East' and 'West', not only imbuing them with cultural and geographical, as well as political, overtones, but also bringing them together in a way that enabled the Olympic movement to move on and forward.

Yet, in retrospect, perhaps the most pervasive legacy for the Koreans themselves is that the Seoul Olympics and the 'Olympic spirit' can still serve as a means to appeal to collective memory and collective mobilization whenever the government and people have to wrestle with another major challenge to the country's self-confidence and image. As such, in this new century, too, it can be expected that recourse to that 'Olympic spirit' will continue to retain its potency in political and cultural discourses within South Korea.

Acknowledgement

Part of the research for this survey was supported by a research grant, DS06A3, from the Social Sciences Research and Postgraduate Studies Panel of Lingnan University, Hong Kong.

Notes

[1] John MacAloon reminds us that '*legacy* – simply anything left behind – is not the same as *heritage* – that which is widely held to be significant in what is left behind.' MacAloon,

'Cultural Legacy', 271. On 'hard' and 'soft' legacies, see, among others, Cashman, 'What Is "Olympic Legacy"', 33.

[2] For the post-war history of the two Koreas, see Hoare and Pares, *Korea: An Introduction*, 67–90, 207–18, and Gills, *Korea Versus Korea*. For Korean sports development, see Ok, *Transformation of Modern Korean Sport*, 298–326.

[3] Ha and Mangan, 'Ideology, Politics, Power', 214.

[4] Hill, *Olympic Politics*, 194–8. Rumours persisted afterwards that the Korean IOC member Kim Un-yong and other lobbyists had been active in giving out various financial incentives to secure votes. See also Oberdorfer, *The Two Koreas*, 180–1.

[5] Ha and Mangan, 'Ideology, Politics, Power', 219–20, 225–31; Park, Seoul Olympics, 1–3; Ok, *Transformation of Modern Korean Sport*, 310–20.

[6] Pound, *Five Rings Over Korea*.

[7] It has been argued that there has yet to be a proper economic impact study, using primary data, carried out on any summer Olympics. See reviews of the literature by Gratton, Shibli and Coleman, 'The Economic Impact of Major Sports Events'; Whitson and Horne, 'Under-estimated Costs'.

[8] Lee, 'Organizing the Games', 148; Larson and Park, *Global Television*, 152–4; Park, *Seoul Olympics*, 95–102.

[9] Payne, *Olympic Turnaround*, 34–6; Barney, Wenn and Martyn, *Selling the Five Rings*, 213–29.

[10] Gratton and Taylor, 'The Seoul Olympics', 55–6.

[11] *Official Report. Games of the XXIVth Olympiad Seoul 1988*. Vol. 1. *Organization and Planning* (1989), available at www.aafla.org/6oic/OfficialReports/1988/1988u.pdf: 223.

[12] See the work of Y.-S. Kang and R. Perdue, cited in Roche, *Mega-events and Modernity*, 141.

[13] Larson and Park, *Global Television*, 143–5.

[14] It should be noted, however, that recent analysis by the HSBC banking group suggests that all host countries tend to exhibit such a slowdown after hosting the games. Tom Holland, 'Olympics Likely to Cause Headaches', *South China Morning Post*, 24 Dec. 2007.

[15] Preuss, *Economics of Staging the Olympics*, 267.

[16] Bridges, *Korea after the Crash*, 15–31, 68–89.

[17] Preuss, *Economics of Staging the Olympics*, 260.

[18] For these various estimates, see Girginov and Parry, *Olympic Games Explained*, 120–1; *Official Report. Games of the XXIVth Olympiad Seoul 1988*. Vol. 1. *Organization and Planning* (1989), available at www.aafla.org/6oic/OfficialReports/1988/1988u.pdf: 221; Gratton and Taylor, 'The Seoul Olympics', 55.

[19] Ha, 'Korean Sports', 11; Larson and Park, *Global Television*, 156–9, 216; Ok, *Transformation of Modern Korean Sport*, 324–5.

[20] Roche, *Mega-events and Modernity*, 186–7; Larson and Park, *Global Television*, 218–27.

[21] Park, *Seoul Olympics*, 31, 43, 74–6.

[22] Larson and Park, *Global Television*, 166–7.

[23] On the Korean fans and the World Cup, see Kwon, 'Korea, Red Devils and the Hiddink Factor'.

[24] See MacAloon, 'Theory of Spectacle', 24–5 for analysis of the thinking underpinning traditional Korean festivals.

[25] Larson and Park, *Global Television*, 231.

[26] Chung, *Between Ally and Partner*, 35; Park, *Seoul Olympics*, 25–31; Pound, *Five Rings Over Korea*, 296 7; Qian, *Ten Episodes*, 115–17.

[27] Sanford, *South Korea and the Socialist Countries*; Oberdorfer, *The Two Koreas*, 189–91.

[28] Gills, *Korea Versus Korea*, 223–4.

[29] Park, *Seoul Olympics*, 15.

[30] Hill, *Olympic Politics*, 204–7; Park, *Seoul Olympics*, 21.

[31] Gills, *Korea Versus Korea*, 221–7.
[32] Bridges, *Playing Games.*
[33] For detailed analyses of the events of 1987, see several chapters in Cotton, *Korea Under Roh Tae-woo.*
[34] Oh, *Korean Politics*, 107–18.
[35] Pound, *Five Rings Over Korea*, 238.
[36] Ha, Korean Sports, 13; Pound, *Five Rings Over Korea*, 237–9.
[37] Pound, *Five Rings Over Korea*, 322; Park, *Seoul Olympics*, 170.
[38] Preuss, *Economics of Staging the Olympics*, 268.
[39] Girginov and Parry, *Olympic Games Explained*, 160–2.

References

Barney, R., S. Wenn and S. Martyn. *Selling the Five Rings: The International Olympic Committee and the Rise of Olympic Commercialism.* Salt Lake City, UT: University of Utah Press: 2004.
Bridges, B. *Korea after the Crash: The Politics of Economic Recovery.* London: Routledge, 1999.
Bridges, B. *Playing Games: The Two Koreas and the Beijing Olympics.* CAPS Working Paper no. 186. Hong Kong: Lingnan University, 2007.
Cashman, R. 'What Is "Olympic Legacy?"' In *The Legacy of the Olympic Games, 1984–2000*, edited by Miquel de Moragas, Christopher Kennet and Nuria Puig. Lausanne: International Olympic Committee, 2003: 31–42.
Chung, J.H. *Between Ally and Partner: Korea–China Relations and the United States.* New York: Columbia University Press, 2007.
Cotton, J. ed. *Korea Under Roh Tae-Woo: Democratization, Northern Policy, and Inter-Korean Relations.* St Leonards, Australia: Allen & Unwin, 1993.
Gills, B.K. *Korea Versus Korea: A Case of Contested Legitimacy.* London: Routledge, 1996.
Girginov, V. and J. Parry. *The Olympic Games Explained: A Student Guide to the Evolution of the Modern Olympic Games.* London: Routledge, 2005.
C. Gratton, S. Shabli and R. Coleman. 'The economic impact of major sports events: a review of ten events in the UK'. In *Sports Mega-Events: Social Scientific Analyses of a Global Phenomenon*, edited by J. Horne and W. Manzenreiter. Oxford: Blackwell, 2006: 41–58.
Gratton, C. and P. Taylor. 'The Seoul Olympics: Economic Success or Sporting Failure?' *Leisure Management* 8, no. 12, (1988): 54–8.
Ha, N.-G. and J.A. Mangan. 'Ideology, Politics, Power: Korean Sport – Transformation, 1945–92'. In *Sport in Asian Society: Past and Present*, edited by J.A. Mangan and H. Fan. London: Frank Cass, 2003: 213–42.
Ha, W.-Y. 'Korean Sports in the 1980s and the Seoul Olympic Games of 1988'. *Journal of Olympic History* 6, no. 2, (1998): 11–13.
Hargreaves, J. 'Olympism and Nationalism: Some Preliminary Considerations'. In *Sport: Critical Concepts in Sociology*. Vol. IV, *Issues in the Sociology of Sport*, edited by E. Dunning and D. Malcolm. London: Routledge, 2003: 18–36.
Hill, C. *Olympic Politics.* Manchester: Manchester University Press, 1992.
Hoare, J. and S. Pares. *Korea: An Introduction.* London: Kegan Paul International, 1988.
Kennet, Christopher and Nuria Puig. Lausanne: International Olympic Committee, 2003. 31–42.
Kwon, Y.-S. 'Korea, Red Devils and the Hiddink Factor'. In *Going Oriental: Football After World Cup 2002*, edited by M. Perryman. Edinburgh: Mainstream Publishing, 2002: 156–67.
Larson, J. and H.-S. Park. *Global Television and the Politics of the Seoul Olympics.* Boulder, CO: Westview Press, 1993.
Lee, C.-S. 'Organizing the Games, Seoul Shows the Way'. *Olympic Review*, no. 269, (March 1990): 146–52.

MacAloon, J. 'Cultural Legacy: The Olympic Games as "World Cultural Property"'. In *The Legacy of the Olympic Games, 1984–2000*, edited by Miquel de Moragas, Christopher Kennet and Nuria Puig. Lausanne: International Olympic Committee, 2003: 271–8.

MacAloon, J. 'The Theory of Spectacle. Reviewing Olympic Ethnography'. In *National Identity and Global Sports Events: Culture, Politics, and Spectacle in the Olympics and the Football World Cup*, edited by A. Tomlinson and C. Young. Albany, NY: State University of New York Press, 2006: 15–39.

Oberdorfer, D. *The Two Koreas: A Contemporary History*, 2nd edn. New York: Basic Books, 2001.

Oh, J.K.-C. *Korean Politics: The Quest for Democratization and Economic Development.* Ithaca, NY: Cornell University Press, 1999.

Ok, G. *The Transformation of Modern Korean Sport: Imperialism, Nationalism, Globalization.* Seoul: Hollym, 2007.

Park, S.-J. *The Seoul Olympics: The Inside Story.* London: Bellew Publishing, 1991.

Payne, M. *Olympic Turnaround: How the Olympic Games Stepped Back from the Brink of Extinction to Become the World's Best Known Brand.* London: Praeger, 2006.

Pound, R. *Five Rings Over Korea: The Secret Negotiations Behind the 1988 Olympic Games in Seoul.* New York: Little Brown, 1994.

Preuss, H. *The Economics of Staging the Olympics: A Comparison of the Games 1972–2008.* Cheltenham: Edward Elgar, 2004.

Qian, Q. *Ten Episodes in China's Diplomacy.* New York: HarperCollins, 2005.

Roche, M. *Mega-events and Modernity: Olympics and Expos in the Growth of Global Culture.* London: Routledge, 2000.

Sanford, D. *South Korea and the Socialist Countries.* London: Macmillan, 1990.

Whitson, D. and J. Horne. 'Underestimated Costs and Overestimated Benefits? Comparing the Outcomes of Sports Mega-Events in Canada and Japan'. In *Sports Mega-Events: Social Scientific Analyses of a Global Phenomenon*, edited by J. Horne and W. Manzenreiter. Oxford: Blackwell, 2006: 73–89.

The Sydney Olympics: Striving for Legacies – Overcoming Short-Term Disappointments and Long-Term Deficiencies

Kristine Toohey

Australian cities have now staged two Olympic Games and others have been unsuccessful applicants. In 1956, Melbourne was the first Australian city to host the Olympic Games. Sydney was the next Australian city to host the Olympic Games, in 2000. The nation has been also been more successful in the Olympic medal count than would be expected of a country with a population of only 21 million in 2007. But the nation's Olympic connections run deeper than this: the International Olympic Committee (IOC) has long had an overrepresentation of members who 'still call Australia home', even though they may have not always been domiciled there. [1] Understandably, then, given its level of successful involvement, the nation prides itself on its Olympic contribution. However, the boundaries between admirable pride and a less commendable hubris can, at times, be blurred, and Australians have at times crossed the line in their Olympic dealings.

There is a logical question that arises from associating the nation's Olympic successes with the theme of Olympic legacy. Has an overemphasis on Olympic achievement meant that Australia has concentrated on this aspect of its Olympic involvement at the expense of leaving a legacy based on the qualities of

'Olympism'? [2] In order to address the nature and extent to which an Australian Olympic legacy exists and what forms this legacy might take, Sydney's hosting in 2000 of the Olympic Games will be used as a case study below. Its post-games outcomes will be investigated in terms of their economic, social, environmental, knowledge, sporting and political legacies. With regard to the last of these, a political legacy emerged even before the Sydney games were concluded. Ric Birch, the director of ceremonies for the Sydney games, noted that 'the seeds of ambition and envy that had been sown during the famous 1993 Monte Carlo announcements [that Sydney had won the right to host the 2000 Olympics] ... flowered into some poisonous blossoms.' [3] In this unflattering appraisal, he was referring specifically to the Australian domestic context, rather than to other nations that had also sought to host the 2000 games.

Background

Australia is a relatively small player in the global economy, and while there is validity to claims that its international status has been enhanced by the operational success of the 2000 Summer Olympic Games, what has become more debatable is whether there have been long-term benefits for the people of Sydney and the state of New South Wales (NSW), the latter of which was the principal underwriter of the 2000 games. Certainly, the highly successful operational aspects of the games validated the Sydney 2000 Bid Limited's claims that the country could efficiently organize an event of this magnitude. [4] However, since October 2000, many politicians, sports managers and businesses, some with only tenuous associations with the event, have capitalized on the Sydney games' kudos to present Australia, and by association themselves, as not merely the organizers of a large sports event, but as a world-class tourist destination, possessing an innovative, capable, technologically advanced culture, with both strong financial and knowledge economies. [5] For example, Phillip Knightly, writing in the *Sydney Morning Herald*, noted:

> Staging the Games was an opportunity to ... show the world the face of new Australia – a modern, prosperous, independent, confident and, above all multicultural country looking to its future. Australia, consciously or not, seized this chance. [6]

The immediate post-games euphoria also resulted in some ambitious claims regarding the effect that the games had on the nation's psyche. Prime Minister John Howard, writing in the *Australian* less than a month after the games, on 25 October 2000, asserted:

> I do not think there is another country that can look to the future with such optimism, or that faces such an array of opportunities. ... We should recommit ourselves to ensuring that the Australian spirit on display during the Olympics is not only maintained during our second centenary of Federation, but is extended so that we can also achieve our full potential as a nation. [7]

Whether any single sporting event has the potential to leave such an enduring legacy is questionable, especially given Sydney's relatively late attention to any legacy planning. [8] Thus, it is appropriate to examine the nature of the Sydney Olympic legacy and how perceptions of its success or otherwise have morphed over the seven years since the games were held. To achieve this, stakeholder theory will provide a suitable theoretical framework to understand why there is not universal agreement on the success or otherwise of Sydney's Olympic legacy.

Stakeholder theory

Essentially, a stakeholder is any organization or person that has something to gain or lose through a relationship and thus can affect or be affected by others involved. [9] Stakeholder theory is based on the premise that an organization's ability to achieve its goals and thus endure is determined by how it adapts to and influences the ever altering needs, goals, motivations and perceptions of the parties with which it interacts internally and externally. [10] Stakeholder theory is based on two premises: first, that stakeholders have legitimate interests, and, second, that the interests of all stakeholders are of intrinsic value. [11]

The theory has been applied in a variety of research contexts. [12] Applications of stakeholder theory to sporting organizations have revealed that there is often a complex network of contiguous stakeholders and an even more convoluted grid of those whose link is more distal. [13] The Olympic Games are no exception. An Olympic organizing committee has multiple stakeholders and can advance or be constrained by their agendas. The Sydney Olympic Games myriad stakeholders are presented in Figure 1. What is problematic for an Olympic legacy is that an organizing committee of Olympic Games (OCOG) disbands within two years of the games' conclusion. Many of its stakeholders have a more permanent tenure and are thus more able to influence long-term public perceptions.

This is especially apposite, as an organization's stakeholders can also include parties with which the organization may not necessarily want to deal, such as the groups who oppose the Olympic Games, or in the case of Sydney's Olympic legacy, its critics, such as those disagree with spending additional money to ensure the legacy is ongoing. Thus, it is imperative to consider such stakeholders' agendas.

Since R. Edward Freeman introduced stakeholder theory in 1984, some critics have proposed that his definition of what constitutes a stakeholder is too broad, and, if taken to its logical conclusion, could extend an organization's responsibility to an entire society. [14] However, T. Donaldson and L.E. Preston reject this criticism, arguing that Freeman never implied that all stakeholders are of equal significance. [15] R.K. Mitchell, B. Agle and D. Wood propose that stakeholders can be prioritized on the basis of three relational attributes: power, legitimacy and urgency. They consider that a stakeholder's power is relative to 'to the extent it has or can gain access to coercive, utilitarian, or normative means, to impose its will in the relationship'. [16]

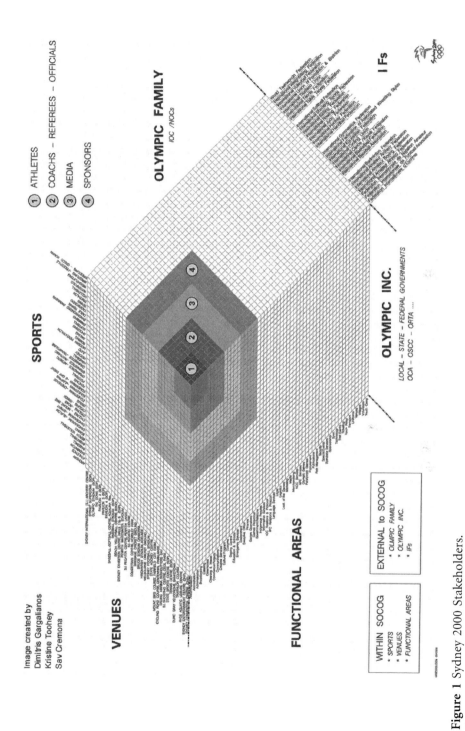

Figure 1 Sydney 2000 Stakeholders.
Source: Dimitris Gargalianos, Kristine Toohey and Sav Cremona.

B. Merrilees, D. Getz and D. O'Brien used stakeholder analysis in a case study of the 2001 Brisbane Goodwill Games. They advanced stakeholder theory as an 'appropriate and possibly stronger method of building inter-organizational linkages than alternatives such as network theory'. [17] While, in a review of stakeholder theory and sport management, M. Friedman, M. Parent and D. Mason argued that it holds 'descriptive and prescriptive value' for sport practitioners and sport management academics alike. [18] Hence its applicability to this contribution of Olympic legacies.

The use of a stakeholder approach is relevant in the context of the legacy of the Sydney games, as there are varied constituents of the concept of an Olympic legacy, involving many different organizations with different agendas, resource bases and philosophies. To best understand this constituent complexity, a brief outline of the general Sydney games legacy is provided before its component parts are examined individually.

The Sydney 2000 Olympic Games

Beginning with its opening ceremony and during the 16 days of competition, the Sydney games organizers, Sydneysiders and indeed many Australians with no involvement or previous interest in the Olympics, or even sport in general, revelled in the triumph of an operational success that impressed the International Olympic Committee (IOC) officials, who had been singularly uninspired by the organization of the previous Atlanta games, as well as the NSW government (which underwrote the games), and also met with the general approval of the world's media. This outcome was especially gratifying to those directly responsible for the games' organization, as, in the years preceding the games, there had been many games detractors. [19]

However, history is more than a 16-day snapshot, and Sydney's smug sense of Olympic accomplishment was relatively short-lived, as, in the years immediately following, when the measure of the Sydney games' success focused more on evaluating its Olympic legacy than its operational factors, there was again less enthusiasm for the venture, especially in terms of the under-utilization of the major venues constructed at Sydney Olympic Park (SOP). Accolades about the games slowed to a trickle, and increasing unease about their financial legacy was the new *cri de coeur*. While there were few comparisons to the 1976 Montreal games' crippling economic burden, the spectre of years of public debt and run-down state health and education systems was raised, as the state government coffers felt the effects of the earlier extra financial injections needed to ensure the games' success. Pronouncements about the inability of the organizers to realize a sustainable legacy came from a variety of sources, including Olympic scholars as well as Sydney taxpayers and the media. For example, in 2001, G. Holloway cautioned: 'Future Olympic city hosts be warned. Despite the stunning sell-out success of the 2000 Games, Sydney's $200 million Olympic Stadium is shaping up as a white elephant of mammoth proportions. And the other sports venues and facilities at Olympic park are not doing much better.' [20]

Thus, even in the space of a year, the dissimilar assessments of the games' success and their subsequent legacy or lack thereof suggest that judging the success of the games is not an absolute but a relative measure, and one related to temporal vagaries. While it is fairly straightforward to judge whether the games have been successfully organized or not (although such pronouncements may themselves depend on a stakeholder's agenda), during the 16 days of competition, the question of whether the legacy provisions of the organizers have been sufficient may be subject to more veiled chronological constraints. So, this raises the difficulty of determining the appropriate time to make pronouncements on the merits or otherwise of an OCOG legacy. The appropriateness of the timing of any evaluation, however, does not mean that evaluation should not be undertaken. In the words of one commentator:

> The post-Games period is as fertile a field for research as the pre-Games period or the Games themselves … there has been a dearth of post-Games analysis. [21]

In terms of the Sydney games, any post-games analysis now has a seven and a half year perspective, and without coming to a conclusion about the ultimate legacy of the Sydney games, it appears that those in the 'we should not have hosted the games' camp (for example, Booth and Tatz; Lenskyj), or the 'failure to provide a legacy' camp (for example, Chappelet), may have been premature in their pessimism. However, while we do not want to rain on the parade of the faction of Sydney Olympic supporters (for example, Gordon, 2003; Webb, 2001), it appears that effort to sustain the positive games' appraisal, most specifically by the reversing of the Sydney Olympic Park 'white elephant' tag, has come at an additional and not unsubstantial cost to the NSW taxpayer.

The following sections describe assessments of the sporting and infrastructure legacies of the 2000 Olympics. A historical view of the lead-up to the Sydney games is provided in order to best understand and contextualize the post-games period.

Sports legacy

In Monte Carlo on 23 September 1993, Sydney won the right to stage the 2000 Olympic Games when the IOC session convened to decide who would host the games of the XXVII Olympiad. It took four rounds of voting for Sydney to defeat the other candidate cities, with Beijing being the second placed city. To reach even this stage in the bidding process took many years and many millions of dollars. [22]

Immediately after the win, Sydney and the Australian Olympic Committee (AOC) signed the Host City Contract with the IOC and were required to establish an OCOG known as the Sydney Organizing Committee for the Olympic Games (SOCOG). Section 37 of the Host City Contract and section 54 of the subsequent SOCOG Act passed by the NSW Parliament stated that any surplus funds from the games would be distributed as follows: 10% to the IOC, 80% to be spent on sport in the host country to be administered by the AOC, and 10% to the AOC. [23] However, before the games, the NSW government (which underwrote the games) and the AOC came to an agreement whereby the AOC would forgo any games profit and also the right of veto over the SOCOG budget. In exchange, after the games, the AOC received A$90m. [24] Ironically, this windfall for the AOC has been used to ensure that it remain independent of government funding. [25]

One way that the AOC has spent its Olympic bounty is by establishing an Australian Youth Olympic Festival (AYOF). One aim of this festival is to give aspiring elite athletes a taste of a large, multi-sport competition, so that if they get to the Olympics they will not be so overawed by its scale. Held biannually, the AYOF foreshadowed a similar initiative by the IOC in terms of its 'Youth Olympics', the first of which is to be held in Singapore. At the 2007 AYOF, there were over 1,600 athletes aged 13–19 years who came from all five continents and competed across 16 Olympic sports. While the AYOF is one positive legacy for elite athletes, the outcome for the average sport participant has not been so encouraging.

As the Olympic Games is a sports contest, it is not unreasonable to expect that a sports legacy should be one of the more robust outcomes for an Olympic host nation, not necessarily in terms of medals won during the games and any prestige which ensues from this, but, more importantly, in terms of increased participation in sport after the event. In terms of the Sydney 2000 sports legacy, the NSW Department of Sport and Recreation planned a policy for the post-Olympic use of sports facilities. Yet, as will be made clear later, it remains doubtful whether Australians have become more physically active as a result of the Sydney Olympics. [26]

Once Sydney had won the right to host the 2000 games, Australian sports officials, especially those of the peak national government sports organization, the Australian Sports Commission (ASC), were eager to promote the possibility of an association between the games and increased participation in sport. In 1997, Barry Houlihan noted that 'the forthcoming Sydney Olympics ... is seen [by the ASC] as a major opportunity to market sports participation to the Australian public.' [27] While the ASC, which had a vested interest in the administration of sport-for-all, advanced the notion of the trickle-down effect (i.e., a successful performance by elite athletes would result in greater participation at the sport-for-all level), it also cautioned that this would not occur without suitable planning and additional funding. Henny Oldenhove of Active Australia (the sport for all division of the Australian Sport Commission) stated:

> The year 2000 presents the sport and recreation sectors with an unprecedented marketing opportunity to capture public interest and new members. Certainly Sydney will benefit from much needed infrastructure, but how will the nation as a whole turn the sport euphoria into an ongoing benefit for every community? Looking at previous Olympics and Paralympics there is a raised motivation and desire to play sport, which unfortunately plateaus after about six months. This is an

opportunity and challenge that Active Australia wants to take up. We need to make sure that when the Games are over this motivation is harnessed and captured by all those groups that provide sport and recreation programs to the community. [28]

Despite the ASC's lofty intent, a study by A.J. Veal, K. Toohey and S. Frawley noted that it was impossible to conclude that the 2000 games left a legacy of active sport-for-all in Australia, and their findings echoed Oldenhove's caution regarding the lack of any trickle-down effect from previous games. [29] Other studies echo this and suggest that there was very little, if any, change to sport participation numbers at the community level, with the exception of a short-term spike after 2000. [30] However, Australian Bureau of Statistics (ABS) figures did not seem to reflect even this small encouragement. The ABS noted that in the 12 months to April 2001, an estimated 4.1 million persons (27.1% of all people aged 15 years and over) were involved in organized sport and physical activity. This involvement included players and others involved in non-playing roles. Only 3.5 million persons (23.5%) were players in at least one organized sport or physical activity. [31] However, these figures indicate that a smaller percentage of the population was physically active than in the pre-games years. For example, during 1998 and 1999, the ABS data indicated that 28.9% of the population had participated in organized sport or physical activity. [32]

Regrettably, it seems that the most substantial sport participation-related impact of the Sydney 2000 Olympic Games was an increase in passive involvement, such as live and television spectating. [33] Similarly disheartening, when the *Official Report of the Games of the XXVII Olympiad* was published in 2002, it made no mention of sport for all in its section detailing the games' legacy. [34] However, it did detail how the games would provide a sports infrastructure for Sydney.

Sports infrastructure

Ironically, then, one of the strongest subjects of criticism of Sydney's Olympic legacy has been the use, or lack thereof, of the facilities that were constructed for the games, especially those at Sydney Olympic Park (SOP); however, Blacktown's Olympic Park baseball facility and the equestrian venue at Eastern Creek have also received censure. Under-utilization of sports facilities after the games is a common issue for Olympic host cities. [35] Sydney is no exception, despite the fact that before the games 'the government had emphasized the benefits to future NSW generations of the world-class sporting facilities' built for the games. It was forecast that world-class, environmentally friendly sports facilities would attract international sporting competitions for decades; that games athletes, media and officials' accommodation for the games would assist the long-term housing needs of Sydney and generate urban renewal; and that the media and business interest generated by the games would improve Australia's international profile as a safe, stable and financially secure economy for other trading nations. [36]

The Sydney Olympic Park Authority (SOPA) was established in 2001 to ensure that SOP maintained its identity as a major event, residential and business precinct

after the games. Essential to this was the drawing up of a master plan for the area. This identified eight major development sites and provided development capacity for 230,000 m2 of commercial, leisure, education, retail, hotel and cultural/institutional uses to support an estimated 20,000 workers. Two residential development sites with capacity for 3,000 residents were also identified. [37] However, this master plan received considerable criticism and has been since been replaced by 'Vision 2025'.

Vision 2025 embodies the following principles:

- preserve and celebrate the Olympic legacy, including identification of the significant infrastructure of the Sydney 2000 Olympic Games;
- build on government investment in SOP to create a poly-functional centre at the heart of metropolitan Sydney;
- reinforce SOP as the venue of choice for hosting major national and international sporting, cultural and entertainment events in NSW;
- introduce a diverse mix of uses to ensure that SOP is an active place all year round;
- transform the low-density land uses, currently occupying large areas of the urban core, into an intense urban centre through establishment of major development opportunities;
- build on the grandeur and spatial generosity of the Olympic Boulevard to form one of the world's great contemporary civic spaces;
- continue the traditions at SOP of creating high-quality urban design, architectural, landscape, and art projects;
- promote environmental best practice in all new facilities and events, further extending the best-practice standards already achieved at SOP;
- create a diverse and inclusive social mix by providing a wide range of uses and activities throughout the urban core;
- retain and enhance high public transport access and use, so that SOP remains a model of sustainable best practice in transport policy and implementation;
- provide better connections to adjoining areas, so that SOP with its surrounding parklands and communities is easily accessible by a range of transport modes, and becomes fully integrated. [38]

All this has come at a cost. Thus, the NSW government, which paid for the initial games infrastructure, has continued to invest large amounts of money in SOP. There is some good news in this. Figure 2, which was produced by the SOP Authority, demonstrates its claim that that there has been a steady increase in visitors to the precinct since the games and demonstrates that the post-games expenditure has had demonstrable outcomes.

Another perceived benefit of hosting the games is increases in inbound tourism to the host nation, resulting in a positive economic impact. Again, Sydney cannot claim great success in this regard.

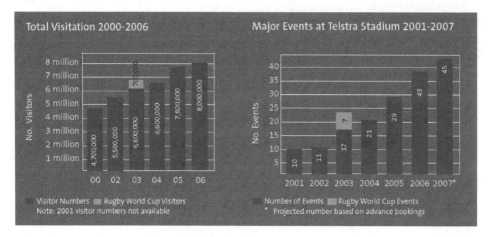

Figure 2 Visitors to Sydney Olympic Park.
Source: *Sydney Olympic Park; a Living Legacy for the People of Australia*, p. 3, available at
http://www.sydneyolympicpark.com.au/corporate/about_us/olympic_legacy.

Tourism

According to Graham Brown:

> Accurate measures of the impact of the Sydney Olympic Games on tourism are not
> available as little research to specifically examine this issue has been conducted. As
> with the case with most major events, considerable effort was spent to gain support
> for and justify the bid and to ensure that the event could be staged successfully.
> However impact analysis received less attention as people with relevant knowledge
> move on to work on the next event. [39]

He also notes that there was duplication of research in the planning stages and that
the research agenda could have been 'more effectively coordinated'. [40] In one of
these studies conducted in the pre-games period, research conducted by the Tourism
Forecasting Council forecast that an additional 1.6 million visitors would come to
Australia in 1997–2004 as a result of the games, generating an extra $A6.1bn in
tourism export earnings. However, these numbers were not realized, partly because of
the effects of the terrorist attacks of 11 September 2001 and the severe acute
respiratory syndrome (SARS) scare on Australian inbound tourism. In summary,
'visitor numbers have increased since 2003 but it is now impossible to determine the
role played by any residual Olympic effect.' [41]

Economic Impact

The difficulty in accurately determining tourism and sport impacts and their link to
possible economic legacies has not deterred various bodies from making claims in

this area. For example, in 2002, the NSW government claimed that the economic impact of the Sydney games could be classified into four major categories: construction of the infrastructure required for staging the games; additional employment for those working either directly on games organization, or with proximal stakeholders; visits to Sydney for the games and for tests and other associated events; and, finally, visits to Australia after the games by tourists as a result of the games. The *Official Report of the Games of the XXVII Olympiad* lists the total net operating revenue of the games as $A2,387m, the total net operating expenditure as $A2,015.7m, and the net profit as $A371.5m. [42] In its 2002 report, the NSW government estimated that while it contributed a total of $A1,326.1m, it had received an additional $653m in tax revenue. [43]

A study by Price Waterhouse Coopers, commissioned by the NSW Department of State and Regional Development, also supported government claims that the games would provide substantial economic benefits. The report concluded that the games led to $A3bn in 'business outcomes'. The report also suggested that the games generated up to $A6.1bn in international publicity for Australia, $A6bn in spending by an additional 1.6 million visitors in 2001, and 210 events for the Sydney Convention and Visitors Bureau. It concluded that the total economic stimuli from the Sydney games were among the highest of any recent games. [44]

The Commonwealth government contributed substantially less to the games than the NSW government. However, it staged 94 'networking events' at games time, to boost Australia's export markets. These were considered to be successful, and the Federal Trade Minister, Mark Vaile, claimed that the programme generated $A1bn for the nation in new business and investment. [45]

While basking in the immediate post-games euphoria, few state taxpayers appeared to begrudge any of the financial expenditure, but now that the economic 'report cards' on the games are beginning to be known, their Olympic rapture appears to have worn off. With the current troubles in NSW health, transport and other state government sectors, some are again questioning the long-term costs and benefits of the games. However, to estimate legacy simply in economic terms is myopic. [46] Apart from the sports legacies mentioned earlier, another important criterion to be gauged is the effect of the social impacts on the host community.

Social impacts

Before the games, a 1995 Keys Young report, the *Social Impacts of the Games*, had identified a number of potential negative outcomes from hosting the games for the people of Sydney and NSW. Because of the report, many NSW government agencies introduced strategies to address the issues raised. However, despite any such attempts to dilute the 'Olympic effect', observers such as Helen Lenskyj were critical of the social cost of the games to some disadvantaged groups such as Aborigines, the political Left, and specific interest groups such as low-rent tenants. [47] She contended that before the games, and even before the bid was won, Olympic

politicians and the games organizers had deliberately deflected protests through a strategic policy of division, which effectively marginalized alternative views about support for the games in the mainstream media.

During the games period, attendance at public protests, such as the 'Aboriginal Embassy' in Victoria Park, were overshadowed in the media and public consciousness by official Olympic social activities. Furthermore, according to G. Waitt's study of the social impacts of the Sydney Olympics, the most positive reaction to Sydney's Olympics intensified from 1998, reaching its peak in September 2000. Waitt noted:

> As clearly demonstrated by Sydney's Olympics, global sporting events provide the opportunity for government and city authorities to (re)establish or increase the attachment and identification of people to place. For Sydney, the possibilities presented by these outcomes are particularly relevant in an era marred by increasing levels of youth suicide, homelessness, and drug addiction as well as accusations of racism against those not conforming to an Anglo-Celtic Australian national identity (Chan and Human). However, a hallmark event's relevance in addressing any of these social issues diminishes if such benefits are not sustained after the 'circus' has left town. [48]

He cautioned that the community spirit that the Sydney Olympics engendered may have only briefly revived a flag-waving form of nationalism, rather than sustaining Olympic supporters' claims of building a new spirit of 'Australianness'. Echoing G. Brown's caution in terms of investigating tourism benefits, Waite called for future research to investigate whether any substantial social impacts really occurred. [49]

Knowledge Legacy

One area in which Sydney can legitimately claim to have made a positive difference has been in the area of transferring Olympic knowledge to the Olympic Movement. Despite the complicated logistics of organizing the Olympic Games, until the 2000 games, there was little knowledge or even information passed from each OCOG to the next, except for those staff who worked on successive games, or a small number of Olympic consultants who sold their tacit knowledge to the next host city. [50] When an OCOG was dissolved, its information, knowledge and experience often vanished. Moreover, the next host cities, understandably, sought to stamp their games with their identity, not that of the games before. Until the Sydney games, this meant that there was not a strategic, IOC-sanctioned, information-transfer programme from one OCOG to another.

The first example of this practice changing occurred in 1998, when a commercial agreement was signed between the IOC and SOCOG, which formalized SOCOG's selling of its explicit and tacit knowledge to the IOC for $A5m. This material was then disseminated to the OCOGs of the Salt Lake City and Athens Olympic Games. This programme was known as the Transfer of Know How (TOK) and established

Olympic knowledge as a corporate asset. [51] The TOK from Sydney 2000 involved both written and oral delivery of intellectual property from over 90 relevant SOCOG managers. The first written material was collected in January 2000. Relevant SOCOG staff were required to complete a series of written templates provided on the corporate intranet site. Over the period of the next 10–12 months, managers were obliged to update and expand their contributions.

The collection of the Sydney templates had varied results. Some SOCOG managers had provided detailed materials as required, while others were less forthcoming, possibly hoarding the future value of their tacit knowledge. Others found it difficult to textually record their operations in meaningful way, and so oral exchanges were an important component of this initiative. The concept behind the TOK was that the knowledge provided would form the foundation of generic Olympic management guides designed to evolve following each successive games. While the results of the TOK were not universally successful, generally it has been accepted that this is an important step forward for the Olympic Movement. Indeed, other mega-sporting events have followed suit. The IOC is still pursuing this programme at subsequent Olympics, and so, from its perspective, the Sydney Games provided a foundation to effectively use the Olympic knowledge that was created for these games.

Political legacy

Essentially, the decision to host the Olympics is driven by 'boosterism' and further championed by politicians. Because of the seven years between gaining and staging the games, the host nation's political landscape can be transformed. In the Sydney Olympic's case, both federal and state governments were voted out. The former from Labor to Liberal, and the latter from Liberal to Labor. Despite this juxtaposition, the governments were supportive, and most politicians were enthusiastic about being involved in the games, whatever their motives. To cement its stake, the NSW government established the position of Minister for the Olympic and Paralympic Games. Michael Knight was appointed to this position in March 1995 and held it until just after the games when he resigned soon after criticism of his treatment of the SOCOG chief executive, Sandy Hollway, during the games.

Despite his reputation and unpopularity with the general public and SOCOG staff, Knight guided much of Sydney's Olympic planning. He formed a strong alliance with John Coates, the president of the AOC, and it was a brave individual who stood up to the two of them. After the games, Coates became an IOC member and Knight continued his earlier commitment as a member of the Athens Coordination Committee. He kept a low profile until 2007, when it was announced he would be the next the chairman of the board of the SOP Authority, a role previously held by his Olympic bureaucratic champion, David Richmond. This was another case of Olympic deckchairs being reshuffled.

Although NSW politicians wanted successful games, as their government was underwriting them, they were also conscious of the budget. This tension, in the case of

Sydney's infrastructure, fell firmly on the side of bigger is better. However, this has implications beyond the host games. It creates benchmarks and expectations for the next host city to improve on, excludes from hosting those nations who cannot bear the cost, or may economically cripple nations who ignore this negative outcome. After the Sydney games, the IOC examined the predicament of escalating costs through the establishment of an Olympic Games Study Commission. This group presented its report to the 115th IOC Session held in Prague during July 2003. The commission's report recommended ways of decreasing of the size, cost and complexity of organizing the Olympic Games in five main areas. It suggested changes to the games' format, venues and facilities, management, the number of accredited persons, and service levels. [52] However, the report conveniently shifted some of the responsibility for the mushrooming overheads away from the IOC when it noted that:

> The enormous increases in Olympic revenues in the past couple of decades, derived principally from the leadership of the IOC, appear to have allowed Games organizers to relax, to some degree, their efforts to control costs, because the revenues to support higher expenditure have been available to them. Also, many stakeholders have become increasingly demanding and have put a great deal of pressure on Games organizers to provide ever bigger facilities and better services, without proper IOC control and approval. [53]

Conclusion

It is obvious that legacy assessments of the Sydney games are fraught with dangers of incorrect assessments and influenced by the perceptions of those who make them, especially when SOCOG has been long disbanded and unable to influence stakeholders. Firstly, there is the likelihood of insufficient time having passed when the pronouncements are made to make any meaningful judgement. Secondly, there is the matter of objectivity depending on the stakeholder relationship. Olympic 'tragics' (to use an Australian term to describe sporting aficionados – especially those who were not talented enough to compete on the elite level) or those with political capital invested in the games are prone to extol their benefits, while trenchant Olympic critics are unlikely to be converted, no matter what the outcome. Much depends on the stakeholder's agenda. Nevertheless, given that that there has been a substantial time period since the games and the brief of Olympic legacies there is not much scope for avoiding an assessment, nor indeed is it necessarily wise to do so. Present assessment might ensure future realism. So, the most obvious conclusion is to break the evaluation down into component parts.

From a sports perspective, elite sport in Australia has profited at the expense of sport for all. Yes, the nation was successful on the field of play, winning 58 medals, including 16 gold. Yet, the sustainability of keeping Australia in the top four nations in the medal count that was achieved at the Sydney games is expensive. K. Hogan and K. Norton estimated the costs to the nation at $A37m per gold and $A8m per medal in general. [54] Is this a price that the nation can continue to afford? What happens if the nation starts to slide down the medal tally? An increase in passive sports consumption is the last thing Australia needs, given its increasing obesity problems. Moreover, in terms of sport, as noted by stakeholder theory, there are also some legacies that are beyond the ability of the organizers to control, but that are nonetheless significant. The Sydney games had pushed forward the boundaries in terms of advancing drug-testing procedures. However, drug testing invariably lags behind drug invention. The confession of steroid use by the US multiple gold medal winner at Sydney, Marion Jones, has soured the sports legacy of the Sydney Olympics. Jones admitted taking a steroid known as 'the clear' for two years from 1999, in the lead-up to the Sydney games. In 2007, she pleaded guilty to two counts of lying to US federal agents about doping and an unrelated financial matter. She was sentenced to six months in prison. While Jones has been stripped of her medals, it is highly likely that she was not the only star of the games to cheat, and other stories of previously undetected drug cheating in Sydney are emerging. [55] The legacy for those athletes who competed without performance-enhancing substances must be one of frustration, and for the general public there must be doubt that some athletes won fairly.

The sports infrastructure legacy is improving, but at continuing cost to the NSW taxpayer. SOP is iconic. It has nine major sporting, event and entertainment venues, and parks surrounded by one of the largest urban parklands in the world. Currently, it hosts nearly 1,800 events each year.

On the other hand, any social impacts that were claimed as a result of the games appear to have dissipated. In this respect, the games have gone on – to the next city, as has the official knowledge transfer, although many Australians have taken their Olympic expertise to the world. It would be difficult to find a mega-sports event being organized anywhere in the world without Australians contributing to it in some form.

Politically, it appears that, at this stage, Australian politicians still believe in a positive Sydney games legacy. Those who were in office during the games have always talked up the benefits of the Sydney games and their messages, and undeniably many of their words are invariably the same. For example, in a speech in 2005, Australian Federal Minister for the Arts and Sport, Senator Rod Kemp, noted:

> There can be little doubt that the Sydney 2000 Games showed to the world the attributes of our country and our people. There are many very good reasons for the Australian Government to support large sporting events like these. As I said before, they showcase and celebrate Australia as a successful, multicultural society. As well as building national pride and being an entertainment spectacular, these events can lead to benefits such as a strengthening of bilateral trade relationships with other countries. The vast experience accumulated and the international attention gained has led to the opportunity to win business in Beijing and in other major sports projects. [56]

Since the 2000 Olympics, Australia has hosted the 2003 Rugby World Cup and the 2006 Commonwealth Games and has just announced that it is going to bid for the

2018 Football World Cup. This suggests that politicians still see large sporting events as a suitable strategy for the nation's international relations.

Richard Cashman noted that 'the challenge for post-Games organizations is not simply to wind down the Olympic infrastructure and to avoid additional costs, but to access new Olympic investment opportunities.' [57] Australia is seeking these opportunities by leveraging off its Sydney Olympic record. For this reason, despite any negative legacy assessments by others, the politicians and sport managers, who are the most crucial stakeholder group bidding for mega-sport events, have been strongly supportive of the outcomes of the 2000 games.

Notes

[1] From the title of a famous Australian song written by Peter Allen ('I Still Call Australia Home') and now the music for an iconic Qantas advertisement.
[2] The philosophy of the Olympic Games, as espoused by the International Olympic Committee and expressed in the Olympic Charter.
[3] Birch, *Master of the Ceremonies*, 306.
[4] Cashman *et al.*, 'When the Carnival Is Over'.
[5] Frawley and Toohey, 'Shaping Sport Competition'.
[6] Knightley, 'The Wizards of Oz'.
[7] Howard, *Australian*. Quoted in Cashman *et al.*, 'When the Carnival is Over', p. 4.
[8] Cashman, *The Bitter-Sweet Awakening*.
[9] Kennelly *et al.*, 'An Investigation of the Relationship Between an Australian National Sport Organisation and a Private Tour Operator'.
[10] Freeman, *Strategic Management*.
[11] Donaldson and Preston, 'The Stakeholder Theory of the Corporation'.
[12] Kennelly *et al.*, 'An Investigation of the Relationship Between an Australian National Sport Organisation and a Private Tour Operator'.
[13] Hoye and Cuskelly, *Sport Governance*.
[14] Kennelly *et al.*, 'An Investigation of the Relationship Between an Australian National Sport Organisation and a Private Tour Operator'.
[15] Donaldson and Preston, 'The Stakeholder Theory of the Corporation'.
[16] Mitchell *et al.*, 'Towards a Theory of Stakeholder Identification and Salience', 865.
[17] Merrilees *et al.*, 'Marketing Stakeholder Analysis', 1060.
[18] Friedman *et al.*, 'Building a Framework for Issues Management in Sport Through Stakeholder Theory', 170.
[19] Toohey and Veal, *The Olympic Games*.
[20] Holloway, 'After the Party, Sydney's Olympic Blues'.
[21] Cashman, *The Bitter-Sweet Awakening*, 273.
[22] McGeogh and Corporaal, *The Bid: How Australia Won the 2000 Olympics*, 199.
[23] Toohey, *Official Report of the XXVII Olympiad*.
[24] Frawley and Toohey, 'Shaping Sport Competition'.
[25] Toohey, 'National Olympic Committees'.
[26] Toohey and Veal, 'The (Sporting) Legacy of the Sydney 2000 Olympic Games'.
[27] Houlihan, *Sport Policy and Politics*, 71.
[28] Australian Sports Commission, 'Developing an Olympic Legacy for Community Sport'.
[29] Veal *et al.*, '"Sport for All".'
[30] National Centre for Culture and Recreation Statistics, 'The Impact of the Olympics on Participation in Australia'; Australian Sports Commission, 'Impact of Hosting the Sydney

2000 Olympic and Paralympic Games on Participating in Sport and Physical Activity in Australia', unpublished paper, Sport Development Unit, Australian Sports Commission, Canberra, 2001; Toohey and Veal, 'The (Sporting) Legacy of the Sydney 2000 Olympic Games'; Beyond the Torch – Olympics and the Australian Culture Conference, Australian Society for Sports history ACT Chapter, April, Canberra.

[31] Australian Bureau of Statistics, 'Involvement in Organised Sports and Physical Activities'.
[32] Ibid.
[33] Veal *et al.*, "'Sport for All'".
[34] Toohey and Veal, The (Sporting) Legacy of the Sydney 2000 Olympic Games'.
[35] Essex and Chalkley, 'The Infrastructural Legacy of the Summer and Winter Olympic Games'.
[36] Sydney 2000, 'Games Info'.
[37] Sydney Olympic Park Authority, 'The Vision'.
[38] Ibid.
[39] Brown, 'The Games of the XXVII Olympiad', 149.
[40] Ibid.
[41] Ibid., 151.
[42] Toohey, *Official Report of the Games of the XXVII Olympiad*.
[43] Olympic Coordination Authority, 'The Sydney 2000 Olympic and Paralympic Games'.
[44] Price Waterhouse Coopers, *Business and Economic Benefits of the Sydney 2000 Olympic Games.*
[45] Shoebridge, 'After the Games'.
[46] Cashman *et al.*, 'When the Carnival Is Over', 14.
[47] Lenskyj, *The Best Olympics Ever?*
[48] Waitt, 'Social impacts of the Sydney Olympics', 213.
[49] Ibid.
[50] Halbwirth and Toohey, 'The Olympic Games and Knowledge Management'.
[51] Ibid.
[52] Toohey and Veal, *The Olympic Games.*
[53] Pound, *Inside the Olympics,* 13.
[54] Hogan and Norton, 'The "Price" of Olympic Gold'.
[55] Toohey and Veal, *The Olympic Games.*
[56] Kemp, 'Impact of the Olympics and Commonwealth Games'.
[57] Cashman, *The Bitter-Sweet Awakening,* 275.

References

Australian Bureau of Statistics. 'Involvement in Organised Sports and Physical Activities', available at http://www.abs.gov.au/Ausstats/abs%40.nsf/46d1bc47ac9d0c7bca256c470025ff87/ea4ba506f23871f4ca256cae0010851a!OpenDocument, 24 Jan. 2003.

Australian Sports Commission. 'Developing an Olympic Legacy for Community Sport' [cited 27 June 2000], available at http://catalogue.ausport.gov.au/fulltext/2000/ascmedia/20000627.html.

——. 'Impact of Hosting the Sydney 2000 Olympic and Paralympic Games on Participating in Sport and Physical Activity in Australia'. Unpublished paper, Sport Development Unit, Australian Sports Commission, Canberra, 2001.

Birch, R. *Master of the Ceremonies.* Sydney: Allen and Unwin, 2004.

Booth, D. and C. Tatz. "'Swimming with the Big Boys"? The Politics of Sydney's Olympic Bid'. *Sporting Traditions* 11, no. 1, (1994): 3–23.

Brown, G. 'The Games of the XXVII Olympiad in Sydney (2000)'. In *Olympic Tourism*, edited by M. Weed. Oxford: Butterworth–Heinemann, 2008.

Cashman, R. *The Bitter-Sweet Awakening: The Legacy of the Sydney 2000 Olympic Games.* Sydney: Walla Wall Press, 2006.

Cashman, R., K. Toohey, S. Darcy, C. Symons and B. Stewart. 'When the Carnival Is Over: Evaluating the Outcomes of Mega Sporting Events in Australia'. *Sporting Traditions* 21, no. 1, (2004): 1–32.

Donaldson, T. and L.E. Preston. 'The Stakeholder Theory of the Corporation: Concepts, Evidence, and Implications'. *Academy of Management Review* 20, no. 1, (1995): 65–91.

Essex, S. and B. Chalkley. 'The Infrastructural Legacy of the Summer and Winter Olympic Games. A Comparative Analysis'. In *The Legacy of the Olympic Games 1984–2000*, edited by M. Moragas *et al.* Lausanne: International Olympic Committee, 2002.

Frawley, S. and K. Toohey. 'Shaping Sport Competition: The SOCOG Sports Commission and the Planning and Delivery of Sport at the Sydney 2000 Olympic Games'. In *Beyond the Torch: Olympics and Australian Culture.* Melbourne: ASSH, 2005.

Freeman, R.E. *Strategic Management: A Stakeholder Approach.* Marshfield: Pitman Publishing, 1984.

Friedman, M., M. Parent and D. Mason. 'Building a Framework for Issues Management in Sport Through Stakeholder Theory'. *European Sport Management Quarterly* 4, no. 3, (2004): 170–90.

Gordon, H. *The Time of Our Lives: Inside the Sydney Olympics.* St. Lucia: Queensland University Press, 2003.

Halbwirth, S. and K. Toohey. 'The Olympic Games and Knowledge Management: A Case Study of the Sydney Organising Committee of the Olympic Games'. *European Sport Management Quarterly* 1, no. 2, (2001): 91–111.

Hogan, K. and K. Norton. 'The "Price" of Olympic Gold'. *Journal of Science and Medicine in Sport* 3, no. 2, (2000): 203–18.

Holloway, G. 'After the Party, Sydney's Olympic Blues'. *CNN.com*, available at http://edition.cnn.com/2001/WORLD/asiapcf/auspac/07/11/sydney.stadiums/index.html, 11 Jul. 2001.

Houlihan, B. *Sport Policy and Politics: A Comparative Analysis.* London: Routledge, 1997.

Hoye, R. and G. Cuskelly. *Sport Governance.* Oxford: Elsevier, 2007.

Kemp, R. 'Impact of the Olympics and Commonwealth Games', available at http://www.minister.dcita.gov.au/kemp/media/speeches/china-australia_media_forum?SQ_DESIGN_NAME=printer%20friendly, 2005.

Kennelly, M., K. Toohey and D. Zakus. 'An Investigation of the Relationship Between an Australia National Sport Organisation and a Private Tour Operator'. Paper presented at the 5th European Association of Sport Management Congress, Turin, Italy, Sept. 2007.

Knightly, P. 'The Wizards of Oz'. *Sydney Morning Herald*, available at www.olympics.smh.com.au, 13 Oct. 2000.

Lenskyj, H. *The Best Olympics Ever?: Social Impacts of Sydney 2000.* Albany, NY: State University of New York Press, 2007.

McGeoch, R. and G. Korporaal. *The Bid: How Australia Won the 2000 Olympics.* Melbourne: William Heinemann Australia, 1994.

Merrilees, B., D. Getz and D. O'Brien. 'Marketing Stakeholder Analysis: Branding the Brisbane Goodwill Games'. *European Journal of Marketing* 39, nos. 9–10, (2005): 1060–86.

Mitchell, R.K., B. Agle and D. Wood. 'Towards a Theory of Stakeholder Identification and Salience: Defining the Principle of Who and What Really Counts'. *Academy of Management Review* 22, no. 4, (1997): 853–86.

National Centre for Culture and Recreation Statistics. Unpublished paper, 'The Impact of the Olympics on Participation in Australia: Trickle Down Effect, Discouragement Effect or No Effect?' Adelaide: Australian Bureau of Statistics, 2001.

Olympic Coordination Authority. 'The Sydney 2000 Olympic and Paralympic Games. A Report on the Financial Contribution by the New South Wales Government to the 2000 Games'. Sydney: Olympic Coordination Authority, 2002.

Owen, K.A. 'The Sydney 2000 Olympics and Urban Entrepreneurialism: Local Variations in Urban Governance'. *Australian Geographical Studies* 40, no. 3, (2002): 323–36.

Pound, D. *Inside the Olympics*. Chichester, UK: Wiley, 2004.

Price Waterhouse Coopers. *Business and Economic Benefits of the Sydney 2000 Olympic Games*, available at http://www.gamesinfo.com.au/pi/ARPICOE.html, April 2002.

Searle, G. 'Uncertain Legacy: Sydney's Olympic Stadiums'. *European Planning Studies* 10, no. 7, (2002): 845–60.

Shoebridge, N. 'After the Games: It Is Time for the Real Gold Rush'. *Business Review Weekly* 6 Oct. (2000): 14.

Sport Accord 2007. 'Legacy and the Olympic Games', available at http://www.olympic.org/uk/news/olympic; http://www.olympic.org/uk/news/olympic_news/newsletter_news/newsletter_full_story_uk.asp?id=21513, May 2007.

Sydney 2000. 'Games Info', available at http://www.gamesinfo.com.au/pubinfoweb.

Sydney Olympic Park Authority. 'The Vision', available at http://www.sydneyolympicpark.com.au/developing_sydney_olympic_park/the_vision.

Sydney Organizing Committee for the Olympic Games. 'Sydney Olympic and Paralympic Games Facts'. Unpublished factsheet.

Toohey, K. *Official Report of the XXVII Olympiad*. Sydney: SOCOG, 2001.

——. 'National Olympic Committees'. In *Aspects of Sport Governance. Perspectives*, vol. V, edited by D.A. Kluka, G. Schilling and W.F. Stier. Oxford: Meyer and Meyer Sports, 2005.

—— and A.J. Veal. 'The (Sporting) Legacy of the Sydney 2000 Olympic Games: Some Observations'. Paper presented at the Beyond the Torch – Olympics and the Australian Culture Conference, Canberra, April, 2004.

—— and A.J. Veal. *The Olympic Games: A Social Science Perspective*, 2nd edn. Wallingford, UK: CABI Publishing, 2007.

Veal, A.J., K. Toohey and S. Frawley. '"Sport for All" and the Legacy of the Sydney 2000 Olympic Games'. Paper presented at the 13th Commonwealth International Sport Conference, Melbourne, Australia, March 2006.

Waitt, G. 'The Olympic Spirit and Civic Boosterism: The Sydney 2000 Olympics'. *Tourism Geographies* 3, no. 3, (2001): 249–78.

——. 'Social Impacts of the Sydney Olympics'. *Annals of Tourism* 30, no. 1, (2003): 194–215.

Webb, T. *The Collaborative Games: The Story Behind the Spectacle*. Sydney: Pluto Press, 2001.

The Athens Olympics: Optimistic Legacies – Post-Olympic Assets and the Struggle for their Realization

Penelope Kissoudi

'You have won. You have won by brilliantly meeting the tough challenge of holding the Games.... These were unforgettable, dream Games.'

Jacques Rogge [1]

Preparing for the Athens Olympics: Urban Infrastructure and New Sports Facilities

Greece's bid for the 2004 Olympic Games and Paralympics was rewarded with success when, in September 1997, Juan Antonio Samaranch, President of the International Olympic Committee, revealed that Athens would host the 28th Olympic Games. The announcement of this positive development, following an unsuccessful bid to host the 1996 Olympics, inspired the Greek public to welcome sport to the top of the national agenda and highlight its benefits. On the other hand, however, they were circumspect about the enormous drain on public funds it would entail. In fact, the Olympic Games, as a major sporting event, can play a very important part in delivering social, economic, environmental and sporting benefits to the host country in general and the host city in particular. It was expected that the Athens Olympics would act as a catalyst promote modern sport and culture in Greece, thereby benefiting the national economy. As such, exploitation of the games' legacy in terms of the facilities and urban infrastructure created should be carefully planned and incorporated into a broad strategy aspiring to cultural and economic development that would have a beneficial impact on the country as a whole. Consequently, the benefits offered by the games, which would provide the Athenians with a unique opportunity to update city infrastructure and acquire new sports facilities to enjoy for years to come, should certainly outlast the two-week celebration. Athens, a densely populated city with very few open and green spaces, needed major urban improvements. Moreover, lack of a modern road transport network resulted in traffic congestion and air pollution. [2] Given the size and magnitude of the event, it was argued, Athens could use the opportunity to accelerate its modernization and briskly increase the pace of economic development. A building boom was initiated with the intention of creating impressive facilities spread around metropolitan Athens. This ambitious preparation project provided new sports facilities, renovation of the existing ones, extension of the Athens metro, modernization of the public transport system, a new tramline linking the city centre to the waterfront, improved transport connections, and motorway and slip roads providing a speedier trip to the Eleftherios Venizelos International Airport, as well as footpaths linking major attractions in the city centre. Since thousands of athletes, team escorts, judges, referees, media and press representatives, spectators, employees and volunteers were expected to travel to the Olympic facilities every day, road and railway network improvement was considered crucial to the success of the games. More significantly, infrastructure and new facilities, it was agreed, should be designed on the basis of a long-term prospect of further improvement and extension. Of the works completed prior to the games, the Athens underground railway (Attiko Metro) considerably improved the quality of city life by allowing Athenians to travel faster and reducing traffic congestion and air pollution. The metro connected more than 20 municipalities of Attica with provision for new lines. Furthermore, the new suburban railway, an integral part of a wide development plan which aimed to update and extend the railway network, was constructed to link Athens to districts in Attica, while the new tramline linked the centre with the southern suburbs, a route providing a good view of the sea. Another ambitious construction plan completed prior to the games was Attiki Odos (Attica Road), a modern motorway of 67 km through 30 municipalities of Attica with 32 junctions of unequal level and 15 pedestrian bridges, while a big part of the existing motorway was renewed or repaired and a large number of underpass complexes together with bridges and tunnels were constructed, thus reducing traffic congestion and journey time. [3] There is little doubt that the preparation project afforded Athens the opportunity to present itself as a modern metropolis, highlighting to the world its classical and modern nature while ensuring long-term benefits. In addition, the Athens Olympic Village was part of an ambitious social programme. It is standard practice that the host country invests large sums of money in the Olympic Village, having post-games uses in view. With the exception of the 1984 Los Angeles Olympics and the 1996 Atlanta Olympic Games, when athletes and sports representatives were accommodated in the student residences of UCLA and Georgia Tech respectively, from

1932 onwards (when, for the first time, the host city of Los Angeles constructed a complex of houses for the athletes' accommodation) the Olympic Village has been part of a long-term business plan. In designing the Olympic Village, Athens aspired to create a modern development area that might both solve environmental problems and meet housing needs. Built at the foot of Parnitha Mountain (in the Acharnes municipality, a short distance from the centre), the village was intended to accommodate 16,000 athletes during the Olympic Games and 6,000 athletes participating in the Paralympics. After the games, it was intended that the houses would be offered at a reduced price to low-income workers, beneficiaries of the Workers' Housing Organization. A modern town of about 10,000 residents was envisaged. [4] Given the scale and complexity of the project, an affiliated company of the Workers' Housing Organization, named the Olympic Village 2004 SA, was established by law in 2000 and was entrusted with the construction of the village. [5] During the work, part of the Hadrian Aqueduct, a significant antiquity which had supplied the ancient city of Athens with water, was restored to embellish the newly constructed village. In fact, Greece, for the first time, implemented a large-scale housing project designed to meet social needs. Additionally, the Olympic Press Village, a model development area named Ilida, inspired by the name of the site of the ancient games, was to accommodate media and press representatives while the International Broadcasting Centre (IBC), heart of the games' global television transmission, was designed as an impressive modern building. [6] New sports facilities and regeneration of the old ones were expected to encourage sport and promote Greece's image at international level. Of the existing sports facilities, the Olympic Sports Centre included the Olympic Stadium with a seating capacity of 80,000 spectators. The renovated stadium hosted track events as well as the opening and closing ceremonies of the games. The Olympic Sports Centre also contained a small gymnasium and outbuildings, two Olympic swimming pools (seating 11,000 and 6,500 spectators respectively), a cycling track with seating capacity of 5,000 people, a big gymnasium (seating 16,000 spectators), and a tennis court which could accommodate 20,000 spectators. Regeneration of the Faliro area, which contained the Peace and Friendship Stadium, yacht facilities, the Karaiskaki Stadium and the old Athens airport, aimed at regional development, a crucial matter which had been neglected for many decades. The Faliro coastline, a place of beautiful beaches, restaurants, cafes and pedestrian streets before the Second World War, had since become a place littered with heaps of discarded construction materials and rubbish. The area remained undeveloped for more than 50 years with the exception of the creation in the 1960s of a race course and a few marinas in the Faliro Delta. In consequence, exploitation of many hectares of abandoned or misused state-owned seaside land was a challenge that the Organizing Committee of Athens 2004 could not overlook. The development project for the Faliro area involved construction of the Sports Pavilion (Tae-Kwon-Do Hall), a modern building of about 4,000 retractable seats (an ideal place for conferences, concerts, commercial exhibitions and film productions in post-Olympic use), as well as the creation of an aquarium, a modern marina, the Olympic beach volleyball courts, an open-air theatre, pedestrian streets and an esplanade. [7] The Schinias Rowing and Canoeing Centre was included in an ambitious environmental and ecological project so that the natural springs and the attractive landscape of the area, which were then threatened by neglect or destruction, would be protected. In addition, the following projects to be built in deprived and downgraded areas were expected to improve the area by promoting tourism and culture, affording local people the opportunity of being involved in sports activities and providing employment: the Agios Kosmas Sailing Centre, the Nikea Weightlifting Centre, the Markopoulo Shooting and Equestrian Centre, the Olympic Tennis Stadium, the Ano Liossia Centre (which was to host the Olympic Wrestling and Judo competitions), the Peristeri Boxing Hall and the Galatsi Hall where the Olympic table tennis and rhythmic gymnastics events were to be held. The preparation project also involved regeneration of the Helleniko Olympic Complex, site of the old Athens airport where, after renovation, the Olympic fencing, basketball, baseball and softball competitions were to take place. The Canoe Kayak Slalom, an impressive artificial lake 2,250 m in length with an auxiliary lake for the athletes' training and warm-up, canals and a bridge, was to be added to the area. The long catalogue of sports facilities also included the Goudi Olympic Centre, a spacious hall for badminton, the restored Equestrian Centre and two open-air venues. Struggling against difficulties and time constraints and faced with harsh criticism from abroad, Greece attempted to realize an ambitious, large-scale construction and reconstruction undertaking. More significantly, viable projects for the post-games exploitation of the Olympic legacy were considered imperative. During the period of preparation, the games' cost in general and the expenditure on the new sports facilities in particular, an onerous burden on the national economy, aroused strong feelings in the public and provoked political dispute. Negative press comments and biting criticism from all the political parties, focusing on the fact that the citizens were burdened with high taxes, were frequent and dampened enthusiasm for the games. Nevertheless, those who keenly supported the Athens Olympics argued that the cost should be judged in the context of the long-term benefits to the country as a whole. [8] Despite criticism and gloomy predictions two years prior to the games, an article entitled 'A Survey of Greece' published in *The Economist*, reported that 'Greece, in spite of economic difficulties, can host the 2004 Games', while in August 2004, another article, entitled 'The Athens Olympics', in *The Economist* said, 'Cassandra was defied and the Greeks hoped to get everything ready on time.' [9] In short, in implementing the ambitious project of preparing the 2004 Olympics, Greece had an opportunity to improve the general quality of life in the host city and promote athletic, economic and cultural development. More specifically and importantly, new sports facilities and improved environmental conditions were expected to give a new look to neglected and downgraded areas, simultaneously providing the local people with fresh opportunities of involvement in sporting and cultural activities and of employment. [10] As a result of winning the bid to host the games, at the turn of the twenty-first century, Greece initiated the largest number of construction works in its modern history. In this way, Athens in 2004 aspired to present itself as a modern, socially, economically and culturally developed metropolis and therefore an attractive tourist destination; an aspiration that was realized at least in part.

The Games' Cost and the Plan for the Olympic Legacy's Utilization: Object of Political Dispute

The Athens games concluded on 29 August 2004, leaving behind a precious legacy of modern facilities. Their post-games use was a challenge to Greece to ensure long-term benefits. However, the Olympic legacy and its realization increasingly became a splitting headache to the government and gave rise to controversy between it and the political parties. [11] Established as a state company, Hellenic Olympic Properties SA (under the control of the Ministries of Finance, National Economy and Culture) was charged with the creation and implementation of a long-term strategy for utilizing each of the Olympic venues after the games. The value of the property that the company was entrusted to administer amounted to 2bn euros, roughly 1.3% of the gross national product, while, in a rough estimate, the cost of the facilities' maintenance after the games was expected to run to 15m euros per annum. The Thessaly University of Economics, which investigated the subject, concluded that the annual cost would finally run to 84m euros. In fact, the maintenance and security costs of the facilities were to be considerably higher. [12] A day after the closing ceremony, the games' cost was already in the news. 'The Olympic Games were excellent but the price is too high,' the newspaper *Eleftherotypia* reported. [13] It was in November 2004 that the government announced that the games' cost actually amounted to 9bn euros. The parties that made up the opposition, the Pasok Party, the Syriza Party and the Communist Party of Greece, doubted the accuracy of the government report, and mutual recrimination between government and the opposition began. [14] High-ranking IOC members did not hide their unhappiness with the report. Tactfully, they said that 'the official report on the cost of the games is off-hand and does not correspond with the money actually spent on the Athens Olympics.' [15] Political dispute was at its height when, in May 2005, the Organizing Committee of Athens 2004 at last gave a detailed account of the Olympic expenditure attributed to the games' organization, leaving out, however, the expense of urban infrastructure and new sports facilities constructed with public funds. According to the report, revenues mainly emanating from television rights and sponsorship ran to more than 20bn euros (2,098.4m euros), whereas the expenses came to less than 20bn euros (1,967.6m euros); the Organizing Committee thus succeeded in its object of ensuring the state a surplus of 130.6m euros. [16] In general, the cost of most Olympic projects exceeds the initial estimate. In the case of the Athens games, however, although the cost was estimated at 4.5bn euros during the bid process, the final expense topped 11bn euros, thus going way over the initial budget with only a small part of the outgoings funded by the private sector of the economy. [17] In contrast, the net cost of the 2000 Sydney Olympics was about A$2.2 bn (about 1.3bn euros), taking into account the outgoings on construction of venues, transport, security, etc. [18] Nevertheless, the cost was not the only crucial issue raised. The post-games use of the facilities was a serious issue that troubled the government, the world of sport, and those who were involved in the games. In August 2004, while the games were in progress, Christos Hadjiemmanuel, President of Hellenic Olympic Properties SA and Reader in Law at the London School of Economics and Political Science, speaking at the Athens Business Club Conference about the future of the Olympic assets, pointed out that 'preparation of an immediately implemented plan for the post-Games use of the facilities on the one hand and cooperation with businessmen on the other are crucial objectives and a challenge that Hellenic Olympic Properties SA is prepared to meet.' Hadjiemmanuel continued, 'The facilities' utilization must deliver long-term benefits, promote economic development and upgrade the areas where the assets are found, affording opportunities for participation in sport and culture. To achieve our goal, we shall have talks with representatives from the public and private sector of the economy, sports officials and the local authorities so that the Olympic facilities are exploited for the local peoples' benefit.' He added that 'there is a lack, for the time being, of a complete development plan. Much time was lost in the past when, during the Games' preparation, the post-Olympic utilization of the assets was of no particular interest. ... The facilities were constructed without a long-term viability plan and every mention of the post-Games use was short and vague.' [19] This statement was a clear dig at the Pasok Party (which was in office until March 2004) and the way it bid for and conceived the Athens Olympics. Political dispute grew as the magnificent facilities were abandoned after the games and caustic press comments were frequently published. 'The Schinias Olympic Rowing and Canoeing Centre has been reduced to a rubbish dump and 200 thousand euros are needed for its cleaning. ... The Nikea Weightlifting Centre is fenced off, weightlifting athletes are locked out while wrestlers and judo athletes are not admitted to the Ano Liossia Olympic Centre since the federations cannot meet maintenance expenses,' the press reported. [20] Controversy over the exploitation of the Olympic legacy was initiated just one day after the closing ceremony of the games (30 August 2004). It was George Papandreou, leader of the opposition, who highlighted the games' success on the one hand and on the other pointed out that 'the Karamanlis government should not keep on blaming the Pasok party which played a very important part in preparation and took great interest in the post-Games use of the facilities when it was in office ... fresh plans for the exploitation of the Olympic legacy and viable development projects must now take priority.' [21] On the same day, in a television message to the Greek people, Prime Minister Kostas Karamanlis first thanked the Greek public and those who contributed to the games' success and then laid stress on the government's interest in the post-games exploitation of the facilities. 'Greece must stand firm on a higher social and cultural plane promoting its image and exploiting in the best way the magnificent Olympic facilities, all incorporating high technology, which the Greek people made sacrifices to fund.' He concluded by saying that 'the success of a major athletic event is not a two-week jamboree but a milestone of a new era.' [22] The Olympic assets exploitation dominated the Premier's address at the 15th Economic Conference held in Athens in November 2004. Among other things, he pointed out that 'by exploiting the legacy the Olympic Games left behind, we aspire to attract investors from abroad and promote development and tourism,' thus making clear that his government recognized the contribution of the games and the Olympic legacy to Greece's economic development. [23] Following harsh criticism for supposed inaction, the assignment of the facilities' use to businessmen on long-term lease was announced by Kostas Karamanlis in November 2004. Although the 'Solomon solution' (as it was dubbed by business sectors) was presented after considerable delay, it demonstrated government determination to make headway with the Olympic assets. [24] Furthermore, in December 2004, a consultation was held at ministerial level, which took place at the Maximum Mansion, the building that houses the rooms of the Premier. Presided over by the Premier, the Minister of Economics and Finance (George Alogoskoufis), the Minister of Environment, Land Use and Public Works (George Souflias), the Deputy Minister of Culture (Fani Palli-Petralia) and the President of Hellenic Olympic Properties SA (Christos Hadjiemmanuel) attended to discuss the future of the facilities and make resolutions to avoid wasting any more time. Following the consultation, Karamanlis, addressing the conference held at the Maroussi Press Centre entitled 'Post-Olympic Utilization of the Olympic Infra-structure: Development, Culture, Quality of Life', outlined the government plan for the post-games use of the assets. 'Exploiting the Olympic facilities, the new transport network and the urban infrastructure, we seek to promote Greece's image, make Athens a desirable tourist destination, attract investors from abroad and first and foremost improve the quality of life in Attica,' the Prime Minister said. He added that 'the new Olympic facilities fulfilled the specifications in terms of function, accessibility and aesthetics and acted as symbols of Greece in the new era.' He then asserted that 'the assets will be under state ownership. ... We will administer and exploit them pursuing economic and cultural development so that, in the short and long-term, Athenians may benefit at both the cultural and economic level.' Finally, he made clear that the intended international competitions for the use of the assets were to take place with complete transparency. [25] The government plan gave rise to fresh negative press comments; a number of them examined the way the facilities were to be exploited with a critical eye. Headlines such as 'the government resolutions lack substance' or 'the Olympic stadiums still remain fenced off and patrolled by security guards, a discouraging and disappointing situation that is not likely to change in the immediate future' deepened public anxiety for the assets' future. Not only the ruling Nea Dimokratia Party but also the opposition Pasok Party became a target of bitter criticism for not having designed a viable project for the post-games use of the facilities when they were in power. [26] By early spring 2005, no government decision had yet been made concerning the facilities' upkeep expense. The government was vague as to whether the expenditure was to come from the public purse or businessmen and whether the facilities' administration and exploitation were to be entrusted to state-run organizations, private enterprises or a combination of the two. [27] There is little doubt that a prompt government decision could have protected facilities from the wear and tear of time. Some positive press comments were published in March 2005 when the newspaper *Kathimerini*, in an article entitled 'Invitation for Post-Olympic Investment', reported that 'the government will assign use of the facilities to businessmen, thus ensuring the state considerable revenues', and stressed the fact that the first step to exploitation of the Olympic legacy will then have been made. [28] In the same month, the Deputy Minister of Culture, Fani-Palli Petralia, presented the draft of the bill which stipulated the post-Olympic use of the facilities for cultural, sporting and commercial activities in an attempt to interest investors. The draft again aroused strong feelings among the political opposition. 'The facilities' utilization will be assigned to business interests which anticipate making big profits from the Olympic assets whereas the Athenians will have no access to them in the future,' the former Deputy Minister of Culture and opposition member, N. Alevras, stated, blaming the government for favouritism and lack of concern for the citizens' needs. [29] According to the law, which was eventually published in June 2005, some of the facilities were to be turned into open-air recreation centres while the remainder would provide indoor cinemas, theatres, restaurants and patisseries. [30] Despite efforts to utilize the facilities, they remained unexploited on the first anniversary of the Athens Olympics, and there was concern that this discouraging situation would continue. Although the games were originally hailed as a good opportunity for Greece to promote its image globally, the sight of the abandoned facilities now caused Greek agitation. 'The Olympic venues have been abandoned while ambitious projects for new parks and regeneration and ornamentation of the seafront areas and central squares fell by the wayside,' the press reported, focusing on the likely gloomy future of the assets which were to be given to businessmen 'unconditionally'. [31] Responding to the negative comments, Dora Bakoyianni, mayor of Athens, argued that 'the benefits are not tangible immediately' and added reassuringly if optimistically that 'Athens changed for the better due to the Games and the Athenians now feel self-assured and optimistic.' [32] Notwithstanding, in a long report, dubbed the 'Black Book', the Pasok Party reproached the government for utilizing the Olympic Games as a 'means to attain narrow party ends'. It alleged, 'The government did not recognize the economic sacrifice of the Greek people and took no interest in the facilities with the view to selling them off.' The Deputy Minister of Culture, Fani-Palli Petralia, responded sharply. 'We do not forget that the Pasok government bid for the Athens Olympics; an enormous national undertaking, unsystematically and with no viable exploitation plan for the Olympic legacy,' she pointed out. 'The much-discussed project for the post-Games use of the facilities, which the Pasok party argues it designed when it was in power, does not actually exist. Six bills concerning the Athens Olympics were passed during its government but not even a draft for the facilities' exploitation was introduced in the Chamber of·Deputies.' [33] Without doubt, the post-Olympic use of the magnificent but expensive facilities engendered political wrangling and recrimination between the government and the opposition, each holding the other responsible for considerable delay, missed opportunities and lack of overall control of the situation.

Implementing the Exploitation of the Olympic Assets: International Competitions and Results

The first step towards the exploitation of the Olympic legacy was made in July 2005 when an international competition was announced for the development of the canoe kayak slalom, the badminton hall and the international broadcasting centre (IBC). Hellenic Olympic Properties SA, established by law in May 2002 and supervised by the Ministries of Finance and Culture, [34] was entrusted to administer and exploit the Olympic assets on behalf of the government. The right to administer, maintain and exploit the facilities (paying annual rent to the Greek state) would be given to the businessmen who made the bid. The canoe kayak slalom, a magnificent white-water facility, would be turned into a recreation centre and venue for sporting and commercial events; the renovated badminton hall would host cultural events (international concerts and ice-skating shows) while the international broadcasting centre, part of which was to house the Hellenic Olympic Games Museum and the International Athletic Museum, would be converted into a shopping and media centre and recreation venue. The important role that a detailed, long-range plan for the post-games use of the assets could play in economic development, specifically at a regional level, was clearly recognized. However, beneficial repercussions of the Athens Olympics and the legacy they left behind in the economy, tourism, sport and culture were only expected in the long run. A fresh competition for the future use of the Agios Kosmas Olympic Sailing Centre and the Galatsi Olympic Hall was announced a month later (August 2005), while competition for the future utilization of the Olympic beach volleyball facilities at the Faliro Olympic Complex was announced in March 2006. [35] The way the beach volleyball facilities were to be used resulted in a dispute between government and the local municipal authority (Kalithea). The mayor publicly reproached the government for misguided intentions and held it responsible for having only commercial ends in view. 'The government, instead of exploiting the modern facilities for the benefit of local people, allots land to business interests, permits them to set up shops and amusement parks excluding the local residents from the facilities,' he stated. The president of Hellenic Olympic Properties SA, Christos Hadjiemmanuel, described the mayor's reproach as 'ungrounded and unjust'. [36] Nevertheless, the assignment of the facilities to businessmen aroused suspicion and fear that they would finally fall prey to business interests. Fresh competition for the use of the Tae-Kwon-Do Hall, which was intended to be converted into an international convention centre after redevelopment, was announced in November 2006. [37] Although the process for the assets' utilization was initiated two years after the Athens Olympics, negative comments once again became front-page news. 'The impressive Olympic facilities remain fenced off and underutilized. ... The stadiums are turned into "museums" which only school-children visit as part of school activities programmes,' the newspaper *Investor's World* reported. It observed, however, that the announcement of the competition for the assets' utilization was an initial positive step. 'Better late than never,' the newspaper concluded. [38] Reporting on the same matter, the newspaper *Eleftherotypia*, in an article entitled 'The Dowry Was Lost; the Debts Are Still Here', wrote that 'two years after the Olympic Games for which the Greek people paid much in anticipation of immediate exploitation of the Olympic venues and growth of regional economy, the facilities remain unexploited.' The newspaper further commented, 'Greece's gamble on a successful Games was finally won, but the gamble on the subsequent use of the assets was lost.' [39] The newspaper *Kathimerini* said much the same. [40]

Clearly, the Athens Olympics, it was widely agreed, should not be just a two-week flash-in-the-pan; they should ensure enduring benefits to the host city and the country. The legacy the games left should be utilized with discrimination and viable long-term considerations. The first results of the international competitions were made known on 15 May 2006. The badminton hall was the first venue to be put to good use. It was leased for a term of 20 years to a business group comprised of George and Panayiotis Georga (of the Half Note Jazz Club), Dimitris Kontoyiannis (entrepreneur and founder of the Allon Fun Park) and Michael Adam (of Adam Productions), who made the bid and paid the sum of 12,500 million euros to the Greek state. After renovation, the badminton hall was turned into a luxurious theatre, the biggest theatre in Greece (with seating capacity of about 2,500 spectators). It opened its doors on 31 January 2007 with a performance of Matthew Bourne's production of *Swan Lake*, a high-quality artistic event. Including an outdoor concert venue with a seating capacity of 700 spectators, the renovation of the badminton hall complex is expected to be completed in the summer of 2008. [41] On 23 May 2006, the Galatsi Olympic Centre (where the Olympic table tennis and rhythmic gymnastics competitions had been held) was leased to the company Acropol Charagiones and Sonae Sierra SGPS SA, which paid the Greek state the sum of about 154m euros for a 40-year use. The renovated facility was to be converted into modern shopping and recreation centre. [42] At least a start on a viable legacy had been made. More importantly, the housing project for the Athens Olympic Village was implemented in July 2006. A total of 2,292 houses were given to beneficiaries of the Workers' Housing Organization, on a lottery basis, in an official ceremony and in the presence of the Minister of Employment and state dignitaries, who also had the opportunity to attend a cultural event entitled Olympic Village: A Town Is Born. [43] In 2006 also, the assignment of the use of the IBC for a term of 40 years, to Lamda Development SA was a further positive development. According to the contract, the main part of the building was to be converted into a shopping centre including offices and restaurants, while in the remainder the Ministry of Culture in cooperation with the International Olympic Committee would house the Museum of the Hellenic Olympic Games and the International Athletic Museum. The outcome boosted the morale of those who were entrusted with exploitation of the Olympic assets and created optimism about further positive results of the international competitions yet in progress. In the meantime, there were discussions between the president of Hellenic Olympic Properties SA and Denis Oswald, president of the International Rowing

Federation (FISA) and the Association of the Summer Olympics International Federation, on a contract for the use of the Schinias Olympic Rowing Centre by FISA. This facility, to be situated in a national environmental park protected by the European Union and an ideal place for international rowing competitions, was to be the third FISA international training centre (after those located in Seville, Spain, and Munich, Germany). [44] These positive developments demonstrated that the eventual plan for the post-games use of the facilities appeared to be designed and implemented carefully and methodically, ensuring considerable revenues for the state. Furthermore, a 30-year contract for the use of the canoe kayak slalom, which was given to J&P Avax-Gek-Bioter-Corfu Water-Parks SA, was announced in January 2007. This unique white-water facility was to be converted into a large water area and amusement park. The total paid to the Greek state by the company ran to 129,799,594m euros, a considerable sum. 'In a relatively short time we accomplished with success four international competitions for long-term lease of the Olympic assets ensuring the Greek state considerable revenues,' the president of Hellenic Olympic Properties SA said, expressing satisfaction at the development. 'Administering the Olympic legacy carefully and prudently we will return to the Greek people a portion of the money they paid for the Games,' he added and expressed optimism about the competitions in process. [45] There were further ambitious plans for a viable legacy. It was intended that the Main Press Centre (MPC), a building incorporating a superb auditorium, was to house the Ministry of Health, while the Nikea Weightlifting Centre, located in south-west Athens, was to house the new Piraeus University. [46] Then the result of the international competition for the use of the Agios Kosmas Sailing Centre was announced in April 2007; Seirios Tech SA won the bid, ensuring the use of the facility for a term of 45 years. It was to be converted into a modern marina of high specifications, capable of hosting 1,170 boats, crews and passengers. Among other provisions of the 2005 bill, the Agios Kosmas facility was to provide luxurious guest houses, shops, offices, restaurants and cafes, playing fields and multi-purpose halls. The new impressive installations were expected to attract high-spending tourists and afford Greece the chance to surpass its regional tourism competitors. [47] 'After the successful resolution of the long-term lease of five of the Olympic facilities, construction expenses are balanced and not only this but the Greeks are free from the burden of running costs, security and maintenance expenditure,' the president of Hellenic Olympic Properties SA stated, yet again stressing his company's efforts to achieve the profitable exploitation of the assets. [48] Harmonious cooperation between government and municipal authority resulted in the assignment of the Pagkretio Stadium in Heraklion, Crete, to the municipality (February 2007). Regional sport and local amateur and professional sports associations were expected to benefit from this. In addition, utilization of the stadium's outbuildings for conferences, concerts and various cultural events was expected to open new possibilities for culture, sport and tourism in the area. In addition, the contract (signed in late June 2007) between Hellenic Olympic Properties SA and S. K. Pazaropoulos SA for the long-term use of the Olympic beach volleyball facilities at Faliro was the starting point of the post-games utilization of the facilities. After the necessary work, it was intended that the bidder company would create a complex of facilities, including an open-air amphitheatre overlooking the picturesque Saronic Gulf, suitable for hosting high-quality performances and musical events. The time, however, that the complex was to be completed was not announced. More significantly, cooperation between S. K. Pazaropoulos SA and ecological organizations was also facilitated as a result of the company's concern for environmental protection. [49] Following the long-term lease of the beach volleyball facilities, Hellenic Olympic Properties SA reported that it had guaranteed Greek state rental revenues running to 1.5bn euros, while the Greek taxpayers were relieved of about 15m euros per annum covering maintenance, security and operation expenses. [50] Nor was this all. In early July 2007, the government initiated the process for transformation of the Tae-Kwon-Do Hall into an international convention centre through a public-private partnership (PPP). Budgeted at 94m euros plus value-added tax, and maintenance and insurance costs, the project included funding, plans, reconstruction and technical management of the building. At the same time, international competition for the facility's lease was in progress. [51] Moreover, the Ano Liossia Olympic Centre, located in a deprived area of northwest Athens, was to house the Arts Academy as well as the National Digital Museum, a modern museum of picture and sound. The academy's intended creation was announced by the Prime Minister himself in May 2007. [52]

Furthermore, exploitation of the basketball, fencing, softball, hockey and baseball facilities at the Helleniko Olympic Complex, which covers an area of 783,000 m^2 and is to be converted into the Athens Metropolitan Park, was provided by the government plan for the realization of the Olympic legacy. However, no international competition for the assignment of the facilities' use was to be announced before completion of the architectural design and issue of the relevant presidential decree. [53] As for the utilization of the Markopoulo Equestrian Centre, international competition for its assignment was in the final stage by August 2007, while the Markopoulo Shooting Centre, located 40 km from the Athens centre, had been designated for use as a police training centre. [54] The post-Olympic Markopoulo Equestrian Centre, a magnificent facility, hosted the modern Pentathlon World Cup in 2005 and the European hurdle championship for children and the international competitions for adolescents on 9–13 July 2008. [55]

As agreed, Denis Oswald, president of FISA, and Christos Hadjiemmanuel, president of Hellenic Olympic Properties SA, met in Munich on 3 September 2007 during the FISA annual general meeting. In the presence of representatives of 128 national rowing associations from around the world, they signed a 5-year contract by which the Schinias Rowing Centre, 43 km from the centre of Athens, would be turned into the FISA International Training Centre as well as a venue for congresses and cultural events. [56] The 2008 European Rowing Championship was scheduled to be held in the Schinias facility and the canoeing centre in Marathon on 18–21 September 2008 after a unanimous decision by the representatives of 25 European national rowing federations, who met in Linz/Ottensheim, Austria, on 1 June 2007 on the occasion of the first 2007 Rowing World Cup. [57] The athletic event is expected to attract athletes from around the globe, opening up new horizons for sports tourism in Greece. According to the Hellenic Olympic Properties SA report of 3 September 2007, the viability of the facility was finally secured and the ecological role of the Schinias area was recognized and promoted. Just one day later, a contract for the assignment of use by the Nikea Olympic Centre to Piraeus University was signed between the rector of the university and the president of Hellenic Olympic Properties SA. This was intended to meet the expanding needs of the university. In this way, the Nikea Olympic Centre was to meet crucial social needs and was to be utilized for the benefit of state higher education. The modern facility would afford the students of Piraeus University spacious classrooms, upgraded research infrastructure, and places for cultural and sporting events. It was to meet the standards of a modern European university and provide the area with opportunities for cultural and economic development. [58]

In summery, the 2004 Athens Olympics were intended to be a good opportunity for Greece to present itself as a modern country with bright prospects for economic investment and development. And, indeed, in all respects, the games did act as a catalyst to the transformation of the city of Athens. Significant infrastructure improvement took place, and projects and construction work that might otherwise have taken decades to complete were delivered within 5 years. Athens acquired the look of a modern city. It became a dynamic, forward-looking, metropolitan capital of the twenty-first century by combining an improved road network, a modern public transport system, high-quality hotel accommodation and improved tourism infrastructure. More significantly, the games left behind a precious legacy of new sports facilities. Their post-games use, however, which was only initiated after considerable delay, aroused political dispute, suspicion and criticism from all the political parties. Nevertheless, from 2006 onwards, a government plan for the assets' utilization was put into practice, resulting in considerable revenues to the state. This positive outcome boosted the morale of those involved in the Olympic legacy's ambitions, eased political dispute and raised hopes of further economic and cultural development. By late 2007, a number of the facilities were assigned to financially influential businessmen after international competition. According to the Hellenic Olympic Properties SA report, the Olympic assets and their utilization afforded the Athenians fresh opportunities for their leisure time, gave further impulse to tourism and upgraded neglected urban areas, improving at the same time the quality of life in Athens. [59] A long-term, positive step towards realizing the Olympic legacy had been made.

So far, so good. In the spring and summer of 2008, however, some of the post-Olympic assets were still deserted and in a state of disrepair. The fact again generated disappointment and indignation, gave rise to negative press comments, and provoked protest meetings. In April 2008, there appeared caustic newspaper articles on intended construction work for the tourist and commercial development of the Agios Kosmas

Sailing Centre, leased to Seirios Tech SA. The construction plan, which provided a hotel, 13 cinemas, cafes, restaurants, a shopping centre and a car park for 2,500 cars, again gave rise to vigorous protest. The newspaper *Eleftherotypia* reported that 'on a surface of 104,000 square metres along the beach, the leaser company will create an immense car park intended to cover half of the size of the Helleniko beach laying the area bare of trees and lawn and replacing them with cement. In this way, the company aspires to meet the needs of thousands of visitors who are expected to reach the complex by car every day. … And on top of all that, walking into the beach volleyball facilities, when there is no security guard, one can see abandoned and ruined installations which have been reduced to a tip where rubbish and old building materials are mounting.'[60] Speaking about the intended construction work at the Olympic Sailing Centre in general and the creation of a car park along the coast in particular, the mayor of Helleniko, Christos Kortsidis, among others, stated that 'the municipality appealed against the assignment of the Agios Kosmas Olympic Sailing Centre to businessmen and we shall dynamically struggle for the protection of the environment and free access to the Helleniko beach.' [61] It is clear that the local society's reaction to new construction that further spoils the environment and prevents citizens from enjoying the beach will escalate in the immediate future.

In the same month, Giannis Kourakis, mayor of Heraklion, Crete, disappointed with the considerable delay in the utilization of the post-Olympic Pagkretio stadium in Heraklion, met Constantino Mattala, the new president of Hellenic Olympic Properties SA, and discussed the matter with him. The mayor expressed his anxiety about the wear and tear on the stadium and the outbuildings, inasmuch as they remained padlocked. 'Any further delay in the facility's use is considered unjustifiable. The modern stadium must open to athletes, the young and the local society as soon as possible,' Kourakis remarked. [62] Following the mayors' demand for immediate utilization of the Pampeloponissiako, Pagkretio, and Panthessaliko stadiums in Patras, Peloponnesus; Heraklion, Crete; and Volos, Thessaly, respectively, Hellenic Olympic Properties SA, on 21 and 22 May 2008, made clear that 'as agreed, we assigned the stadiums to the respective municipalities on condition that the sports facilities will be self-supporting. For this reason, we have meetings with the mayors of Heraklion and Patras so that a viable solution may be found. If the municipalities of Heraklion and Patras wish to take possession of the stadiums immediately and engage themselves to finance maintenance and administration, then we have no objection. If they cannot do that, then the mayors are asked to continue discussing with us so that we may reach an agreement for the benefit of the local society.'[63] In the summer of 2008, discussions for the stadiums' maintenance and administration were still in progress.

Negative comments on the Athens post-Olympic assets and their utilization were published in the foreign press too. In early June 2008, in an article entitled 'Ruined Athens Olympic Facilities a Warning to London', the *Daily Telegraph* reported that 'of the 22 venues in the city, 21 are in a state of disrepair and under guard to prevent vandalism. … The infrastructure, which was installed in such haste, has proven to be far too extravagant for the city. It is difficult to imagine there was ever much local interest in continuing to use the baseball, kayaking, fencing, and handball facilities down the coast at Hellenikon. A few miles outside the city centre, the sprawling Faliro complex that once hosted the beach volleyball and taekwondo competitions is deserted. . . . Elsewhere at Hellenikon, piles of rubbish are mounting behind heavily padlocked gates and electrical cables hang loose from the walls.' [64] Following criticism from the Greek and foreign press, Hellenic Olympic Properties SA, in the same month, hastened to report progress in the utilization of the post-Olympic assets:

> The International Broadcasting Centre (IBC) was leased to the Lamda Development SA in August 2006 intended to be converted into a shopping and recreation centre. The delivery protocol was signed on 30 April 2007. Moreover, the design for the creation of the Museum of the Hellenic Olympic Games and the International Athletic Museum was completed.
>
> The renovated Badminton Hall at Goudi is in full use.
>
> The Galatsi Olympic Centre was given to the Sonae Sierra SA and Acropol SA. The two companies established the Park Avenue SA which is expected to initiate further construction work in the facility.
>
> The Canoe Kayak slalom at Helleniko was given to J&P Avax-Gek-Bioter-Corfu Waterparks SA. The construction work license for the creation of a water area and amusement park is anticipated to be issued.
>
> The Agios Kosmas Sailing Centre was given to the Seirios Tech SA on 2 July 2007. The construction work license is expected to be issued.
>
> The first stage of the competition for the commercial exploitation of the Faliro Tae Kwon Do Hall intended to be transformed into an international convention centre was completed. At the same time, the General Secretariat of Olympic Exploitation completed the competition for the selection of technical advisers who will be in charge of the facility's reconstruction.
>
> In September 2006, the marina at Faliro was given to the Hellenic Sailing Federation which now makes use of the facility.
>
> The Main Press Centre (MPC) at Maroussi will house the Ministry of Health and Social Solidarity in the course of 2008. In the meantime, the facility temporally houses the Committee for the 2013 Mediterranean Games' bid. The National Centre of Health is housed in the reconstructed part of the building. As for the remaining part that will house the Ministry of Health, the reconstruction work license was issued.
>
> The Nikea Olympic Centre was given to Piraeus University in April 2008.
>
> A contract was signed, on 10 July 2007, between the Hellenic Olympic Properties SA and the Ministry of Public Order for the utilization of the Markopoulo Olympic Shooting Centre as Police training centre and as headquarters of the Police Special

Forces. The plan for the facility's reconstruction was completed; assignment of the use to the Police will be realized soon.

The baseball, fencing, softball, hockey and baseball facilities at the Helleniko Olympic Complex are leased on short-term contract and host conferences, commercial exhibitions and concerts. The baseball facility was given to the Ethnikos Football SA for a term of three years.

The Schinias Olympic Rowing Centre was turned into the FISA International Training Centre by a contract signed on 6 September 2007.

The Anno Liossia Olympic Centre is intended to house the Arts Academy. Until then it is leased on short-term contract.

The Markopoulo Olympic Equestrian Centre was given to the Hellenic Equestrian Federation. The facility hosts international athletic events. [65]

In short, in the summer of 2008, a number of the post-Olympic assets are in either full or partial use, reconstruction work is in progress on some of the facilities, and a building work licence is expected to be issued for some assets, while a number of sports facilities are leased on short-term contract or remain deserted and under guard, awaiting completion of international competition or deliberation. More significantly, disagreement and dispute between the municipal authorities and Hellenic Olympic Properties SA resulted from the fact that the post-Olympic sports facilities were leased to businessmen to convert them into shopping centres and recreation places for their profit, while no particular provision for the protection of the environment was made. No doubt, the spectacle of modern, expensive Olympic assets in a state of disrepair is at least disappointing and understandably provokes the indignation of the Greek people, who have paid dearly and will long continue paying for these facilities. Nevertheless, that the matter again got publicity is hoped to sensitize and activate politicians, sports associations and representatives, and a large number of sports fans and citizens. In this way utilization of the facilities may be expedited to some extent, and bureaucratic formalities and deliberation in abeyance may be completed. The common reality, however, is that four years after the games, the enduring benefits of the post-Olympic use of the facilities to the economy, culture, sport and tourism in Greece still remain to be seen.

Acknowledgement

Many thanks are due to Professor J. A. Mangan for his editorial support.

Notes

[1] 'The Closing Ceremony', *Kathimerini*, 30 Aug. 2004.
[2] Synadinos, *O Agonas mias Polis*, 57; Lunzenfichter, *Athenes ... Pekin (1896–2008)*, *Choix Epiques des Villes olympiques*, 195–206.

[3] Tziralis *et al.*, 'Economic Aspects and the Sustainability Impact of the Athens 2004 Olympic Games'.

[4] Synadinos, *O Agonas*, 194, 200.

[5] Law 2819, 15 Aug. 2000, *Official Gazette*, vol. 1, no. 84.

[6] Synadinos, 'He megali simassia tou Olympiakou choriou', 8.

[7] Synadinos, *O Agonas*, 200–1.

[8] Ibid., 183–203.

[9] 'A Survey of Greece', *The Economist*, 12 Oct. 2002; 'The Athens Olympics', *The Economist*, 18 Aug. 2004.

[10] Hellenic Ministry of Culture, *Just Before the Finish Line*, 50–5; Synadinos, 'Post-Olympic Use', 41.

[11] 'Olympic Legacy Exploitation', *Apogevmatini*, 30 Aug. 2004.

[12] 'The Cost of the Olympic Installations', *Vima*, 22 Aug. 2004.

[13] 'The Cost of the Games', *Eleftherotypia*, 30 Aug. 2004.

[14] 'How much did the Games Cost?', *Vima*, 20 Nov. 2004.

[15] 'The Cost of the Games', *Investor's World*, 20 Nov. 2004.

[16] 'Report of the Organising Committee of the Olympic Games, Athens, 2004', *Kathimerini*, 14 May 2005, 5; 'Report of the Organising Committee, Athens, 2004', *Investor's World*, 14 May 2005, 3.

[17] Tziralis *et al.*, 'Economic aspects', 26. According to another estimate, the total cost reached the sum of 13 bn euros. See 'The Economic Dimension of the Games', *Vima*, 19 Aug. 2005; 'The Games and the Cost', *Investor's World*, 12 Aug. 2006.

[18] Hollway, 'Enduring Benefits of the Olympic Games for Australia', 29.

[19] 'The Post-Olympic Utilization of the Olympic Facilities', *Kathimerini*, 24 Aug. 2004.

[20] 'Abandoned Olympic Assets', *Ta Nea*, 7 Dec. 2004; 'Olympic Assets in Abeyance', *Macedonia*, 8 Dec. 2004.

[21] 'The Day After the Games', *Ethnos*, 30 Aug. 2004. In March 2004, the Nea Dimocratia Party assumed the reins of government.

[22] 'Post-Olympic Assets and their Exploitation', *Kathimerini*, 31 Aug. 2004.

[23] Ibid., 3 Nov. 2004.

[24] 'Olympic Assets', *Investor's World*, 13 Nov. 2004.

[25] 'Consultation on the Olympic Assets', *Express Time*, 7 Dec. 2004. A detailed development programme entitled *Greece 2005–2007* was presented by the Deputy Minister of Culture, Fani Palli-Petralia. See 'Post-Olympic Utilization of the Assets', *Ta Nea*, 7 Dec. 2004; 'Post-Olympic Utilization of the Olympic Assets', *Macedonia*, 8 Dec. 2004; 'Olympic Installations and their Exploitation', *Investor's World*, 11 Dec. 2004.

[26] 'Locked Olympic Stadiums', *Ta Nea*, 7 Dec. 2004; 'The Olympic Stadiums Remain Locked', *Macedonia*, 8 Dec. 2004; 'Olympic Stadiums in the Dark', *Investor's World*, 11 Dec. 2004.

[27] Synadinos, 'He metaolympiaki chrissi ton egatastasseon'; *Ethnos*, 29 April 2004, 8.

[28] 'Invitation for Post-Olympic Assessment', *Kathimerini*, 31 March 2005.

[29] According to the 2005 bill, the Secretariat General of the Olympic Games was renamed Secretariat General of Olympic Exploitation, which, in collaboration with Hellenic Olympic Properties SA, was to manage the exploitation of the facilities. See *Kathimerini*, 31 March 2005.

[30] Law 3342, 6 June 2005, *Official Gazette*, vol. 1, no. 131.

[31] 'A Year After the Games', *Ta Nea*, 13 Aug. 2005.

[32] 'The Athens Olympics: A Year After the Games', *Vima*, 19 Aug. 2005.

[33] 'The Back Book of the Pasok Party', *Ethnos*, 13 Aug. 2005.

[34] Law 3016, 17 May 2002, *Official Gazette*, vol. 1, no. 110.

[35] 'International Competitions for the Olympic Assets' Utilization', *Express Time*, 27 June 2005; Olympic Properties, *Press Release*, 8 July 2005; 30 Aug. 2005; 15 March 2006.

[36] 'The Olympic Assets are Assigned to Businessmen', *Ta Nea*, 12 April 2006.

[37] Olympic Properties, *Press Release*, 22 Nov. 2006.

[38] 'Two Years After the Games', *Investor's World*, 12 Aug. 2006.

[39] 'The Dowry was Lost: The Debts are Still Here', *Eleftherotypia*, 13 Aug. 2006.

[40] 'Post-Olympic Exploitation of the Assets', *Kathimerini*, 13 and 30 Aug. 2006. Sidney took two years to open Homebush Bay, which is the biggest recreation park in the world. The government assigned the right of use of the Olympic Stadium's name to a big telecommunication company and invested the money raised in the creation of a company entitled Sydney Olympic Park, which is charged with management and exploitation of the park. The Australians also assigned the use of a large number of facilities to businessmen, who converted the stadiums to shopping and conference centres and built hotels in the allotted land. See Hollway, 'Enduring Benefits', 29; *Kathimerini*, 13 Aug. 2006.

[41] Olympic Properties, *Press Release*, 15 May 2006; Rigopoulos, 'The Biggest Theatre in Athens', *Kathimerini*, 6 Jan. 2007, 12.

[42] Olympic Properties, *Press Release*, 23 May 2006; 'Exploitation of the Galatsi Olympic Centre', *Investor's World*, 12 Aug. 2007.

[43] 'The Olympic Village to the Beneficiaries of The Workers' Housing Organization', *Kathimerini*, 19 July 2006; 'The Athens Olympic Village was Given to the Beneficiaries of the Workers' Housing Organisation', *Macedonia*, 19 July 2006.

[44] Olympic Properties, *Press Release*, 28 May 2006; 28 Aug. 2006; 19 Sept. 2006; 'The Schinias Olympic Rowing Centre will be used as FISA Training Centre', *Investor's World*, 12 Aug. 2007.

[45] 'Exploiting the Olympic Legacy', *Kathimerini*, 3 Jan. 2007; Olympic Properties, *Press Release*, 4 Jan. 2007.

[46] 'Utilization of the Olympic Assets', Olympic Properties, *Press Release*, 6 July 2007; *Investor's World*, 12 Aug. 2007.

[47] Olympic Properties, *Press Release*, 11 April 2007; 6 July 2007; 'Utilization of the Agios Kosmas Sailing Centre', *Ethnos*, 12 April 2007; 'The Agios Kosmas Olympic Facility and its Exploitation', *Investor's World*, 12 Aug. 2007.

[48] *Ethnos*, 12 April 2007; *Hemerissia*, 12 April 2007.

[49] Olympic Properties, *Press Release*, 28 Feb. 2007; 22 June 2007; 'The Assignment of the Use of the Olympic Beach Volley Facilities at Faliro to S. K. Pazaropoulos', *Kathimerini*, 26 June 2007. The new Lyric Scene and the National Library, both funded by the Stavros Niarchos Institute, were intended to be constructed in the Faliro area. See 'The New Lyric Stage and the National Library in the Faliro Area', *Investor's World*, 12 Aug. 2007.

[50] Olympic Properties, *Press Release*, 22 June 2007.

[51] 'The Tae-Kwon-Do Hall will be Converted into an International Convention Centre', *Kathimerini*, 5 July 2007.

[52] 'Art Academy will be Established at the Ano Liossia Olympic Centre', *Vima*, 13 May 2007; 'Academy of Art will be Founded in the Ano Liossia Centre', *Kathimerini*, 13 May 2007; Olympic Properties, *Press Release*, 6 July 2007; 'Art Academy is to be Created at the Olympic Center of Ano Liossia', *Investor's World*, 12 Aug. 2007.

[53] Olympic Properties, *Press Release*, 6 July 2007.

[54] 'The Markopoulo Olympic Centre and its Utilization', *Investor's World*, 12 Aug. 2007.

[55] Ibid.; Olympic Properties, *Press Release*, 9 July 2008.

[56] Olympic Properties, *Press Release*, 3–4 Sept. 2007.

[57] Ibid., 2 June 2007.

[58] Ibid., 3–4 Sept. 2007.

[59] Ibid., 6 July 2007; 'The Olympic Assets and their Exploitation', *Investor's World*, 12 Aug. 2007; 'The Olympic Assets and their Exploitation', *Vima*, 12 Aug. 2007; 'The Olympic Assets and their Exploitation', *Kathimerini*, 12 Aug. 2007.

[60] 'An Immense Car Park Instead of Green in the Helleniko Beach', *Eleftherotypia*, 1 April 2008.
[61] Ibid.
[62] Heraklion Municipality, *Press Release*, 23 April 2008.
[63] Olympic Properties, *Press Release*, 21–22 May 2008.
[64] Moore, 'Ruined Athens Olympic Facilities a Warning to London', *Daily Telegraph*, 2 June 2008.
[65] Olympic Properties, *Press Release*, 16 June 2008.

References

Hellenic Ministry of Culture. *Just Before the Finish Line*. Athens: Hellenic Ministry of Culture 2003.
Hollway, S. 'Enduring Benefits of the Olympic Games for Australia'. *Olympic Review* 27 (2001): 28–33.
Lunzenfichter, A. *Athenes ... Pekin (1896–2008). Choix Epiques des Villes olympiques*. Atlantica: Anglet, 2002.
Synadinos, P. 'Post-Olympic Use: A Picture of the Future'. *Olympic Review* 27 (2001): 39–41.
——. *O Agonas mias Polis*, [The Struggle of a City]. Athens: Kastanioti, 2004.
Tziralis, G., A. Tolis, I. Tatsiopoulos and K.G. Aravossis. 'Economic Aspects and the Sustainability Impact of the Athens 2004 Olympic Games'. *Environment Economics and Investment Assessment* 98 (2006): 21–33.

Los Angeles is *the* Olympic City: Legacies of the 1932 and 1984 Olympic Games

Mark Dyreson and Matthew Llewellyn

Los Angeles is, from its own vantage, *the* Olympic city. No city has bid more frequently or more furiously for the Olympics. No city has made the Olympics as central to its core identity. The Olympics have left a more powerful legacy in Los Angeles than in any other city they have visited since 1896. Conversely, Los Angeles has, according to its own chroniclers, left a more powerful legacy for the Olympic movement than any other modern host. According to its own local histories, Los Angeles has twice saved the Olympic movement from fiscal disaster and cultural decay. [1] Even scholars concede the significance of Los Angeles to the modern games. Los Angeles provided in 1932 the original blueprint for transforming the Olympics into one of the globe's most important events. Five decades later in 1984, Los Angeles revitalized the Olympics and provided a new template to keep the games relevant into the twenty-first century. [2]

The claims by Los Angeles that modern Olympic legacies begin and end in southern California reveals the commanding role of the games in the region's collective imagination. *Los Angeles Times* sportswriter Bill Dwyre, recounting an anecdote from the city's urban mythology, illustrates the power of the Olympics in the public memories of the metropolis. Dwyre contends that during the globally televised 1992 Los Angeles riots sparked by the acquittal of the white officers charged with beating African-American motorist Rodney King, a small band of unarmed security guards fended off huge hordes of looters targeting the building housing the Amateur Athletic Foundation of Los Angeles, the repository of much of the city's Olympic legacy. The defenceless watchmen performed the miracle by simply appealing to the hooligans' sense of respect for the Olympic history that resided in the museum's bowels. 'Even the looters understand,' Dwyre proclaimed. 'Los Angeles is an Olympic city.' [3]

Another powerful sign that Los Angeles is indeed 'an Olympic city' resides in the history of the ubiquitous palm tree. Many love the image of Mediterranean paradise that the arboreal palm canopy lining the city's boulevards and open spaces evokes. Others loathe the fact that the tree, a non-native, invasive species that heightens the illusions of paradise on which the city rests, has come to symbolize Los Angeles. Neither the palm's defenders nor its detractors, however, dispute that palm-lined, asphalt-paved streets symbolize the city. [4] Indeed, one urban critic, gripped by an overdeveloped sense of irony, suggests that a bullet-riddled palm tree represents the truest version of Los Angeles reality. [5] Los Angeles' palm tree forests date to the city's first Olympics. In 1932, local boosters persuaded the city to spend more than $100,000 of the Olympic budget to plant 30,000 palms to spruce up the already extensive urban sprawl that blighted the area. To get ready for the world once again in 1984, Los Angeles spent even more money to plant considerably fewer trees in a new phase of its urban forestry, or, as some viewed it, urban fantasy project. [6]

The Olympics and palm trees symbolize Los Angeles. They evoke images of southern California for the area's residents and for the multitudes of tourists who flock to the city. They stand as iconic representations of the meaning of Los Angeles in the minds of billions of the planet's inhabitants who regularly view Los Angeles through the lenses of television and cinema, two industries that make their world headquarters in the California metropolis. The palms and the Olympics are also fundamentally linked. The palms appeared to gild the original Los Angeles games, and then five decades later were replanted to re-gild the city for its second Olympic chapter. This gilding represents a deliberate attempt to manufacture an Olympic legacy for Los Angeles. The palms highlight two key components of Olympian legacies. First, as the palm-planting plans illustrate, host cities manufacture legacies. Second, as the spread of the palm into a Los Angeles icon reveals, global audiences mediate legacies. Well-manufactured legacies that endure capture the world's imagination, even if they are as fictitious as the common notion that the palm tree is native to southern California. Out of such fictions has Los Angeles woven its legacy as *the* Olympic city.

To comprehend the legacies of the Los Angeles Olympics requires grasping the fact that the city perfected the modern bid process. [7] The first few modern Olympic games went to metropolises that allowed Baron Pierre de Coubertin's fledgling International Olympic Committee (IOC) to connect to the mythologies of Olympic antiquity, Athens in 1896 and 1906, and Rome, in an even more dramatic misreading of classical history, in 1908 – before an eruption of Mount Vesuvius required a relocation of the Roman games. In addition to sites that evoked collective memories of Western antiquity, Coubertin and the IOC also planted the early games in the cosmopolitan capitals of Europe such as Stockholm (1912) and Berlin (the never-held 1916 games), or indentured them to world's fairs as in St Louis (1904), or did both at the same time, as in the case of Paris (1900) and London (1908, Rome's replacement). Coubertin and his IOC vassals selected these cities as they met in glittering European salons and made what they considered cosmopolitan decisions without benefit of any formal bid process. [8]

After the Great War interrupted the Olympic cycle and cancelled the 1916 Berlin games, the IOC entered a new phase in site selection. For the next three instalments of the games, they made the Olympics monuments to Allied triumph and sacrifice in the victory over Germany and the other Central Powers. They honoured Antwerp (1920), Paris (1924), and Amsterdam (1928) with Olympian beneficence and without any serious consideration of other aspirants. [9] Antwerp, Paris, and Amsterdam did not supplicate the IOC potentates, seeking to acquire an Olympics as a centrepiece for advertising their climate, culture, and cachet in the global marketplace. The European capitals merely waited for the wisdom of the IOC to anoint them with the games. One unsuccessful bidder for the games of the 1920s, however, pioneered the new art of Olympian seduction in its quest to win hosting rights. This new strategy was developed by real-estate developers, mortgage bankers, corporate lawyers, and used-car salesmen from Los Angeles, a city that stood far outside the orbit of the IOC's aristocratic universe. In their ardour to garner the games, they radically changed the modern Olympic movement by establishing a new archetype for campaigns to win the games.

Los Angeles actually began its Olympic quest during the Great War. It started with the invention by the city's aggressive boosters of the bid process itself, the now familiar courting of IOC doyens by municipalities, regions, and nations eager to win the Olympics in order to advertise themselves to the world. The Los Angeles group that invented this strategy recognized that the Olympics were about far more than sport. The Olympics offered a chance to 'brand', in the lingo of contemporary marketing, a host for the globe's consumers. The California bidders sought the games not for the intrinsic value of staging an international sporting competition but as a glossy addition to the most ambitious real-estate development in American history – the construction of modern Los Angeles.

William May Garland, one of southern California's biggest land speculators and the only two-term president of the industry's most powerful lobbying group, the National Association of Realtors, spearheaded Los Angeles' drive to win the Olympic

Games. [10] Los Angeles before the 1930s was a new and unknown city, even in the United States, though for decades prior it had been promoting itself as the epitome of the American 'good life'. [11] Governed by an oligarchy of entrepreneurs interested in promoting rapid growth, the city mushroomed at an amazing pace in the first half of the twentieth century, climbing from thirty-sixth to fifth place on the list of the nation's largest urban areas from 1900 to 1930. [12] The real-estate, petroleum, and movie industries fuelled the boom. Indeed, the huge expansion in new home construction made Los Angeles during the 1920s the largest importer of lumber in the world. [13] This new metropolis that had sprouted seemingly overnight on the Pacific Coast lacked a clearly defined identity. Hosting the Olympics seemed to the oligarchs a perfect way to advertise their new urban development to the world. [14]

Los Angeles began seeking the Olympics in 1915, while the Great War consumed Europe. Rumours swirled around North America that the IOC might move the 1916 Berlin Games to the 'neutral' United States. [15] American Olympic Committee (AOC) executives entertained feelers from several US cities about the prospects of relocating the 1916 games. Newark, Cleveland, Chicago, Philadelphia, and San Francisco joined Los Angeles in a frenzied effort to capture Berlin's Olympics. [16] Los Angeles city officials devised a bid highlighted by the promise of superior climate and scenery as well as the construction of a huge stadium with seating for at least 100,000. [17]

The brief bidding war to move the 1916 games to the United States proved a futile quest. Coubertin and the IOC never entertained serious thoughts of moving the 1916 Olympics anywhere. With the Berlin games officially cancelled, American cities turned their attention to 1920. New Yorkers announced a proposed Central Park Olympic stadium in a ploy to garner the games. [18] When that plan collapsed due to a lack of enthusiasm among Gotham's taxpayers for the Olympics, AOC officials and federal bureaucrats in Washington sought the construction of a national stadium to garner the 1920 Olympics for the nation's capital. Fiscal realties scuttled those schemes as well. [19] Meanwhile, in Los Angeles, civic boosters organized a political action group, the Community Development Association (CDA), that won support for their stadium. Construction began on the Los Angeles Coliseum, original dubbed the 'Olympic Stadium'. [20]

With a grand California coliseum rising from a construction pit near downtown Los Angeles, the AOC decided to endorse California's efforts to host an Olympics. At the IOC meetings in Antwerp in 1920, the Los Angeles delegation sought to win the 1924 Olympics for their city, promising the IOC $300,000 to cover event expenses. [21] Los Angeles lost to Coubertin's hometown, Paris, the first city to win a second Olympics. At the same meeting, Los Angeles also lost the 1928 Olympics to Amsterdam. Garland returned to Los Angeles, frustrated by his failure but confident he could win a future bid. Paris, still hungover from the war effort and facing a variety of internal and external challenges, had a difficult time staging the 1924 games. A year before the Paris Olympics opened, the French government warned that France might not be able to manage the event. The Third Republic's

announcement so startled Baron de Coubertin that he began to negotiate with Los
Angeles to move the 1924 Olympics to California. The crisis dissipated and Paris kept
its Olympics. Repaying American loyalty, Coubertin promised Los Angeles the 1932
Games. [22]

With William May Garland ensconced in 1922 as a member of the IOC and the Los
Angeles Coliseum completed and open for business in 1923, Coubertin delivered on
his pledge. At the 1923 IOC Congress in Rome, the Baron announced Los Angeles as
the host for the games of the Xth Olympiad. The Los Angeles Olympic Organizing
Committee (LAOOC), headed by Garland and his fellow boosters from the CDA, ran
the 1932 Olympics. They expanded the coliseum to 105,000 seats and made it the
linchpin of the spectacle. Additional venues sprouted, some near the coliseum and
others on the metropolitan fringes of Los Angeles. [23]

In addition to the sporting infrastructure they built across California, Garland and
his team sought to ensure that their Olympics left several legacies. Garland grandly
announced that the Olympics would bring southern California $10 million of free
advertising. [24] Garland received some perks as well. The 30,000 palms the city paid
for lined Wilshire Boulevard, the gateway to Garland's personal real-estate empire.
Tourism agents flooded the media with announcements that an Olympic trip was the
best vacation deal seen in decades. They promoted California's faux-Mediterranean
climate, scenic splendour, and romantic history as at least the equal of ancient
Greece's Olympian splendour. Not satisfied merely with making the region into a
neo-Olympia, they also packaged the allure of Hollywood, the promise that Los
Angeles was a dazzling modern metropolis, and the image of California as the leader
in American lifestyle trends to gild their promotions. The Olympic sporting
programme played only a small role in their advertisements for their Olympian
extravaganza. [25]

To advertise their city for national and international consumption, the LAOOC
focused on the themes of dynamic modernity and social harmony. In his 'official'
invitation to the world, California's governor assured visitors that the state was not
an untamed wilderness and promised to welcome everyone 'regardless of race, color,
or creed'. [26] Although Los Angeles, like the rest of the United States in the early
1930s, was fractured by ethnic and class divisions, the city boosters built an Olympic
Village and organized tourist attractions that advertised Los Angeles as a land of
frictionless racial unity. Although the rapid modernization of Los Angeles had created
a host of problems, the LAOOC structured the Olympics to promote the illusion that
the process had been an unmixed blessing for the region. [27]

The onset of the Great Depression in 1929 threatened the survival of the Los
Angeles Olympics and made advertising southern California to the world more
difficult. The LAOOC pushed forward and promised success in spite of the economic
calamity. LAOOC administrators arranged for cuts in travel costs and helped to
subsidize living expenses on site in order to make sure foreign teams made the
journey to California. They also began to tout the Olympics as a 'depression buster',
an event literally powerful enough to affect the global economy. [28]

The fortnight-long Olympic spectacle that opened on 30 July 1932 did not loosen the grip of the depression on the United States or the world, though it did provide an economic stimulus and produce some jobs in southern California. The games proved a great success on many levels, drawing record numbers of spectators and producing the first profit in Olympic history. The $1.5 million surplus eventually flowed back into the community, but not before several years of legal wrangling – a legacy Los Angeles would later repeat. [29]

The 1932 Olympics left many other legacies. The Olympics created an image of Los Angeles as a vibrant, modern metropolis characterized by ethnic and racial harmony. During the games, palm trees swayed in Pacific breezes, traffic flowed, Angeleños celebrated, and the urban infrastructure functioned smoothly. Whether these images matched everyday Los Angeles realities mattered little. The world witnessed a city that worked, producing an unparalleled marketing opportunity. [30]

The massive public-relations machine set up by the LAOOC broadcast images of a thriving Los Angeles to global audiences. Print, radio, and newsreel media chronicled Olympian feats. The media coverage fuelled the efforts to build durable Olympic legacies for Los Angeles. [31] The world press corps, as well as German Olympic organizers in Los Angeles to learn how to stage their 1936 Olympics, concurred that the Olympic Village, the Olympic Cauldron's monumental flame, and many of the other spectacular features of the Los Angeles production should become permanent features of future Olympic pageants. [32]

Indeed, the notion of a 'California style', so effectively packaged and marketed by the LAOOC, created legacies that extended far beyond the new pomp that organizers had sprinkled on the Los Angeles games. On the sporting front, Los Angeles fused the Olympics with the entertainment and leisure industries, two modern economic colossi that had set up headquarters in the city. Metro-Goldwyn-Mayer's (MGM) Louis B. Mayer served on the LAOOC, while other movie moguls and stars helped to stage the 1932 games. Hollywood's celebrities flocked to Olympic events. Talent scouts from the film conglomerates roved the venues, in search of athletes who might make a splash on the silver screen, as former American Olympic gold medallist Johnny Weissmuller had done just a few months before the Los Angeles Olympics opened, when he debuted in MGM's blockbuster, *Tarzan, the Ape Man*. [33] The LAOOC showcased sports such as swimming and diving that evoked connections to the notion of California as a paradise of play. The media also eroticized male and female athletes at the Los Angeles games. Print and pictorial coverage of the games depicted Olympians as the beautiful citizens of a new version of Eden, a modern utopia devoted to leisure. [34]

Through the focus on style, the 1932 Olympics built legacies in unexpected ways. The games introduced the nation and the world to the California lifestyle and to the many products consumers could purchase in the quest to acquire the modern ideal. California clothing companies used the Olympics to push their new leisure and sportswear designs. Swimming, tennis, and golf costumes invaded everyday fashion, as did a new palette of bright 'California' colours. [35] The Olympics provided a perfect opportunity to advertise casual clothing as a staple of modern haberdashery. Southern Californians developed an entire magazine, entitled *Game and Gossip*, devoted to their lifestyle. The glossy monthly promoted the intersections between sports, fashion, and show business. The Olympic numbers of *Game and Gossip* promoted Olympic-themed California casual wear and touted the region as the globe's new 'playground'. [36]

The Olympian confluence in 1932 of sport, fashion, and show business seduced not only the makers of sportswear but also the makers of American foreign policy. The United States tried during the interwar years to globalize the American national trinity of pastimes – baseball, basketball, and American football – in a quest to Americanize the globe through sport. Winning a spot on the Olympic programme represented an essential component of the plan to globalize American culture. At the beginning of the 1930s, none of the American trio had a place on the Olympic programme. The Los Angeles organizers made 'college football' a demonstration sport in at the 1932 Olympics, but the world found the American version of football too strange for more than a single Olympic sideshow. [37] A few years later, a coalition led by Babe Ruth tried to push baseball into the Olympics. After initially winning a slot for baseball as an exhibition sport in 1936 at Berlin, they failed in their quest to make it a medal sport in that epoch. [38] In a more successful lobbying effort, Americans propelled basketball onto the official Olympic programme in 1936. [39] Still, a global basketball culture would not develop for decades thereafter.

While failing to establish beachheads for the three great American national games at the heart of the Olympic programme, the 1932 games still inspired bureaucrats at the US Department of State and Department of Commerce to imagine that the affluent American lifestyle, showcased in swimming and swimwear, could convert the rest of the globe to Americanism. Exporting California-inspired versions of American aquatic sports and American swim fashions, the federal agents believed, would serve the interests of US statecraft. [40]

The American swimmer Johnny Weissmuller, ineligible to compete in Los Angeles after trading his amateur status for a career in entertainment, became the face of the federal advertising campaign. The role of Tarzan catapulted Weissmuller into a career as a celebrity. Weissmuller's fame helped to transform swimming, according to sportswriter Paul Gallico, from a 'colorless sport' into a global passion. [41] Weissmuller, who had moved to Hollywood shortly before the games commenced, conspicuously attended the 1932 Olympics, as did a host of other movie stars. The Hollywood glitterati lent an additional lustre to the spectacle. [42] The movie industry scouted the Olympics intensively, signing swimmers Clarence 'Buster' Crabbe, Helene Madison and Eleanor Holm, and several other American athletes to contracts after the closing ceremonies. [43] Indeed, in the wake of the Los Angeles Olympic extravaganza, some speculated that the quickest route to film stardom was a successful athletic career. [44]

For Los Angeles, the marriage of film, fashion, and athletics represented an Olympian legacy that helped to define the California lifestyle for future generations of global consumers. [45] Since the 1920s, when the region's film industry began to boom, southern California has, in the words of a Los Angeles public-relations firm, aspired to serve as 'the *style-setting center* of the world'. [46] The Olympics helped to make that desire a reality. The legacy of glamour and stardom spawned in Los Angeles affected the Olympic movement as well. After 1932, the Olympics became a featured destination on the international celebrity circuit. In Berlin in 1936, Nazi potentates mingled with movie stars and European royalty, as the newsreel paparazzi filmed their cavorting. [47] Over the next several decades, the parade of celebrities that continually swirled through the Olympics helped the IOC eventually to garner enormous television contracts. The 1932 Los Angeles games started the Olympic movement on the path to becoming an attractive commodity in the international entertainment industry. [48] While the 1936 Berlin Olympics would complete the transformation of the Olympics into a global 'mega-event', the 1932 Los Angeles Olympics provided the blueprint for that evolutionary leap. [49]

In the immediate afterglow of the Olympics, Los Angeles congratulated itself on staging the greatest spectacle in modern Olympic history. Local scribe Bill Wise predicted that the games of the Xth Olympiad would live forever in the hearts of southern Californians. Wise dubbed the Los Angeles games the 'most successful – the most memorable – in the history of this honorable sports tradition reaching back, deep into the archives of mythology'. [50] Efforts by Angeleños to make Wise's sentiments the collective memory of the 1932 Olympics began as soon as the games closed. Looming near downtown, the splendid Los Angeles Coliseum became the central architectural legacy of the games. The construction of the Olympic stadium, according to one local reporter, 'gave to California, the playground of the world, a playground'. [51]

That 'playground' went back to multiple uses after the Olympics. The University of Southern California (USC) returned to play football there in the autumn of 1932, and it has remained the home of that famed collegiate programme ever since. The city's other major institution of higher education, the University of California at Los Angeles, also played its home schedule at the coliseum until the 1980s. Beginning in the 1940s, six different professional football teams called the coliseum home for various periods of time. [52] The coliseum hosted two Super Bowls (numbers I and VII in Super Bowl numerology). It also hosted a World Series and a Major League Baseball All-Star game when the Los Angeles Dodgers played within its confines. In addition, it housed outdoor basketball games, championship prize fights, midget auto races, and, somehow, a ski jumping contest. [53]

The coliseum anchored Los Angeles in non-sporting ways as well. California celebrated the end of the Second World War in the coliseum, cheering appearances by the military heroes General George Patton and General Jimmy Doolittle. In later decades, John F. Kennedy and Nelson Mandela held political rallies in its mammoth confines. The Rolling Stones and Pope John Paul II drew – on separate occasions – huge gatherings of fervent disciples. Billy Graham's 1963 Christian crusade set the all-time attendance record for the edifice, drawing 134,324 spectators. [54]

Although football games, war memorials, political speeches, rock concerts, religious rallies, and a variety of other events were held at the coliseum, it remained fundamentally associated with the Olympics. Looking back at the legacy of the coliseum as the building marked its fiftieth anniversary, *Los Angeles Times* columnist John Hall put the Olympics in the first slot on his list of the top 10 moments in the stadium's history. [55] Coliseum managers sought every opportunity to reconnect their stadium with its Olympic heritage. Beginning in the 1930s, the city put on a series of 'junior' Olympic meets on the stadium's track. [56] The coliseum also staged major international track meets and served as the site for US Olympic track and field trials in 1952, 1956, 1964, and 1984. [57]

The coliseum became the main place for Los Angeles' residents to commemorate their Olympic memories, particularly through the tradition of relighting the Olympic Cauldron on opening day of every new Olympics and letting the flame burn for the duration of each games. The reignition ceremonies began for the 1936 Berlin Olympics and continued whenever the games were celebrated. [58] Los Angeles occasionally relit the Olympic Cauldron for a great variety of other reasons, including the fourth quarter of USC football games, a track meet in 1941 preparing American youth for the Second World War, a ceremony in 1986 to remember the victims of the *Challenger* space shuttle disaster, and a homage to the dead in the 11 September 2001 World Trade Center attack. [59]

The main focus of relighting the cauldron, though, has been Olympic commemoration. In 1936, a large-scale re-enactment of the opening ceremonies accompanied the flame's return, a custom Los Angeles leaders hoped would become a standard feature of Olympic legacies at all host cities. [60] The ceremonies staged initially by a group called the Olympic Memorial Committee, made up mainly of the 1932 LAOOC membership. [61] This group comprised the first bureaucracy designed specifically to promote legacy in the history of the Olympic movement. In 1939, the Olympic Memorial Committee evolved into the Southern California Olympic Organizing Committee (SCOOG). That group continues to relight the coliseum's cauldron to mark each new opening of an Olympics. [62]

From its origins in 1939, SCOOG has sought to promote the legacy of the Los Angeles Olympics both at home and abroad. Created, according to its founders, for 'insuring that the spiritual flame lighted by the Olympic Torch should continue to glow', the civic group cloaked its designs in the gaudy homilies of Olympism. [63] SCOOG grandly promised from its inception to 'produce, promote and advance knowledge and appreciation of the noble, chivalric, patriotic, educational and social character of the International Olympic movement and ideals as practiced in the quadrennial Olympic Games'. [64]

The group raised funds to support US Olympic teams and southern California Olympians. They also sought and staged US Olympic trials and international track meets. SCOOG's early leadership included William May Garland (who also served as an IOC member from 1922 to 1948), Louis B. Mayer of MGM, Paul Helms of Helms Bakery, and William M. Henry, sports editor of the *Los Angeles Times*, all veterans of the LAOOC's 1932 crew. [65] Indeed, SCOOG helped Henry distribute his popular *An Approved History of the Olympic Games*, a tome endorsed by founding father Baron de Coubertin, which lauded Los Angeles' contribution to the Olympic movement, to an international audience. [66] In 1948, William May Garland bequeathed his positions at SCOOG and in the IOC to his son, John Jewett Garland. The organization remained active under the leadership of Garland the younger, entertaining IOC members when they travelled to California and helping to run the 1960 Olympic Winter Games at Squaw Valley. [67]

SCOOG's main endeavour was a seemingly eternal quest to bring the Olympics back to Los Angeles. True believers in the legacy for Los Angeles they had created, including the fundamental article of faith that the 1932 Olympics had been the greatest ever staged, the group committed itself to returning the Olympics to southern California. From its inception in 1939, SCOOG bid for every single Olympic Games. For four decades, they lost those bids, all the while eagerly informing the IOC of their 'readiness to act as a "standby" host city, ready to accept on short notice, the responsibility of holding the Games should some unforeseen misfortune overtake the chosen city'. [68]

Year after year, SCOOG implored the IOC to return. California newspapers chronicled the losses as the Olympics went to Helsinki (1952), Melbourne (1956), Rome (1960), Tokyo (1964), Mexico City (1968), and Munich (1972). During the bid wars of the 1950s, 1960s, and 1970s, Los Angeles was not even the first choice of the United States Olympic Committee (USOC). The USOC consistently chose Detroit over the southern California metropolis, even as Los Angeles surged past the centre of the American car industry in population and grew to become, by 1960, the third largest city in the nation. [69]

Undaunted by losing bid after bid, SCOOG set its sights on the 1976 Olympics, calculating that the bicentennial of US independence would predispose the IOC to selecting an American city as host. Finally, Los Angeles vanquished Detroit to win the USOC's favour. [70] Advancing to the final round of the IOC contest against Florence, Montreal, and Moscow, SCOOG promised the Olympian oligarchy a huge profit. [71] Unimpressed with the monetary guarantees, the IOC awarded the 1976 Olympics to Montreal, which eventually recorded a mammoth loss on the games. [72] Los Angeles boosters next tried for the 1980 Olympics, promising an even larger profit. SCOOG lost again, this time to Moscow. [73]

Conditioned by decades of bidding, Los Angeles threw its hat in the ring once again for the 1984 Olympics. Los Angeles beat New York to win the USOC's endorsement, and then moved into the IOC's main event. [74] SCOOG soon discovered that it would have an easy path to victory, as Teheran, the only other city to mount a bid effort, pulled out of the race as Iran began its descent toward the 1979 revolution. [75] Although Los Angeles still coveted the Olympics, the rest of the world's cities had become leery of the spectacle. Political controversies and boycotts by various nations had plagued the 1968 Mexico City Olympics, the 1972 Munich Olympics, and the 1976 Montreal Olympics. The 1980 Moscow Olympics would suffer the largest boycott yet as the United States and much of the West refused to compete in order to protest Soviet incursions into Afghanistan. [76]

In addition to the political controversies swaddling the Olympic movement, the games had since the 1960s become increasingly expensive financial obligations that left host cities and nations with monumental deficits. Montreal's games, which incurred a $1.2 billion shortfall, scared away every potential suitor for the 1984 Olympics except for Los Angeles, where bidding for the games had become an established fact of life. Los Angeles was, after all, by its own estimation, *the* Olympic city. SCOOG's optimists pointed out that the 1932 Olympics turned the first and only profit in Olympic history. They predicted that even in the new era of gigantically expensive Olympic extravaganzas they could turn a profit. Even in southern California, however, sceptics wondered whether or not the bid was worth the cost, in spite of the clear field that loomed in front of Los Angeles for the prize. [77]

To the surprise of no one, Los Angeles won the 1984 Olympics. A protracted negotiation between a newly formed LAOOC and the IOC earned a variety of financial concessions from the international group, which had little leverage since no other city wanted the games. Southern California municipalities indemnified themselves against financial risks and turned the spectacle over to the privately financed LAOOC. [78] The LAOOC, chaired by Paul Ziffren, a veteran SCOOG leader, scion of the Los Angeles establishment, and prominent lawyer, hired an unknown travel industry mogul named Peter Ueberroth to stage the games. Movie producer David Wolper also played a key role on the committee. As in 1932, the quest to advertise California and its culture, to generate tourism and commerce, and to confirm the city's status as the 'style centre' of the world took precedence in staging the Olympics. This time, a travel agent rather than a realtor ran the show. [79]

By the 1980s, Los Angeles faced considerable challenges in rehabilitating its image. The metropolis had continued to grow since the 1930s, ranking as the third largest city in the nation, just behind Chicago, according to the census of 1980. By the next census, Los Angeles would surge to 'second city' status. [80] With its gigantic size came enormous problems, including the typical urban maladies of crime, entrenched poverty, and overcrowding typical of any megacity, combined with certain deficiencies many associated especially with Los Angeles, from smog, brush fires, mud slides, and earthquakes to serial killers, wacky cults, narcissistic citizens, and mind-numbing materialism. While Los Angeles remained an attractive location in some ways, boosters increasingly had difficulty in overcoming the popular notion that the city harboured the dark as well as the bright side of the American dream. The titles of two popular texts on the history of California highlighted the growing cynicism that clouded Los Angeles. In the 1960s, California remained *Everyman's Eden*. By the 1980s, it had become *The Elusive Eden*. [81]

As the 1984 Olympics approached, Angeleños inhabiting the 'elusive Eden' remembered the glory days of 1932. Indeed, an article in the *Los Angeles Times* credited the many legacies of the 1932 Olympics, from profit and publicity to the desire 'instilled in the hearts of many Angeleños' to recapture the pageant for bringing the 1984 games to Los Angeles. [82] Newspaper columnist Carolyn Murray granted the 1932 Olympics 'an ongoing legacy' in the history of the city. She proclaimed that the original Los Angeles Olympics had defined the new metropolis for the world. A few built legacies survived, she noted, most importantly the coliseum where the 1984 Olympics would soon kick off. The trees and flowers planted in 1932 still beautified Los Angeles, she observed. The spectacular landscapes and brilliant climate first advertised in 1932 still drew tourists. The 'city of the future' became a reality in the present in 1932, she argued. She hoped the 1984 Olympics would perform a similar urban miracle for her city. [83]

Los Angeles sportswriter Paul Zimmerman, who five decades earlier had covered the original southern California Olympics, recollected that the 1932 games had left 'an unmatched legacy' for both Los Angeles and the Olympic movement. Zimmerman labelled the 1932 games 'the most competitive, artistic and innovative ever staged'. [84] In a special issue of the journal *California History* dedicated to memories of 1932, [85] Zimmerman reinforced the notion that the original Los Angeles games elevated the Olympics to 'world acceptance'. One of the key legacies that had been overlooked, Zimmerman insisted, was that the 1932 Olympics had spawned generations of California athletes who came to dominate US Olympic rosters. For the 1964 Tokyo Olympics, Zimmerman noted, 101 of the 365-member American team came from California. At the 1968 Mexico City Olympics, Zimmerman added, 20 of the 36 gold medals the US garnered were earned by Californians. Zimmerman asserted that in terms of both participants and medallists such a 'ratio persists to this day' on US Olympic teams. [86]

The 1984 Olympics opened on 28 July at the coliseum and ran through 12 August. In spite of a Soviet-led boycott, the Los Angeles Olympics drew 140 nations and more than 7,000 athletes. Millions of fans attended. Billions watched on television. US athletes won 174 medals, including 83 gold medals. American audiences embraced the games in a patriotic rhapsody. The US Olympic team roster at the 1984 Olympics confirmed Zimmerman's contentions about California's role in securing Olympian gold. Among the American medallists who had strong roots in southern California were diver Greg Louganis, gymnast Peter Vidmar and volleyball star Karch Kiraly. Significant segments of the US swimming, gymnastics, diving, cycling, track and field, and women's and men's basketball and volleyball teams hailed from California as well. [87]

In the years following the second Los Angeles Olympics, the 1984 games exerted a powerful influence over their successors. Olympic scholar Wayne Wilson has forcefully argued that Los Angeles again proved that an Olympics could make money, raising the expectations for future hosts substantially. He has traced the influence of the 1984 model on future revenue-sharing arrangements between host cities, the IOC, and national Olympic committees. Wilson contends that the first two legacies produced a third, crucial legacy for Los Angeles. Much like the 1932 games, the 1984 games once again convinced the world that the Olympics represented a valuable commodity. Following the Los Angeles production, cities and nations came to the conclusion that the Olympics could bring economic, political, and cultural capital to their hosts. After 1984, the number of bidders for the Olympics climbed dramatically. No longer would the IOC be courted, as it had been after Teheran pulled out of the contest for the 1984 games, by a single suitor. [88]

The 1984 Olympics left some marks on the city similar to those from the 1932 Olympics. A refurbished coliseum and a host of other new Olympian venues continued to make Los Angeles a coveted host of national and international sporting contests. The organizers of a variety of events, including both the men's and women's World Cup association football contests, chose Los Angeles as a main venue. [89] Continuing the tradition started after the 1932 Olympics, the flame in the Olympic Cauldron at the coliseum continued to come to life during each succeeding Olympian celebration. The commercial innovations introduced by the 1984 LAOOC, including the selling of the Olympic torch relay to corporate sponsors, a gambit that had produced $10.9 million in revenues, influenced future hosts. The next US host of an Olympics, Atlanta in 1996, borrowed wholesale from the 1984 Los Angeles blueprint, including copying the use of the torch relay as a revenue generator. [90] Symbolically, the torch relay in the United States started at the Olympic Cauldron in Los Angeles and then made its way across the continent to Atlanta. [91]

The focus on finance stemmed from the fact that, for the first time since 1932, the 1984 Olympics turned a profit. In fact, the second Los Angeles games made at least $222.7 million, and some later reports pegged the net gain as $232.5 million. [92] About 60% of the profit went to the USOC and the sports federations under its umbrella, providing an enormous endowment for future US Olympic teams. The remaining 40% went to the newly chartered Amateur Athletic Foundation of Los Angeles (AAFLA), later spared by looters in the Rodney King riots, to preserve the Olympic legacy of Los Angeles. [93]

The more than $90 million generated to start the AAFLA left one of the most visible legacies for the city. Peter Ueberroth initially led the AFFLA. He later turned it over to one of his LAOOC lieutenants who had become a major figure in the USOC and a member of the IOC, former Olympic rower Anita DeFrantz. The AFFLA sponsored state-of-the-art youth sports programmes throughout the region, though not without some wrangling among the many constituencies that constitute contemporary Los Angeles political culture. The AFFLA also built the Paul Ziffren Sports Resource Center for Olympic scholars and students, named after the long-time SCOOG and LAOOC leader. [94] By 2004, the AAFLA's endowment had grown to $140 million. [95]

Beyond the profit turned by the LAOOC, economists estimated the entire financial impact of the 1984 Olympics on southern California as totalling $2.376 billion, or 1.6% of the 1984 gross domestic product of the area. The Olympics, boosters proclaimed, added dozens of new sports venues to the region, improved the telecommunication infrastructure of Los Angeles by the installation of fibre optics technologies to serve the global media coverage of the games, helped southern

California book future national and international sporting competitions, developed new cultural facilities for tourists and residents, increased the 'hosting capacity' of Los Angeles for future mega-events, and amplified the city's status as a vacation destination in domestic and foreign markets. [96]

The success of the Los Angeles Olympics, particularly in financial terms, set the standard for future hosts. As Los Angeles Olympic scholar Wayne Wilson has observed, the economic success of the 1984 games produced 'a legacy of raised expectations'. [97] The head of the organizing committee for the 1988 Seoul Olympics publicly admitted that he hoped to imitate Los Angeles but warned Koreans not to expect the same financial windfall. [98] Commentators shrewdly noted that the IOC, having witnessed the profit potential of Olympic spectacles in Los Angeles, would never again fail to negotiate a cut of the lucre, a mistake they made in 1984, never dreaming that anything but a deficit would result from an Olympics. The IOC's hard-won experience made Seoul's effort in 1988 and those of future host cities to make sure the Olympics ran in the black even more difficult. [99]

As in 1932, 'California style' represented a legacy as important as the financial windfall in measuring impacts on the modern Olympic movement. Indeed, beginning in 1984, California culture helped to restructure Olympic sport radically. The changes came from new rather than venerated pastimes, as illustrated by the contrast of the fates of baseball, synchronized swimming, and windsurfing after the 1984 Olympics. Baseball, the old American national pastime that US interests had been pushing as an Olympic sport since the 1930s, appeared as a demonstration sport at the 1984 games, on its way to medal sport status in 1992. By 2005, however, the IOC, citing a lack of global appeal, dropped baseball off the Olympic programme. [100] Baseball did not meet the 'California style' requirements for a long run as an Olympic sport. Two other contests that debuted in Los Angeles possessed a stronger connection to essential elements of California fashion, particularly to the entertainment, sex appeal, and sunshine components of beach culture. Synchronized swimming, a sport that seemed to have sprung from the old Hollywood aqua musicals of the 1940s and 1950s that starred California-born swimmer Esther Williams, made its initial splash at Los Angeles. Windsurfing, a beach-inspired adventure sport with a strong California core, joined the staid yachting classes at the Los Angeles games. [101]

Indeed, windsurfing became the first 'extreme sport' to win a spot at the Olympics. Since then, several other 'California-style' extreme sports have made huge inroads into the Olympic programme. Seeking to capture the interest of younger television viewers, the IOC has added not only windsurfing but also the 'Generation X' spectacles of snowboarding, short-track speed skating, mountain biking, beach volleyball, and triathlon. BMX cycling, another California-inspired neo-sport, became a medal contest at the 2008 Beijing Olympics. [102] The IOC and a variety of commentators have explained the inclusion of these new sports as evidence that the Olympics has created a cosmopolitan and transnational new world sporting culture rooted not in any particular cultural or national tradition but in the common thirst for leisure and excitement among the youth of the world. While promoters of these 'extreme sports' recognize the Western origins of many older Olympic events, they point to the supposedly global reach of newly added contests, claiming that they are equally accessible in the United States and Uganda, in France and Fiji, in South Africa and South Korea, or in New Zealand and Nicaragua. [103]

The notion that these extreme sports represent the unfettered triumph of globalization over nationalism ignores the fact that these pastimes originated in a particular culture, in a particular place, at a particular time. Mountain biking, snowboarding, triathlon, and beach volleyball rose to popular acclaim in California, as have so many other cultural practices with global reach since the middle of the twentieth century, from surfing and cinema to personal computers and the 'summer of love'. [104] The Olympic chimera of 'globalization' surrounding these sports masks a particular brand of Americanization that has always suffused the Olympics. [105] *Les sports californiens*, as some French social critics label these pastimes, have created a 'postmodern' empire of leisure centred in California. [106] Beach volleyball, which debuted at the 1996 Atlanta Olympics, represents the classic version of a southern California innovation that has spread throughout the world's coastal cultures. This new Olympic spectacle pitting scantily clad, well-oiled men and women in sun-dappled battles clearly reveals the power of 'California style' in shaping the twenty-first-century Olympic *zeitgeist*. The IOC has fallen in love, as reporter Chris Hogg noted in a report from the 2004 Athens Olympics, with such mergers of 'sport with lifestyle'. [107]

Reforging the links between the Olympics and 'lifestyle' originally built in 1932 thrilled Americans. In 1985, Peter Ueberroth, the director of the Los Angeles Olympic production, made the cover of *Time* as the magazine's 'person of the year'. [108] *Time*, a leading compendium of mainstream American opinion, made Ueberroth's games into the central symbol of the recovery of American national pride and national will in the 1980s. The magazine claimed the 1984 Olympics dovetailed neatly with the optimism of President Ronald Reagan's 'revolution' overturning the 'Spenglerian' gloom that had descended on the United States during the 1970s. 'There was a kind of magic about the Games, a brilliance of performance and setting, as if not only the athletes but the place itself and the weather, blue and golden, all rose to the occasion,' confessed Lance Morrow, the *Time* correspondent who penned the cover story. [109] The Los Angeles Olympics, it seemed, had restored faith in American exceptionalism throughout the nation.

The 1984 Olympics restored not only American faith in the nation but the also the faith of Angeleños in their own city. The games, city boosters proclaimed, allowed Los Angeles to reclaim its rightful place among the globe's great cities. In 1985, Los Angeles staged an Olympic Legacy Day, on which luminaries glorified the 1984 games. Former UCLA chancellor Franklin D. Murphy contended that the 'Olympic Games personified what this city can do ... if it makes up its mind collectively to do it.' A city that had once been the butt of international jokes now shined in the reflective light of Olympic glory. [110] Southern California's chroniclers constantly sang the praises of the 1984 Olympics as a rejuvenator of the Olympic movement. They claimed that

Los Angeles had saved the Olympics from its long time of troubles, an epoch which began in Mexico City in 1968 and stretched through Moscow in 1980. [111]

In the minds of many Angeleños, the 1984 Olympics stood as a symbol of Los Angeles at its best. During the decades following the Olympics, as the city descended into another epoch during which the media depicted a southern California gripped by horrific riots, escalating crime rates, interminable gang wars, a series of municipal corruption scandals, massive traffic snarls, mushrooming environmental disasters, unchecked urban sprawl, undemocratic class divisions, and interminable political wars between ethnic constituencies, Los Angeles developed a reputation as a virtually unlivable metropolitan disaster. [112] In that context, the 1984 Olympic fortnight appeared as a utopian dream, a brief, shining moment when Los Angeles functioned. Urban reformers looked to the Olympics for lessons while the city's intelligentsia wondered whether the communal goodwill that seemed to descend on the city like beneficent smog could be resurrected in a non-Olympian context. [113] Following the 1992 riots, the city even brought back Olympic mastermind Peter Ueberroth to head the massive Rebuild LA project, an attempt to unite the private and public sectors in an effort to refurbish the deteriorating core of the metropolis. Ueberroth, however, could not return Los Angeles to the halcyon days of the summer of 1984 and soon resigned from Rebuild LA. [114]

Two decades after the 1984 Olympics, the *Los Angeles Times* published a 'legacy' series that assessed the impact of the city's second games on the region. Olympic beat reporter Bill Dwyre began the essays by describing a Los Angeles 'larger than many countries and so diverse that coffee being ordered in five languages at Starbucks on any given morning doesn't turn a head'. Los Angeles, Dwyre asserted, 'isn't a community bake sale place'. Indeed, he contended, Los Angeles typically manifested no discernible sense of commonweal, lamenting that Angeleños knew 'their freeways better than their neighbors'. Dwyre argued that no event but the Olympics had ever forged communal bonds in Los Angeles. In 1984, as in 1932, the Olympics united 'SoCal' – as local lingo dubbed the region. 'The city that is too big to work, worked,' Dwyre insisted, if only for 16 short days in the summer of 1984. [115]

Many Angeleños shared Dwyre's sentiments. They dreamed that another Olympics might descend on southern California and replicate the harmonic convergence of 1984. They continued to believe that the IOC considers their city the permanent back-up site should a host fail in its obligations. When speculation grew that Athens might not be able to finish construction in time to stage the 2004 Olympics, SCOOG officials publicly stated their readiness to step into the breach. 'The IOC knows that there is no city in the world that could stage an Olympics successfully with less advance notice than Los Angeles,' announced SCOOG leader David Simon. [116]

Just as in 1932, the 1984 Olympics convinced Los Angeles boosters that they needed other Olympics. SCOOG continues to thrive in southern California, lusting after another Olympic spectacle like addicts with an unquenchable thirst. The Olympian desires of Angeleños shape the politics of urban renewal. Developers who want to tear down the more than 80-year-old coliseum in order to build a new edifice to lure another professional football franchise to the city (six teams, of greater and lesser lifespan, have already come and gone in the stadium) have failed to outmanoeuvre those who see preserving the historic landmark as the keystone for a third Olympics. California architectural conservationists and SCOOG potentates have argued that the only stadium in the world to have hosted two Olympic opening and closing ceremonies represents an essential ingredient in getting the IOC to grant a third prize to the city. [117] In anticipation of a third Olympic chapter, the city has refurbished the old 1932 swimming complex next door to the coliseum as well. [118]

London's victory in the bid sweepstakes for the 2012 Olympics heartened Los Angeles' many Olympic boosters, convincing them that they might also win a trifecta. Shortly after London's third victory, the president of SCOOG, Barry Sanders, chirped that the 'idea that going to the Olympics can be a generational experience can be true in L.A.' [119] By 2005, Sanders and Los Angeles Mayor Antonio Villaraigosa announced that southern California would bid for the 2016 Olympics. 'The Olympics are in our DNA,' contended Sanders. [120]

By 2007, Los Angeles city officials and SCOOG leaders had unveiled a $112 million coliseum refurbishment scheme to dress up the stadium for a new Olympic bid. SCOOG's Sanders touted the plan by declaring that the 'Coliseum is a revered Olympic landmark and represents hallowed ground around the world.' [121] Los Angeles and Chicago quickly emerged as the frontrunners for the USOC's endorsement to move into the IOC's final round for 2016 hosts. [122] In April 2007, the new USOC president, none other than Los Angeles' Peter Ueberroth, opened an envelope containing the winning American bid. Ironically, the man who had been largely responsible for staging the 1984 Los Angeles Olympics had to announce that Chicago had won the right to represent the United States in the 2016 host competition. [123] *Los Angeles Times* correspondent Bill Dwyre complained that Chicago had no facilities built and no hope of turning an Olympic profit while Los Angeles had nearly every venue in place and a track record of producing excellent Olympic returns. Still, Dwyre groused, the USOC had chosen the new and potential over the tried and true. Dwyre gave Chicago little chance of impressing the IOC. [124] SCOOG remained undaunted. 'Someday, the Olympics are coming back to L.A.,' SCOOG President Sanders predicted. [125]

Many Angeleños share that vision of an Olympian legacy, believing that Los Angeles is still *the* Olympic city. From many vantages, the Olympics have left a more powerful legacy in Los Angeles than in any other city they have visited since 1896. In no other host city has the Olympic moment coincided so completely with the global debut moment as in Los Angeles, as a brief survey of built environments reveals. From the historic architecture of the Los Angeles Coliseum, the only stadium to have hosted two modern games, to the palm-tree-lined boulevards, planted to beautify the city for its two spectacles, the Olympics have given Los Angeles its iconographic landmarks. The architectural signatures of other host cities do not begin nor end with their Olympic venues. Paris, London, Berlin, Tokyo, Rome, Moscow, Sydney, Melbourne, Montreal, Helsinki, Antwerp, Amsterdam, Munich, Seoul, Barcelona, even St Louis and Atlanta, do not depend on their Olympic buildings for trademark sights. Even Athens, which, as scholars have recently demonstrated, has coveted the Olympics nearly as fervently as Los Angeles, [126] has the Parthenon and other jewels of antiquity rather than its 1896 and 2004 Olympic stadiums to mark its architectural brilliance. Los Angeles, beyond its distinctive Olympic edifices, many still intact from 1932 and even more from 1984, has little to distinguish its contributions to architecture beyond the vast stucco tracts of single-family homes that stretch endlessly across the enormous Los Angeles basin.

Los Angeles has left a more powerful legacy for the Olympic movement than any other Olympic city. Los Angeles invented the modern bid process, perfected the Olympic village concept, married the games to the modern entertainment industry, and turned the first two profits in the history of the spectacle. Los Angeles rescued the games from the perils of the Great Depression and the chaos of the Cold War. The Los Angeles Olympics sparked a thorough and long-lasting 'California-style' Americanization of the Olympics. Though Greek boosters have wished that Athens would stand as the epitome of the modern Olympics, Los Angeles has exerted a more consistent influence. Though a gaggle of scholars have elected Berlin as the birthplace of the modern Olympics as mega-event, the Nazis followed a template crafted by Los Angeles real-estate developers, movie moguls, and used-car dealers in staging the 1936 Berlin Olympics. Half a century later, with the Olympic movement rocked by internal and external political controversies and roiled by financial turmoil, Los Angeles reinvented the spectacle and provided a revitalized template for staging the games. A chorus of Angeleños have twice congratulated themselves for staging the greatest Olympics in modern history. A review of these claims reveals that such contentions are not entirely without merit. Los Angeles is, after all, *the* Olympic city. Someday, the Olympics might even come back to 'SoCal'. Certainly, Los Angeles will keep bidding until they do return.

Acknowledgements

The authors thank Dr Wayne Wilson, the Vice President for Education Services and the Director of the Paul Ziffren Sports Resource Center at the LA84 Foundation in Los Angeles, for his invaluable help in locating sources for this essay.

Notes

[1] Bill Henry, the *Los Angeles Times* sports editor who helped to stage the 1932 Olympics made that claim in the aftermath of the first Los Angeles games. Kenneth Reich, a *Los Angeles Times* scribe who covered the 1984 Olympics in more detail than any other beat reporter, offered similar sentiments in the aftermath of the second Los Angeles games. Henry. *An Approved History of the Olympics*; Reich, *Making It Happen*.

[2] A series of recent articles have argued that Los Angeles deserves more credit for pouring the foundation for the Berlin Olympics. Dinces, 'Padres on Mount Olympus', 137–66; Dyreson, 'Marketing National Identity', 23–48; Keys, 'Spreading Peace, Democracy, and Coca Cola®',

165–96; White, 'The Los Angeles Way of Doing Things', 79–116. Standard histories credit Los Angeles in 1984 with changing the Olympic template. Senn, *Power, Politics, and the Olympic Games*, 202; Wilson, 'Los Angeles 1984', 207–15.

[3] Bill Dwyre, 'L.A. and the Olympics Were a Golden Match', *Los Angeles Times*, 30 March 2006.

[4] Gregory Rodriguez, 'Nothing Says Pretend Like a Palm Tree', *Los Angeles Times*, 15 Aug. 2007.

[5] Peter King, 'Under the Unlovely L.A. Palms', *Los Angeles Times*, 28 Jan. 1992.

[6] Robert Smaus, 'An Urban Forest by 1984', *Los Angeles Times*, 25 July 1982; Josine Ianco-Starrels, 'Frond Memories of L.A.'s Palm Trees', *Los Angeles Times*, 29 July 1984; Cassy Cohen, 'Wilshire Boulevard—The Palms', *Los Angeles Times*, 18 Nov. 1984; Mark Ehrman, 'Palm Latitudes', *Los Angeles Times*, 29 Sept. 1991.

[7] In fact, another American city, Chicago, inaugurated the modern bid process in its quest for the 1904 Olympics that eventually went to St Louis. Chicago's efforts to woo the IOC included the use of documents that very closely resemble the now standard 'bid books' that provide a basic outline for a city's campaign to win the games. Chicago also had the first organized bid committee in Olympic history. Evidence of Chicago's pioneering efforts will soon be published by the noted Olympic scholar, John J. MacAloon. Personal conversation with John J. MacAloon, 30 March 2008, Oxford, England.

[8] MacAloon, *This Great Symbol*; Guttmann, *The Olympics*; Senn, *Power, Politics, and the Olympic Games*.

[9] Ibid.

[10] For an interesting biography of Garland, see the appendix to the legal documents contained 'In the Matter of the Funds Realized from the Olympic Games held in California in 1932'. Legal Documents, Paul Ziffren Sports Library, Archives of the Amateur Athletic Federation, Los Angeles, California. See also William May Garland at http://www.realtor.org/vlibrary.nsf/pages/president1917 (accessed 25 Jan. 2008).

[11] Davis, *City of Quartz*; Fogelson, *The Fragmented Metropolis*; Starr, *Material Dreams*; Sitton, *Metropolis in the Making*; Caughey, *Los Angeles*; Tygiel, *The Great Los Angeles Swindle*.

[12] By the US census rankings of 1900, Los Angeles ranked thirty-sixth among the nation's cities, with a bit more than 100,000 inhabitants. By 1910, it had grown to seventeenth, at more than 300,000. In 1920, it ranked tenth, with more than half a million people. By 1930, Los Angeles had shot up to fifth, with 1.2 million residents. It remained fifth in the census of 1940, with 1.5 million inhabitants. It moved into fourth in 1950 with 1.9 million. By 1960, it was third, with nearly 2.5 million residents. US Census Bureau at http://www.census.gov/population/documentation/twps0027/tab13txt; http://www.census.gov/population/documentation/twps0027/tab14txt; http://www.census.gov/population/documentation/twps0027/tab15txt; http://www.census.gov/population/documentation/twps0027/tab16txt; http://www.census.gov/population/documentation/twps0027/tab17txt; http://www.census.gov/population/documentation/twps0027/tab18txt; http://www.census.gov/population/documentation/twps0027/tab19txt (accessed 25 Jan. 2008).

[13] Carey McWilliams, *Southern California Country*, 135–7; Lillard, 'International City', 5–7.

[14] The argument that the Los Angeles boosters were far more interested in the advertising and entertainment possibilities of the Olympics than they were in the sporting events has been made quite forcefully in three excellent recent articles: Riess, 'Power Without Authority', 50–65; White, 'The Los Angeles Way of Doing Things', 79–116; Dinces, 'Padres on Mount Olympus', 137–66.

[15] 'Cuba Asks for Olympics', *New York Times*, 24 Dec. 1915; 'Still Hope for Games', *New York Times*, 2 Feb. 1915; 'More About Olympic Games', *New York Times*, 9 March 1915; 'Olympic Games in U.S.', *New York Times*, 10 March 1915; 'Doubts of Olympic Meeting', *New York*

Times, 11 March 1915; 'No Olympic Games Here', *New York Times*, 12 March 1915; 'Olympic Games Denial', *New York Times*, 10 April 1915; 'No Olympic Games Until War Ends', *New York Times*, 11 April 1916.

[16] 'No Games Until War Ends', *New York Times*, 13 March 1915.

[17] 'Los Angeles Wants Olympic Games', *New York Times*, 5 April 1915.

[18] 'No Stadium in the Park', *New York Times*, 17 Jan. 1917.

[19] Dyreson, 'If We Build It, Will They Will Come?'

[20] Riess, 'Power Without Authority', 50–65; Cecilia Rasmussen, 'L.A. Then and Now: Colossal Undertaking Left an Enduring Landmark', *Los Angeles Times*, 18 May 2003.

[21] 'California Bids $300,000 for 1924 Olympics', *New York Times*, 14 July 1920; AOC, *Report*, 422–4; Riess, 'Power Without Authority', 50–65.

[22] Guttmann, *The Olympics*, 41–4; Senn, *Power, Politics, and the Olympic Games*, 38–40.

[23] Wise, 'These Things You Should Know About the Tenth Olympiad', 9, 42.

[24] Dinces, 'Padres on Mount Olympus', 144.

[25] Dinces, 'Padres on Mount Olympus', 137–66; White, 'The Los Angeles Way of Doing Things', 79–116; Dyreson, 'Marketing American Culture', 23–48; Welky, 'Vikings, Mermaids, and Little Brown Men', 24–49.

[26] Official Proclamation from Governor James Rolph of California, *Game and Gossip* 10 (June 1932): 1.

[27] Dinces, 'Padres on Mount Olympus', 137–66; White, 'The Los Angeles Way of Doing Things', 79–116; Dyreson, 'Marketing American Culture', 23–48; Welky, 'Vikings, Mermaids, and Little Brown Men', 24–49.

[28] 'Olympic Games as a Depression Buster', 28–31.

[29] 'In the Matter of the Funds Realized from the Olympic Games Held in California in 1932'. Legal Documents, Paul Ziffren Sports Library, Archives of the Amateur Athletic Federation, Los Angeles, California.

[30] In fact, quite a few scholars have pointed out the discrepancies between image and reality created by the 1932 Olympics in regards to race relations, urban amity, and a host of other issues. Dinces, 'Padres on Mount Olympus', 137–66; White, 'The Los Angeles Way of Doing Things', 79–116; Dyreson, 'Marketing American Culture', 23–48; Welky, 'Vikings, Mermaids, and Little Brown Men', 24–49.

[31] Spencer, 'Records Crashed and Heroes Soared', 22, 44; Wise, 'Afterglow of the Olympiad', 13, 46–8; Wise, 'Behind the Xth Olympiad' 7, 38–41; Xth Olympiade Committee, *The Games of the Xth Olympiad*.

[32] Large, *Nazi Games*; Dinces, 'Padres on Mount Olympus', 137–66'.

[33] 'Picturing Wild Beasts', *New York Times*, 27 March 1932; Mordaunt Hall, 'The Screen', *New York Times*, 28 March 1932.

[34] Dyreson, 'Johnny Weissmuller and the Old Global Capitalism', 268–83; Dyreson, 'Marketing Weissmuller to the World', 284–306; Dinces, 'Padres on Mount Olympus', 137–66; Pieroth, *Their Day in the Sun*.

[35] Starr, *The Dream Endures*, 18–19; Fleishman, 'Made in California', 80–3.

[36] Ivar, 'Olympian Motifs Sway Fashions of Autumn', 32–3; Rice, 'You're Lucky California!', 9, 41.

[37] 'Demonstrations – American Football and Lacrosse', *The Games of the Xth Olympiad*, 739–47.

[38] Dyreson, 'Mapping an Empire of Baseball', 143–88.

[39] Grundman, 'AAU-NCAA Politics', 111–26.

[40] Dyreson, 'Marketing Weissmuller to the World', 284–306; Dyreson, 'Globalizing American Sporting Culture', 145–51.

[41] Gallico, *The Golden People*, 223–4.

128   *M. Dyreson and M. Llewellyn*

[42] John Scott, 'Film Celebrities to Mix with Crowds at Games', *Los Angeles Times*, 31 July 1932; Alma Whitaker, 'Society Seethes with Sparkling Functions', *Los Angeles Times*, 6 Aug. 1932; Bob Ray, 'Japanese Take Honors in Swimming Events', *Los Angeles Times*, 7 Aug. 1932.
[43] Muriel Babcock, 'Olympic Champions Hear Siren Song of Screen', *Los Angeles Times*, 7 Aug. 1932; 'Movie Move by Madison', *Los Angeles Times*, 15 Aug. 1932; Grace Kingsley, 'Olympic Stars Take Tests', *Los Angeles Times*, 25 Aug. 1932; 'Miss Madison Throws Lot in Screen World', *Los Angeles Times*, 12 Sept. 1932; Erickson, 'Where Fancies Flicker', 66–70.
[44] Erskine Johnson and Victor G. Sidler, 'The Quickest Way into the Movies', *Los Angeles Times*, 2 Oct. 1932.
[45] California historian Kevin Starr argues that the region has dominated the modern 'search for the good life' since the 1930s. Starr documents the potent combination of cinema, sport, and fashion that shaped images of the California 'lifestyle' in global imaginations. Starr, *The Dream Endures*, 3–57.
[46] Lillard, 'International City', 54.
[47] Large, *Nazi Games*.
[48] Barney, Wenn and Martyn. *Selling the Five Rings*, 31–50.
[49] On the role of Berlin in making the Olympics a 'mega-event', see Roche, *Mega-Events and Modernity*. For scholars who have argued that Los Angeles laid the groundwork for Berlin's 'mega-event', see Keys, *Globalizing the Olympics*; Dinces, 'Padres on Mount Olympus', 137–66; Dyreson, 'Marketing National Identity', 23–48; White, 'The Los Angeles Way of Doing Things', 79–116.
[50] Wise, 'Afterglow of the Olympiad', 13. Other local reporters concurred. Spencer, 'Records Crashed and Heroes Soared', 22, 44.
[51] Wise, 'Behind the Xth Olympiad', 41.
[52] Kenneth Reich, 'Critics of Coliseum Tear-Down Line Up Raiders', *Los Angeles Times*, 6 Feb. 1990.
[53] John Hall, 'Coliseum Strikes 50', *Los Angeles Times*, 17 Dec. 1970; 'Proposed L.A. Coliseum Enhancements Combine Historic Integrity and Modern Offerings', *PR Newswire*, 22 Feb. 2007; Epting, *Los Angeles Memorial Coliseum*.
[54] Rasmussen, 'L.A. Then and Now'; 'Fighting Generals Return in Triumph to City's Cheers', *Los Angeles Times*, 10 June 1945; Tom Cameron, 'Los Angeles Conquered by Charm of Warriors', *Los Angeles Times*, 10 June 1945; Ray Zeman, 'Patton, Doolittle "Capture" City', *Los Angeles Times*, 10 June 1945.
[55] Hall, 'Coliseum Strikes 50'.
[56] 'Boy Olympics to Be Staged in Coliseum', *Los Angeles Times*, 7 Aug. 1936; Bill Henry, 'Los Angeles Gets American Olympic Games', *Los Angeles Times*, 6 May 1940; John de la Vega, 'Records Fall in Junior Olympic Meet', *Los Angeles Times*, 5 June 1948; 'Junior Olympics in Coliseum Today', *Los Angeles Times*, 27 May 1950.
[57] Paul Zimmerman, 'USA-USSR Track Meet July 23–24', *Los Angeles Times*, 27 Feb. 1966; 'Spectacular Action Climaxes Olympic Tryouts at Coliseum', *Los Angeles Times*, 29 June 1952; Braven Dyer, 'U.S. Trials End in Record-Smashing Spree', *Los Angeles Times*, 29 June 1952; Braven Dyer, 'L.A. to Stage Olympic Trials', *Los Angeles Times*, 14 Dec. 1955; 'Relays Meet Combined with Olympic Trials', *Los Angeles Times*, 25 Jan. 1956; Paul Zimmerman, 'Olympic Track Trials Start Tonight', *Los Angeles Times*, 29 June 1956; 'U.S. Track Trials Set for Weekend', *New York Times*, 6 Sept. 1964; Paul Zimmerman, 'Olympic Trial Spikers Begin Drills Today', *Los Angeles Times*, 24 June 1968; Paul Zimmerman, 'Glittering Field Opens Final Olympic Trials Today', *Los Angeles Times*, 29 June 1968; Chris Baker, 'Olympic Track Trials', *Los Angeles Times*, 15 June 1984; 'Olympic Trials Notes', *Los Angeles Times*, 18 June 1984; Mal Florence, 'U.S. Track and Field Trials', *Los Angeles Times*, 18 June 1984; Bill Shirley, 'A Torrid 800 Won by Jones', *Los Angeles Times*, 20 June 1984; Mal Florence, 'Olympic Track Trials', *Los Angeles Times*, 21 June 1984; Mal Florence, 'Lewis Completes Coliseum Clean Sweep', *Los Angeles Times*, 22 June 1984;

Mal Florence, 'Olympic Trials Roundup', *Los Angeles Times*, 25 June 1984; Scott Ostler, 'U.S. Olympic Track and Field Trials', *Los Angeles Times*, 25 June 1984.

[58] 'Opening of Olympics to Be Re-enacted Here', *Los Angeles Times*, 30 July 1936; 'Coliseum Torch Hails Games' Start Abroad', *Los Angeles Times*, 2 Aug. 1936; 'City Lights Own Olympic Torch to Honor Games', *Los Angeles Times*, 30 July 1948; 'Significance of the Olympic Games', *Los Angeles Times*, 31 July 1948.

[59] 'Coliseum's Olympic Torch to Be Lighted on Monday', Los Angeles Times, 15 May 1941; Marita Hernandez and Edward J. Boyer, 'Olympic Flame Relit to Honor Shuttle Victims', *Los Angeles Times*, 30 Jan. 1986. Historian Richard Cashman has argued, from material provided by AAFLA scholar Wayne Wilson, that the 'Los Angeles cauldron has developed a new post-Olympic life as a community and even a healing symbol.' Cashman notes its re-ignition following 11 September 2001. Richard Cashman, 'What Is "Olympic Legacy"?' in *The Legacy of the Olympic Games, 1984–2002*. Documents of the Olympic Museum. Miguel de Moragas, Christopher Kennett, Noria Puig, editors. Lausanne: International Olympic Committee, 2003. Paul Ziffren Sports Library, Archives of the Amateur Athletic Federation of Los Angeles. Los Angeles, California.

[60] 'Once Again Olympic Torch Flares in Sky', *Los Angeles Times*, 1 Aug. 1936.

[61] 'Opening of Olympics to Be Re-enacted Here'.

[62] 'City Lights Own Olympic Torch to Honor Games'.

[63] 'Southern California Committee for the Olympic Games, Presentation to the 62nd Session of the International Olympic Committee, Tokyo, Japan, October 4–10, 1964'. Pamphlet produced by SCOOG. Paul Ziffren Sports Library, Archives of the Amateur Athletic Federation of Los Angeles. Los Angeles, California.

[64] 'The Southern California Committee for the Olympic Games Invites You to Become a Member of the Advisory Board'. Pamphlet produced by SCOOG, 1950. Paul Ziffren Sports Library, Archives of the Amateur Athletic Foundation of Los Angeles. Los Angeles, California.

[65] Ibid.

[66] Ibid. The first edition of Henry's *An Approved History* appeared in 1948.

[67] 'The Southern California Committee for the Olympic Games Invites You'.

[68] Ibid.

[69] Paul Zimmerman, 'U.S. Logical Olympic Site', *Los Angeles Times*, 19 March 1947; 'We're Still in There Pitching', Los Angeles Times, 8 March 1949; Paul Zimmerman, 'Chances for '56 Games in Los Angeles Dim', *Los Angeles Times*, 30 Oct. 1951; 'Olympic Bids from Four U.S. Cities Considered', *Los Angeles Times*, 17 Nov. 1954; Braven Dyer, 'Los Angeles to Bid for '64 Games', *Los Angeles Times*, 12 July 1958; 'Los Angeles Sends 1964 Olympic Bid', *Los Angeles Times*, 3 Sept. 1958; Paul Zimmerman, 'L.A. Moves in Quest of 1968 Olympics', *Los Angeles Times*, 21 Oct. 1960; 'L.A. to Seek 1968 Olympics', *Los Angeles Times*, 21 Oct. 1960; 'Deal for '68 Olympics Offered Here', *Los Angeles Times*, 10 Feb. 1962; Paul Zimmerman, 'Detroit Choice Weakens U.S.', *Los Angeles Times*, 17 Oct. 1962; 'Detroit Gets Nod Over L.A. for '68 Olympic Bid', *Los Angeles Times*, 17 Oct. 1962; '$50,000 OKd in L.A. Drive to Get Olympics', *Los Angeles Times*, 6 Dec. 1962; Paul Zimmerman, 'L.A. in Contention for 1968 Olympic Games', *Los Angeles Times*, 20 June 1962; 'The Best Site for the Olympics', *Los Angeles Times*, 15 March 1963; 'L.A. Group Makes New Bid for Games Today', *Los Angeles Times*, 12 Feb. 1963; Paul Zimmerman, 'L.A. Gets New Chance for Olympic Bid', *Los Angeles Times*, 13 Feb. 1963; Paul Zimmerman, 'Detroit Lags', *Los Angeles Times*, 3 March 1963; Paul Zimmerman, 'L.A. Olympic Bid', *Los Angeles Times*, 17 March 1963; Paul Zimmerman, 'L.A. Olympic Hopes Dimmed by L.B. Fair', *Los Angeles Times*, 18 March 1963; Paul Zimmerman, 'L.A. Loses Olympics Bid to Detroit', *Los Angeles Times*, 19 March 1963; 'L.A. to Renew Olympic Bid', *Los Angeles Times*, 13 Dec. 1965; Paul Zimmerman, 'L.A. to Make Determined Push for 1972 Olympics', *Los Angeles Times*, 3 Nov. 1965; 'L.A. Thwarted Again in Bid for Olympics', *Los Angeles Times*, 16 Jan. 1966.

[70] 'Coliseum Goal: Olympics in '76', *Los Angeles Times*, 24 Sept. 1967; Bob Oates, 'Spirit of '76: L.A.'s Fight to Stage Olympics', *Los Angeles Times*, 2 April 1970; 'Yorty Seeks Funds to Push Olympic Bid', *Los Angeles Times*, 9 Feb. 1968; Don Shannon, 'Asian Bloc Backs L.A.'s Olympic Bid', *Los Angeles Times*, 16 Oct. 1969; 'L.A. Olympic Bid Progress Told by Yorty', *Los Angeles Times*, 21 Nov. 1969; 'Yorty Will Tout City Olympic Bid in Panama City', *Los Angeles Times*, 26 Feb. 1970.

[71] 'L.A. Olympic Bid Rapped by Soviet Official', *Los Angeles Times*, 16 April 1970; Chuck Garrity, 'L.A.'s Olympic Bid Ready', *Los Angeles Times*, 23 April 1970; Thomas J. Foley, 'Rejection of Russ Olympic Bid Urged by Congressmen', *Los Angeles Times*, 8 May 1970; 'Council Sends 3 to Olympic Talks', *Los Angeles Times*, 12 April 1970.

[72] Senn, *Power, Politics, and the Olympic Games*, 160–72.

[73] Erwin Baker, 'L.A. Opens Battle to Host Olympics in 1980', *Los Angeles Times*, 22 Sept. 1974; Erwin Baker, 'Bradley Names 9 for Vienna Trip to Seek '80 Olympics for L.A.', *Los Angeles Times*, 27 Sept. 1974; 'L.A. Olympic Bid Stresses Freedom', *Los Angeles Times*, 23 Oct. 1974; 'Moscow Voted Site of 1980 Olympics', *Los Angeles Times*, 24 Oct. 1974.

[74] 'L.A. Has "Assurances" to Host '84 Olympics', *Los Angeles Times*, 26 April 1977; Bob Oates, 'L.A. Can Have the 1984 Olympics … for a Price', *Los Angeles Times*, 6 July 1977; Bob Oates, 'Target: Olympics', *Los Angeles Times*, 6 July 1977; Kenneth Reich, 'L.A. Delegation Confident on Bid for '84 Olympics', *Los Angeles Times*, 24 Sept. 1977; Kenneth Reich, 'L.A. Picked for Olympic Bid', *Los Angeles Times*, 26 Sept. 1977; Kenneth Reich, 'Wrapping Up the Olympics', *Los Angeles Times*, 13 Nov. 1977; Rodney W. Rood, 'Consider, for a Moment, the Benefits of Hosting the Olympics', *Los Angeles Times*, 4 Dec. 1977.

[75] Kenneth Reich, 'It's Official: L.A. Is Only Candidate for Olympics', *Los Angeles Times*, 2 Nov. 1977.

[76] Senn, *Power, Politics, and the Olympic Games*, 174–87.

[77] Ronald L. Soble, 'Olympics Debt: Could It Happen in L.A.?', *Los Angeles Times*, 1 July 1977; Ronald L. Soble, 'Huge Deficit: Olympics Still Have Canada Seeing Red', 1 July 1977; Art Seidenbaum, 'Shall We Bear the Torch?', *Los Angeles Times*, 26 Aug. 1977; Bill Shirley, 'Los Angeles Shapes Up as World Watches', *Los Angeles Times*, 12 Dec. 1982; Scott Ostler, 'An Olympics Minus a Deficit', *Los Angeles Times*, 23 Dec. 1982.

[78] Kenneth Reich, 'Bradley Insists There Will Be No Olympics Deficit', *Los Angeles Times*, 2 Dec. 1977; Kenneth Reich, 'Key Olympic Talks to Begin in Mexico City', *Los Angeles Times*, 10 April 1978; Kenneth Reich, 'Bradley Says L.A. Can Veto Olympic Costs', *Los Angeles Times*, 13 April 1978; Kenneth Reich, 'Killanin Cool to L.A. Spartan Olympic Bid', *Los Angeles Times*, 12 Feb. 1978; Kenneth Reich, 'L.A. Cables Tough Contract to Olympic Games Headquarters', *Los Angeles Times*, 5 May 1978; Kenneth Reich, 'L.A.'s Olympic Bid Not Acceptable, IOC Indicates', *Los Angeles Times*, 9 May 1978; Kenneth Reich, 'L.A. Gets Ultimatum on Olympic Games', *Los Angeles Times*, 15 May 1978; Kenneth Reich, 'L.A. Officials Conditionally Give in to IOC', *Los Angeles Times*, 17 May 1978; Kenneth Reich, 'IOC Members Stress They Won't Accept Compromise', *Los Angeles Times*, 20 May 1978; Kenneth Reich, '1984 Games Provisionally Go to L.A.', *Los Angeles Times*, 19 May 1978; Kenneth Reich, 'Fate of Olympics Seems to Rest With L.A. City Council President', *Los Angeles Times*, 24 May 1978; Kenneth Reich, 'Bradley Set to Drop Olympic Bid If Offer Is Rejected', *Los Angeles Times*, 12 July 1978; Kenneth Reich, 'IOC Willing to Renew Talks, Bradley Told', *Los Angeles Times*, 20 July 1978; 'OK of L.A. Olympic Bid Predicted', *Los Angeles Times*, 29 Aug. 1978; Kenneth Reich, 'Bradley, Killanin Will Sign 1984 Olympics Pact in Special White House Ceremony', *Los Angeles Times*, 18 Oct. 1978.

[79] Wilson, 'Los Angeles 1984', 207–15; Reich, *Making It Happen*; Ueberroth, *Made in America*.

[80] US Census Bureau at http://www.census.gov/population/documentation/twps0027/tab21.txt; http://www.census.gov/population/documentation/twps0027/tab22.txt (accessed 10 Feb. 2002).

[81]   Roske, *Everyman's Eden*; Rice, Bullough and Orsi, *The Elusive Eden*.

[82]   '1932/1984 Olympic Games: A Case of Déjà Vu', *Los Angeles Times*, 18 Sept. 1983.

[83]   Carolyn S. Murray, 'Olympics: An Ongoing Legacy', *Los Angeles Times*, 25 July 1982.

[84]   Paul Zimmerman, 'Olympic Games in Los Angeles', *Los Angeles Times*, 23 July 1984.

[85]   Frances Ring served as guest editor for the winter 1984 number of volume 63 of *California History* entitled 'Champions in the Sun'.

[86]   Zimmerman, 'The Story of the Olympics—B.C. to A.D.', 10–12.

[87]   Perelman, *Olympic Retrospective*.

[88]   Wayne Wilson, 'The Legacy of Raised Expectations', in *The Legacy of the Olympic Games, 1984–2002*. Documents of the Olympic Museum. Miguel de Moragas, Christopher Kennett, Noria Puig, editors. Lausanne: International Olympic Committee, 2003. Paul Ziffren Sports Library, Archives of the Amateur Athletic Federation of Los Angeles. Los Angeles, California.

[89]   'LA 84: Games of the XXIII Olympiad', 1–36; Lisa Dillman, 'New Recreation Complex Accepts Olympic Torch', *Los Angeles Times*, 4 May 2003; Rasmussen, 'L.A. Then and Now'.

[90]   'Olympic Flame Dispute', *New York Times*, 31 Jan. 1984.

[91]   '$10 Million in Torch Funds Distributed', *Los Angeles Times*, 4 Sept. 1984; Elizabeth Kurylo, 'Torch for '96 Games Unveiled – Eternal Olympic Flame to Be Carried in Relay from Los Angeles to Atlanta', *Atlanta Journal*, 6 April 1995.

[92]   The lower estimate comes from *Los Angeles Times* reporter Kenneth Reich's book on the 1984 Olympics, *Making It Happen*, 265. The higher, later estimate comes from a 2004 newspaper report that purports to accept Reich's tally. Bill Dwyre, '1984 Olympics: The Legacy', *Los Angeles Times*, 25 July 2004.

[93]   Wilson, 'The Legacy of Raised Expectations'.

[94]   Edward J. Boyer, 'Bishop Mahony Backs Youths' "Olympic Legacy"', *Los Angeles Times*, 25 Oct. 1985; Joe Drape, 'Putting the Kids First', *Atlanta Constitution*, 19 Sept. 1993; Ron Dungee, 'The Amateur Athletic Foundation: Ten Years Old and Going Strong', *Los Angeles Sentinel*, 18 Aug. 1994; Kenneth Reich, '1984 Olympics/The Legacy: The Ring Leader', *Los Angeles Times*, 25 July 2004.

[95]   Dwyre, '1984 Olympics: The Legacy'.

[96]   'Executive Summary: Community Economic Impact of the 1984 Olympic Games in Los Angeles and Southern California'. Los Angeles Olympic Organizing Committee. Oct. 1984. Paul Ziffren Sports Library. LA84. Amateur Athletic Foundation of Los Angeles. Los Angeles, California.

[97]   Wilson, 'The Legacy of Raised Expectations'. For an excellent interpretation of how the 1984 Olympics fundamentally transformed the economics of the Olympic movement, see Barney, Wenn and Martyn, *Selling the Five Rings*, 153–202.

[98]   Bill Dwyre, 'Los Angeles Set Example for Seoul '88 – South Korea Is Seeking to Duplicate Success of 1984 Olympic Games', *Los Angeles Times*, 23 Jan. 1986.

[99]   Kenneth Reich, 'Reflections of the L.A. Games', *Los Angeles Times*, 11 Sept. 1988. Indeed, as Brian Bridges points out in another essay in this collection, estimates of the economic impact of the Seoul Olympics vary widely, though most chroniclers think it had a positive impact on the Korean economy. Bridges, 'The Seoul Olympics'.

[100]   Bob Hohler, 'Olympic World Turns with Ever-Less American Influence', *Boston Globe*, 20 Feb. 2006.

[101]   *Official Report of the Games of the XXIIIrd Olympiad*, vol. 2, part 2, pp. 45–54; part 3, p. 107, p. 184.

[102]   Dan Giesin, 'Next Up for BMX: Some Heavy Medal', *San Francisco Chronicle*, 9 Sept. 2006; Robert Marquand, 'Even Pop Culture Must Get a Stamp of Approval in China', *Christian Science Monitor*, 14 June 2005.

[103]   Dyreson, '"To Construct a Better and More Peaceful World" or "War Minus the Shooting"?', 337–51.

[104] I have used the term 'incubated' with great care (I think), since using a phrase such as 'gave birth' falsely implies that features of these phenomena do not have several geographical development points. For instance, snowboarding originates both in California and Vermont, or cinema gets started in New York, London, Paris, Berlin, Vienna and Hollywood, to provide two examples. California might not have given each movement 'birth' in the strict sense, but it certainly nurtured all of the sports and trends to global fruition.

[105] Dyreson, 'Globalizing the Nation-Making Process', 91–106; Dyreson, *Making the American Team.*

[106] Guttmann, *Sports*, 323–5.

[107] Chris Hogg, 'Sport, Sand and Sex: Olympic Beach Volleyball the Newest Craze', *Digital Journal*, http://www.digitaljournal.com/article/35455 (accessed 10 Jan. 2008).

[108] *Time* cover, 7 Jan. 1985.

[109] Morrow, 'Feeling Proud Again', 21–30.

[110] Beverly Bevette, 'Los Angeles Reflects on Legacy of the Olympics', *Los Angeles Times*, 4 Aug. 1985,

[111] Reich, *Making It Happen*; Ueberroth, *Made in America*; Bill Dwyre, 'Ueberroth Watches Torch Being Passed', *Los Angeles Times*, 20 July 1996.

[112] Starr, *Coast of Dreams.*

[113] Peter H. King, 'Waiting for You Know What', *Los Angeles Times*, 14 April 1993; Joyce Miller and Barbara Thornburg, '25 Ways to Fix L.A.', *Los Angeles Times*, 6 Aug. 1989; 'Tom Bradley: 1917–1998', *Detroit News*, 30 Sept. 1998; Jack Burby, 'The Master Planners: For Mark and Jane Pisano, There's No Time Like the Future', *Los Angeles Times*, 6 Aug. 1989.

[114] Dwyre, '1984 Olympics: The Legacy'; Alan Abrahamson, '1984 Olympics/The Legacy: Light Touch', *Los Angeles Times*, 28 July 2004; Starr, *Coast of Dreams*, 548.

[115] Dwyre, '1984 Olympics: The Legacy'.

[116] Ibid.

[117] Reich, 'Critics of Coliseum Tear-Down Line Up Raiders'; Leon Whiteson, 'Could Face Lift Make the Coliseum a Contender?', *Los Angeles Times*, 10 June 1996; Rasmussen, 'L.A. Then and Now'.

[118] Dillman, 'New Recreation Complex Accepts Olympic Torch'.

[119] Alan Abrahamson, '1984 Olympics/The Legacy: Stage Awaits Encore', *Los Angeles Times*, 25 July 2004.

[120] Barry A. Sanders, 'Olympic Dreams', *Los Angeles Times*, 20 Sept. 2005.

[121] 'Proposed L.A. Coliseum Enhancements'.

[122] Lisa Dillman, 'L.A. Hopes Its Charm Is Good for a Third Time', *Los Angeles Times*, 3 March 2007; Lisa Dillman, 'L.A. Submits Detailed Bid to USOC', *Los Angeles Times*, 23 Jan. 2007.

[123] Helene Elliott, 'Chicago Spirit Steals Show', *Los Angeles Times*, 15 April 2007.

[124] Bill Dwyre, 'An Olympic Bid Where Fresh is Flat', *Los Angeles Times*, 17 April 2007.

[125] Abrahamson, 'Stage Awaits Encore'.

[126] Georgiadis, *Olympic Revival*; Koulouri, ed., *Athens: Olympic City*; Kitroeff, *Wrestling with the Ancients.*

References

American Olympic Committee. *Report of the American Olympic Committee: Seventh Olympic Games, Antwerp, Belgium, 1920.* Greenwich, CT: Conde Nast, 1920.

Barney, Robert K., Stephen R. Wenn, and Scott G. Martyn. *Selling the Five Rings: The International Olympic Committee and the Rise of Olympic Commercialism.* Salt Lake City, UT: University of Utah Press, 2002.

Bridges, Brian. 'The Seoul Olympics: Economic Miracle Meets the World'. *International Journal of the History of Sport* 25 (Dec. 2008): forthcoming.

Carr, Harry and E.H. Suydam. *Los Angeles, City of Dreams*. New York: D. Appleton-Century, 1935.

Caughey, John Walton. *Los Angeles: Biography of a City*. Berkeley, CA: University of California Press, 1976.

Davis, Mike. *City of Quartz: Excavating the Future in Los Angeles*. New York: Verso, 1990.

Dinces, Sean. 'Padres on Mount Olympus: Los Angeles and the Production of the 1932 Olympic Mega-Event'. *Journal of Sport History* 32 (Summer 2005): 137–66.

Dyreson, Mark. 'Globalizing American Sporting Culture: The U.S. Government Plan to Conquer the World Sports Market in the 1930s'. *Sportwissenschaft: The German Journal of Sport Science* 34 (June 2004): 145–51.

——. 'Globalizing the Nation-Making Process: Modern Sport in World History'. *International Journal of the History of Sport* 20 (March 2003): 91–106.

——. 'If We Build It, Will They Will Come?: Washington National Stadium Schemes and American Olympic Desires'. *International Journal of the History of Sport* 25 (Nov. 2008): forthcoming.

——. 'Johnny Weissmuller and the Old Global Capitalism: The Origins of the Federal Blueprint for Selling American Culture to the World'. *International Journal of the History of Sport* 25 (Feb. 2008): 268–83.

——. *Making the American Team: Sport, Culture and the Olympic Experience*. Urbana, IL: University of Illinois Press, 1998.

——. 'Mapping an Empire of Baseball: American Visions of National Pastimes and Global Influence, 1919–1941'. In *Baseball in America and America in Baseball*, edited by Donald Kyle and Robert R. Fairbanks. College Station, TX: Texas A&M University Press, 2008: 143–88.

——. 'Marketing National Identity: The Olympic Games of 1932 and American Culture'. *Olympika: The International Journal of Olympic Studies* 4 (1995): 23–48.

——. 'Marketing Weissmuller to the World: Hollywood's Olympics and Federal Schemes for Americanization Through Sport'. *International Journal of the History of Sport* 25 (Feb. 2008): 284–306.

——. '"To Construct a Better and More Peaceful World" or "War Minus the Shooting"?: The Olympic Movement's Second Century'. In *Onward to the Olympics: Historical Perspectives on the Olympic Games*, edited by Gerald Schaus and Stephen Wenn. Waterloo, Ontario: Wilfrid Laurier University Press, 2007: 337–51.

Epting, Chris. *Images of America: Los Angeles Memorial Coliseum*. Chicago: Arcadia, 2002.

Erickson, Steve. 'Where Fancies Flicker'. *California History* 63 (Winter 1984): 66–70.

Fleishman, Sue. 'Made in California'. *California History* 63 (Winter 1984): 80–3.

Fogelson, Robert M. *The Fragmented Metropolis: Los Angeles, 1850–1930*. Cambridge, MA: Harvard University Press, 1967.

Gallico, Paul. *The Golden People*. Garden City, NY: Doubleday, 1965.

Georgiadis, Konstantinos. *Olympic Revival: The Revival of the Olympic Games in Modern Times*, trans. Richard Witt. Athens: Ekdotike Athenon, 2003.

Grundman, Adolph H. 'AAU-NCAA Politics: Forrest "Phog" Allen and America's First Olympic Basketball Team'. *Olympika: The International Journal of Olympic Studies* 5 (1996): 111–26.

Guttmann, Allen. *The Games Must Go On: Avery Brundage and the Olympic Movement*. Urbana, IL: University of Illinois Press, 1984.

——. *The Olympics: A History of the Modern Games*. Urbana, IL: University of Illinois Press, 1992.

——. *Sports: The First Five Millennia*. Amherst, MA: University of Massachusetts Press, 2004.

Henry, William M. *An Approved History of the Olympic Games*. New York: G. P. Putnam's Sons, 1948.

Ivar, Paul. 'Olympian Motifs Sway Fashions of Autumn'. *Game and Gossip* 10 (Aug. 1932): 32–3.

Keys, Barbara. *Globalizing Sport: National Rivalry and International Community in the 1930s.* Cambridge, MA: Harvard University Press, 2006.

——. 'Spreading Peace, Democracy, and Coca Cola®: Sport and American Cultural Expansion in the 1930s'. *Diplomatic History* 28 (April 2004): 165–96.

Kitroeff, Alexander. *Wrestling With the Ancients: Modern Greek Identity and the Olympics.* New York: Greekworks, 2004.

Koulouri, Christina, ed. *Athens: Olympic City.* Athens: International Olympic Academy, 2004.

'LA 84: Games of the XXIII Olympiad'. *Design Quarterly* 127 (1985): 1–36.

Large, David Clay. *Nazi Games: The Olympics of 1936.* New York: W. W. Norton, 2007.

Lillard, Richard. 'International City'. *California History* 63 (Winter 1984): 52–7.

MacAloon, John J. *This Great Symbol: Pierre de Coubertin and the Origins of the Modern Olympics.* Chicago: University of Chicago Press, 1981.

McWilliams, Carey. *Southern California Country: An Island on the Land.* New York: Duell, Soan & Pearce, 1946.

Morrow, Lance. 'Feeling Proud Again'. *Time* 125 (7 Jan. 1985): 20–31.

'Official Proclamation from Governor James Rolph of California'. *Game and Gossip* 10 (June 1932): 1.

Official Report of the Games of the XXIIIrd Olympiad, Los Angeles, 1984. 3 vols. Los Angeles: LAOOC, 1984.

'Olympic Games as a Depression Buster', *Literary Digest* 113 (18 June 1932): 28–31.

Perelman, Richard B. *Olympic Retrospective: The Games of Los Angeles.* Los Angeles: LAOOC, 1985.

Pieroth, Doris. 'Los Angeles 1932'. In *The Historical Dictionary of the Modern Olympic Movement*, rev. 2nd edn, edited by John Findling and Karen Pelle. Westport, CT: Greenwood Press, 2004: 95–103.

——. *Their Day in the Sun: Women of the 1932 Olympics.* Seattle, WA: University of Washington Press, 1996.

Reich, Kenneth. *Making It Happen: Peter Ueberroth and the 1984 Olympics.* Santa Barbara, CA: Capra, 1986.

Rice, Grantland. 'You're Lucky, California!' *Game and Gossip* 10 (Sept. 1932): 9, 41.

Rice, Richard B., William A. Bullough and Richard J. Orsi. *The Elusive Eden: A New History of California.* New York: Knopf, 1988.

Riess, Steve. 'Power Without Authority: Los Angeles = Elites and the Construction of the Coliseum'. *Journal of Sport History* 8 (Spring 1981): 50–65.

Roche, Maurice. *Mega-Events and Modernity: Olympics and Expos in the Growth of Global Culture.* London: Routledge, 2000.

Roske, Ralph Joseph. *Everyman's Eden: A History of California.* New York: Macmillan, 1968.

Senn, Alfred Erich. *Power, Politics, and the Olympic Games.* Champaign, IL: Human Kinetics, 1999.

Sitton, Tom. *Metropolis in the Making: Los Angeles in the 1920s.* Berkeley, CA: University of California Press, 2001.

Spencer, Emerson. 'Records Crashed and Heroes Soared'. *Game and Gossip* 10 (Sept. 1932): 22, 44.

Starr, Kevin. *Coast of Dreams: California on the Edge, 1990–2003.* New York: Knopf, 2004.

——. *The Dream Endures: California Enters the 1940s.* New York: Oxford University Press, 1997.

——. *Material Dreams: Southern California Through the 1920s.* New York: Oxford University Press, 1990.

Tygiel, Jules. *The Great Los Angeles Swindle: Oil, Stocks, and Scandal During the Roaring Twenties.* New York: Oxford University Press, 1994.

Ueberroth, Peter, with Richard Levin and Amy Quinn. *Made in America: His Own Story.* New York: William Morrow, 1985.

Welky, David. 'U.S. Journalism and the 1932 Olympics'. *Journal of Sport History* 24 (Spring 1997): 24–49.

White, Jeremy. 'The Los Angeles Way of Doing Things: The Olympic Village and the Practice of Boosterism'. *Olympika: The International Journal of Olympic Studies* 11 (2000): 79–116.

Wilson, Wayne. 'Los Angeles 1984'. In *The Historical Dictionary of the Modern Olympic Movement*, rev. 2nd edn, edited by John Findling and Karen Pelle. Westport, CT: Greenwood Press, 2004: 207–15.

Wise, Bill. 'Afterglow of the Olympiad'. *Game and Gossip* 10 (Sept. 1932): 13, 46–8.

——. 'Behind the Xth Olympiad'. *Game and Gossip* 10 (Oct. 1932): 7, 38–41.

——. 'These Things You Should Know About the Tenth Olympiad'. *Game and Gossip* 10 (Aug. 1932): 9, 42.

Xth Olympiade Committee. *The Games of the Xth Olympiad, Los Angeles, 1932*. Los Angeles: Woffler, 1933.

Yamamoto, Eriko. 'Cheers for Japanese Athletes: The 1932 Los Angeles Olympics and the Japanese American Community'. *Pacific Historical Review*, 69 (Aug. 2000): 399–429.

Zimmerman, Paul B. 'The Story of the Olympics—B.C. to A.D.' *California History* 63 (Winter 1984): 8–21.

Beijing Olympics Legacies: Certain Intentions and Certain and Uncertain Outcomes

Dong Jinxia and J. A. Mangan

Recent host cities to the Olympic Games have left legacies with both intended and unintended consequences. To concentrate on the positive: the 1956 Melbourne games, for example, introduced the now standard practice in the closing ceremony of athletes entering the stadium in mixed parties; satellite and colour TV coverage, now normal, were first introduced in the 1964 Tokyo games; the 1984 Los Angles games made private sponsorship and marketing a common practice; the 1988 Seoul games had, *inter alia*, twin legacies: South Korean economic and political advance; the opening ceremonies of the 2000 Sydney games and the 2004 Athens games metonymically raised the bar for ceremonial spectaculars – and so on. [1]

Beijing will be no different in some ways but very different in others. The 2008 games, arguably, will prove both unexceptional and exceptional in the creation of Olympic legacies. However, one thing is certain, that, as Jacques Rogge, the present president of the International Olympic Committee (IOC) presciently, and perhaps with unconscious irony, announced at the one-year countdown celebration in Beijing earlier this year, '*The staging of the Olympic Games will leave people a legacy of far-reaching influence*' [italics mine]. [2] In fact, Beijing will leave multiple legacies rather than just the singular legacy Rogge mentioned. What are the intended legacies of Beijing 2008 and what could be the consequences both intended and unintended? These are the questions that intrigue people both in China and around the world. This brief discussion, *inter alia* in a review, partially, but not exclusively, of the stated Beijing Organizing Committee of the Olympics Games (BOCOG) policies, their implementation and their putative possibilities for Chinese and the global society, seeks to chart the potential social, economic and political impact on Beijing and China and, indeed, the world, of hosting the world's largest sports event, and to reflect upon some of the intangible and tangible legacies that Beijing 2008 could bequeath to the host city, the host nation and the international community.

The intangible positive legacies, with the necessary caveat that precise measurement will be difficult if not impossible, from a Chinese perspective will include the internal absorption and dissemination of Olympic ideals and values, the sharing of multiple cultural experiences, the accumulation of positive memories, and the experience of community cohesion and patriotic pride through national accomplishments. One hoped-for intangible legacy should be singled out for special mention – the publicity China will attract globally from hosting a virtually no-expense-spared Olympics – unique in cost, and arguably, in effort. Beijing 2008, many Chinese hope, will entrance, astound, amaze and seduce the globe – and announce the arrival of China on the international stage as the coming global superpower. In China, this is a publicly unspoken but privately much spoken about intended legacy. Beijing 2008 is a political exercise in global diplomatic public relations, ostensibly, on an unprecedented scale.

Tangible Legacies?

The intended tangible legacies of Beijing 2008, obvious and measurable, including new buildings, new sports structures, new traffic infrastructure, a massive influx of tourists, and many other changes, are well publicized and well known. The Olympic Games are an international sports festival that involves virtually all sectors of society. To host the event, therefore, brings many concrete legacies to the host city and country.

Towards a Twenty-First Century International City

'New Beijing, Great Olympics' was the self-assured slogan when Beijing bid for the games. The slogan mirrors Chinese confidence in a great city soon to become greater – and the determination to transform Beijing, a historic capital for more than 800 years, into a modern metropolitan city that will impress the world. 'New' is a hypnotic term in China, as the nation harnesses, rides and thrusts forward on the back of political, social and economic changes begun in the early 1980s. Via the games, Beijing intends to showcase to the entire world a dynamic, glittering and advanced metropolis. Will this be achieved?

Immediately after the successful bid in 2001, Beijing at once embarked on a vast investment and construction programme. More than 290bn yuan (about US$40bn) – 10 billion yuan (US$1.4bn) more than initially intended due to the increased budget for security and other escalating costs – is required to deliver the games; specifically, it is needed to modernize Beijing's airport and other infrastructure, build the required 31 competition venues, and clean up pollution and environmental hazards. [3] Will capital investment on this massive achieve its ends – certainly some of them? At least one is already realized!

The world is taking note of China's achievements and aspirations. A leading Western newspaper recently wrote of the hugely impressive new terminal at Beijing Airport, now the largest airport in the world: 'No project is more symbolic of how China is using the Olympic Games this year to refashion its image and prepare for a future once only dreamed of by Chairman Mao's exuberant, but ill-advised, economic planners.' [4]

Other legacies are more problematic and less desirable. Without exaggeration, Beijing has become one of the most eye-catching, cosmopolitan cities in Asia – and increasingly a city of cars. With rising living standards, cars have steadily replaced bicycles, but this has brought a predictable problem in its wake, traffic congestion. This is being tackled, but the extent of any eventual success is uncertain. Beijing will invest 90bn yuan (about US$11.25bn) in the construction of underground railways, light railways, express ways and airports. Eight new underground lines have been constructed in the urban area and the number of public transit lines will increase to over 650 by 2008. It is intended that by adopting 3S-based core technology a highly effective, intelligent traffic network system will be created, and the capacity and efficiency of Beijing's passenger and freight transport will rank with the rest of the advanced world. [5] In part, this prodigious effort is driven by the games – certainly the speed of implementation is! This effort, the Chinese hope, sooner rather than later, will greatly reduce present and future transport problems. However, these multiple innovations are essentially untested. Many commentators are concerned about the possible collapse of the transport system during the games. [6] Ambition is one thing; success is another.

Optimism is more apparent in other directions. To stage the 'best ever' games in Olympic history – the unabashedly declared intention – state-of-the-art venues and facilities have been built in Beijing and other co-host cities. Of the required 37 stadiums, 31 are located in Beijing, including 11 new stadiums, 9 temporary stadiums and 11 old stadiums that have been modernized. In addition, about 45 training venues and other specialized facilities that are directly related to the games will be made available. Thus, direct investment in the construction of Olympic venues and facilities will amount to about 13bn yuan (US$1.7bn) in the lead-up to the games. [7] The National Stadium, now known internationally as the 'bird's nest' because of its giant lattice-work structure of irregularly angled metal girders, as has been well publicized, will cost about 3.5bn yuan (about US$488m). It was to have cost even more, but the IOC got cold feet. [8]

In addition, the latest technological innovations will be used in construction, communications, transportation, food delivery and competition management. The construction of information technology alone, ranging from a digital communication system and a software and intelligent management system for competition to a fibre-optic network for journalists or officials to obtain video pictures of what is happening at any site, will cost some 30bn yuan (US$3.8bn). Surely, the Chinese declare, 'iconic stadiums, architectural designs, infrastructure improvements ... [will] be the legacy of Beijing'. [9] As a result, the capital city will become as vibrant and dynamic as any in the world. If this intended legacy is achieved, it will be a legacy handed on to future generations of which the present generation will be justly proud. Time will tell. The intention is clear: the realization is awaited. Unintended legacies, like Banquo's ghost at a rather different feast, are not to be ruled out. For example, if charges for use of the post-Olympic facilities are so high that grass-roots sport fails to benefit, then post-Olympic euphoria could swiftly turn to post-Olympic exasperation.

Accelerated Economic Growth, Increased Employment Opportunities and Improved Living Standards – and Possible Complications

Beijing's successful bid for the 2008 games coincided with Chinese entry to the World Trade Organization in 2001. This has had a significant impact on China. First, billions of dollars of direct investment in infrastructure building and related activities have boosted China's annual GDP by 0.3% [10] – a valuable legacy from expenditure on the games. Beijing has benefited more than any other city in the country. Investment has resulted in a two-digit growth for 9 years in terms of GDP, which has been accompanied by an increase of house prices – 11.4% in 2007. [11] Beijing's economy has grown by 12% annually over the past 5 years, increasing its GDP from 433bn yuan (US$60bn) in 2002 to 900bn yuan (US$113.9bn) in 2007. [12] By 2006, Beijing had fulfilled the goal of about 44,400 yuan (US$6,000) per capita GDP 2 years earlier than planned, and well above the average per capita GDP of 12,876 yuan (US$1,740) of the country. [13] A year later, Beijing's GDP rose to 51,800 yuan (US$7,000). It is estimated that the 2008 games will continue to boost Beijing's GDP by 2–3% annually. It created, incidentally, about 1.94 million new jobs between 2002 and 2007. [14] The city is aiming for a 71,000 yuan (US$10,000) per capita GDP in 2012. [15] Some of this anticipated growth will be the direct result of hosting the games.

In the lead-up to the games, the structure of industries has changed, and will change further, over time. It is anticipated that service industries will become the main contributor to the national economy. In 2005, their industrial output was 67.7% of the total. In 2008, it will increase to 72%. The tourism and services, insurance and sports industries will be the major beneficiaries of the games. The Beijing construction industry has also increased its gross production by 135.115bn yuan (about US$19bn) between 2004 and 2008. This has led to an extra 795,900 jobs. In addition, between 2002 and 2007, some 1.92 million jobs were created in the

Beijing hospitality industry. [16] Tourism is an industry that has developed very quickly in the twenty-first century. By 2005, foreign tourists reached 4.68 million, a 41% increase over 2001. China ranked fourth in the world for foreign visitors. The revenue from inbound tourism was 29.3bn yuan (US$3.66bn) – a 64% rise over 2001. In fact, China ranked sixth in the world for inbound tourist revenue. Chinese tourism overseas has also increased from 3.69 million in 2001 to 28.55 million in 2005, and the countries and regions visited have expanded from 18 to 132. [17] In 2006, incoming tourist numbers rose again by 3.87%. Outgoing tourist numbers rose by 11.3%. Foreign currency revenue from inbound tourism reached about 251bn yuan (US$33.949bn), up over 15.88% from the previous year. [18] The World Travel and Tourism Council (WTTC) has forecast that China will become the world's fourth-largest tourist outbound country by 2020. [19] Meanwhile, the games have helped already, and will certainly help further in the future, to promote Beijing at home and abroad.

There is a downside to the Beijing boom. While housing prices in Beijing have soared in recent years, the games have injected additional tremendous growth in the cost of Beijing real property. In 2001, following the award of the 2008 games, investment in real property surged dramatically, growing by 50.12%. [20] By 2006, investment had increased to 171.99bn yuan (US$21.77bn), 51% of the whole investment in fixed capital. [21] The price of land, homes and home rentals in Beijing, as in Sydney prior to its 2000 games, has rocketed. The annual percentage increases of house prices in Beijing in 2001 and 2004 were 3% and 6.7%, respectively, but in 2005 it leapt to 20%. [22] This is in part an unfortunate legacy of the games. The escalating price of land and property in Beijing, and other cities, has raised great concern about the impact on inflation, employment and equilibrium. In recent years, the inflation rate has risen to such a dangerous level that the central government has taken measures to curb the 'overheated' economy and dangerous inflation. Whether the latter can be curbed effectively will determine the level of social stability across this huge country. Whatever the situation ahead with regard to both these aspects of life, the games, in conjunction with other forces, might well leave a regrettable legacy.

Thankfully, not all is potential doom and gloom. The BOCOG claimed in 2004 that Beijing 2008 would reach a cost-profit balance, requiring an input of about 13.65bn yuan (US$1.625bn) and enjoying an output of about 13.52bn yuan (US$1.609bn). In 2007, after excellent Olympic marketing, [23] the IOC believed that the revenue from the games would reach a record in excess of 20bn yuan (US$3bn) – double that of the 2004 Athens games. [24] This is a more positive legacy of Beijing 2008.

It should be noted that preparations for the games stand against a background of rapid urbanization of China. The urban population was only 30.1% of China's total population in 1999; by 2006, it had reached 43.92%. China had 666 cities in total in 1999, of which 32 were very large, 43 were large, 192 were middle-sized, and over 400 were small. [25] It is predicted that by 2010 there will be 125 large cities with a population of one million or more. As virtually all Olympic competitions will take place in cities (some football preliminary matches will be staged in Shanghai, Tianjin, Shengyang, and Qinghuangdao, the windsurfing in Qingdao and the equestrian events in Hong Kong), the Beijing games will unquestionably accelerate the development of benevolent urbanization in these locations – a relatively minor but advantageous legacy.

Sport at Elite and Grass-Roots Levels: Ambitions, Aspirations and Potential Obstacles

To be wholly optimistic for a moment, the games will be a golden opportunity for the Chinese to fulfil their long-standing dream of becoming a foremost, if not *the* foremost, Olympic power. They are only too well aware of this and have no intention of letting the chance slip from their grasp. To change the metaphor for effect – no stone will be left unturned. To ensure this, the 'Plan to Win Glory in the 2008 Olympics' [2008 ao yun hui zheng guang ji hua] was drafted in 2002. According to the plan, Chinese athletes will participate in all 28 sports competitions and obtain more medals in more events than in past games, aiming at least to be one of the top three medal winners. China plans to capture no less than 180 medals from the 302 events. [26]

 To secure Olympic success, the Chinese are making a stupendous effort to ensure the finest domestic performances ever at these 'home' games. The sports budget has risen annually since 2001, for example, from about 1.55bn yuan (about US$0.187bn) in 2003 to over 2.15bn yuan (about US$0.272bn) in 2006. [27] Nor are these all the funds appropriated. To prepare for the 2008 games, a special budget from the state has reached over 4bn. [28] Since 2002, a special budget for Olympic-related research projects has been available. In addition, national policies on the management of sport have been adjusted. Each sports management centre has put forward its own 'Project to Implement the Plan to Win Glory in the 2008 Olympics' [guanche 2008 aoyun zhengguang jihua gongcheng]. Countdown training plans for the key athletes of many sports have been fine-tuned and competition arrangements programmed to fit in with the games schedules. Special workshops on the prevention and treatment of athletes' injuries have been provided. To guarantee 'match fitness', Olympic-type competitions were organized for a number of relevant sports in August, 2007. To ensure that athletes are perfectly honed by August 2008, pre-games training has been arranged with meticulous care. Nothing has been overlooked. To motivate athletes to commit themselves totally to the Olympics, for example, an athletes' insurance system has been established, and their incomes have been increased following the reform of the athletes' income distribution system. 'Insurance standards are classed into 12 categories, the top one is 300,000 yuan RMB; the 11th category will be 2000 yuan RMB yuan,' as stated by Article 15 of the Provisional Measures of Mutual Funding Insurance for Elite Athletes' Injuries and Disability [xiuyou yundongyuan shanchang huzhu baoxian shixing banfa], issued by the State Sports Administration. [29]

In 2007, athletics was included as an independent occupational category for the first time in the National Management System of Public Enterprises' Staff [guojia shiye dangwei gongzuo renyuan guanli tiyu]. Furthermore, a series of educational and psychological activities were organized for national teams and individuals to assist them in their mental preparation for the games. [30] No effort has been spared to guarantee that Olympic athletes concentrate on all aspects of training without distraction. There are two potential legacies arising out of these superlative preparations, one positive and the other negative: elevated personal and national self-regard and pride if the athletes are successful *or* lowered self-esteem and humiliation for both athletes and people if the athletes are unsuccessful. Indeed, if the athletes do not perform well, further negative consequences could include hostility to and criticism of coaches, management, and even government. The psychological and practical stakes are high.

One trumpeted legacy of phenomenally expensive new facilities is the long-term advantage to grass-roots sport. Authorities proclaim that mass sport, if all goes swimmingly at the games, will benefit. [31] Given that the majority of the sports venues and facilities that have been built for the games, organizers assert, will be used for public recreation and leisure after the games, [32] dispute over resources between 'elite' and 'grass-roots' sport, characteristic of the past, could be markedly alleviated. Corruption, though not unknown in China on a substantial scale, may scuttle the effort to bring Olympic benefits to the masses. Time will tell.

Grass-roots sport, incidentally, has already a positive games' legacy. China has combined a national fitness programme with the build-up to Beijing 2008, encouraging people to enthusiastically support the Olympics by getting a feel for sport through participation in it. A 'National Fitness and Move with the Olympics' [quanmin jianshen yu aoyun tongxing] campaign was launched across the country in 2006. Nearly 100 million people now participate in a variety of programmes. Recently, an annual National Fitness Week (quanmin jianshen zhou) was extended to an annual National Fitness Month [quanmin jianshen yue] and has become a very popular event. Various kinds of activities such as the Ice and Snow Event for a Million Teenagers [baiwan qingshaonian bingxue huodong], a National Display of Hundreds of Millions of Women Fitness Enthusiasts [yiwan funv jianshen zhanshi dahui], a National Sunshine Physical Education and Sport for Hundreds of Millions of Students [yiwan xuesheng yangguang tiyu yundong], and a National Display of Exercises for Hundreds of Millions of the Aged [quanguo yiwan laonianren jianshen huodong], have been established. In addition, attention is now being given to the fitness of farmers. In 2003, the 'Construction Plan of the Sports and Fitness Projects for Peasants During the 11th Five-Year Period' [shi yi wu qijian nongmin tiyu jianshen gongcheng shishi fangan] was issued jointly by the General Administration of Sport and the Financial Ministry. Some 180m yuan (US$22.5m) will be invested in this. To cater for these mammoth innovations since 2002, 'public sports venues have increased by 20 million square metres [and] financial input into such projects has reached 2bn yuan (US$270m).' [33] There can be no doubt that staging the games has helped raise the generally low level of popular participation in sports, especially among the young. [34] That legacy is already in place.

Intended and Crucial Intangible Legacies

Consolidation of a Confident Chinese National Identity

The *most* important legacy the Beijing games, asserts He Zhenliang, chairman of the IOC Commission for Culture of Olympic Education, is 'the elevation of our Chinese people's self-confidence and sense of pride'. [35] There is a bitter background to this ambition. The Chinese are very proud of their five millennia of documented history and cultural traditions. However, China suffered 'the century of shame and humiliation' during the domination first by the Western nations [36] and then by Japan, from the mid-nineteenth century until the end of the Second World War. This traumatic experience has been a driving force, some say *the* driving force, behind Chinese exertions to press urgently for global status, in economics, in science and technology, in sport – and in global politics. It is widely believed that, if successful, the games will serve to restore China's national greatness [37] by helping to erase the old memory of a humiliated and subordinated people and replacing it with a new memory, the beneficent gift of the games, of a confident, powerful and respected nation. [38] The Chinese consider the games an opportunity to herald China's emergence as a major world power on many levels. The importance of Beijing 2008 in this regard simply cannot be exaggerated. A legacy of retribution and assertion is anticipated. However, by way of counterpoise, as the games approach, China's external policies in Africa and elsewhere closer to home in turn attract international opprobrium. A steadily ballooning legacy has already risen and may well rise further. The full extent of its ascent is not yet clear, but it could well result in a legacy of international recrimination – and even action.

The games, then, have won complete support from government, party and citizens. Both the Chinese central and Beijing municipal governments have promised to guarantee the funding of any shortfall in the construction of infrastructure and venues and working costs. In addition, the games have received a promise of strong support from the general public. A survey showed that about 95% of residents in Beijing wish to volunteer their services for the games. [39] Incidentally, the games needs 100,000 volunteer workers, but more than 930,000 people have applied, and over one million people want to be city service volunteers. Finally, 30% of Beijingers have said that, if necessary, they would donate to the games. [40] A legacy of community cohesion is in the making. Will it survive 2008?

China entered the economic development fast track in the 1980s. By 2003, China had earned about 7,148bn yuan (US$851bn) in exports and at the same time surpassed Japan as the world's third-largest market. [41] The games, as noted earlier, are expected to be a harbinger of China's economic world elevation. China, however, expects much more from the Olympics than a brief advertisement of its growing economy. They expect that the Olympics will power a national drive toward modernization, provide a broad bridge to the West, and pave the way for China to play a greater part in world affairs. Through the games, China will make the clearest of political statements. This brings the possibility of a negative legacy – possibly, chauvinism that could damage China's global image if Chinese athletes, as expected and intended, dominate the games. Some foreigners have voiced their fears of this possibility. A group of Japanese students visiting Peking University in 2007 asked pointedly, 'Will Japanese and other nations' athletes again be harassed by Chinese spectators, as has happened before, if Chinese do not do well in the 2008 games?' The fear is real – even among the Chinese. [42] Selected schools have been instructed to cheer for designated incoming national teams. Will America be among them? On the other hand, some foreigners are more sanguine, expecting a more measured reaction. One has declared that 'China will act more confidently on the world stage, [but] it will still be at the starting block in the journey for great "powerdom".' China, he added, is well aware of this. [43]

In summary, on the positive side, what the games may provide is a legacy of a successful bid that involves an upsurge in national spirit, pride, morale and cooperation; on the negative side there is a danger of nationalistic over- reaction and not far from hyperbolic chauvinism.

China: Global Integration

China has become increasingly more open to the outside world and better known throughout it after 30 years of economic reform. Chinese brands such as Lenovo, TCL, Haier, Huawei and ZTE are now recognized worldwide. China's direct investment overseas is rising rapidly. By the end of 2006, China made about 555bn yuan (US$75bn) in direct investments in more than 160 countries. Chinese artists, such as the film director Zhang Yimou, the composer Tan Dun, the cellist Yo-Yo Ma and the artist Cai Guoqiang, are internationally acclaimed. The Olympic Slogan, 'One World, One Dream' [tong yi ge shijie, tong yi ge mengxiang], a metaphor of oneness, demonstrates Chinese eagerness to be part of the global community. Those words have already been put into action. Foreign experts in design, security, environmental protection, competition administration and publicity have been employed as advisers, consultants and evaluators. The Australian Bob Elphinston, with extensive Olympic organizational expertise, [44] for example, serves as an international consultant to BOCOG. [45] Foreign coaches have been employed in increasing numbers to train Chinese national teams. In the Chinese delegation to the 2004 games, the coaches for archery; canoeing; women's handball, hockey and softball; and men's basketball were all foreign coaches. The Athens games, regarded as a stepping stone to the Beijing games, saw more foreign coaches employed, especially in men's and women's football, rhythmic gymnastics, synchronized swimming, cycling, fencing and tae kwon do. Since the Athens games in 2004, nearly 60 foreign coaches have been employed by China to improve the performance of 21 sports. These coaches have brought to China not only fresh training ideas and techniques, but also new management skills and practices. They have ensured the transformation of both sports skills and sports management. [46] 'One world, one dream' – globalization in short, in China's interest – is a legacy that will be in evident during the games and after the games.

While Chinese are learning from foreign countries, how is the world reacting? What might the emerging global legacy be after the games? In recent years, the world has turned its attention to China with evermore intensive concentration. Some 30 million non-Chinese are learning Mandarin. After years of superior indifference, the West now celebrates China: 'In 2004, Parisians looked at a red Eiffel Tower in honour of Chinese President Hu Jintao's visit, which coincided with the "Year of China in France".' A 'China in London 2006' event was the largest celebration of Chinese culture ever seen in the British capital. In 2007, Russia held its own 'Year of China'. Perceptively and imaginatively, the French journalist Erik Izraelewicz in 2005 wrote *Quand la Chine change le monde* (*When China Changes the World*). He argued with some justification that 'China is succeeding in having non-Chinese framing the debate in a way that is advantageous to it.'

Studies on China flow off the world's presses. To name merely four recent ones that have attracted special attention, Will Hutton's *The Writing on the Wall: China and the West in the 21st Century* (2007), Susan L. Smith's *China: Fragile Superpower* (2007), Ted Galen Carpenter's *America's Coming War with China* (2006), and Giovanni Arrighi's *Adam Smith in Beijing* (2008). There are many more. Adding to the volume of publications, the University of California Press has launched a series Focus on China – all literary straws in the wind. The airlines of the world carry a constant stream of politicians and businessmen, not to mention tourists, to China. A legacy of a new, multi-structured familiarity with 'the Sleeping Dragon' is being established at this very moment; one huge building block is the Beijing games and the world publicity it has occasioned. One extraordinary example illustrates this power trend. For the first time in Olympic history, invitation letters to the games were delivered personally by IOC President Rogge to the Olympic committees of more than 200 countries and regions from a host country (Beijing, China) rather than from the IOC headquarters in Lausanne, Switzerland. [47]

China has clearly become an important part of the IOC 'global village'. The games arguably will have far more influence than any other games in history, on both China and the world. [48] The Beijing games are a declaration of full global involvement; a metonym of absorption. Will one legacy be the removal in due course of the IOC headquarters from West to East?

Blending Olympic Culture and Chinese Traditional Culture – Inspirational Momentary Fusion

After Beijing was awarded the games, one immediate and quite astonishing domestic legacy resulted: an unprecedented Olympic Education Project involving 400 million students from 500,000 schools throughout the nation was launched. [49] Olympic courses for students were established at many universities and schools across the country. Olympic research centres were created in higher education institutions. In addition, since 2005, Olympic Education Model Schools have been set up across the country to ensure that many of the young will be familiar with Olympic issues prior to the games. In Beijing, some 200 model schools are charged with welcoming foreign teams, cheering for them even against Chinese athletes, and raising their National Olympic Committee (NOC) flags at ceremonies. [50] In addition, textbooks have been produced to introduce students to the history of the Olympic Movement, the Olympic Games, the Olympic symbols and the role of Olympism in international peace. Photography, painting, poetry, calligraphy and foreign-language speech contests are being used at this very moment to promote an understanding of Olympism in schools throughout China. [51] Beijing 2008 has provided the impetus for this unique and gargantuan pedagogical endeavour.

This nationwide campaign has wider ambitions linked directly with the education [52] of character [sushi jiaoyu] advocated forcefully by the Ministry of Education in the early 1990s: 'The efforts to implement character education call for comprehensive changes in orientation, functions, content, institutions and approaches. They call for sweeping changes in our understanding of values, talent and the quality of education.' However, by 2005, due to a deeply rooted preference for academic performance and the examination-centred educational systems of schools and universities, character education had not achieved its intended impact. An investigation sponsored by the Ministry of Education and several other ministries and institutions in the same year discovered that the implementation of various policies and practices associated with character education faced serious obstacles, mainly because educational systems had not adapted to government advocacy; the system of college entrance examination, in particular, was a major obstruction. [53]

China is thus taking advantage of the Olympic opportunity to address the lack of success of the 1990s policy. Olympic education with its stress on the all-around development of body, mind and will, which is, in essence, identical with the aim of character education, is presently strongly encouraged in educational institutions – at all levels. With the full support of educational administrators in Beijing and China as a whole, Olympic education with character-training implications has been introduced on an unprecedented scale. These efforts have led IOC President Rogge to state euphorically: 'To bring the Olympic values to the one-fifth world population is indisputably the most exciting thing in the Olympic history.' [54] For Chinese character training, the games' arrival has been a serendipitous outcome – it could result in an opportunistic legacy of earlier intent! The intent is praiseworthy; the impact, of course, remains to be evaluated in the future.

The national Olympic Education Project has been matched by more popular media programmes directed at all sections of society, from the well educated to the less well educated. To popularize the Olympics, CCTV introduced *Beijing 2008*; on its sports channel in 2005 and other local TV stations also transmitted Olympic theme programmes such as '*My 2008*' on Hunan Satellite TV. Numerous newspaper columns have been also devoted to Olympic topics, especially in the *Beijing Evening Daily* and *Competition Daily*. At least one media venture has attracted international audiences and acclaim. The Olympic promotion video *New Beijing, Great Olympics*, directed by the internationally acclaimed Zhang Yimou, won three top awards at the Milan international festival in 2003. [55] When the games are long past, these visual totems will comprise part of a vivid visual legacy bequeathed to future generations.

Potentially another even more commendable legacy of the successful games bid is the promise of greater media openness and less government censorship. It is estimated that 20,000 registered journalists and 30,000 non-registered journalists will travel to Beijing to cover the Olympics by August 2008. The Chinese government has attempted already to live up to its promises, made in 2001, of greater press freedom prior to and during the games. In late 2006, China issued a new set of rules entitled 'Regulations on Reporting Activities in China by Foreign Journalists During the Beijing Olympic Games and the Preparatory Period' [ao yun hui qijian he zhun bei jieduan qaiguo jizhe zai zhongguo baodao huodong de guiding]. According to the new regulations that came into force on 1 January 2007 but will expire 2 months after the games, 'Foreign reporters will be allowed to travel anywhere in the country without prior permission from local authorities.' [56]

Prior to January 2007, these journalists were required to obtain prior approval to travel to certain parts of China and have frequently been refused access. Clearly, the games will have at least a short-term positive influence on media freedom. However, regression to the pre-2007 situation after the games will not seem to the world a progressive action. There is more evidence of present goodwill. On 17 January 2007, the State Council issued 'The Regulations on Government Disclosure of Information [zhengfu xinxi gongkai tiaoli]', which took effect on 1 May 2008. The new regulations make freedom of disclosure a statutory obligation whose implementation can be overseen by courts. [57] The games appear to have played a part in the acceleration of the process of media freedom and transparency of government action. The efficacy of these regulations, as well as their full influence, will only be apparent over time.

These developments – temporary as they are – are important not just for the sake of abstract principles of free speech but also for the practical creation of a Chinese media industry that is professional, credible, respected and able to provide an informed Chinese perspective on domestic and international affairs. With foreign media companies keen to access China's markets (and already supplying content to Chinese media outlets, albeit subject to restrictions), and 'with chat rooms and blogs only a click away, boring "official" media will not be competitive in China, let alone the wider world.' [58] Without doubt, the international media drawn to China by the games will provide at least some impetus for change. Possibly, they could help the Chinese embrace more extensively the universal values of human rights, curb malpractice, reduce corruption and limit exploitation. To be realistic, this is, of course, a tall order given the extent of these indigenous anti-social practices. But in time, and assisted by uncensored international media brought to China by the games,

Chinese society could become more liberal, could press successfully for greater political reform, and could bring about increased respect for human rights. At least this is an Olympic legacy of hope.

Will the introduction of global expertise, new management practices, universalistic education projects, exposure to media freedom, and, not least, the extensive use of English during the games significantly affect Chinese culture? The answer is yes and no! History has demonstrated that Chinese culture has enormous conservative resilience. Buddhism and Christianity were introduced to China at different times, but they were both adjusted to fit the Chinese philosophical, pragmatic and linguistic traditions. Confucianism, which is wholly Chinese, is making a sustained comeback! An overwhelming majority of Chinese feel proud of their long historical heritage and wish not only to retain it but also to revive it. One demonstration of this is the emphasis on Chinese traditional culture via the symbols of the Beijing games. The Olympic emblem, entitled 'Chinese Seal – Dancing Beijing' [zhongguo yin, wudong de Beijing], features a single Chinese character on a traditional red Chinese seal with the words 'Beijing 2008' written in an *eastern-style* brush stroke. The official mascots of the 2008 games are five little children [Fuwa] embodying the natural characteristics of the fish, the panda, the (Tibetan) antelope and the swallow together with the Olympic Flame. Collectively and individually, they carry a Chinese message of friendship, peace and blessing to children all over the world. [59] The opening and closing ceremonies of Beijing 2008, though details and arrangements have not yet been disclosed, will 'emphasise the five-thousand-year splendid Chinese culture', in the words of the world-renowned film director and chief designer of the Beijing 2008 opening and closing ceremonies, Zhang Yimou. He added diplomatically, 'and of course, more importantly, display the Olympic spirit'. [60]

The design of the Beijing Olympic medals revealed on the occasion of the 500-day countdown to the opening of the games is also indicative of the Chinese mindset. The medals are made of gold and jade, marking the first time that jade will be used for medals in Olympic history. With inspiration from 'bi', China's ancient jade piece inscribed with a dragon pattern, the medals symbolize nobility and virtue and are an embodiment of traditional Chinese complementary values of ethics and honour. [61] Jian Xiaoyu, the executive vice-president of the BOCOG, has stated: 'The medals embody Chinese art of style and elegance, but are a harmonious combination of Chinese culture and Olympic culture, making them a vehicle for the dissemination of the Olympic spirit and the Olympic concept of the Games, as well showcasing Chinese culture and arts, at high levels of design and technology.' [62] These fused, talismanic images will conjoin the legacies of historical continuity and change, serving as consecrated repositories of enduring national symbols and modern innovatory principles.

BOCOG has also held various contests for the design of sports venues, for sculpture, for the motto, for the mascots, for the theme songs, and for the choreography of the opening and closing ceremonies: emblematic manifestations of the Olympic spirit and Chinese culture that constitute semaphores of nationalism and globalism that China hopes will become legacies of a triumphal moment in Chinese history.

In short, the Beijing games will be a bonding agent fusing Olympic culture with Chinese culture. Chinese culture changes but its essence remains and furnishes legacies for the China of the future, reinforcing national pride and linking past and present through sustaining memories caught in film, song, dance, art – and, of course, athletic performance.

Improved Consciousness of Environmental Priorities

There is one legacy in the process of construction that is especially compelling to the contemporary world and its concerns – environmental protection. A 'Green Olympics' was one of the three aims put forward by Beijing in its bid. To advance harmony between citizen and environment by means of the games in 2002, the Beijing municipal government introduced the 'Beijing Olympic Ecological Environment Protection Specific Plan' [Beijing aoyunhui shengtai huanjing boahu tebie jihua], and the 'Beijing Olympic Energy Development and Energy Structure Adjustment Specific Plan' [Beijing aoyunhui nengyuan fazhan he nengyuan jiegou tiaozheng tebie jihua]. Beijing set a demanding target: by 2008, the days of air quality were to reach second or above grades for 75–80% of the whole year. Accordingly, a series of measures, including adjusting the industrial economic structure, controlling industrial pollution, suspending or closing seriously contaminated plants, removing the most pollutant plants from within the four ring-road systems, intensifying industrial pollution source management, publicizing clean manufacture and recycling, have been taken. In addition, the emission of waste gases has been reduced and environmental friendly methods adopted in several renovation projects, while about 200 factories threatening potentially empoisoning pollution were moved out of the city completely between 2002 and 2005. [63]

As a consequence, the air quality has improved. However, there is no complacency. Much remains to be done, but there have been achievements. The number of days with air quality reaching second or above grade was 48.4% in 2000, and the figure rose to 64.1% by 2005. Beijing hope to meet its stated Olympic target on time, although some have doubts. [64]

Furthermore, modern digital, network-broadband, environmental, energy, and water-saving technologies are being applied to the construction of venues and the installation of telecommunications and transportation facilities. By the time of the games, electric motor automobiles will be used in the Olympic village and competition venues to reduce air pollution. The physical environment around the venues and approach roads will also be improved aesthetically by landscaping, architectural renovation and other methods. [65]

In spite of these efforts, the environment is certainly still far from ideal. Beijing is faced with severe challenges due to China's rapid economic development. Between 2001 and 2007, the industrial production of China rose by 80%, while the number of privately owned cars increased from 1.5 million in 2001 to 11.49 million in 2006. [66] Worries about pollution are actually growing among ordinary citizens, as years of breakneck growth take their toll on the country's air and water. The Olympic measures seem to many to be Canute-like gestures. The positive legacies to the pessimists appear minimal, but there have been some and the intention is that there will be more. Promises about an improved environment are not mere tokenism. Nevertheless, the challenges should not be underestimated and the people's growing exasperation should not be ignored. A survey entitled '2007 Environmental Protection and People's Livelihood Index' [2007 nian huanjing baohu he renmin shenghuo zhishu] showed that 32.3% of the 9,011 respondents from 29 provinces and autonomous regions were dissatisfied with the local water environment while 20% were not content with the quality of drinking water in public places. [67] The remedial efforts taken must constitute measurable positive environmental legacies both related and unrelated to the games.

One issue illustrates dramatically the extent of the challenges ahead. China appreciates only too well that it has to clean up its major lakes, which are choked with pollution and over-exploited. So great, however, is the problem that the target date for returning them to a pristine condition is 2030! [68] The State Council has recently approved three large, state-funded programmes for research into and the development of environment-friendly water technologies. Paradoxically, in the meantime, in order to ensure that a 'green' Beijing greets the world in August 2008, some 300 million cubic metres of 'emergency' water for the 'Green Olympics' will be pumped from the canals that link the city with neighbouring regions. Self-evidently, 'to draw water from its parched neighbour ... dramatises the environmental blowback from the country's explosive, city-skewed growth'. [69] This will prove to be a negative legacy of the games for areas beyond Beijing. China's shrinking water supplies will increasingly prove a contentious legacy.

In a tripartite strategy to improve environmental conditions in time for the games, to turn the skies bluer, to make the water cleaner and to ensure that the earth is greener, Beijing has recently increased its budget for environmental projects from the initially agreed 45bn yuan (US$5.696bn) to 57bn yuan (US$7.215bn). [70] One of these projects is a monitoring system to check the day's air pollution, and more than 20 test sites have been set up in Beijing. [71] This could be construed as an immediate and subsequent positive legacy of being awarded the games.

Beyond any doubt, much needs to be done about the environment, but as least the Chinese are increasingly aware of this need. The games have accelerated this awareness. Since the establishment in 1994 of the Friends of Nature, China's first non-governmental environmental protection organization, similar organizations have grown rapidly. In Beijing to date, several dozen such groups have sprung up. [72] One of the consequences is that in early 2008 China launched an unexpected crackdown on plastic bags, banning production of ultra-thin bags and forbidding its supermarkets and shops to hand out free carrier bags from 1 June 2008. [73] Given that up to 3 billion plastic bags are used each day in the country and 5 million tonnes

(37 million barrels) of crude oil every year has to be refined to make the plastic for packaging, this act will have an immediate and obvious impact on Chinese sensitivity to the need for environmental protection and the sensible use of resources. The games, without question, have helped the Chinese to become more conscious of the need to balance economic development and environmental protection.

In summary, Beijing 2008 has been a major stimulus to China's efforts to tackle serious environmental problems. Solutions will take years but they are being attempted, and the games have played a part.

A Pool of Talent for the Future

To host the Olympic Games requires thousands of qualified personnel in architecture, marketing, finance, trade, transport, the environment, tourism, sport and many other fields. BOCOG alone has developed more than 30 departments with a total of over 4,000 staff. Some were recruited from the Communist Party, internal government departments, the State Sports Administration, the Foreign Affairs Ministry and Xinhua News Agency. Most of the staff, however, were recruited through public advertisements. In addition, BOCOG has accumulated some 10,000 specialists covering 27 specialties such as marketing, foreign languages, media and law. In short, the successful bid will leave a legacy of professional expertise.

There is certainly more to the legacy than recruiting staff to run the games. There is also domestic training. That legacy had another dimension – personnel in technology, appropriate sciences and administration were selected by BOCOG for study abroad. Competition administrators, for example, were attached to the Athens Organizing Committee for 6 months. [74]

In spite of BOCOG's efforts, since this is the first time China has organized such a leviathan of a sports event as the games, there still remained a shortage of quality sports managers, sports marketing agents, journalists and lawyers who understood international rules and practices, and indeed a plethora of those with other requisite skills. [75] Competence training, therefore, over and beyond that already mentioned, was an early priority. [76] A Coordination Committee for Competence [ren cai xietiao weiyuan hui] was set up in 2005. It provided programmes at four levels. The competence committee trained general officials and staff, sports managers, coaches and referees; special ceremony officials and the like; media, security, service and related industries personnel; and general public hosts and hostesses. [77]

Nor was this all. While BOCOG has taken responsibility for competence training, including training for hundreds of thousands in 11 industries since 2006, individual national sports management centres have also organized courses for their personnel in Olympic Studies and English. Universities have also played a part in training required personnel. In 2006, for example, Beijing Industry and Technology University signed a 'Memorandum on Jointly Cultivating Postgraduate Students Specializing in Applied Computer Science' [lianhe peiyang yingyong jisuanji kexue shuoshi yanjiusheng beiwan lu]. This has been only the tip of the iceberg. And then, there is the crucial matter of communication. A pronounced effort is being made to communicate with guests in the major international languages, English, in particular. Many Beijingers, including taxi drivers, [78] are learning English. Needless to say, the language barrier will not be easily overcome. Misunderstandings could easily occur. One survey has revealed that about half of the foreign journalists consider that language will be a barrier during the games. Nevertheless, to an extent, the games will result in a legacy of increased linguistic competence.

Conclusion

Since 13 July 2001, not a single day in China has gone by without news of, or comments on Beijing 2008. Much is expected of the games in terms of positive legacies – quantitative and qualitative, tangible and intangible. China seeks to use the Olympics to embrace both the national 'village' and the 'global village'. Without doubt, there will be some negative legacies. Perfection is not the customary human condition. As a caveat; this essay constitutes, metaphorically at least, more than a toe in the water but not full immersion. Space precludes the latter. Finally, the Chinese consider, with some justification that they have prepared an astonishing, impressive and successful games with lasting indelible constructive legacies. Is the world prepared for the games that will bring a sea change of Chinese characteristics and Chinese consequences? This is a legacy China keenly awaits!

Notes

[1] Dong Jinxia, 'Prospect of the Legacy of the Beijing Olympic Games: Comparative Perspective'.
[2] 'Rogge Satisfied with Beijing's Preparation for 2008 Olympics', 2006-11-28, CRIENGLISH. com.
[3] Zhonggong Beijing shiwei zhuzhi bu, Beijing shi renshi ju, Beijing shi kexue jishu weiyuan hui, eds. 'Xin Beijing, xin aoyun' zhishi jiangzhuo [Lectures on New Beijing, Great Olympics]. Beijing Chuban she [Beijiing Publishing Press], 2006, 60.
[4] 'Beijing Terminal Breaks Size Barrier', Daily Telegraph, 27 Feb. 2008, 16.
[5] 3S-based refers to a system run by GIS (geographic information system), GPS (global positioning system) and RS (remote sensing) technologies. By the year 2008, the urban railway system is expected to carry 1.8–2.2 billion passengers per year, the capacity of Beijing's buses and trolleys will reach 4.5 billion passengers per year, and the number of vehicles will reach 18,000.
[6] Min Jie and Ding Yimin, 'Diaocha faxian, shijie yulun pubian guanzhu Beijing aoyunhui saishizhi wai de shiqing' [Surveys Show that the World Is Concerned About the Issues Beyond the Olympic Games], Guoji xianqu daobao [International Herald Tribune], 18 Dec. 2006.
[7] 'Aoyun changguan jianshe chengben bu chaoguo 130 yi, niaochao touzi 35yi yuan nei' [The Cost of Constructing the Olympic Venues Will Not Be More Than 13bn Yuan and the Investment for the 'Bird-Nest' Will Be Within 3.5bn Yuan], http://sports.sina.com.cn, accessed 28 Jan. 2008.
[8] The IOC felt that he intended Chinese expenditure on the stadium would set too high demands on future Olympic hosts.
[9] Olympic legacy discussed in Bookworm, Beijing Today, 27 July 2007.

[10] '1417 yi yuan aoyun touzi tisu Beijing jingji' [141.7 Billion Investment Speeds Up Beijing Economy], www.jingbaonet.com, accessed 24 March 2005.

[11] Wang Hailiang, 'Renjun GDP tupo qi qian meiyuan, qunian quanshi renkou zeng 52 wan' [Per Capita GDP Breaks Through the Record of Seven Thousand US Dollars and the Population of the City Increased 520,000 in the Last Year], *Beijing Chenbao* [*Beijing Morning Post*], 22 Jan. 2008.

[12] 'Beijing's Per Capita GDP Expected to Top $8,000 This Year', *China Daily*, 2008-01-21.

[13] 'Beijing tiqian liangnian shixian renjun GDP liuqian meiyuan' [Beijing Fulfilled the Target of GDP US$6,000 per Capita Two Years Ahead], available at http://www.build.com.cn/hangyedongtai/ShowArticle.asp?ArticleID=1596Liu yan; 'Aoyun dacan shui yu zhenggeng' [Who Will Compete for the Olympic Market?], *Beijingxiandai shangbao* [*Beijing Modern Commerce Post*], 4 April 2003.

[14] Beijing shi zhengfu yanjiu shi jingji chu [Economics department of Beijing Municipal Research Office], 'Beijing aoyun jingji de wu da yingxian' [Five major economic impacts of the Beijing Olympics], jinian Beijing shen ao chenggong liang zhou nian zhuanjia luntan [Presentation at the Expert Forum of Celebrating the Two Anniversary of Beijing's Successful Bid to Host the Olympic Games], 25 May 2004.

[15] Liu Dili and Xu Di, 'Hu Angang: wu nian nei beijing renjun shouru jiang dadao shijie gao shouru shuiping' [Within 5 Years the Per Capita Income of Beijingers Will Reach the Level of High Income in the World], *Beijing Qingnian Bao* [*Beijing Youth Daily*], 18 May 2007.

[16] Zhonggong Beijing shiwei zhuzhi bu, Beijing shi renshi ju, Beijing shi kexue jishu weiyuan hui, eds, *Xin Beijing, xin aoyun' zhishi jiangzhuo* [Lectures on New Beijing, Great Olympics], Beijing Chuban she [Beijiing Publishing Press], 2006, 69.

[17] Guojia liyou ju yinxi zhongxin [Information Centre of National Tourism Administration], 'Woguo lvyou ye zai fazhan zhong zhuangda' [Chinese Tourist Industry Has Developed and Expanded Over Time], http://www.cnta.gov.cn/news_detail/newsshow.asp?id, 2006-12-11.

[18] Guojia xinxi zhongxin [National Information Centre], *2007nian zhongguo lvyou hangye niandubaogao* [The 2007 Yearbook of the Tourist Industry in China], zhongjing wang guanli zhongxin [Management Centre of China Economy Network].

[19] 'Travel Market Opens Ahead of Schedule', *China Daily*, 30 Nov. 2004.

[20] Zhonggong Beijing shiwei zhuzhi bu, Beijing shi renshi ju, Beijing shi kexue jishu weiyuan hui, eds (see note 16 above), p. 69.

[21] Yin Lijuan, 'Beijing fangdichan kaifa touzi zhan guding zichan touzi guoban' [Beijing's Property Investment Accounts for More Than Half of the Fixed Asset Investment], http://news.xinhuanet.com/local/2007-01/24/content_5648172.htm, 25 Jan. 2007.

[22] 'Baogao cheng quanguo fangjia jiang changqi shangzhang, Beijing qunian shangzhang jin 20%' [The Report Claims That the House Prices of the Country Will Grow for a Long Time and It Rose Nearly 20 Percent in Beijing], http://www.sina.com.cn, 25 April 2006.

[23] In 2002, BOCOG began sponsorship negotiations with major domestic and international enterprises in such industries as telecommunication, banking, insurance, automobiles, petrifaction, electronic appliances and aviation. In April 2004, a promotion conference was convened in Beijing. BOCOG has signed deals with 11 companies making them official partners at the games, appointed 10 sponsors and 15 exclusive suppliers, and approved more than 300 licensed products.

[24] 'Beijing aoyunhui zanzhu jihua wancheng, yuqi shouru 30 yi meiyuan' [The Sponsorship Plan for the Beijing Games Has Been Implemented and the Input Is Anticipated to Reach US$3bn], *Diyi caijing* [*China's Business Newspaper*], 7 Aug. 2007.

[25] 'Jianshe bu fu buzhang: 2015 nian zhongguo chengzheng renkou jiang tupo ba yi' [The Deputy Minister of the Ministry of Construction: By 2015 the Urban Population in China

Will Be More Than 800 Million], http://news.xinhuanet.com/newscenter/2008-09/03/content_9764679.htm, 3 Aug. 2007.

[26] Guojia tiyu zongju jingji tiyu si [Department of Competitive Sport in the National Sports Administration], 'Ge sheng zizhiqu zhixia shi beizhan 2004 nian 2008 nian aoyunhui diaoyan qingkuang baogao' [Survey Report on the Preparation of Provinces, Autonomous Regions and Municipalities for the 2004 and 2008 Olympic Games], Quangguo jingji tiyu gongzuo huiyi canyuan cailiao zhiyi [One of the Reference Materials for the National Work Conference of Competitive Sport], 2003.

[27] Date from the Economics Department of the State Sports Administration.

[28] Global Financial Observer, 'Yi kuai aoyun jinpai de chengben gusuan: 3000–8000 wang' [The Estimated Cost of an Olympic Gold Medal: 30–80m yuan], *Quanqiu caijing guancha* [Observer], 21 Aug. 2004.

[29] Mutual Funding Insurance for Elite Athletes' Injuries and Disability [youxiu yundongyuan schanchang huzhu baoxian shixing banfa] (tiren zi (20021)), No. 137, 15 April 2002, http://www.sport.gov.cn/n16/n1092/n16879/n17366/37673.html, 18 Sept. 2003.

[30] 'Guojia tiyu zongju juzhang dangzu shuji liupeng zai 2008 nian quanguo tiyu juzhanghuiyi shang zuo zhuti baogao' [The Director and the Party Secretary General of the State Sports Administration, Liu Peng, Makes Keynote Speech at the National Conference of the Sports Directors], tiyu xinxi zhongxin wangzhang bu [Sports Information Net], 7 Jan. 2008.

[31] Ti zong wang, 'Hu jia yan: quanmian lijie choubei aoyun shi 'zhong zhong zhi zhong' hang yi' [Hu Jia Yan: Fully Understanding the Meaning of Preparing the Olympic Games Being the 'Centre of Focus'], http://zhuanti.sports.cn.06tiyujuzhang/xckb/2006-01-20/778709.html.

[32] Li Chungen, 'Beijing aoyun chouban zhuanfang zhi ba: san xiang chuoshi cujin aoyun changguan saihou liyong' [No. 8 of the Series of Interviews for the Office of Preparation for the Beijing Olympic Games: Three Measures to Promote the Post-Games Utilisation of Stadiums and Facilities], *Shanxi Ribao* [*Shanxi Daily*], 28 April 2006.

[33] 'China Encourages People to Exercise More', 2007-10-13 15:11:56 CRIENGLISH.com.

[34] 'Chinese IOC member stresses good manners', 20 March 2006, available at http://www.boston.com/sports/other_sports/olympics/articles/2006/03/20/chinese_ioc_member_stresses_good_manners/.

[35] Ni Han, 'Duihua he zhengliang: aoyunhui jiang tisheng minzhu zixinxin he zihao gang' [Dialogue with He Zhengliang: The Olympic Games Will Boost the National Confidence and Pride], http://news.xinhuanet.com/sports/2007-11/09/content_7041336.htm, 8 Feb. 2007.

[36] The First Opium War erupted in 1840. China lost the war; subsequently, Britain and other Western powers, including the United States, forcibly occupied 'concessions' and gained special commercial privileges. Hong Kong was ceded to Britain in 1842 under the Treaty of Nanking, and in 1898, when the Opium Wars finally ended, Britain executed a 99-year lease of the New Territories, significantly expanding the size of the Hong Kong colony.

[37] Garver, *Foreign Policy of the People's Republic of China*, 20.

[38] Ibid.

[39] 'Liu Qi tan Beijing aoyun "qiantu" zhengqian tongshi yao rang minzhong dedao shihui' [Liu Qi mentioned that the Beijing Games should benefit the citizens while marketing to earn money], http://www.tongxin.org/j-sys-news/page/2005/1116/17331_106.shtml, 16 Nov. 2005.

[40] Du xinda, 'Beijing aoyunhui saihui zhiyuan zhe baoming chao 93wan' [The Applicants for the Competition of the Olympic Games Reach Over 930,000 in Number], *Beijing wanbao* [*Beijing Evening News*], 14 Feb. 2008.

[41] Ernesto Zedillo, 'Current Events: On China's Rise', 05.24.04, http://www.forbes.com/columnists/free_forbes/2004/0524/043.html.

[42] The author Dong Jinxia gave a lecture to the visiting students at Peking University in 2007.

[43] Kevin Bergquist, 'As Olympics Approach, China Still in Flux, Journalist Says', Regents of the University of Michigan, 19 Sept. 2003.

[44] David Gosset, *A Century with Chinese Characteristics*. He successively assumed the posts of Physical Education Officer of Sydney 2000 Olympic Games, Secretary-General of the Australian Olympic Committee, Sports Consultant of the International Olympic Committee (IOC) and Vice-President of the International Basketball Federation (FIBA). He also took part in four Summer Olympic Games, i.e., Los Angeles (1984), Barcelona (1992), Atlanta (1996) and Sydney (2000), and three Winter Olympic Games, i.e., Lillehammer (1994), Nagano (1998) and Salt Lake City (2002).

[45] Zhang Yu, 'Bob Elphinston Becomes the Sports Consultant of BOCOG', http://en.beijing-2008.org/92/71/article211667192.shtml.

[46] Lai zheng, Shen Nan, 'Duowei waiji jianlian zheng zai dailing zhongguo yundongyuan beizhan aoyun' [A Number of Foreign Coaches Are Helping Chinese Athletes to Prepare for the Olympic Games], http://xinhuanet.com/sports/2007-11/09/content_7041336.htm, 8 Nov. 2007.

[47] David Gosset, *A Century with Chinese Characteristics*, 'Whole Nation Countdown for Beijing Olympic Games', 2007-08-29, http://olympics-2008.blogbus.com/logs/7987035.html.

[48] Michael Penn, 'Aoyun: rang shijie chongxin renshi "zhongguo" pingpai' [The Olympic Games: Let the World Know 'China' Brand], *Fortune China*, no. 1, (2008): 80–1.

[49] Huang Yong, 'Zhongguo jiang zai gengduo de xuexiao zhong kaizhan aolinpike jiaoyu' [China Will Promote Olympic Education in More Schools], http://www.xinhuanet.com, 18 Sept. 2007.

[50] 'Beijing 2008: Games of Education, Enlightenment', http://english.peopledaily.com.cn/90001/90779/90867/6342261.html, 21 Jan. 2008 10:44 Xinhua.

[51] 'IOC Chief Says Daily Pollution Tests for Beijing Games', New York, Reuters News Service, 5 Nov. 2007. For example, *Beijing aoyunhui zhong xuesheng duben* [*Textbook of the Beijing Olympic Games for the Middle School Students*], *Beijing aoyunhui xiao xuesheng duben* [*Textbook of the Beijing Olympic Games for Primary School Students*] and *aoyun zhishi guatu* [*Illustrative Books of Olympic Knowledge*] have been published. Beijing aoyunhui he canaohui jiexiang wu zhengji sheji dasai [Competition for the Design of the Mascots for Both the Summer Games and Paralympics Games], aolinpike kouhao zhengji huodong [Competitions for the Olympic Motto], Beijing 2008 nian aoyunhui diaosu sheji bisai [Competition for Sculpture Designs for Beijing 2008 Olympics], and many others have been organized.

[52] Li Lan Qing, *Education for 1.3 Billion – Former Chinese Vice Premier Li Lan Qing on 10 Years of Education Reform and Development*, Foreign Language Teaching and Research Press, 2004.

[53] 'Sushi jiaoyu sitong diaoyan: gaokao ye nan tixian sushi jiaoyu yaoqiu' [Institutional Survey of Character Education: the College Entrance Examination is Hard to Embody the Requirement of Character Education], http://www.jyb.com.cn/ks/gk/gksx/t20061110_48034.htm, 1 Dec. 2006.

[54] Li Guanyun, 'Aoyunhui, shi zhongguo yu shijie jianshe xing duihua de cuihuaji' [The Olympic Games Are the Catalyst for the Constructive Dialogue Between China and the World], 21 shiji jingji baodao [21st Economic Report], 8 Aug. 2007.

[55] http://english.people.com.cn/200311/13/eng20031113_128200.shtml.

[56] Kirsten Sparre, 'China Relaxes Rules on Foreign Reporters in the Run-Up to the Olympics', 22 Dec. 2006, http://www.playthegame.org/News/Up%20To%20Date/China_relaxes_rules_on_foreign_reporters_in_the_run_up_to_the_Olympics.aspx.

[57] 'Open Government: A Step Forward, But with Sideways Shuffles Too', *China Development Brief*, 2007-05-24.

[58] 'Editorial: Press Freedom Is Good News for Business', http://www.chinadevelopmentbrief.com/node/905, 17 Dec. 2006.

[59] 'The Official Mascots of the Beijing 2008 Olympic Games', http://en.beijing2008.com/80/05/article211990580.shtml.

[60] 'Zhang yimou: kaimushi dianhuo fangan chubu queding, kaimushi yu niaochao tianren heyi' [Zhang Yimou: The Programme for the Opening Ceremony Is Preliminarily Fixed and the Ceremony Will Be in Harmony with the 'Bird-Nest'], www.beijing2008.cn, 9 Aug. 2007.

[61] 'Beijing 2008: aoyun jiangpai liangxiang' (Beijing 2008: Olympic Medals Unveiled), 27 March 2007.

[62] Ibid.

[63] Zhu Ying,' Wei 'lvse aoyun' ranglu, Beijing 40 jia gongchang qianchu sihuan' [40 Factories in Beijing Moved Out of the 4th Ring Road for the Requirement of the Green Olympics], http://www.chinanews.com.cn, 30 Oct. 2002.

[64] Zeng Yun, 'Beijing kongqi zhiliang qi nian gaishan, zhuyao wuran wu nongdu xiajian' [The Air Quality in Beijing Has Improved for Seven Successive Years and the concentration of Infectants Has Decreased], *Beijing Ribao* [*Beijing Daily*], 5 Sept. 2005.

[65] 'Olympic Projects Progress on Course', beijing2008.com, 8 Dec. 2006, http://www.china.org.cn/english/sports/191730.htm.

[66] '2007–2010 nian zhongguo qiche fuwu ye shichang yuce yu touzi qianjing fenxi baogao' [Report on the Forecast of the Automobile Service Market and Its Investment Prospect Between 2007 and 2010], http://www.chinaccm.com/06/0612/061202/news/20080307/095233.asp, 8 Nov. 2007.

[67] 'China to Invest Billions to Remedy Water Pollution. Updated: 2008-01-14 From: CRIENGLISH.com.

[68] Emma Graham-Harrison, 'China Sets 2030 Target to Clean Up Lakes', Reuters News Service, Planet Ark.

[69] 'China to Invest Billions to Remedy Water Pollution', CRIENGLISH.com, 2008-01-14; Chris Buckley,' Beijing Olympic Water Scheme Drains Parched Farmers', Reuters News Service, Planet Ark.

[70] 'Beijing aoyunhui touru 300 yi yuan yongyu xinxi hua jianshe' [The Beijing Games Invest 30 Billion Yuan for Information Construction], *Diyi caijing ribao* [*China Business Newspaper*], 25 Jan. 2007.

[71] Shi Xi, 'Beijing: xuejian xinshi cheliang ceshi kongqi zhiliang' [Beijing: Reducing the Number of Vehicles on the Road and Testing the Air Quality], *Beijing qingnian bao* [*Beijing Youth Daily*], 10 Aug. 2007.

[72] 'Huanbao NGO jieshao, zhongguo huanbao NGO – cunzai dailai gaibian' [NGO of Environmental Protection Introduction: China's NGO for environmental protection – Existence Leads to Changes], http://www.bjee.org.cn/news/index.php?ID=17119, 29 March 2007.

[73] 'Liu yue 1 ri qi quanguo jingzhi mianfei tigong suliao gouwu dai' [From 1 June, Providing Plastic Bags Will Be Banned], http://www.chinanews.com.cn, 8 Jan. 2008.

[74] www.chinatradenews.com.cn. Cite sources on pool of talent hired by BOCOG; Yuan Tiecheng, 'Dapi zhongguo guanyuan yi aoyun mingyi chuguo "kaocha"' [A Number of Chinese Officials Go Abroad to 'Review' in the Name of the Olympic Games], *Zhongguo qingnian bao* [*China Youth Daily*], 31 Aug. 2004.
Cite sources on those BOCOG programs.

[75] Yang yunsheng, 'Aoyun cuisheng duozhong xin zhiye' [The Olympics Create Many New Occupations], *Jingbao* [*Competition Post*] 29 Aug. 2005.

[76] 'Beijing aoyun rencai "jiao ke", daibiao jianyi quanmian qidong peixun gongcheng' [The Beijing Olympics Are Short of Talent. Delegations Propose to Start a General Training Project], http://news.xinhuanet.com/newscenter/2005-03/06/content_2659524.htm.

[77] Ibid.

[78] Taxi drivers must be able to speak the 100 most frequently used English sentences for taxi services. Thus, they have to pass an English test to get a taxi licence.

References

Jinxia, Dong. *Women, Sport and Society in New China*. London: Cass, 2003.

Fortune China, no. 1, (2008): 80–1.

Garver, John W. *Foreign Policy of the People's Republic of China*. Englewood Cliffs, NJ: Prentice-Hall, 1993.

Li Lan Qing. *Education for 1.3 Billion – Former Chinese Vice Premier Li LanQing on 10 Years of Education Reform and Development*. Beijing: Foreign Language Teaching and Research Press, 2004.

Quangguo jingji tiyu gongzuo huiyi canyuan cailiao zhiyi [One of the Reference Materials for the National Work Conference of Competitive Sport], 2003.

Regents of the University of Michigan, 19 Sept. 2003.

Zhonggong Beijing shiwei zhuzhi bu, Beijing shi renshi ju, Beijing shi kexue jishu weiyuan hui, eds. 'xin Beijing, xin aoyun' zhishi jiangzhuo [Lectures on New Beijing, Great Olympics], Beijing: Beijing Chuban she [Beijing Publishing Press], 2006.

Olympic Legacies in the IOC's 'Celebrate Humanity' Campaign: Ancient or Modern?

Joseph Maguire, Sarah Barnard, Katie Butler and Peter Golding

While it is evident that the modern Olympics is a global event that acts as a carrier of cultural meanings that are available to international audiences and markets, what is less clear is the status of such meanings. Though the heritage of the Olympics is claimed to be derived from the ancient world, in fact contemporary legacies are very modern. Here, attention is paid both to the broader and more specific aspects of these legacies. For instance, the development of the modern Olympic games is bound up in broader globalization and sportization processes. [1] As such, the Olympics and its related movement have reinforced and reflected both the diminishing of contrasts and the increased varieties of body cultures available to different peoples. Bound up in sportization processes that are characterized by a series of phases and structured processes, the modern games have produced an Olympic legacy that expresses what Heinilä termed 'total sport'. [2]

More specifically, the meanings associated with the modern Olympics, and the legacy thereby attached, are re-represented, distributed, and marketed by a media-sport complex predicated less on a legacy expressed through *arete* and much more on a consumption ethos. To demonstrate the validity of this claim, the initial formulation, development and use of the 'Celebrate Humanity' programme is investigated. This programme and the wider Olympic movement highlight the basic contradiction between the ideals of 'Olympism' and the realities of the modern Olympics in practice. One of the legacies of the modern games is consumption. Indeed, the legacy 'message' becomes embedded in a broader process of commerce whereby the media/marketing/advertising/corporate nexus is concerned less with the heritage values underpinning Olympism per se and more with how such values can help build markets, construct and enhance brand awareness, and create 'glocal' consumers/identities.

Globalization, Sportization and Olympic Legacies

The emergence of the modern Olympics and its subsequent diffusion worldwide are bound up in the more recent phases of globalization processes. Its formation in 1896 can arguably be located within the third phase of sportization processes and the more general 'take-off' phase of globalization. The subsequent diffusion of Olympic ideology, its movement and the games during the twentieth century both reflects and has reinforced the fourth and fifth sportization phases. [3] The Olympic movement and the games were and are shaped by wider global flows of people, finance, media images, ideologies and technologies that permeated these phases. Taken as a whole, the Olympic movement, and the International Olympic Committee (IOC) in particular, can be seen as symptomatic of the emergence of transnational movements more generally. The IOC can thus be viewed as a transnational organization – with an ideology that purports to be internationalist and have global appeal and relevance.

Yet, the Olympic movement as a whole, and the games more particularly, did, and continue to, as part of these broader sportization and globalization processes, reflect Western values, ideologies and corporate activities – and, as such, have led to greater homogeneity. For some, one distinct legacy of the Olympics has been to reinforce Western cultural imperialism. [4] In fact, de Coubertin himself was seemingly well aware of the civilizational struggles that were at stake when he wrote, in 1931, on this issue of athletic colonization:

> If one wishes to extend to natives in colonized countries what we will boldly call the benefits of 'athletic civilization', they must be made to enter into the broad athletic system with codified regulations and comparative results, which is the necessary basis of that civilization. More than one colonizing country balks at this decisive step. Yet we are going to have to reach a decision, or the natives will end up organizing on their own. After all, perhaps they would not be any the worse off that way, but perhaps so for those who direct them. [5]

Its competitive structure has subsequently been standardized globally and accepted universally – the games, summer and winter, are global media events that cut across cultures and as such can be said to form a 'global idiom'. Yet and seemingly paradoxically, this movement has led to new varieties of meanings and activities associated with the experience of global sport. Tracing the changes and continuities since its establishing at the 1896 Athens games, the Olympic movement can thus be seen to have both reinforced and reflected broader global sport processes. Further exploration of this legacy is required. In this regard, it would be worthwhile assessing the degree to which the Olympic legacy, through its ideology, content, organization, production and consumption, has contributed to several interlocking processes. These include the following:

1. The emergence and diffusion of achievement sport and the Olympic Games have ensured the decline of both Western and non-Occidental folk body cultures. Irrespective of time period or society, the impact of achievement sport and the Olympic games has been to marginalize indigenous games. While such folk practices have not disappeared, and may, in some societies, be undergoing some revival, the overall trend is for folk games to become residual features of body cultures. [6]
2. Given that modern sport was devised by and for men, we should not be surprised that global sport reflects, through to the present day, a gendered ideology and content. Power at the IOC remains the preserve of men. [7]
3. Concomitant with the globalization of modern achievement sport and the Olympic movement, we have seen the development of a set of practices for schooling the body. Here it is possible to trace the shifts from nineteenth and early twentieth century forms of 'drill', European forms of gymnastics and dance, physical training, and physical education, through to late twentieth-century trends such as human movement studies, sports science, and kinesiological studies. [8] The state, through its compulsory schooling policies, has thus played an active role in the reinforcement of global sport and the Olympic games.
4. From its inception through to its high-tech manifestations of the present day, achievement sport and the Olympic games have reflected and reinforced the medicalization, scientization and rationalization of human expressiveness.

The athlete has increasingly been seen as an enhanced, efficient machine, adhering to a sport ethic associated with the 'ultimate' performance. The logic at work may well be leading the athlete towards genetic modification and a cyborg coexistence. [9]

5. The impact of global sport and the Olympic games has not only been on the habits of people of different societies, but also on the habitats in which they live. Over the long term, as sport practices move from small to large scale, from low intensity to high intensity forms, and from 'natural' materials to synthetics, the athlete, spectator, viewer and employers become consumers of scarce resources and threats to the environment. The need to proclaim the Sydney Olympics as a 'green games' and the marketing of the Beijing games along similar lines, highlight the issues of sustainability that confront us now, and – if present trends continue – will plague us in the future. [10]

6. The global diffusion of sport has reflected the balance of power within and between nations. Up to the present day, the sport power elite have not only maintained their grip on power, but have also been joined by a range of representatives from big business. These include media moguls, marketing personnel and the representatives of transnational corporations (TNCs). [11] Demands for democratic control, transparency and accountability in decision-making within the International Olympic Committee (IOC) remain unfulfilled.

7. Both in the making and ongoing formation of global sport and the Olympic games, notwithstanding the hosting of the Beijing Olympics, we have witnessed the reinforcement and enhancement of global inequalities within the West and between the West and non-Occidental societies. Here, questions of cultural power and civilizational struggles are to the fore. [12]

These are some of the interlocking, structured processes through which people experience sport and which help to explain why the modern sporting world and global body cultures emerged in the way they did. An emphasis on achievement striving was closely connected to and reinforced by a quest for excellence embodied in the notion of the 'ultimate performance'. The quest for the ultimate performance rests on what might be termed the myth of the *superman* – a performance so great that it eclipses the efforts of 'mere mortals'. Though varying in intensity across time and different societies, this subculture is also marked by rationalization and scientization processes. The most efficient and technically competent display has to be developed that would produce the 'optimal performance'. Through the sports industrial complex, various national sports bodies seek Olympic success: the logic of *citius, altius, fortius* requires it.

Exploration of these interlocking trends would also need to be conducted in conjunction with an investigation of the degree to which the primary legacy of the Olympics, as part of broader globalization processes, is to extend, or contract, emotional identification between members of different societies – not within the Olympic village but within the global village at large. [13] Certainly, the IOC claim that the primary legacy of Olympic games is to build such identification, and through the Celebrate Humanity campaign it is purported to find expression. But is this the case?

Celebrate a Legacy of Humanity or Consumption?

This paper sets out to examine how exponents of global mega-sport events, while claiming that they foster and develop unity, friendship and cosmopolitan identities, are in fact increasingly concerned more with our identities as consumers. In this connection we focus on the seemingly contradictory nature and problematic vision of the IOC's 'Celebrate Humanity' campaign. While this paper represents an initial, largely exploratory, and preliminary analysis of this campaign, it is part of a wider project examining the Athens Olympics and global sport. [14] Thus, though global sport is commonly associated with the nation and is beset by the fault lines of gender, racism and geopolitics, claims are also made as to the positive role that sport plays in building social capital and international understanding. On the one hand, and reinforcing the views of proponents of the sports-industrial complex, global sport is viewed as a thoroughly progressive and liberating phenomenon that opens up the potential for greater human contact, dialogue and friendship. Global sport events, such as those planned for the 2008 Beijing Olympics, are said to promote the spread of human rights and democracy, improve intercultural understanding, and, as in the IOC's slogan, 'Celebrate Humanity'.

In contrast to such sentiments, the present structure of global sport can also be seen as symptomatic of a new, consumer-dominated phase of Western capitalism. As such, global consumer sport imposes its cultural products on vulnerable communities across the globe. One consequence of this imposition is the eradication of cultural difference – identities are constructed through consumption. The West dominates the economic, technological, political and knowledge resources and controls the levers of power of global sport. Global sport is thus tied to the opening up of new markets, including that of labour, and the commodification of cultures – its consumption is a hallmark of late capitalism in the early twenty-first century. [15]

These contradictions can be highlighted with reference to how the campaign Celebrate Humanity was linked to the Athens Olympic Games and the comments made by Jacques Rogge, IOC president, are particularly revealing when he observed:

> 365 days a year, the true spirit of the Games is demonstrated by our Worldwide Corporate Sponsors. Because our athletes can't run, jump or swim until they are fed, housed and trained. For that, we – and everyone who loves the Games – owe them our deepest gratitude. [16]

Such comments may be no surprise to academics critical of the IOC, but it is worth noting the emphasis placed by Rogge on the role of private enterprise, it is the Olympic Partner (TOP) Programme sponsors that count. This is the context in which to understand Celebrate Humanity. Despite Rogge's silence regarding the role of public investment, Greek and other European Union (EU) taxpayers spent $300m helping to run the games, nearly $1.5b keeping them secure, and some $7b preparing facilities for them. Indeed, the development of the London 2012 Olympic Games has already run into cost escalation, with public monies being drawn away from arts budgets and from grass-roots sports – schemes which directly improve the health of the nation and which were the claimed legacy benefits of the London bid.

Clearly, such publicity does not help the IOC. So what, then, does suit the marketing department of the IOC? Throughout the 1990s, 'harnessing and better understanding the power of the Olympic brand became an increasing focus for the IOC.' [17] Developed in this climate and against the backdrop of the Salt Lake City crisis, Celebrate Humanity was launched in New York in June 2000. Though ostensibly highlighting the specific non-commercial qualities and ideals associated with the games, what Michael Payne, then head of marketing for the IOC, called, its 'Olympic DNA', Celebrate Humanity was conceived in its marketing department and was part of a broader attempt to 'better understand the *consumer's* true perception of the Olympic brand'. [18] It is significant that the campaign was developed within the IOC's marketing department (rather than, say, its educational section), in order to attract and maintain the interest of sponsors, and provide the 'metaphoric empty flask' that the Olympics has come to represent. [19] Here, we seek, then, to trace the emergence and development of the campaign, and we do so with reference to IOC documents and interviews with personnel from TOP sponsors and representatives from their advertising agencies.

How, then, can Celebrate Humanity be understood? Here, we focus on how the values highlighted in the Celebrate Humanity campaign, far from acting as a counterbalance to 'the international commercial sport entertainment complex', play a more subtle and invidious role. [20] Not only do the campaign's explicit values go hand-in-hand with the development of Olympism as a brand sold to sponsors and the wider public, but they also allow TOP sponsors to reposition themselves and ensure that their brands can compete globally. [21] This analysis is informed by critical political economy and process sociology. [22] We make sense of the campaign by reference to how the Olympic Games have become incorporated into the media-sport complex 'circuits of promotion' and the mechanisms of marketing, advertising and sponsorship through which Celebrate Humanity itself was framed and experienced. [23] In addition, in order to make sense of the IOC's rationale that underpins the campaign, we refer to research on brands in business studies. [24]

Drawing on these various strands, our argument is that Celebrate Humanity is an exercise in enhancing brand equity – for the benefit of the IOC and TOP sponsors. It is best understood as celebrating consumers, not humanity. Our analysis suggests that the IOC, while claiming to promote the ideals of Olympism, has accommodated itself to commercial pressures to ensure the success of the games, thereby reinforcing capitalist social relations and practices. [25] Thus, the Celebrate Humanity campaign is an attempt to enhance the brand rather then promote the values of Olympism per se. However, the enhancement of the brand is linked specifically to the particular qualities and values for which the Olympics is perceived to stand. In relation to this point, it has been argued that

> the overt commercialism of the Olympics has come at a price: it has threatened a legitimation crisis for the Olympic movement and its buttressing Olympic ideals. The problem then, for Olympic officials, is not so much how to *maximize profit* but rather how to *recapture mystique*. [26]

This recapturing of 'mystique' is something that the IOC's 'Celebrate Humanity' campaign seeks to address. Our approach, then, shares some common ground with several writers in that we view, as noted, Celebrate Humanity as part of the media-sport complex, embedded in 'circuits of promotion', and as part of the broader reshaping of global sport. [27] Yet, our critique is not of the contemporary need to market 'respectable human values'. This may be unavoidable and thus campaigns, such as that launched by the UN regarding development through sport, that promote humanitarian values are important. In addition, while our critique is fairly bleak, we do not quite return to the vision offered by exponents of the Frankfurt school. That is, we do not wish to give up on the need to show how the Olympics and global sport could serve humanitarian purposes. [28] However, we see that the market/consumer research conducted by the IOC to identify core values was designed to ensure that the IOC and TOP sponsors could more effectively compete as global brands, and not to promote humanitarian values per se. Let us consider this in more detail.

Methods and Olympic marketing research

Attention here focuses on the details of IOC-commissioned market research undertaken over the last two decades: use is made of information provided by the IOC in internal documentation and IOC publications, such as *Olympic Marketing Matters*, and interviews with various personnel involved in IOC marketing research and the development of the Olympic brand. We will also offer an analysis of the IOC's general research conception and design. In addition, we look at how the research that has been conducted has been used to legitimize corporate positioning, reflects the increased dependency upon corporate sponsorship, and has led to the development of Olympism as an international brand in the 'Celebrate Humanity' campaign. The relationship between IOC research and the broad marketing strategy of the Olympic brand is a close one. As stated in the *Olympic Marketing Fact File*,

> As part of its commitment to its commercial partners and to better understand the dynamics of the marketplace and the effectiveness of an Olympic Sponsorship as a marketing tool, the IOC and its marketing partners have commissioned an extensive programme of research over the last ten years. [29]

In fact, the IOC has been involved in extensive marketing research since 1985. The research, while looking specifically at the attitudes and perceptions of the general public, tends to wholly understand the participants in terms of consumers and thus seeks to generate data that are used to support Olympic partners and make the Olympic brand more attractive to potential sponsors and audiences. [30] However, the Olympic ideals promoted within the Olympic branding exercise itself are seemingly at odds with this interpretation of the public. Thus, a more fitting tag line for the marketing campaign could be, as noted, 'Celebrate Consumers', rather than 'Celebrate Humanity', as this is the overwhelming framework within which IOC-commissioned research and the subsequent marketing campaign was developed.

During the late 1990s, the IOC placed a greater emphasis on the utilization of attitudes and perceptions that people have of the Olympic movement in order to develop the Olympic brand. This was mainly due to the influence of Terrence Burns, then senior vice-president of Meridian Management SA (who previously worked for Delta Airlines, sponsors of the 1996 Atlanta Games, and currently president and chief executive officer of Helios Partners, Inc.), who was hired by the IOC marketing arm in 1996 precisely because of his strong marketing background. He thought it was crucial to explore the recognition of the Olympic brand and the attitudes and perceptions of the Olympic movement in order to update the Olympic Charter for the modern world. In order to identify these and develop an effective marketing plan, the IOC commissioned a series of studies to be conducted by an a variety of global market research agencies – initially, they turned to Sponsorship Research International (SRi), but they also used Meridian Management SA (of which the IOC had 25% ownership, 100% since 2004), Edgar Dunn & Co, Sports Marketing Surveys (SMS), Ipsos Reid, and, more recently, Sponsorship Intelligence.

The agencies are chosen by tender and the research conducted is benchmarked to other organizations' sports marketing research. As outlined above, the desire to develop Olympic marketing research was directly linked to the increased importance of the Olympic Sponsorship programme to the success of the movement. As noted in *Olympic Marketing Matters*, 'The research provides insight into how a company's business plan can be assisted by a partnership featuring these unique qualities and images. [...] The IOC Marketing Department supports its Partner's sponsorship with global research and studies.' [31] Specifically, in 1998, the IOC commissioned an Olympic brand and image research project to help develop a strategic marketing plan that uses the core values of Olympism as its foundation. Meridian Management SA (now IOC Television and Marketing Services) and Edgar Dunn & Company conducted over 5,500 interviews with participants in 11 countries and 250 in-depth interviews with members of the Olympic family, sponsors and broadcasters. This project was used as a springboard for further research on the Olympic brand/image conducted in 2000, 2002, 2004 and 2006.

There are, however, several problems that can be detected with such research. Firstly, the countries chosen for the research activity always include the USA, as this is where most corporate sponsors are based; future host countries; and countries that represent the other major markets in the world (Head of Marketing Strategy, IOC Television and Marketing Services; interviews conducted 23–24 October 2006). In the 2004 research, the countries chosen accounted for one-third of the world population. However, as choices are based upon economic marketability, huge regions of the world are ignored, most notably the African nations. Clearly, the IOC argues that the economic objectives of the research determine how the research is conducted; thus, the IOC is primarily interested in participants in developed countries who are already well-versed consumers of global products and brands. Yet, in failing to investigate how African or Middle Eastern countries interpret the attributes and values of the Olympic Movement, the IOC seems to be celebrating only particular parts of humanity.

Secondly, while the participants are chosen randomly by the research agencies and are representative of the wider population (or bodies of consumers) of those countries, the nature of the questions asked is slanted towards positive interpretations: when respondents are asked to select which phrase best describes how they perceive the Olympic Games, all of them are to varying degrees positive statements. [32] Thus, the participants are not given the opportunity for negative or even contradictory responses, as the questions are closed. More details of the methodology and data generated by the IOC's research would be useful for this analysis, but the IOC does not permit public access to the research, and only sanitized 'snippets' are available in the public domain. Indeed, when questioned about the variety of responses and the possibility of contradictory interpretations of Olympic attributes, the head of marketing strategy for IOC Television and Marketing Services stated that 'contradictory responses don't come into it' (head of marketing strategy, IOC Television and Marketing Services; interviews conducted 23–24 October 2006); instead, the data generated by the research merely allocate strength of agreement to predefined statements. Obviously, more access to the research may uncover more varied interpretations by respondents than acknowledged by the IOC publicly, particularly in the qualitative research conducted, but one should be clear of the IOC's objectives. The marketing research is about building the Olympic brand and maintaining relationships with sponsors, so it is unlikely that a more nuanced and complex discussion of the Olympic image will be conducted publicly by the IOC marketing department – save for internal consumption.

Thirdly, the level of involvement of the TOP sponsors in the marketing research itself raises some issues. Not only is the overall research premise based upon the desire to strengthen the Olympic brand to offer 'a better investment for sponsors' (head of marketing strategy, IOC Television and Marketing Services; interviews conducted 23–24 October 2006), but the research agencies also liase, with regard to the form and content of the research, with the sponsors, who may suggest that particular questions be added to the interview schedule to investigate participants' support for the Olympic sponsors. Representatives from the IOC television and marketing services department visit sponsors annually to present the findings of the research and receive feedback. Not only is the research important to the TOP sponsors, but results are also disseminated widely to the National Olympic Committees (NOCs) and Organizing Committees for the Olympic Games (OCOGs) to be incorporated into the annual planning of the whole Olympic family. A clear example of the importance to the IOC of the marketing research conducted is evident in its relationship to the IOC's flagship marketing campaign, 'Celebrate Humanity'. Let us examine this more closely.

The Olympic Brand and How Global Brands Compete

The aim of branding is for the company or product to accumulate symbolic meaning through various associations, which serve to differentiate the brand from competitors who are essentially providing very similar products or services. [33] Synergies are created between brand identity, the corporation and the media, which eventually affect consumer spending habits. [34] The symbolic and global nature of branding and marketing means that 'the challenge of truly international brands therefore is to stand for something that appeals to "all" people, while incorporating opportunities to extend the brand for cultural niche markets.' [35] The media facilitate the communication of international brands in the global marketplace, and sport business is an important arena in which this process takes place.

Sport and business have always had a close relationship. However, this relationship has flourished within the media-sport complex, fostering the now crucial role that sport branding and marketing play in the success of global sporting events such as the Olympics. The symbiotic relationship of media/sport/business does not, however, exist without drawbacks; the success of a brand such as the Olympics is dependent upon the integrity of the event and the wider organization. The integrity of the Olympic movement has recently come under criticism for questionable dealings and overtly commercial activities. It is the commercial nature of global sporting events and the IOC's desire to negate, at least symbolically, the commercial nature of the Olympic enterprise that makes this particular campaign an interesting case for analysis. How does what is essentially a marketing campaign, promote the 'core values' of the Olympic movement – hope, dreams and inspiration, friendship and fair play, and international understanding?

The contradictions apparent in the Celebrate Humanity campaign can be said to epitomize the seemingly paradoxical relationship between the ideals of 'Olympism' and the realities of the modern Olympics in practice. The IOC purports to promote a message of internationalism, cosmopolitanism, environmentalism and 'fair play'. [36] To achieve this, IOC officials defend their involvement with commercial interests on pragmatic grounds. Without such commercial support, officials argue, their movement would not achieve its goals of disseminating the ideals of Olympism. However, the development of the TOP programme and the policing of ambush advertising demonstrate the IOC's current take on commercial activity. Thus, 'the Olympic movement has sought to control commercialization on its own terms' [37] and purportedly to maintain the 'integrity' of the Olympic brand in order to offer 'value' to TOP sponsors. Despite this desire to exert control over the level of overt business involvement, the adoption of a commercial strategy in the 1980s resulted in the Olympic 'message' becoming embedded in a broader process of commerce. [38] That is, the media / marketing / advertising / corporate nexus is concerned less with the IOC message, and more with building markets, constructing brand awareness and creating local and globalized consumers and identities. [39] This much is fairly well established. Here, however, we wish to extend the analysis and suggest that the assumptions underpinning the marketing of the Olympic brand in general and Celebrate Humanity in particular are based on a business-oriented rationale about how global brands compete. While there are apparent contradictions within the Celebrate Humanity campaign between the ideals celebrated and commercial realities, for those involved there is no paradox. Celebrate Humanity is good business practice. Let us explain.

'Celebrate Humanity' was the first fully global marketing campaign to attempt to communicate the values embodied within the Olympic movement. The campaign was devised as a result of the Olympic brand/image research outlined above. The IOC's decision-making with regard to the campaign coincided with the Salt Lake City crisis, though Payne, then IOC Marketing Director, is keen to dismiss accusations that the IOC was trying to advertise its way out of the crisis. [40] The context of the campaigns development is, however, crucial to understanding the motivation behind the campaign and to measure its subsequent success or failure. Payne's desire to reassert Olympism as a truly global brand capable of capturing the lucrative sports sponsorship market and ensure the success of the Olympic movement was apparently not greeted initially with open arms by the IOC: 'I had my hands full convincing the IOC about the principle of the campaign to begin with.' [41]

The brand and image research undertaken, as noted, in 1998 and 1999, formed the foundation of the key themes for the campaign. Terrence Burns of Meridian Management SA, worked on the data generated by focusing on the 30 or so core perceptions or attributes identified in relation to the Olympics. [42] These attributes were then organised into 'communication platforms' or the core messages of the Olympic image that required conceptualizing into a marketing campaign. The core messages devised were as follows:

- *Hope*: 'The Olympic Games offer hope for a better world, using sport competition for all without discrimination as an example and a lesson.'
- *Dreams and Inspiration*: 'The Olympic Games provide inspiration to achieve personal dreams through the lessons of the athletes' striving, sacrifice and determination.'
- *Friendship and Fair Play*: 'The Olympic Games provide tangible examples of how humanity can overcome political, economic, religious and racial prejudices through the values inherent in sport.'
- *Joy in effort*: 'The Olympic Games celebrate participation and the universal joy in doing one's best, regardless of the outcome.' [43]

Six advertising agencies were invited by the IOC to pitch for the account, lured not by the promise of huge financial rewards, but by the 'considerable prestige' that would go along with winning the account. [44] The pressure was on to develop a campaign that communicated the core values that provide the foundation of the Olympic image message, which would also translate internationally in the global market. Initial formulations by the winning advertising agency TBWA/Chiat Day, based upon the tag line 'Go Humans', while headed in the right direction, was deemed too American by Payne. Following this, many months were spent in devising the ultimately successful 'Celebrate Humanity' tag line for the campaign. The American actor, Robin Williams, was approached by the advertising agency to do the voice-over for the campaign. As he had never done advertising voice-over work before, it is implied by Payne that he undertook the work because of the special nature of the campaign itself. [45]

The Celebrate Humanity campaign was launched in New York in January 2000 prior to the Sydney games later that year. The campaign included six broadcast spots, eight radio spots and a series of print advertisements, the contents of which will be described and analysed in more detail below. Apparently, 'even the most cynical commentators were moved' [46] by the campaign, and media companies around the world ran the advertisements for free as public service announcements worth an estimated total of $120m. CNN international aired the campaign around the world an estimated 6,500 times, and the print advertisements appeared in over 30 publications and were carried by over 30 airlines. [47] The deemed success led to the continuation of the campaign in Salt Lake 2002, Athens 2004 and Torino 2006, updating and revising the original campaign each time.

In considering developments in global brand marketing, two main trends stand out. First, a shift to a more 'glocalized' brand strategy and, second, a growing sensitivity to the need to manage the global characteristics of the brands of TNCs. With regard to the first trend, it is clear that hand in hand with the intensification of globalization processes over the past two decades, TNCs have sought to grow by selling standardized products across the globe. The American National Football League is a case in point. [48] The development of the TOP programme can also be understood in this way. The Olympic Games thus provide a globalized and globalizing arena in which TNCs linked to the TOP programme can advertise and market their brands. The use of universal messages, combined with local appeal, is the prevailing mantra. Yet, such corporate links have not remained unchanged.

Over time, both the IOC and TNCs have modified their strategies – for their own and mutual benefit. TNCs have sought to 'glocalize' their marketing strategies, customize product features, and develop selling techniques tailored to local tastes and customs. The IOC's Celebrate Humanity campaign is no exception. In its marketing brief for the 2004 campaign linked to the Athens Olympics, the IOC noted that the television component highlights how the 'Olympic experience touches all people and that the Olympic ideals are universal'. Similarly, the print component of Celebrate Humanity, while containing personal testimonials by global celebrities, also 'reflects a universal truth about the Olympic spirit'. [49] Significantly, however, the marketing brief also contains a section, 'how to localize the announcements', which notes that each 'broadcaster also has the option to customize either "Heart" or "Play" for their specific market by replacing the global spokesperson with a local/regional celebrity that represents the same message as the global celebrity.' This glocalization strategy is also combined with the desire to control the brand; in this vein, the marketing brief goes on to instruct potential users that 'it is essential the interpretations and delivery of the message be consistent with the global campaign' and that copies of all announcements be lodged with Meridian Management SA – the IOC's marketing agency. Such centralization is, of course, is essential to the branding process, which requires consistency and coherence across various facets and corporate activities.

The IOC's actions in globalizing the Olympic brand followed strategies similar to those of TOP sponsors (indeed, Melinda May, the current head of marketing strategy, formerly worked for the marketing department at Coca-Cola). Their marketing personnel have also followed the trend of TNCs who seek to 'manage' the characteristics and perceptions of their brands. Such brand management is an integral part of the glocalizing strategy; because of the pervasiveness of these brands, consumers in different parts of the world form positive or negative associations and 'use these attributes as criteria while making purchase decisions'. [50] Three dimensions of these attributes stand out: signal quality (the perception of excellence and innovation), global myth (imagined global identities and shared cultural ideals) and social responsibility (to address social problems linked to what they sell and how they conduct their business). In this regard, a 'brand's global dimensions have a significant impact on its value in the consumer's eyes.' While quality signal remains the most significant factor, taken together, these dimensions explain some 64% of the variation in brand preferences worldwide. [51]

It is no coincidence that the themes underpinning Celebrate Humanity – identified by the brand analysts Edgar Dunn & Co, and Terrence Burns from the IOC's marketing agency, Meridian – dovetail neatly with these global dimensions. There is a neat corporate synergy at work between the IOC and TOP sponsors. Indeed, this synergy was recognized by Payne when he noted:

> We needed to give our marketing and broadcast partners far greater insight into what the Olympic brand really represented. They had to understand what made the Games so unique and special. They needed stability and, more than anything, a clear long-term vision. [52]

Celebrate Humanity, via both its market research and campaign, gives this greater insight and provides the IOC with a 'long-term vision' of its brand. Crucially, it also commodifies the values that are constructed as the non-commercial universal features of the games. This is evident in several ways. A closer examination of a brand's global dimension reveals how clearly it links to Celebrate Humanity and how embedded is corporate logic in the articulation of 'Olympism'. For example, the 'signal quality' of Celebrate Humanity relates to the games per se and to its motto *citius, altius, fortius* – this is an example of quality and innovation par excellence. Indeed, the modern Olympics has been constructed as *the* global benchmark for achievement in sport and sporting success and is rooted in a sports-industrial complex that celebrates human performance, not human development. [53]

TNCs have proved adept at developing marketing strategies to persuade consumers that their brands are symbols of global cultural ideals that unite people across the globe and give them a sense of belonging. The IOC has proved to be no less adroit with its 'universal' key propositions of hope, dreams and inspiration, friendship and fair play, and joy in effort that echo these dimensions of global branding. For example, the global myth dimension is evident in the proposition 'hope' – that the Olympic Games offer hope for a better world. Similarly, the 'dreams and inspiration' theme identified in Celebrate Humanity conveys a broad message that the Olympic Games have the power to inspire humanity to achieve things not possible in everyday life. Thus, the IOC and Celebrate Humanity's key propositions echo the global myth dimension of global brand marketing.

The sense of 'social responsibility' that TNCs cultivate in order to avoid the attention of anti-globalization movements also finds expression in Celebrate Humanity. In terms of 'friendship and fair play', we are led to believe that only in the context of the Olympics can humanity overcome the inequalities evident beyond the boundaries of sport. The proposition 'joy in effort' also enables Celebrate Humanity to position the games as an opportunity to celebrate honour and human dignity – and that, as such, the Olympics has moral lessons for humanity as a whole. The dark side of sport is sidestepped and a veil drawn over the Salt Lake City scandal and the ongoing issues surrounding drugs.

Lee Clow, the Chairman of TBWA (the agency responsible for originally conceiving the campaign) claimed at the outset of Celebrate Humanity that it 'is not about advertising in the traditional sense, it's about reminding the world of the values and dreams the Olympics represent.' [54] Indeed, Celebrate Humanity is far from traditional; it is at the cutting edge in its approach to advertising; its message is more subtle and in tune with recent strategies that allow global brands to compete more effectively. In one sense, the IOC is quite clear about this. In the 2004 Celebrate Humanity marketing brief, cited earlier, the IOC concludes that both Olympic broadcast and marketing partners 'can benefit from the Celebrate Humanity campaign in a variety of ways'. This claim is reinforced by sports management research conducted by Séquin and Preuss that focused on the Olympic brand and its assets and liabilities. In this, they noted, in interviews with TOPs and industry experts, that the Olympic ideals were the 'essence' of the Olympic brand and that

> the ideals provided partners with a unique marketing platform, not available on other properties, which defined meanings and context of values towards consumers. Consequently, the offering of brand associations that other properties can't offer or imitate provided the partners with a point of differentiation or competitive advantage. [55]

Despite this explicit recognition of mutual self-interest, the IOC has managed to convey to a wider public the idea that Celebrate Humanity is not, as noted, about advertising in the traditional sense; indeed, that its marketing strategy is about *controlling* commercialization on its own terms. Yet, such control seems more about managing the characteristics of the brand and avoiding 'ambush advertising'. Given this success in disguising the real intent of Celebrate Humanity, the IOC can be seen to have passed what Holt *et al.* term as 'the litmus test for social responsibility initiatives'. That is, 'will consumers perceive the actions to be motivated primarily by self-interest – or by an interest in the welfare of people and the planet?' [56]

Olympic Heritage and Legacies

In adopting a form of historical sociology or sociological history, it is possible to probe both how the meaning, structure, organization, production and consumption of the Beijing Olympic games have emerged out of the heritage of the past and what legacy trends are evident for the future. The heritage of the ancient world seems to matter less in practice than the extent to which the history of modern games reinforces and expresses the broader globalization of Western achievement sport. Bound up in the sportization phases identified, this past ensures that the legacies of the Beijing games will deepen and intensify the interlocking processes identified earlier. Though the heritage of the ancient games is claimed to find expression in the DNA of Olympism, in practice the legacy of the Celebrate Humanity campaign is more focused on twenty-first-century consumption and the opening up of new markets.

The marketing campaign that underpins the Beijing Olympics can also be understood in this light. With its slogan 'One World, One Dream' and the Chinese claim that this 'reflects the essence and the universal values of the Olympic spirit – Unity, Friendship, Progress, Harmony, Participation and Dream', the rhetoric of the Beijing games, not surprisingly, dovetails well with the Celebrate Humanity campaign and the Olympic DNA detected by Payne. [57] While the full nature and extent of the legacies of the Beijing Olympic games are difficult to predict, if the Athens games are any guide, the legacy will be less about the ancient heritage of Olympism, invented or otherwise, and more to do with the thoroughly modern consumption processes that characterize global sport more generally. [58]

Notes

[1] Maguire, *Global Sport*; Maguire, *Power and Global Sport.*
[2] Heinilä, 'The Totalization Process in International Sport'.
[3] Maguire, *Global Sport: Identities, Societies, Civilisations.*
[4] Eichberg, 'Olympic Sport – Neocolonization and Alternatives'.
[5] De Coubertin, *Olympism*, 704.
[6] Renson, 'The Reinvention of Tradition in Sport and Games.'
[7] Hargreaves, *Sporting Females.*

[8] Kirk, *Schooling Bodies.*

[9] Berryman and Park, *Sport and Exercise Science*; Hoberman, *Mortal Engines.*

[10] Maguire *et al.*, *Sport Worlds.*

[11] Miller *et al.*, *Globalization and Sport.*

[12] Maguire, *Global Sport*; Maguire, *Power and Global Sport.*

[13] Maguire, *Power and Global Sport.*

[14] Barnard *et al.*, '"Making the News"'; Maguire, *Power and Global Sport.* The project, entitled 'Branding, Identity and the Athens Olympic Games: A Case Study of Global Media-Sport', was directed by Joseph Maguire and Peter Golding and funded by the Economic and Social Research Council. The initial findings of our examination of the Celebrate Humanity campaign are found in this paper.

[15] Miller *et al.*, *Globalization and Sport*; Maguire, *Power and Global Sport.*

[16] IOC, 'Celebrate Humanity'.

[17] Payne, *Olympic Turnaround*, 111.

[18] Ibid., 113.

[19] Wamsley, 'Laying Olympism to Rest', 232.

[20] Ritchie, 'Cool Rings', 67.

[21] Holt *et al.*, 'How Global Brands Compete'.

[22] Golding and Murdock, 'Culture, Communications and Political Economy'; Maguire, *Global Sport.*

[23] Wernick, *Promotional Culture.*

[24] Holt *et al.*, 'How Global Brands Compete'.

[25] Budd, 'Capitalism, Sport and Resistance'.

[26] Magdalinski *et al.*, 'Recapturing Olympic Mystique', 47.

[27] Giardina and Metz, 'Celebrating Humanity'; Wamsley, 'Laying Olympism to Rest'; Whitson, 'Olympic Sport, Global Media and Cultural Diversity'.

[28] Maguire, *Power and Global Sport.*

[29] IOC, *Olympic Marketing Fact File.*

[30] See section 6.6 of the *IOC Marketing Fact File*, 2002, for a clear demonstration of this.

[31] *Olympic Marketing Matters*, 11, 4.

[32] 'The Olympic Games is …' – just a sporting event; a multi-national sporting event; a sporting event with ceremonial traditions; an international entertainment festival; an opportunity for peace' *Olympic Marketing Fact File*, 2002, or 'The Olympic Games are special because …' – the whole world competes; they are steeped in tradition; all of the world's top athletes compete; there's something for everyone to enjoy'. *Olympic Marketing Matters* 11, 4.

[33] Leiss *et al.*, *Social Communication in Advertising.*

[34] Shank, *Sports Marketing: A Strategic Perspective.*

[35] Westerbeek and Smith, *Sport Business in the Global Marketplace*, 189.

[36] IOC, website, 2002.

[37] Magdalinski, 'Recapturing Olympic Mystique', 45.

[38] Real, 'The post-Modern Olympics'; Roche, *Mega-Events and Modernity*; Tomlinson, 'The Commercialisation of the Olympics'.

[39] Rowe, *Sport, Culture and the Media*; Silk, 'Corporate Nationalism(s)'; Slater, 'Changing Partners'; Moragas Spa *et al.*, *Television in the Olympics.*

[40] Payne, *Olympic Turnaround*, 119.

[41] Ibid., 118.

[42] These include friendship, multicultural, honourable, trustworthy, unity, dignified, participation, global, peaceful, striving, respectful, integrity, fair competition, determination, patriotic, being the best, dynamic, and celebration (source: *Olympic Marketing Fact File*, 2002: section 6.4).

[43] Ibid., section 6.2.

[44] Payne, *Olympic Turnaround*, 118.
[45] Ibid., 118–19.
[46] Ibid., 120.
[47] IOC, Marketing Fact File, section 6.9.
[48] Maguire, *Global Sport.*
[49] IOC, 'Celebrate Humanity', 3.
[50] Holt *et al.*, 'How Global Brands Compete', 70.
[51] Ibid., 70–2.
[52] Payne, *Olympic Turnaround*, 112.
[53] Maguire, *Power and Global Sport.*
[54] http://www.prnewswire.com/cgi-bin/stories, accessed 20 Oct. 2006.
[55] Séquin and Preuss, 'Olympic Brand – Assets and Liabilities', 193.
[56] Holt *et al.*, 'How Global Brands Compete', 75.
[57] http://en.beijing2008.cn/17/25/article, accessed 18 Feb. 2008.
[58] Maguire *et al.*, 'Olympism and Consumption'; Maguire, 'Civilised Games'.

References

Barnard, S., K. Butler, P. Golding and J. Maguire. '"Making the News": The Athens Olympics 2004 and Competing Ideologies?' *Olympika: The International Journal of Olympic Studies* 15 (2006): 35–56.
Berryman, J.W. and J. Park, eds. *Sport and Exercise Science: Essays in the History of Sport Medicine.* Urbana, IL: Human Kinetics, 1992.
Budd, A. 'Capitalism, Sport and Resistance: Reflections'. *Sport in Society* 4, no. 1, (2004): 1–18.
De Coubertin, P. *Olympism: Selected Writings.* Lausanne: International Olympic Committee, 2000.
Eichberg, H. 'Olympic Sport – Neocolonization and Alternatives'. *International Review for the Sociology of Sport* 19, no. 1, (1984): 97–106.
Giardina, M. and J. Metz. 'Celebrating Humanity: Olympic Marketing and the Homogenization of Multiculturalism'. *International Journal of Sports Marketing and Sponsorship* June/July (2001): 203–21.
Golding, P. and G. Murdock. 'Culture, Communications and Political Economy'. In *Mass Media and Society*, edited by J. Curran and M. Gurevitch. London: Edward Arnold, 1991/2000: 15–32.
Hargreaves, J. *Sporting Females: Critical Issues in the History and Sociology of Women's Sports.* London: Routledge, 1994.
Heinilä, K. 'The Totalization Process in International Sport'. In *Sport in Social Context*, edited by K. Heinilä. Jyväskylä: University of Jyväskylä Press, 1998: 123–40.
Hoberman, J. *Mortal Engines. The Science of Performance and the Dehumanization of Sport.* New York: Free Press, 1992.
Holt, D.B., J.A. Quelch and E.L. Taylor. 'How Global Brands Compete'. *Harvard Business Review* 82, no. 9, (2004): 68–75.
International Olympic Committee (IOC). *Olympic Marketing Matters* 11 (Aug.) (1997): 4.
——. *Olympic Marketing Fact File*, spring (1998).
——. *Olympic Marketing Fact File* (2002), available at http://multimedia.olympic.org/pdf/en_report_556.pdf.
——. 'Celebrate Humanity' (2004), available at http://multimedia.olympic.org/pdf/en_report_808.pdf.
——. IOC website, available at http://www.olympic.org, accessed 26 March 2006.

Kirk, D. *Schooling Bodies: School Practice and Public Discourse 1880–1950*. London: Leicester University Press, 1998.

Klein, N. *No Logo*. London: Flamingo, 2000.

Leiss, W., S. Kline and S. Jhally. *Social Communication in Advertising. Persons, Products and Images of Well-Being*. London: Routledge, 1997.

Magdalinski, T., K.S. Schimmel and T.J.L. Chandler. 'Recapturing Olympic Mystique: The Corporate Invasion of the Classroom'. In *The Political Economy of Sport*, edited by John Nauright and Kimberly Schimmel. London: Palgrave, 2005:

Maguire, J. *Global Sport: Identities, Societies, Civilisations*. Cambridge: Polity Press, 1999.

——. '"Civilised Games"?: Beijing 2008, Power Politics and Cultural Struggles'. In *Power and Global Sport: Zones of Prestige, Emulation and Resistance*. London: Routledge, 2005: 145–58.

——. *Power and Global Sport: Zones of Prestige, Emulation and Resistance*. London: Routledge, 2005.

——, K. Butler, B. Barnard and P. Golding. 'Olympism and Consumption: An Analysis of Advertising in the British Media Coverage of the 2004 Athens Olympic Games'. *Sociology of Sport Journal* 25, no. 2, (2008): 167–86.

——, G. Jarvie, L. Mansfield and J. Bradley. *Sport Worlds. A Sociological Perspective*. Champaign, IL: Human Kinetics, 2002.

Miller, T., G. Lawrence, J. McKay and D. Rowe. *Globalization and Sport: Playing the World*. London: Sage, 2001.

Moragas Spa, M., N. Rivenburgh and J. Larson. *Television in the Olympics*. London: Libbey, 1995.

Nauright, John and Kimberly Schimmel. *The Political Economy of Sport*. London: Palgrave, 2005.

Payne, M. *Olympic Turnaround: How the Olympic Games Stepped Back from the Brink of Extinction to Become the World's Best Known Brand – and a Multi-Billion Dollar Global Franchise*. London: Greenwood, 2005.

Real, M.R. 'The Post-modern Olympics: Technology and the Commodification of the Olympic Movement'. *Quest* 48 (1996): 9–24.

Renson, R. 'The Reinvention of Tradition in Sport and Games'. In *Ancient Traditions and Current Trends in Physical Activity and Sport*, edited by G. Doll-Tepper and D. Scoretz. Berlin: ICSSPE, 1998: 8–13.

Ritchie, I. 'Cool Rings: Olympic Ideology and the Symbolic Consumption of Global Sport'. In *The Global Nexus Engaged. Sixth International Symposium for Olympic Research*. Ontario: University of Western Ontario, 2002: 61–70.

Roche, M. *Mega-Events and Modernity: Olympics and Expos in the Growth of Global Culture*. New York: Routledge, 2000.

Rowe, D. *Sport, Culture and the Media*. Buckingham: Open University Press, 1999.

Séquin, B. and H. Preuss. 'Olympic Brand – Assets and Liabilities'. *Pre-Olympic Scientific Congress*, Abstracts, p. 193. Thessoloniki, Greece, 2004.

Shank, M.D. *Sports Marketing: A Strategic Perspective*. Upper Saddle River, NJ: Prentice-Hall, 1999.

Silk, M., D. Andrews and C.L. Cole. 'Corporate Nationalism(s): The Spatial Dimensions of Sporting Capital'. In *Sport and Corporate Nationalisms*, edited by M. Silk, D. Andrews and C.L. Cole. Oxford: Berg, 2005: 1–13.

Slater, J. 'Changing Partners: The Relationship Between the Mass Media and the Olympic Games'. In *Fourth International Symposium for Olympic Research*, edited by R.K. Barney, K.B. Wamsley, S. G. Martyn and G.H. MacDonald. Ontario: University of Western Ontario, 1998: 49–69.

Tomlinson, A. 'The Commercialisation of the Olympics: Cities, Corporations and the Olympic Commodity'. In *Global Olympics: Historical and Sociological Studies of the Modern Games*, edited by K. Young and K.B. Wamsley. London: Elsevier, 2005: 179–200.

Wamsley, K.B. 'Laying Olympism to Rest'. In *Post Olympism: Questioning Sport in the Twenty-First Century*, edited by J. Bale and M.K. Christiansen. Oxford: Berg, 2004: 367–84.

Wernick, A. *Promotional Culture: Advertising, Ideology and Symbolic Expression*. London: Newbury Park, CA: Sage, 1991.

Westerbeek, H. and A. Smith. *Sport Business in the Global Marketplace*. London: Palgrave, 2003.

Whitson, D. 'Olympic Sport, Global Media and Cultural Diversity'. In *Fourth International Symposium for Olympic Research*, edited by R.K. Barney, K.B. Wamsley, S.G. Martyn and G.H. MacDonald. Ontario: University of Western Ontario, 1998: 1–9.

'Legacy' as Managerial/Magical Discourse in Contemporary Olympic Affairs

John J. MacAloon

The appearance in 1996 of the third and final volume of the official centennial history of the International Olympic Committee (IOC) was a watershed marker of the organization's new, if somewhat grudging willingness to have its own composition and internal memory publicly inspected. [1] Subsequently, the scandal surrounding the Salt Lake City bid process and the consequent Olympic reform effort greatly accelerated this development, creating a much broader public awareness of the structure and functioning of the IOC. [2] A new emphasis on administrative efficiency and transparency under the ensuing Jacques Rogge regime has extended a self-proclaimed 'world's best practices' style of management outward from the IOC itself to relations with Olympic bid and organizing committees and a wide variety of other stakeholders. [3] On the scholarly front, as led by the work of Olympic policy expert Jean-Loup Chappelet, an insightful professional scholarship on this new IOC governance has now appeared. [4] A number of IOC insider memoirs have also indicated (albeit in a more tendentious fashion) that these new managerial styles and practices were already being forwarded in the commercial marketing and broadcast rights arenas, though in a fashion generally less visible to public scrutiny because of corporate contractual secrecy. [5] One thing that did become only too apparent within IOC corridors and in public discussions of these external Olympic commercial relations was the appearance of the transnational marketing language of 'brand', 'brand value', and 'brand management' during this period.

The underlying purpose of this paper is to remind us of how patterns of organizational discourse are sensitive indicators of changing institutional arrangements and shifting power relations among stakeholders. As a very broad scholarly literature has long since demonstrated, organizational discursive routines are powerful modes of social control as well. To properly get at them requires an ethnography of speaking, that is, the recording and analysis of speech in its lived context. Interpretation of published or unpublished documents alone, even a properly semiotic analysis, can never get at the full range of meanings apparent only in the social contexts of speaking. [6] In this paper, I present a partial ethnography of 'legacy' speech in Olympic circles today, that is, of talk about what the Olympic Games bring and leave behind. I analyse its contribution to the continued penetration of managerial rationality into Olympic affairs, through what I describe as the magical properties of legacy discourse in attaining in a very short time a cross-functional, cross-contextual, transnational hegemony denied even to Olympic brand speech in its heyday.

'Olympic Brand' to 'Olympic Legacy'

With respect to Olympic brand speech, official IOC marketing department reports, commissioned studies by IOC contractors and subsidiaries such as Meridian Management, and the memoirs of key agents such as Michael Payne and Dick Pound try to make it seem that the appearance of 'Olympic brand' conceptualization and language was a straightforward, unproblematic, and uncontested importation into Olympic affairs of the normal professional speech of the transnational marketing and business communities. My ethnography of speaking in IOC and related Olympic settings, however, makes it absolutely clear that this development was anything but 'normal' and consensual. To other IOC members, administrators, and interlocutors throughout the 'Olympic Family', this lexicon was taken to be offensive, and it remains highly resented and resisted among such parties today. Their attitude can be summed up in the exasperated expression I once heard from an IOC member during a Lausanne meeting: 'The Olympic Movement is not a brand, damn it, it's a peace movement! We're not selling toothpaste!'

Marketing professionals respond to such objections in highly patterned ways. The first is with tongues clucking over the ignorance of their critics, who are said simply to fail to understand what real professionals mean by 'brand' today. Far from selling a product, the concept is deployed in a highly creative way, the professional adepts insist, to capture the accumulated value of an entire firm or organization in all of its dimensions. To suggest that the concept remains in any way narrowly tied to market segmentation and sales is merely to display one's ignorance. This conceptual inflation is also a key tactical means by which non-profit communications and marketing specialists circumvent objections that it is unseemly to tie organizations with noble social, civic, and charitable purposes to purely profit-driven corporations by adopting the shared language of branding. The brand managers respond that for-profit and not-for-profit entities are merely recognizing, in their different modalities, the characteristics common to good organizations in general. Hence, 'brand-speak' is perfectly appropriate in both domains. I myself have spent many hours in Lausanne not only as the recorder but also as the object of this lecture, as Michael Payne and other Olympic marketing professionals patiently tried to relieve me of my own ignorance. [7] I will return to their specific arguments and tactics later in this paper.

A second typical response to criticism is to commission marketing studies, the drama of whose ostensible findings conceals the fact that the real action is in how the study problem is defined in the first place. A most extraordinary example of this was a late 1990s study of 'the global Olympic brand' arranged by Meridian Management. This study found a higher recognition and status for the Olympic brand than any of the others tested. These others included the FIFA World Cup and the Red Cross/Red Crescent, as well as commercial entities, thus jointly normalizing both sports and humanitarian organizations as brands by pre-defining them as such. As part of the counter-offensive to the Olympic bribery scandals, it was judged politically wise to publicly release and promote this study. But this action only further alienated Olympic circles that found it shocking to see not just the Olympic movement but also the Red Cross subjected to such consumerist characterizations and associations. Later studies in this series included the Christian Cross, the United Nations, and the World Wildlife Fund. [8]

Still, the IOC marketers recognized that they had a persistent problem with 'Olympic brand' language that they could not overcome, for all of their efforts to make it normal and hegemonic. Michael Payne and others have admitted to me (and other Olympic studies colleagues have observed) their own tactical avoidance of brand talk around certain IOC members and officers in other departments of the IOC. [9] I have reason to believe that Juan Antonio Samaranch himself was not entirely comfortable with brand language outside of strictly marketing settings and discussions, because it threatened to demean, by reducing all else to the field of commercial reference, what was most important to him, namely the complex international diplomacy and political work that had been required to bring about the changes in the Olympic system for which he most wished to be credited and remembered. Brand talk was inadequate, in other words, to encompass even the Samaranch legacy, much less the whole of Olympic heritage and current situation.

Thus, while brand speech both evidenced and instrumentally furthered the penetration of managerial rationality in Olympic institutions through the 1990s, its ineradicable association with a commercial base left it unable to spread across all functional areas and organizational networks in the Olympic system. That was to be the rather magical accomplishment of legacy discourse in the present decade.

An Ethnographic Vignette

In late 2006, I happened to be in Lausanne doing research in the Olympic archives, when it was suggested to a newly formed Olympic Games applicant city committee that it might want to get some early exposure to the Olympic movement by sending representatives to do a short seminar with me in the Olympic capital. Since this committee had little prior Olympic experience, and it would be useful for it to have word filter around Lausanne that it really was interested in learning about the Olympic movement prior to bidding, I was eager to oblige. Because no official meetings would be taken and because of the familiarity of my presence in Lausanne and imagined relations with the visitors, the current IOC ethics rules for Olympic applicant cities presented no barrier.

As it turned out, the persons sent to me in Lausanne were employees of a large multinational consulting company, recently seconded *pro bono* to this bid committee as part of their firm's global effort to secure influence and future contracts in the Olympic world. In Lausanne, I gave them interpretive tours of the Olympic headquarters and museum installations and arranged for the ever-resourceful and patient staff of the Olympic Studies Centre to provide them with whatever documentation they wished to work with in the library. Drinks and meals were taken in the Olympic Museum cafe and neighbouring hotel sites, where so much Olympic business actually gets conducted. Casual encounters with IOC staffers were thus accomplished, helping to get the word around, and meetings were taken with independent but highly influential Swiss veterans of past bid campaigns. In the interstices, I tried to keep up a running seminar on Olympic history, institutional culture, administrative organization, and current politics that would be substantive yet clear and comprehensible to rank and rushed beginners.

While the junior member of the delegation took to the process (perhaps because of a family heritage linked with Olympic history), the senior member clearly did not. At first I thought his impatience was due to quotidian business routines, as he interrupted conversations and study sessions I had arranged in order to take BlackBerry calls from corporate superiors, for example. But as I listened to the questions he asked of the experts he was introduced to, I realized that he had arrived in Lausanne with an agenda quite different from contextualization and general learning about the Olympic movement. Instead, he had been charged with or had taken his charge to be discovering and bringing home a 'bottom-line' answer to the question, 'What is most on the IOC's mind these days? What's its single greatest concern that as a bid committee, we should be prepared to address?'

Now management consultants in general and his firm in particular are infamous for this particular *modus operandi*: determine what the client wants to hear; read or talk to a few real experts; write up the report as your own findings; deliver it to the client with speed, efficiency, and bottom-line economy; collect your fee while proposing additional services. There is space in this paper neither to take up the extensive literature on these practices nor to consider the overall encounter of the contemporary Olympic movement with them. An entire scholarly study could and should be devoted to a topic so central to the historical penetration of managerial rationality in current Olympic circles, and yet so rich with ambiguities and ironies. As exemplified by the second member of the visiting team in my story, there are competing epistemic practices at work in the multinational consulting firms today, and as hiring increases outside the narrow confines of professional business schools, their dominant methodology is being newly challenged from within these firms. Moreover, in today's IOC, key members and administrators most identified as agents of the new managerial rationality are at the same time privately sceptical and even in some cases contemptuous of the work being done by the big consulting firms for bid committees, OCOGs, and other international sport organizations. [10]

The point of my ethnographic vignette is less what this management consultant turned Olympic bid official brought to his first encounter with the Olympic centre and more the fact that he actually came away with what he wanted: a one-note chord on what the IOC cares most about today. 'Legacy,' he reported back to his superiors, 'the IOC is going to want to know about our legacy plan more than anything. Everyone says so.' Over a year later, this refrain now dominates the organizational speech of officials and contractors of this bid committee, as it does among its rivals around the world.

Some Characteristics of Legacy Discourse Today

I am not sure I could give an adequate account of the history of this development, even were there space here to do so. Obviously, legacy or heritage awareness has been present from the beginning of the modern Olympics. The 1896 Athens Olympic Games drew aspects of the ancient Greek heritage into modern transformation, and these games left that city with a refurbished Panathenaic stadium ('hard legacy' in today's parlance) and a renewed national Greek self-confidence ('soft legacy', as it would be said today, though this binary opposition is both gender-overdetermined and categorically foolish, since it was the latter not the former that helped propel Greece into a disastrous war). [11] Jumping forward to recent years, a host of heritage cultivation enterprises – the Olympic Museum, documentary and visual archive work, collaboration with independent Olympic Studies Centres, the IOC and Olympic Games centennial celebrations among them – were made possible by the IOC's new levels of income under Samaranch. Jean-Loup Chappelet has stressed the particular contributions of Olympic Winter Games bid and organizing committees to this development. [12] Laudable IOC concerns under Rogge with ensuring that actual or potential Olympic host cities no longer be saddled with unnecessary investments and white elephant facilities have given legacy analysis additional impetus. The consolidation of executive leadership in Olympic Games Executive Director Gilbert Felli's office – with its preferred franchiser/franchisee model of IOC/OCOG relations and its plethora of technical manuals now attached to the Olympic host city contract – has likewise supported a new atmosphere stressing the resources the IOC administration provides to Olympic partners and therefore the legitimacy of asking them in return to better specify what they will add as lasting benefits not just to their own local communities but to the Olympic heritage as a whole. Doubtless there are other factors that will turn out to have been important in the rise of the discourse we are presently analysing.

Not a bit of this history was known to the gentleman featured in my vignette, nor did he need to show any real interest in acquiring it, yet he was able to pick up on the importance of getting his organization to start talking about legacy. Legacy talk is now all around the IOC and the apparent simplicity of the concept – I will discuss differences between *héritage* and legacy in a moment – is the first thing to note in accounting for its attraction and ready diffusion among Olympic neophytes (including, I must add, the conveners of the Oxford Olympic Legacies conference at which this paper was originally delivered).

Another key feature is the desirability of the discursive object. Speaking just of Olympic Games legacy, who could be against commitment to and careful planning for how to leave something good and reasonably long-lasting behind for both the local community and the international Olympic Family? The IOC's emphasis on legacy planning can even be seen to be progressive, through its forcing Olympic bid committees to be far more circumspect with their rhetoric and promises to domestic publics because of current IOC oversight and attention to legacy matters. The IOC executive and administration today closely and independently monitor popular as well as press opinion in candidate cities, and bid committees know this well. A certain discipline is thus being introduced against bid leaderships promising their citizens only the vaguest fiscal, image or development benefits, while actually offering only real estate or political projects masquerading as Olympic legacy but probably benefiting only the few, or else presenting grandiose schemes of urban renewal and development unlikely ever to be funded or completed on budget.

OCOGs are furthermore showing themselves innovative in this direction. Vancouver 2010 is credited with having introduced the slogan and a concerted programme of 'Legacy Now' (though this programme derives largely from the Toronto 2008 bid [13]), meant to mark and encourage the delivery of lasting community benefits at each stage of an Olympic project, not just when the games are concluded. The 'legacy now' concept and expression have spread very quickly through younger Olympic bodies, such as the 2016 applicant cities. This is an exceptionally important development, in my opinion, because it encourages communities not to focus so exclusively on longer-term bricks and mortar projects and cost/benefit projections that they lose sight of the real pay-off in new social and political capital that can be created in early stages of a bid, as normally segregated urban status segments and class fractions are very nearly forced into communication with one another.

'Legacy' as a general term is referential enough to seem substantive and readily hypostasized, yet it is open enough to attract the claims and particular attentions of paid specialists. Indeed, nearly everyone who has had a planning role in large events and who wishes to continue in the field can now proclaim him- or herself a legacy expert and hang out a shingle. The burgeoning population of international consultants seeking to sell their services to Olympic, Paralympic and other mega-event planning bodies has seized upon legacy discourse with a special eagerness and aplomb. Beginning in London in 2007, continuing on Barbados in January 2008, and planned for Vancouver in 2009, whole conferences called 'Legacy Lives' are being convened for these 'international legacy experts' to discuss and self-advertise their strategies for 'the development of best practice in major event legacy planning and delivery'. [14]

Stakeholders within the Olympic system have not been slow, either, to seize the legacy standard to rally their traditional interests. Take the International Federations (IFs) as an example. The IFs have for a long time tortured – some would say blackmailed – Olympic bid committees by demanding larger venues and better perquisites in return for support. 'This other bid is offering us thus and such; will you match or exceed it?' The problem became especially acute when Samaranch determined to incorporate a number of IF presidents as voting IOC members, a development certified and extended by the IOC 2000 reforms, despite the fact that these 'representative' members have clear conflicts of interest. (You get re-elected as IF president on the basis of what you get for your particular sport, not how you serve the interests of the Olympic movement as a whole, the core responsibility of an IOC member.) To its great credit and under the mission of avoiding white elephant venues that are a negative legacy to host cities, the IOC administration of Jacques Rogge has succeeded in significantly tempering the power of the IFs to blackmail candidate cities in this way. But legacy discourse has given the IFs a new weapon and cover in this perpetual struggle. Bid cities proposing temporary venues for sports that have no follow-on local use or funding source are now confronted by IF complaints that this violates the new legacy ethos. In the name of legacy, every sport is now claiming the right to have a substantial venue and sports programming left behind after the games are concluded.

Héritage and Legacy

Having charted some of more obvious semantic features and consequent pragmatics of legacy discourse in today's Olympic affairs, I wish to turn now to some deeper questions of legacy semantics that, I would argue, underlie further magical effects of this discourse that are probably not so benign.

As is well known, the official languages of the Olympic movement are French and English. The fact that all IOC directors and other key administrators are fluent in both languages frequently leads Anglo-Saxon interlocutors (as they are called in Eurocentric Olympic discourse) to overlook the fact that some key IOC departments think primarily in French, including those most associated with promoting legacy management. A cursory reflection might judge the French word *héritage* and the English word *legacy* to be semantic equivalents. In English, we can speak of a 'legacy' coming from the past to the present as well as of the present leaving a legacy for the future. So, too, in French, the past offers its *héritage* to the present, which in turn leaves an *héritage* for the future. But this superficial comparison conceals an important statistical difference in the semantic weighting of the two terms in ordinary speech. In actual usage, the French term is more encompassing and more weighted in more contexts toward the accumulated capital of the past arriving in the present, while the English term is more narrowly specified – e.g. through its legal referents – and tilted towards the present's contribution to the future. Moreover, there is contextual evidence specific to the field of Olympic speech that clearly shows how this apparently subtle semantic difference undergirds and helps reinforce important pragmatic differences, including unintended but no less pernicious consequences of legacy speech.

As a native speaker and more practised ethnographer of francophone IOC speech than I, Jean-Loup Chappelet has pointed out to me that use of *le leg*, the French term much more equivalent in semantic weighting to the English 'legacy', is far less frequently heard in francophone Olympic discourse. [15] Instead, *héritage*, with its semantic emphasis on the accumulated historical, cultural, and moral capital that comes to the present from the past, absolutely dominates. By the same token, we do not find the group of consultants previously discussed – who incidentally are almost entirely anglophone – billing themselves as 'international heritage experts' or holding conventions titled 'Heritage Lives'. They are not historians or museum curators, after all, but professionals selling expertise as to how current and upcoming events managers can convince their constituencies about what will be left to them in the future!

This echoes the effect illustrated in my vignette of a newly minted proponent of legacy discourse actually using this fact as reason to downplay any responsibility to learn about the actual heritage of the Olympic movement. I can add, moreover, that this person remains today allied in his organization with other 'future-oriented', 'results-oriented' seconds from the business consulting world who are preoccupied with a 'legacy planning' that consists of lists of possible future pay-offs and projects, and who are dismissive of or at best indifferent to the organization's need to acquire real knowledge of the Olympic heritage. Their general attitude is 'historical experience is nice, but we have a job to do as legacy managers'.

In my judgement, such persons are now in large part mistaking what the relevant IOC figures precisely mean when asking them to explain 'how they will make a serious contribution to Olympic heritage'. It rarely crosses these newcomers' minds that they are being asked how their city will understand, rethink, and rework in a serious and deeply informed way the great themes of the Olympic historical experience. Instead, they spend their time drawing up urban project lists and 'messaging' the promotion of Olympic values. For their part, francophone IOC officials are clearly underestimating the ways in which legacy discourse in anglophone contexts can actually undermine respect for, actual learning about, and cultivation of the overall and hard-won Olympic heritage, the inherited cultural capital that distinguishes Olympic from other international sport and is the general source of value that makes anyone want to bid for the Olympics in the first place. This brings us back to Olympic brand management discourse, whose relationship with legacy discourse we can now further specify.

Synecdoche and the Fate of the Olympic Movement

When he was Olympic marketing chief and lead 'brand manager', Michael Payne liked to play a ritual game with me. He would take me into his office for a private preview of a spot newly created for the 'Celebrate Humanity' series of Olympic public service messages commissioned for international television by the IOC. [16] After I would tear up at a particularly effective and close-hitting one – say, Derek Redmond's father coming out of the stands in Barcelona to help his stricken son across the finish line – Michael would say something to the effect of 'You see, we are on the same page about the power of the Olympic brand,' and I would say, 'Yes and no, Michael, yes and no.' In analysing Olympic brand or legacy discourse, it is not necessary and in my experience usually wrong-headed to challenge anyone's personal commitment to values that are shared; rather, different theories of value itself are the thing at issue here.

Payne makes his own theory of value explicit in his memoir. 'A key element of the Olympic brand is its heritage,' he writes. Therefore, for Michael Payne and others like him, it can only be a puzzling 'paradox' that 'non-commercial values provide the Olympic brand with its true commercial value to the marketing partners.' [17] Payne is puzzled because he has gotten things exactly backwards. The commercial branding of the Olympics and everything associated with it is now part of Olympic historical heritage, not the other way around. Just so, it is no paradox whatsoever that money and business follow meaning, here as elsewhere. [18] The error is a synecdochal one, the mistaking of the part for the whole, and the whole for the part.

Today's Olympic 'legacy managers' betray their hidden relationship with the Olympic 'brand managers' here, and not just in their common origins in business culture. Far too aware of the antagonism created by brand-speak among 'Olympic movement types', they and their international consultant allies have adopted the seemingly more encompassing and innocent language of legacy, under whose cover they can commit their own version of the same synecdochal error. For them, Olympic heritage – the sum total of accumulated Olympic cultural, historical, political, moral, and symbolic capital – is merely one part, indeed an instrumental background factor in the creation of future Olympic legacies. The actual fact of the matter is the reverse: future legacies are added to or subtracted from the existing heritage accumulation, without whose capital no further legacy projects (much less any legacy management) would be possible at all.

Conclusion

I recognize that such sociolinguistic and discursive analysis of Olympic organizational speech as I have presented here might seem abstract and uninteresting to colleagues preoccupied (as I usually am) with the particular historical and political outcomes of specific Olympic events and initiatives. However, it is my strong conviction that without confronting the magical properties of today's highly fetished legacy talk in Olympic circles, history will not come to matter much for anyone but the historians and curators. One of my points has been to suggest how this legacy discourse can in an uncanny way actually contribute to sending real Olympic movement expertise – in Lausanne and among, in Bruce Kidd's phrase, 'critical partisans' – to the sidelines in favour of neophytes who happen to learn 'what is on the IOC's mind'.

Managerial rationality is in several respects an unquestionable good in Olympic affairs, but as Max Weber taught us some time ago, charismatic social movements rarely survive their rationalization. If the Olympic movement is to have any chance of surviving its increasing penetration by the Olympic sports industry, whether in its commercial or its managerial forms, 'movement types' must become much more alert, in my opinion, to how dominant organizational languages are now threatening to reposition our own knowledges and activities.

Notes

[1] Landry and Yerlès, *The International Olympic Committee, Vol. III.* The previous volumes appeared in 1994 and 1995. Though officially sanctioned by the IOC, these books were prepared by independent scholars, and the negotiations with IOC officials over final texts were frequently vexed. Since their volume edged onto the ground of current Olympic structures, personalities, and affairs, Fernand Landry and Magdeleine Yerlès faced a particularly vexatious struggle to defend the values of scholarly research and to teach fearful bureaucrats of the IOC old school that the reputation of the organization and its leaders was better served by transparency than by censorship. In my judgement, the heroic success of our two Laval University colleagues and the IOC leadership's discovery that the sky did not fall upon them when this text was published already had paved the way for the changes in IOC culture that would soon be greatly accelerated by the Salt Lake City scandal.
[2] The present author served as a member of the Executive Committee of the IOC 2000 Reform Commission.
[3] On the contemporary penetration of Olympic ritual practice by IOC 'world's best practices' orientation, see MacAloon, *Bearing Light.*
[4] Chappelet, 'Governance of the IOC'. Chappelet's work in this area is distinctive because it combines scholarly expertise in public administration and management, knowledge of the Swiss and European legal contexts, and extensive ethnographic experience with the IOC.
[5] For example, Pound, *Inside the Olympics.* Payne, *Olympic Turn Around.* It is interesting to note that the IOC has not proved kind to those who have claimed in such ways to have 'saved it' through their commercial activities. Dick Pound, for many years the IOC's chief negotiator on television and sponsorship contracts, was humiliated in the 2001 elections for IOC president, garnering barely more than a score of votes. Michael Payne, long-time IOC marketing director, had to leave his position shortly after Jacques Rogge assumed the presidency. Neither fate was remotely that of another IOC officer who had earlier (and with infinitely less credibility) claimed in a memoir (Kim Un-yong, *The Greatest Olympics*) to have personally saved the Olympics through his commercial prowess. Kim Un-young, another candidate for the IOC presidency in 2001, was later expelled from the organization and ended up in a South Korean prison after conviction on corruption charges.

[6]   This is not at all to say that inspection and analysis of IOC and other Olympic publications containing legacy talk would not be a worthwhile endeavour. Indeed, just entering 'legacy' into the IOC website search engine will give the researcher evidence of just how widespread and institutionally marked this discourse has become. In this paper, I largely limit my evidence to the ethnography few others have managed to conduct.

[7]   I also happen to live with the chief communications officer and brand manager of a leading disability services charity. The shape of my conversations with her on the issue is quite identical to those I have in Lausanne, illustrating the transnational professional hegemony of this speech.

[8]   The IOC has held various ownership stakes in Meridian over the years, while the company has maintained its chief purpose of managing TOP and other Olympic sponsorships and supporting their activation. The company has served as a professional go-between and mediator for the IOC administration and its global corporate partners. In his book, Payne notes the commissioning of a second such study 'of 10,000 people across nine countries and five continents [that] found that the Olympic rings enjoyed recognition levels of over 90% (99% in Japan) – compared with Shell 88%; McDonald's 88%; Mercedes 74%; Christian Cross 54%; United Nations 36%; World Wildlife Fund 28%'. Payne, *Olympic Turn Around, 132.*

[9]   I am grateful to Michael Payne for our conversations on this matter. While more bemused by my concerns than anything else (once joking to his staff in my hearing, 'No brand management today, Prof. MacAloon's here'), he and Meridian colleagues like Terence Burns did sincerely try to overcome my reservations. I shall discuss their tactics further below.

[10]   The restraint against open criticism, in my experience, derives from a recognition by these key IOC directors that some bid committees and OCOGs now fiscally rely on such seconded consultants and managers to keep their own labour costs down. This is in tune with general policy commitments concerning cost control recommended by the IOC 2000 Reform Commission and strongly pushed by the Rogge administration. Sensitivity to other IOC directors and managers who have consultant firm experience on their résumés probably also plays a role.

[11]   Bruce Kidd, personal communication, May 2008.

[12]   Jean-Loup Chappelet, 'Olympic Environmental Concerns as a Legacy of the Winter Games', 1898–916.

[13]   See MacAloon, *This Great Symbol.*

[14]   See www.legacylives.com/04ConfSpeakers.php for the prose and sample résumés of this occupational group. Though marketed as an opportunity for decision-makers and potential clients to meet legacy services providers, the former show up in very small numbers (some three in Barbados) at these 'Legacy Lives' meetings, leaving them a convention and trade show for the consultants themselves. Top IOC officials have repeatedly expressed how extremely concerned they are about this proliferating tribe of transnational consultants, particularly with respect to Olympic bid committees. As one IOC administrator put it to me, 'We have not worked so hard to cut costs for Olympic applicant cities only to see them turn around and spend so much money on so-called experts.' But the IOC itself bears responsibility for setting the conditions of escalation in which candidate cities fear being outgunned by their rivals' roster of international consultants. The consultants themselves have become masterful at playing bid cities off against one another, and it is further testimony to the magical properties of legacy discourse that it is under this beneficent rubric that this occupational group chooses to meet to plot and scheme as to how the next set of commissions will be distributed. Once hired, consultants frequently team up with bid officers, especially those so new to the process as to be mesmerized by the legacy concept – like the fellow in my vignette. By driving a bid or organizing committee to obsess about this topic, consultants build their own résumés as 'international legacy experts' preparing in the future to make exaggerated claims about their own role in the successes of organizations that will not outlive the events they seek or manage.

[15] Personal communication, Lausanne, Dec., 2007.
[16] The series, including the particular spot I mention, is readily reviewable on YouTube.
[17] Payne, *Olympic Turn Around*, 114, 122.
[18] For a classic discussion, see Sahlins, *Culture and Practical Reason*.

References

Chappelet, Jean-Loup. 'The Governance of the International Olympic Committee'. In *International Perspectives on the Management of Sport*, edited by Trevor Slack and Milena Parent. London: Elsevier Academic Press, 2006: 207–27.

——. 'Olympic Environmental Concerns as a Legacy of the Winter Games'. *International Journal of the History of Sport* (this issue) 25, no. 14, (2008): 1898–916.

Kim, Un-yong. *The Greatest Olympics: From Baden-Baden to Seoul*. Seoul: Sisayongosa Press, 1990.

Landry, Fernand and Magdeleine Yerlès. *The International Olympic Committee: One Hundred Years. Vol. III.* Lausanne: International Olympic Committee, 1996.

MacAloon, John J. ed. *Bearing Light: Flame Relays and the Struggle for the Olympic Movement*. London: Routledge, forthcoming.

——. *This Great Symbol: Pierre de Coubertin and the Origins of the Modern Olympic Games*, 2nd rev. edn. London: Routledge, 2008.

Payne, Michael. *Olympic Turn Around*. London: London Business Press, 2005.

Pound, Dick. *Inside the Olympics*. Toronto: John Wiley, 2004.

Sahlins, Marshall. *Culture and Practical Reason*. Chicago: University of Chicago Press, 1976.

The Regeneration Games: Commodities, Gifts and the Economics of London 2012*

Iain Macrury and Gavin Poynter

Introduction

Legacy has assumed a considerable significance to the International Olympic Committee (IOC), host cities and governments over recent decades. In the wake of their victory in the 2012 Olympic bid sweepstakes, British leaders have proposed an ambitious social-economic legacy for East London through the Olympic construction projects. The London 2012 organizers will face the consequences of reconciling their ambitions with recent public concern over the cost of the games. We propose that it is only possible to achieve productive reconciliation of these ends and ambitions through reframing the conceptualization of the games as a catalyst of urban renewal.

Contemporary government policy and business and academic literature tend to focus upon cost/benefit approaches to evaluate the impact of the games upon East London and the wider economy. Such approaches are derived from marginalist economics and are consistent with the currently fashionable public/private partnership 'models' of working between the state and private enterprise. The dominance of such ways of thinking merely affirms the process of commodification of the Olympics that has occurred over recent decades and, most importantly, serves to subordinate ideas of 'city building' to the exigencies of the market and the direction of the state. 'Good city building', if it is to be catalysed by a mega-event, demands a different perspective on the games and the marketplace that it currently serves. [1]

The proposed reframing examines two modes of social and economic relationship, both of which are enacted in modern Olympism through its association with programmes of urban regeneration and city building. The first and dominant is the 'commodity-mode', typically reflected in cost-benefit economism. A secondary mode is also in evidence as 2012 approaches – which imbricates IOC and other cultural discourses of Olympism. The 'gift-mode' describes a conception of the nature and impact of an Olympic economy embedded in socio-cultural life and relations – notably in the various accumulations and effects corralled under the term 'legacy' – a term which owes its semantic potency to socially embedded (familial) economies.

Examining press-based reporting, governmental and delivery authority policy statements, and other cultural conceptions of 'Olympism', 'legacy' and 'the Olympic economy'; and with close attention paid to the specificities of the 2012 budget and its contexts, we distinguish the tensions and anxieties attaching to and emerging from the necessities of operating a 'commodity Olympics' in the space of a 'gift Olympics'. The Olympic 'brand' and the gift will also be discussed – with an analysis positing branding as a daily version of the (fantasized) transformation of commodity relations into human/gift relations. This transformation leads to the routinized absorption of the 'real' Olympic movement into the commodified, 'fantasy world' of the Olympic brand. The anthropologist Christopher Gregory draws out the distinction in a useful way:

> Commodity exchange is an exchange of alienable objects between people who are in a state of reciprocal independence that establishes a quantitative relationship between the objects transacted, whereas gift exchange is an exchange of inalienable objects between people who are in a state of reciprocal dependence that establishes a qualitative relationship between the subjects transacting. [2]

This contribution illustrates the conflicting political, social and personal relations entailed in thinking, managing and delivering both a 'legacy' and a 'profit' – the elusive 'Olympic Gold' sought by organizers, politicians, communities and sponsors – not to mention athletes. We argue that the 'golden legacy' of 2012, if it is to be delivered through the vectors afforded by the games, requires sensitivity to the 'mixed economies' of commodity and gift. The fate of, and prospects for, a 2012 'legacy' are imperilled in proportion to the extent to which the commodity modality dominates the gift and where their socio-economic dynamics are unthought and ungoverned. We draw on a number of sources in order to argue that legacy – or 'legacy momentum' – is predicated upon and ensured by governance processes sensitive to the tensions in operation between 'commodity Olympism' and 'gift Olympism'. This dialogism is placed at risk by the primacy of a foreclosing discourse of contractual relations that permeates both economic and cultural life in the mega-project that is London 2012.

'Cost Benefit' Games

On 29 January 2008, the House of Commons Culture, Media and Sport Committee met to discuss 'London 2012' with Tessa Jowell, the government minister with responsibility for the games and London. The committee was questioning government ministers, civil servants and 2012 officers for the fourth time about the games in a little over three months. On opening the meeting, the chair, John Whittingdale MP, immediately raised the main issue: 'Chairman: Thank you. Inevitably, we are going to get into the money quite rapidly. Can I turn to Helen Southworth?' [3]

The committee's concerns about 'the money' reflected a wider media and public interest in the cost of the games, an interest that was stirred, in particular, by government announcements in March 2007 that the cost of the games was set to rise from an initial estimate of £2.4bn to a revised budget of £9.3bn. The additional money was to be raised through a further commitment by government of £6bn (including £2.2bn from the national lottery, of which £675m was extra funding). The revised costs were driven by several factors, including the rising price of land remediation, the increased allocation to contingency, tax (the imposition of Value Added Tax (VAT)) and the rising costs of security. [4] To address this cost problem, government and the mayor of London, committed themselves, in November 2007, to the sale of parkland after 2012 to offset any deficits that might arise from the event not covering its costs. Hence, Department for Culture, Media and Sport (DCMS) Select Committee member Helen Southworth's interest in the rigour of the business planning for 2012 and the form that the agreement between government departments might take to ensure the 'realization of assets' to pay back the monies owed to the lottery fund:

> This is something you will understand absolutely, Minister, that those of us from outside London have a very particular interest in. Can I ask you if you can focus around the new memorandum of understanding which is setting out some of the processes by which Lottery monies will be repaid from the benefits of realization of assets rather than profits. Could you actually take us through some of those things? We are very particularly interested in how focused organisation is currently on having a very robust business planning process to ensure that there is an actual return on assets, that the amounts are delivered and that the memorandum will actually operate, that it is not going to be a gentleman's agreement that starts disappearing into the future. First of all, how robust is the business planning going

to be to ensure that there is a return? Secondly, how guaranteed is it that that is actually going to be paid and we are going to see the benefit of it? [5]

The words used by Helen Southworth to interrogate the minister reflects a broader consensus among many business and academic authors on how best to evaluate the economics of the 2012 games. [6] In turn, the minister, Tessa Jowell's reply responded reassuringly on the 'rigour' of the business case while also indicating that the social or regeneration 'legacy' of the games could be accommodated within the framework of the business model:

> *Tessa Jowell*: Let me take that in two parts. First, the robustness of the assumptions and therefore the business case on which the agreement about disbursement was then reached between me and the Mayor. The LDA [London Development Agency] undertook through the work of a surveying and estate agency which has a national reputation an assessment of trends in land prices and they concluded that there was a likely range by the time at which land would be available for sale after 2012 of between £800 million, the most pessimistic case, and £3.2 billion, the most optimistic case. Again, based on the increase in land values over the last 20 years, of which the average has been 19.5 per cent, we went for the midpoint, which by general agreement is a prudent and realistic assumption. So our assumption about the return from the sale of the land is £1.8 billion. In relation to how that will be repaid, because it is our intention that the Lottery should be reimbursed for the £675 million most recent diversion, which is currently being considered by the House, the agreement is that the first tranche, £650 million, will be repaid to the LDA, which is the cost of land acquisition. Seventy-five per cent of the next tranche, £531 million, from memory, will go to the Lottery and 25 per cent to the LDA. From the third tranche, 25 per cent will come back to the Lottery, completing the repayment of the Lottery, and the remainder will go to the LDA and of course, it is the LDA's intention that that money is used for the further regeneration of the Lower Lea Valley, so for the construction of more homes in the development of the community that will be a very important part of the legacy there. [7]

The exchange in the House of Commons DCMS Committee is perhaps unsurprising. The committee was tasked to investigate the preparation for the games and the implications of government policies for achieving its objectives and managing public funds to meet the games costs. The exchange does, however, reveal the dominance of the 'business case' mode of analysis and how regeneration, in this case of the Lower Lea Valley, may arise as perhaps a fortunate 'remainder' or residual consequence of the contractual approach. This contractual approach to the games as a mega-project has shaped the initial public debates regarding the impact of proposals for urban regeneration on the economics of London 2012.

The London 2012 Bid

In 2002, a consultancy company, ARUP was commissioned by the government to provide a report on the capacity of London to host the 2012 Olympic and Paralympic

Games. A summary report was published in May 2002 and provided a financial analysis of the cost of hosting the event. Consistent with the cost/benefit approach, the analysis focused upon the costs and income for bidding, preparing and staging the games, provision for risk, and 'an estimation of the residual values of the assets created'. [8] The report estimated total expenditure at £1.79bn with income estimated at £1.3bn, leaving a shortfall of about £0.5bn that could be reduced significantly according to ARUP, since the report's authors had been conservative in their estimates of income. The government established a cabinet subcommittee to examine the ARUP report and requested a senior civil servant to review carefully ARUP's estimation of costs. The civil servant, Robert Raine, found the ARUP report to underestimate costs by about £800m. [9] A revised figure of $3.8bn (£2.4bn) was eventually agreed, and that figure was submitted in the candidate file to the International Olympic Committee (IOC) by the London bid team: [10] (7):

> The UK Government, the Mayor of London and the BOA [British Olympic Association] have created a successful partnership to oversee the preparation by London 2012 of London's bid. Support from national, regional and local government is detailed below. This support includes a funding package for specific Olympic costs from the UK Government and the Mayor of London totaling $3.8 billion. The Chancellor of the Exchequer has guaranteed that the UK Government will provide all necessary financial support to ensure successful Olympic and Paralympic Games. This includes:
> - Acting as ultimate guarantor of the construction costs of infrastructure, venues and facilities necessary to hold the Games.
> - Ensuring that funds are made available from the $3.8 billion funding package to pre-finance the [London Organizing Committee for the Olympic Games] LOCOG's expenditure prior to receiving Games revenue.
> - Bearing the cost of providing security, medical and other Government-related services for the Games. Legislation is currently progressing through Parliament that will enable up to $2.4 billion of National Lottery revenue to be used towards the preparation and delivery of the Games. The UK Government will bring forward legislation to ensure the delivery of the Games by creating the ODA [Olympic Development Authority], and to align UK legislation with IOC requirements, for example by introducing strict regulations to counter ambush marketing, as soon after July 2005 as possible (as detailed in sections 3.3 and 3.5). [11]

The successful London bid primarily based its financial estimates on the costs required to fund the event. The £2.4bn did not include the non-event-related expenditures required to enable East London to host the games – these infrastructure costs were, in part, already guaranteed by government as a component of the infrastructure development of the wider Thames Gateway and, in particular, the completion of the Eurostar high-speed train project with its upgraded Stratford station located adjacent to the proposed Olympic park. [12] The complementarity of regional regeneration plans with the proposal to locate the games in an Olympic Park centred in East London provided a compelling, technically strong, bid.

The bid's success was widely attributed to the commitment to locating the games in a deprived area of East London, with the regeneration theme appealing to an IOC that was chastened by the Olympic movement's recent history of being criticized for its embrace of commercialism – especially in the wake of the Atlanta 1996 games. [13] The London bid appeared to draw inspiration from Barcelona (1992), a city that had successfully allied social regeneration and economic development to its hosting of the games. [14] London's success, however, has subsequently revealed the hazards associated with combining schemes for urban regeneration and renewal with a bid to host a mega-event. These hazards constitute the ingredients for the complex interplay of the concepts of the 'gift' and 'commodity' economies – and the likely subordination of the former to the latter in the context of the contemporary UK economy.

The Hazards of the Regeneration Game(s)

The programme of urban regeneration associated with hosting the 2012 games is perhaps the most ambitious for a host city in the history of the modern Olympics. East London's status as the poor relation to the West of the city has long historical roots in the industrialization and urban expansion of the city. Historically, the East housed the city's working class, and employment and economic activity relied heavily upon the docks and the manufacturing industries that spread around them. The closure of the docks and the demise of manufacturing in the area in the 1970s and 1980s reinforced the divide between the rich West and the poor East. [15] The Docklands development, initiated in the 1980s, was designed to extend the more dynamic service sector, especially financial service industries, into the East. The development – mainly focused upon the Isle of Dogs and, in particular, Canary Wharf – though subject to boom–bust–boom, eventually achieved its stated goals. It extended the financial centre of the city eastwards and provided a boost to mainly private sector housing development, with many luxury homes attracting the relocation of professional dwellers. The future of London as a global centre for financial services was secured. The development, initiated in the neo-liberal climate of the 1980s, did little, however, to address the underlying social problems of East London. Indeed, critics have rightly argued that the Docklands development has served to reinforce the polarization between rich and poor communities in East London. [16]

It is precisely this divide that the organizers of 2012 claim to address, the legacy of the games being linked to challenging the underlying social and economic problems of East London – the skills deficit, chronic unemployment, health inequalities and lack of available and affordable housing for local people. In addition to these social objectives, the Olympic Park construction seeks to be a showcase for environmental and sustainable development. Government, the Mayor of London and the London Organizing Committee for the Olympic Games (LOCOG) have published a significant number of policy documents containing promises and pledges relating to achieving a positive social, economic, cultural and environmental legacy. [17]

When allied to the local council's plans for the development of 'Stratford City', a public/private funded initiative aimed at constructing a new housing and retail centre adjacent to the Olympic Park, the programme of regeneration for the Lower Lea Valley area almost achieves the scale of creating a new town:

> Stratford City ... will result in one of the largest mixed-use developments in the UK for many years to come. Covering 73 hectares of largely derelict land, the next 15 years will see the creation of a new £4bn metropolitan centre in East London, with more than 100 shops, three big department stores, cafés, schools, hotels, parks and health centres. There will be a new commercial district with landmark towers and new leisure facilities, all in a quality setting with water features. New urban districts will house an extra 11,000 residents and 30,000 workers. It will also house most of the 2012 Olympic athletes. [18]

As the promises and policies relating to achieving a 'sustainable legacy' have been elaborated by government, regeneration agencies and 2012 organizers over the past two years, the costs associated with the 2012 games have, it seems, soared. At the same time, legacy aspirations have been firmly placed within the nexus of the 'cost/benefit', commodity economy for several reasons.

First, the evolution of the IOC approach to the bidding process for hosting the games has shifted focus away from the 'Disney world' model of the commercialization of the mega-event toward a more nuanced, socially responsible attachment to economic development and urban renewal. This distancing from the commodity-style games, which began in 1984 in Los Angeles, has been reflected in candidate files and the IOC's own evaluation process for the games, the Olympic Games Global Impact (OGGI) study. [19] Second, prospective host cities have incorporated social goals into bids without undertaking the detailed tasks associated with evaluating such large-scale projects. The bids are designed to win the competition – the reconciliation of aspirations set down in the candidate file with the financial framework required to deliver them really commences after the winning city is announced. The potential gap between aspiration and reality is filled, according to IOC regulations, by guarantees underwritten by the host city and national government. [20] The bidding process itself creates the capacity for the confusion of event- and non-direct-event-related investment – the former being expenditure related to putting the event on and the latter being the investment in infrastructure that may strengthen the bid but not be attributable to meeting its direct costs.

Finally, the partnership of political institutions and agencies that are formed to put on the event attaches social, economic, cultural and environmental goals to its bid to win domestic public support and, most importantly, legitimate the expenditure required to host a 'gigantic' games. The social dimensions of legacy are caught in the gap between aspiration and affordability. Paradoxically, the IOC's concern to contain the commercialization of the games, in practice, ensures that the process of city building or urban regeneration is 'commodified' within a specific spatial and temporal context, typically in circumstances where the host city population has little capacity for democratic intervention in shaping the outcomes of the regeneration process itself. [21]

These 'hazards' have certainly shaped the early debates regarding London 2012. A National Audit Office Report into the risk assessment and management of the 2012 games (2007) identifies the non-event-related infrastructure costs (£9.9bn) and specifies an additional sum (£1.04bn) set aside by government for non-Olympic-related infrastructure costs arising from construction work in the Olympic Park that was required to regenerate the area even if the games were not taking place. In particular, this expenditure involved the expense associated with moving overhead power lines underground and the construction of bridges, tunnels and roadways, the costs for which were designated as '75 percent Olympic and 25 percent non-Olympic': [22]

> **43** The Candidate File described capital investment for venues and facilities, Olympic Park infrastructure, and roads and railways, which was to be financed by a combination of the public sector funding package to the extent that the work was Olympic related (for Olympic related costs see paragraph 70), and further contributions from the public and private sectors. The costs were estimated in pounds sterling and converted into US dollars for the Candidate File, using an exchange rate of £1 = $1.6. The Candidate File showed that the capital investment amounted to $15.8 billion (£9.9 billion) and stated that funding for some $11 billion of this total related to transport investments for which funding was already committed at the time of the bid.
>
> **44** In May 2003 the Government and the Mayor of London agreed a memorandum of understanding which provided for a 'public sector funding package' of up to £2.375 billion to meet the costs of the Olympic and Paralympic Games (Figure 5). The Government is also to provide £1.044 billion towards the costs of 'non-Olympic' infrastructure (see paragraph 71) on the site of the Olympic Park. [23]

The additional cost attributed to the Olympic Park (£1.04bn) caused the government to announce a revision to the games budget in 2006, a revision that amounted to an increase from £2.4bn to £3.4bn. By 2007, a further revision was announced to include contingency (£2.747bn), £836m for tax, a rise in security costs to £600m, an increase in the Olympic Development Authority (ODA)'s programme delivery budget from £16m to £570m, and a decrease (from £738m to £165m) in the anticipated private sector contribution to meeting the costs of the games. The consequence of these adjustments was that the public sector funds available to meet the costs of the games and associated infrastructure development were required to increase by about £4.7bn net, including £2.7bn contingency. [24] The 'gap' of £2–4bn in the public funding estimated to be needed at the time of the bid and that required by spring 2007 was primarily attributable to the underestimation of tax (VAT – a cost to the games paid out by government but returned to the Exchequer) and the poor initial assessment of security costs, park remediation costs and the expenditure associated with the logistics costs of the ODA (the initial budget for ODA costs had been estimated as if it were a small urban development corporation, the complexity of delivering the project management for the games was ignored). [25]

The 'technically' polished London bid was deeply flawed in relation to estimating clearly identifiable, event-related costs, including contingency and the attribution of tax; the expenditure required to clean up the highly contaminated parkland was also, more understandably, underestimated. Such errors, however, are not unusual in the planning and construction of major projects and mega-events, especially when such events are related to a wider process of urban regeneration or development, as the Athens and Beijing games have revealed. Event-related and infrastructure costs in Beijing, for example, have, according to several estimates, exceeded the bid book by over $20bn and, as a recent study of mega-projects and risk has revealed, across the world nine out of every ten transport infrastructure project costs exceed initial estimated costs by 50–100%. [26]

A benign observer could suggest that the overall event- and non-event-related infrastructure costs of hosting the Olympics and developing a part of East London – a figure of around £18bn, including a cost overrun of approximately £5bn – places the '2012' mega-project at the lower end of the spectrum of the 'calamitous history of cost overruns'. [27] This was not, however, the interpretation or response typically to be found in the UK media. The initial acclaim arising from the UK's successful bid was quickly replaced by articles critical of the uncertainties surrounding the budget, the continual revisions of budget costs by government, and the elaboration of more specific criticisms of the costs associated with the creation of the widely derided Olympic logo, the design and cost of the Olympic Park sporting arenas, the salary costs of LOCOG senior staff, and, by early 2008, the revised estimates of land values emerging from the economic problems posed by the credit crunch. [28] One journalist from the popular press summed up much of the media's perspective on the games and 'money' in concluding that Olympic funding had gone from 'joke to scandal':

> London's Mayor Ken Livingstone has dropped the 2012 Olympics into a billion pound black hole. He has overestimated the value of sporting facility land that can be sold when the event finishes. So the £9.3bn costs will climb even higher. Olympic funding has gone from joke to scandal. The nation is being ripped off years before a single race has been run. In July, we will celebrate the 60th anniversary of the 1948 London Games. Those Olympics cost £761,888 (£77 million in today's money) and they made a profit of £29,420 (£3m today). Times are different, I know. But that was a real Labour government, not one conned rigid by the money men. [29]

From the arguments of countless media articles to the critical reports of Parliamentary select committees, the rising costs associated with hosting the 2012 Olympics have come to dominate public discussion about the games and their eventual legacy. The discourse has been conducted entirely within the framework of the commodity economy, with many concluding that the costs outweigh the benefits of hosting the event. This hostile press and public criticism by politicians has gathered considerable momentum in the UK over the past two years, despite the IOC's generally positive evaluations of London's preparations, evaluations informed by the IOCs own values of 'Olympism'.

The Olympic 'Family' and Olympism

The IOC evokes the attributes of an alternative, socially responsible approach to hosting the Olympic Games, adopting the language of the gift economy. The Olympics is not merely a global sporting event but one that projects universal human values and that promotes, for example, cultural exchange, educational development and international understanding as major components of the participation in the world's leading sporting event. Such values are represented in the ethos of the Olympic 'family'. [30]

It is within the family that theorists of the gift economy observe the origins of an alternative to the commercial economy. The commercial economy is based upon the alienation of labour, the creation of commodities and their exchange as equivalents in the marketplace; this exchange masks a deeply unequal social relationship inherent in the process of their production. By contrast, the family is the location in which alienation through exchange is replaced by social bonds arising from the conferral not of commodities but of 'gifts' which do not acquire the character of alienated labour and which enable social bonds to be forged across generations. Obligation is not defined by a commercial contract but arises from social interactions that confer authenticity and social regard or respect – non-market-related attributes of positive human relations. [31]

The IOCs evocation of the 'family' and the mutuality of its social relations are central to the philosophy of modern Olympism. [32] Olympism, however, seeks to transfer this mutuality from the family to civil society. It is in this process that the IOC and the wider Olympic movement have created a *simulation* of the gift economy within the context of a highly commercialized or commodified form; simulation is now represented in the form of the Olympic 'brand'. The brand is purchased by sponsors, who in turn receive the right to the use of the Olympic logo. The 'gift' of sponsorship provides the basis for the contractual obligations to be set between host cities and the IOC; sponsorship is an important source of income to offset the cost of staging the games. In turn, over recent games, sponsors have engaged with both commercial (Atlanta 1996) and social and environmental agendas (Sydney 2000, London 2012), to influence decisions about legacy and achieve competitive advantage through the promotion of their adherence to programmes of social responsibility. [33]

The Olympics becomes a vehicle for enterprise to practise 'pseudoregard', while the underlying contractual obligations between host city, national government, the IOC and enterprise exact an increasing hold over the wider process of urban development and city building. The discourse of city building is trapped in the immediacy of market relations (costs and benefits) to the exclusion of the 'gift' – the transformative character of which is premised upon the passing between groups, group members and generations of building and elaborating social capital, rather than the immediacy inherent in the relations of commodity exchange.

London's 'Gift'

On 6 July 2005, when London won the 2012 Olympics, there was a moment of collective euphoria that cannot quite be properly explained retrospectively. The scenes in Trafalgar Square were echoed in Stratford and elsewhere, and even while the euphoria was tragically cut short by the terrorist attacks on 7 July there was not a long delay before popular articulations of refusal or indifference emerged about the distribution of the Olympic 'Gold'. The recipient of the gift becomes the *host* – and the host, as recipient of the gift, soon becomes one who is required to give in turn. There is a responsibility attaching to receiving the gift – it must be passed on. As cultural theorist Lewis Hyde intimates: *The gift must always move.* [34] If it is not passed on (within Hyde's logic), the gift becomes a burden – or even a curse.

The transformational nature of the (dynamic) gift is at the heart of a number of accounts of 'bounty' that comes as a reward, but also as a trial or test for the protagonists of folktales. Hyde builds a compelling synthesis of myths and theories of gifts as 'transformative' and creative interventions in individual and collective life. [35] While the folktales and fairy tales Hyde cites hardly constitute sociological evidence, his line of argument is traced equally through the detailed anthropological fieldwork of Bronislaw Malinowski as well as accounts by Marcel Mauss and Marshall Sahlins. [36] Hyde's central proposition that, unlike the commodity, 'the gift keeps on moving', synthesized from his eclectic range of academic and folkloric sources, provides a powerful critique of the commodity as a static; an exhausted and exhausting modality for human and social relations – lacking narrative and futurity. Elliptically, Hyde's argument, derived from his general account of cultural creativity, offers a relevant set of insights for thinking about the 'movement'/momentum (or otherwise) of the Olympic 'gift' of legacy.

> In folktales the gift is often something seemingly worthless – ashes or coals or leaves or straw – but when the puzzled recipient carries it to his doorstep, he finds it has turned to gold. Typically an increase inheres in the gift only so long as it is treated as such – as soon as the happy mortal starts to count it or grabs his wheelbarrow and heads back for more, the gold reverts to straw. The growth is in the sentiment; it can't be put on the scale. [37]

Hyde's analysis provides a valuable tool for opening up thinking about the desire for and anxiety about Olympic 'Gold', not least because Olympism stakes its claim as connected to a (no doubt mythologized) ancient past – of ritual and collective solidarities. The modern Olympics constitutes a mega-event and, in its vast scale, perhaps speaks more of modernity, or, to follow the anthropologist Mark Auge's lead, 'supermodernity', [38] than of the ancient festivals of religion, sport and culture from which it derives its name. Nevertheless, as the classical Greek philosopher Philostratus describes, a component of the ancient games was this:

> When the people of Elis had sacrificed, then the ambassadors of the Greeks, whoever happened to be there, were expected to offer a sacrifice. [39]

It is clear that the Olympic festivals were in some respects reminiscent of some of the pre-modern gifting ceremonies that inform modern anthropological accounts of gift economies. [40] Notwithstanding the tenuousness of such telescopic 'history' – the games' explicit engagements with the languages of familial connection, community building, regeneration, and, lately, legacy construct (if they do not affirm) a genealogy connecting the games more precisely to gift economies – and their 'powers' of cultural restoration/regeneration – and more than other types of mega-events (Expos/world fairs and even extended tournaments, such as the FIFA world cup or national sports festivals, such as the Super Bowl), which are unashamedly festivals of the commodity. [41] The passing of the Olympic flame – the 'spirit' in which the Olympic asset is at once enshrined and let free/passed on – from hand to hand – from host to host – is the most potent symbol of this aspiration, and it ritualizes Hyde's maxim that *the gift must always move*. As Hyde argues: 'There are other forms of property that stand still, that mark a boundary or resist momentum, but the gift keeps going.' [42]

Even without this antecedent connection to such ritualism and collective and public sacrifice and feasting, the Olympics – as both a 'brand' and a 'movement' – poses for us the dichotomy of gift and commodity exchange – a prominent articulation of a dichotomy that is constitutive within contemporary everyday life. [43]

We are not arguing for the Olympics to become a kind of public gift or sacrifice, a national endowment upon the East End of London from a beneficent government and the IOC. [44] But we *are* suggesting that a foregrounding acknowledgement of the necessarily hybrid gift and commodity Olympics is a worthwhile precursor and frame for thinking and planning for the kinds and types of public and private investments around 2012, and also for better ensuring the *social* character and modalities of disbursement/accumulation that can be hoped for and facilitated under the headings 'Olympic' and 'legacy'. It is to the extent that the 'gift mode' is to the fore that the games might induce a dynamic and transformational set of legacies – tangible and intangible – whereby the definition of the Olympic 'Gold' is informed in accountabilities to and engagements of community and political visions and imperatives, rather than in accountabilities of standard, corporate-style accounting.

There is inevitably a co-mingling of 'gift' and 'commodity'-centred conceptions of the Olympics. The anthropologist Arjun Appadurai warns against 'exaggeration and reification of the contrast between gift and commodity', pointing at anthropological writings in particular. [45] Certainly, it is important to acknowledge a degree of necessary 'concurrency' (if that is the right word) across and between these two modalities of exchange and engagement. The modes are hard to conceive of in isolation from their shadow opposites. Frow comments that social life is permeated by just this tension: 'The realm of the everyday is the place where, through the constant transformation of commodity relations into gift relations, it becomes difficult to hold the two terms in their categorical purity.' [46]

However, we argue that this necessary hybridity can be acknowledged without accepting, as Appadurai seems to, Bourdieu's insistence that 'practice never ceases to conform to economic calculation even where it gives every appearance of disinterestedness by departing from the logic of interested calculation (in the narrow sense) and playing for stakes that are non-material and not easily quantified.' [47]

Even if this is the case, there is a value in keeping open the space of the gift as a significant and qualitatively different order of activity, since not to do so – to collapse too readily the distinctions between narrow contractualism (driven by money) and variously elaborated reciprocities and engagement – is, we argue, to foreclose the (optimistic) possibility of a genuine accumulation of social and collective benefit from the 2012 games for London. The social philosopher Marcel Mauss makes a general point in his classic examination, *The Gift*, which is prescient in the run-up to this, our twenty-first-century version of an ancient festival transplanted from Athenian society:

> It is a good thing possibly that there exist means of expenditure and exchange other than economic ones. … I believe that we must become, in proportion as we would develop our wealth, something more than better financiers, accountants and administrators. The mere pursuit of individual ends is harmful to the ends and peace of the whole, to the rhythm of its work and pleasures, and hence in the end to the individual. [48]

The Olympics project awakens an anxiety about what it is that 'survives' and what 'withers' outside the spreadsheets and forecasting technologies through which, often with impressive efficiency, and sometimes not, the abstract vision – of a stadium, a cultural venue or a piece of restored land – materializes. Indeed, the very materiality – the quality of the space – opened up by the Olympics – is, we argue, a matter partly of the successful and integrative conjunction of modalities of provision and appropriation (gift and commodity) that will underpin them.

The commodification of space in regeneration is a problem explored in detail by, for instance, the contemporary critics of the modern city, Stephen Graham and Simon Marvin, in the thesis of their excellent study *Splintering Urbanism*. [49] London 2012 has become a part of the everyday lives of many Londoners, and, will be so for many more as the games approach, notably as volunteers *give* up their time and labour to the successful running of the event. We argue that the planning, delivery and conceiving of the games (and not just their anticipation) should be actively cultivated as a component of the time/space of the East London everyday – so as to stay 'in touch' in its pristine 'figured' [50] future in just the way that undoubtedly the yet-to-be refiguring and disfiguring processes of construction are 'in touch' with the inhabitants of the five boroughs. The Olympic infrastructure – the facilities and the park – must not become redundant – everyone agrees on that. It is a truism of legacy planning. But there are modes of use and modes of engagement that, to reiterate, materialize in the contexts of entailed provisioning and appropriation – especially in the instituted give-and-take of the facility at hand.

Conclusion: The Park and the Gift

As Hyde contends in his theory of gifts and commodities, 'the assumptions of market exchange may not necessarily lead to an emergence of boundaries, but they do in practice.' [51] In Barcelona, the Olympic Park stands as a monument to the legacy of the games. It is both a symbolic and functional component of the cityscape and of its everyday life. It has a function for tourism and for place-making. It is of the city – part of the fabric of Barcelona. Other event venues at other games have attracted the dreaded 'white elephant' tag. We think 'use' and 'non-use' do not adequately get to the point. Utilitarianism provides necessary but not sufficient criteria for evaluating legacy, just as the usefulness of the gift does not fulfil or exhaust its function. The closing off of a utility from its communities might ensure use – but if the privatization of the gift means that accessibility is a matter for only a few who can afford premium prices – the utility will mask significant exclusion. If in London we witness a primarily commodity Olympics, the park will become a series of splintered fragments – premium assets disconnected from the public spaces of city and community within the urban realm, and the gift-based catalytic effects will not materialize. The gift will cease to move. The Olympic park, site of memory and the evolving history/legacy of London's games, will become instead a non-place.

Two of Mark Auge's concepts underscore our prediction. The first is his well-known notion of 'non-place'; the second is his understanding of the kind of contractual relating that inheres in a non-place environment:

> Clearly the word 'non-place' designates two complementary but distinct realities: spaces formed in relations to certain ends (transport, transit, commerce, leisure), and the relations that individuals have with these spaces. Although the two sets of relations overlap to a large extent, and in any case officially (individuals travel, make purchases, relax), they are still not to be confused with one another; for non-places mediate a whole mass of relations, with the self and with others, which are only indirectly connected with their purposes. As anthropological places create the organically social, so-non-places create solitary contractuality. [52]

The park – and its extended facilities – extended geographically into the five boroughs, and temporally, in the emerging modalities of legacy – risk becoming non-space facilities bound to the logics of market exchange. The fear of 'white elephant' non-utilization – of the commodity not being bought or the gift not being received – might encourage those responsible (the London Development Agency) into arrangements whereby the park becomes a functional non-space. Will we see the construction of Putnam's bowling alley in the future park? [53] That is one scenario for the commodified utilization of a corner of the post-games space.

A governance structure confident to pass the Olympic assets on in part in the mode of a gift, and translated into the political economy of contemporary city building, depends upon dialogic reciprocities emergent from open and political processes and local engagements. [54] These are a necessary complement to the cost/benefit planning and project management attached to the delivery of the games and their legacy. To split the two apart in the development phase, as seems to be happening, risks instituting a disconnection 'down the line' and stunting the dynamism of the Olympic gift. As Lewis Hyde observes in *The Gift*:

> When a gift passes from hand to hand in this spirit, it becomes the binder of many wills. What gathers in it is not only the sentiment of generosity but the affirmation of individual goodwill, making of those separate parts a *spiritus mundi*, a unanimous heart, a band whose wills are focussed through the lens of the gift. Thus the gift becomes the agent of social cohesion, and this again leads to the feeling that its passage increases its worth, for in social life at least, the whole really is greater than the sum of its parts. [55]

It is the material and redistributive circulation of the Olympic asset – through the properly appointed materiality of the legacy assets – that will ensure this accumulation of positive affect around the Olympic Games. It is upon such accumulation, among a number of other things, that a lasting legacy depends.

Notes

[1] See, for example, Sennett, who argues that 'good city builders of the past ... did more than just represent the existing social and political conditions of their times. They sought to interpret and so to transmute the material conditions of the political economy through the expressive medium of walls and windows, volumes and perspectives – an art that concentrated on details, compounded specific discoveries about space into an urban whole. The art of urban design is a craft work' (Sennett, 'Capitalism and the City', 121). Other authors (Parkinson and Boddy, 21) have identified the characteristics of good city building as being linked to enhancing social cohesion, while those seeking to develop a 'new urbanism' have focused upon the potentiality for renewed forms of democracy to create cities that are built upon disagreement and conflict 'but within a framework of universal rights designed to build disciplines of empowerment' (Amin and Thrift, *Cities*, 6).

[2] Gregory, 'Kula Gift Exchange and Capitalist Commodity Exchange'. Further relevant discussions of 'gift economies' include Hyde, *The Gift*; Polanyi (1944); Polanyi *et al.*, *Trade and Markets in the Early Empires;* Mauss, *The Gift*. 'Legacy momentum' is a concept developed as part of an assessment undertaken by London East Research Institute as part of a broad analysis of the prospects for a good legacy from the London 2012 games. This was published (May 2007) by the London Assembly in a report: *A Lasting Legacy for London? Assessing the Legacy of the Olympic Games and Paralympic Games*. London, Greater London Authority (May 2007).

[3] Department of Culture, Media and Sport, Transcript of Oral Evidence.

[4] National Audit Office, 'Preparations for the London 2012 Olympic and Paralympic Games.

[5] Department of Culture, Media and Sport, Transcript of Oral Evidence.

[6] On this consensus among business and academic authors, see, for example, Donovan, *East London's Economy and the Olympics*; Evans, 'London 2012'.

[7] Department of Culture, Media and Sport, Transcript of Oral Evidence.

[8] 'ARUP London Olympics 2012 Costs and Benefits Summary'.

[9] Lee, *The Race for the 2012 Olympics*.

[10] For a detailed 'insider' analysis of this process, see Lee, *The Race for the 2012 Olympics*. Lee was Communications Director for the London 2012 bid team.

[11] International Olympic Committee, London Candidate File, vol. 1, 36.

[12] See Department of Communities and Local Government (2007), Thames Gateway Delivery Plan, available at hhtp://communities.gov.uk/publications/thamesgateway/deliveryplan, accessed 18 April 2008, and National Audit Office, 'Preparations for the London 2012 Olympic and Paralympic Games'.

[13] Barney *et al.*, *Selling the Five Rings*, 275–88.

[14] Poynter, 'From Beijing to Bow Creek', 7–8.

[15] See Hamnett, *Unequal City*, 1–21 and Poynter, 'From Beijing to Bow Creek', 288–316.

[16] Hamnett, *Unequal City*, 243.

[17] See, for example, London Organizing Committee of the Olympic Games, *Towards a One Planet 2012*; and Mayor of London. *Five Legacy Commitments'*.

[18] Newham Council, *Regeneration Projects: Stratford City*.

[19] 'What Is the Olympic Games Global Impact Study?', *Olympic Review*, June 2006, available at http://multimedia.olympic.org/pdf/en_report_1077.pdf, accessed 15 June 2008; Philippe Furrer, *Sustainable Olympic Games, a dream or a reality?*

[20] See, for example, the IOC regulations governing the procedure for selecting the host city for 2008: IOC, 'Games of the XX1X Olympiad, in 2008 Host City, Candidate Acceptance Procedure', available at http://multimedia.olympic.org/pdf/en_report_295.pdf, accessed 15 June 2008.

[21] Burbank *et al.*, *Olympic Dreams*.

[22] National Audit Office, 'Preparations for the London 2012 Olympic and Paralympic Games'.

[23] Ibid., 13.

[24] Flyvberg *et al.*, *Megaprojects and Risk*.

[25] National Audit Office, 'Preparations for the London 2012 Olympic and Paralympic Games', and 'Preparing for Sporting Success at the London 2012 Olympic and Paralympic Games and Beyond'.

[26] Flyvberg *et al.*, *Megaprojects and Risk*.

[27] Ibid., 11.

[28] See, for example, *The Metro*, 'The London 2012 Logo, the Blogosphere Is Angry', available at http://www.metro.co.uk/news/article.html?in_article_id=51740&in_page_id=34, accessed 20 April 2008; Ross Lydall, 'The London Assembly, the Olympics and More Doom and Gloom for Ken', *Evening Standard* 25 Feb. 2008, available at http://lydall.thisislondon.co.uk/2008/02/the-london-asse.html; Paul Kelso, 'Parliament and Public Misled over Olympics Budget says MPs', *Guardian*, 22 April 2008.

[29] Paul Routledge, 'Ken's Gold Muddle', *London Daily Mirror*, 18 Jan. 2008.

[30] See, for example, Booth, 'Gifts of Corruption: Ambiguities of Obligation in the Olympic Movement', 43–68.

[31] Offer, 'Between the Gift and the Market, the Economy of Regard', 450–76.

[32] The lyrics from the Beijing opening ceremony song provides recent evidence of BOCOG and IOC commitments to a strong articulation of these ideas (of family, sharing and mutuality). For example: 'you and me, from one world, heart to heart, we are one family, for dreams we travel, thousands of miles we meet in Beijing, come together, the joy we share, you and me, from one world, forever we are one family'. Lyrics and music were composed by Chen Qigang. These commitments are instituted in the daily working of the IOC – in the work, for instance, of Olympic Solidarity (Chappelet and Kubler-Mabbott, 2008).

[33] Barney *et al.*, *Selling the Five Rings*, is the most detailed account of the emergence of a commercialized Olympic movement.

[34] Hyde, *The Gift*, 4.

[35] Ibid.

[36] For instance, Malinowski, *Argonauts of the Western Pacific*; Sahlins, *Stone Age Economics*; and Mauss, *The Gift*.

[37] Hyde, *The Gift*, 35.

[38] Auge, *Non-places: Introduction to an Anthropology of Supermodernity.*

[39] Philostratus, 'On Athletics', 214.

[40] Sacrifices, for Mauss, are gifts of a particular kind: given to the gods: 'The relationships that exist between these contracts and exchanges among humans and those between men and the gods throw light on a whole aspect of the theory of sacrifice. First, they are perfectly understood, particularly in those societies in which, although contractual and economic rituals are practised between men, these men are the masked incarnations, often shaman priest-sorcerers, possessed by the spirit whose name they bear. In reality, they merely act as representatives of the spirits, because these exchanges and contracts not only bear people and things along in their wake, but also the sacred beings that, to a greater or lesser extent, are associated with them. This is very clearly the case in the Tlingit potlatch ... and in the Eskimo potlatch.' Mauss, *The Gift*, 20.

[41] On the Olympics and the World Cup as mega-events, see Roche, *Mega-Events and Modernity.* On the Super Bowl as a 'potlatch', or, in the terminology of the iconoclastic American economist Thorstein Veblen, a spectacle of 'conspicuous consumption', see Hopsicker and Dyreson, 'Super Bowl Sunday', 30–55.

[42] Hyde, *The Gift*, 4.

[43] For cultural theorist John Frow, everyday life can be usefully understood as a conjunction of commodity and gift relations. Everyday life is 'a realm permeated by the archaic patterns of gift-obligation – the dangerous, fluid, subtle generosities that bind members into crystallized orders of relation, in all dimensions of human life, from which they cannot easily be released. These patterns of obligation are, at the same time, in tension with the contractual rationality of the commodity, which produces quite different forms of the everyday. It may produce greater equalities as well as greater inequalities; it may enhance the sharing of wealth, or it may reduce it. It can be seen as a liberation from the 'antiquated and dangerous gift economy', or as a destruction of human sharing.' Frow, 'Gift and Commodity', 217.

[44] Nor, however, would we argue for the games to become an entirely private affair, as in Los Angeles in 1984, or, in one extreme scenario, as might emerge from a global auction of the supposed 'brand equity' locked in the IOC's five-ring symbolism and other intellectual property assets. Both an entirely public gift-based Olympics mode and a totally commodified Olympics would be untenable ... although the privatization of a global asset seems the more plausible scenario.

[45] Appadurai, *The Social Life of Things*, 11.

[46] Frow, 'Gift and Commodity', 217.

[47] Bourdieu, *Outline of a Theory of Practice*, 177.

[48] Mauss, *The Gift*, 98.

[49] Graham and Marvin, *Splintering Urbanism.*

[50] Bowyer, 'The Great Frame Up', 81–109.

[51] Hyde, *The Gift*, 23.

[52] Auge, *Non-Places*, 94.

[53] Putnam, *Bowling Alone.*

[54] Contemporary city-building requires community-driven, planned public amenities and access to soft benefits in the form of skills and training – assets circulating and able to carry on giving within and beyond the local economy.

[55] Hyde, *The Gift*, 36.

References

Amin, A. and N. Thrift. *Cities, Reimagining the Urban.* Cambridge: Polity, 2002.

Appadurai, Arjun, ed. *The Social Life of Things: Commodities in Cultural Perspective*. Cambridge: Cambridge University Press, 1986.

'ARUP London Olympics 2012 Costs and Benefits Summary'. London: ARUP 21 May 2002, 4, available at http://www.arup.com/transactionadvice/project, accessed 20 April 2008.

Auge, Mark. *Non-places: Introduction to an Anthropology of Supermodernity*. London: Verso, 1995.

Barney, R., S.R. Wenn and S. Martyn. *Selling the Five Rings: The International Olympic Committee and the Rise of Olympic Commercialism*. Salt Lake City, UT: University of Utah Press, 2002.

Boddy, M. and M. Parkinson, eds. *City Matters*. Bristol: Policy Press, 2004.

Booth, D. 'Gifts of Corruption: Ambiguities of Obligation in the Olympic Movement'. *Olympika* 8 (1999): 43–68.

Bourdieu, P. *Outline of a Theory of Practice*. Cambridge: Cambridge University Press, 1977.

Bowyer, M. 'The Great Frame Up: Fantastic Appearances in Contemporary Spatial Politics'. In *Spatial Practices*, edited by Helen Liggett and David Perry. London: Sage, 1995: 81–109.

Burbank, M., G. Andranovitch and C. Heying. *Olympic Dreams: The Impact of Mega Events on Local Politics*. Boulder, CO: Lynne Rienner, 2001.

Chappelet, J.-L. and B. Kubler-Mabbot. *The International Olympic Committee and the Olympic System*. London: Routledge, 2008.

Department of Culture, Media and Sport. Transcript of Oral Evidence (uncorrected), House of Commons Culture, Media and Sport Committee, 29 Jan. 2008, HC104v, available at http://www.parliament.uk/parliamentary_committees/culture__media_and_sport/cmsfm080129.cfm, accessed 20 April 2008.

Donovan, P. *East London's Economy and the Olympics*. London: UBS Global Economic Perspectives (mimeo), 2006.

Evans, G. 'London 2012'. In *Olympic Cities: City Agendas, Planning and the World's Games, 1896–2012*, edited by John Gold and Margaret Gold. London: Routledge, 2007.

Flyvberg, B., N. Bruzelius and W. Rothengatter. *Megaprojects and Risk*. Cambridge: Cambridge University Press, 2003.

Frow, J. 'Gift and Commodity'. In *Time and Commodity Culture: Essays in Cultural Theory and Postmodernism*. Oxford: Oxford University Press, 1997: 102–17.

——. *Time and Commodity Culture: Essays in Cultural Theory and Postmodernism*. Oxford: Clarendon Press, 1997.

Furrer, P. *Sustainable Olympic Games, a Dream or a Reality?* available at http://www.omero.unito.it/web/Furrer%20(eng.).pdf, accessed 15 June 2008.

GLA/LERI. 'A Lasting Legacy for London: Assessing the Legacy of the Olympic and Paralympic Games'. London: Greater London Authority (May 2007), available as pdf file at http://www.london.gov.uk/assembly/reports/econsd.jsp, accessed March 2008.

Gold, John and Margaret Gold, eds. *Olympic Cities: City Agendas, Planning and the World's Games, 1896–2012*. London: Routledge, 2007.

Graham, S. and S. Marvin. *Splintering Urbanism: Networked Infrastructures, Technological Mobilities and the Urban Condition*. London: Routledge, 2001.

Gregory, Chris. 'Kula Gift Exchange and Capitalist Commodity Exchange: A Comparison'. In *The Kula: New Perspectives on Massim Exchange*, edited by Jerry W. Leach and Edmund Leach. Cambridge: Cambridge University Press, 1983: 103–17.

Hamnett, C. *Unequal City*. Abingdon: Routledge, 2003.

Hopsicker, Peter and Mark Dyreson. 'Super Bowl Sunday'. In *The Historical Dictionary of American Holidays*, edited by Len Travers. vol. I, Westport, CT: Greenwood Press, 2006: 30–55.

Hyde, L. *The Gift: How the Creative Spirit Transforms the World*. Edinburgh: Canongate, 2006.

International Olympic Committee. *London Candidate File*, vol. 1, p. 36, available at http://www.olympic.org/uk/games/london/election_uk.asp, accessed 20 April 2008.

Komter, A. *Social Solidarity and the Gift.* Cambridge: Cambridge University Press, 2005.

Lee, M. *The Race for the 2012 Olympics.* London: Virgin, 2006.

London Organizing Committee of the Olympic Games (LOCOG). *Towards a One Planet 2012.* London: LOCOG.

Malinowski, B. *Argonauts of the Western Pacific.* New York: E.P. Dutton, 1961 [1922].

Mauss, M. *The Gift: The Form and Reason for Exchange in Archaic Societies.* London: Routledge, 2002.

Mayor of London. *Five Legacy Commitments.* London: Mayor of London, 2008.

National Audit Office. *Preparing for Sporting Success at the London 2012 Olympic and Paralympic Games and Beyond*, Report by the Comptroller and Auditor General, HC 434, Session 2007–08; SG/2008/22, 20 March 2008, accessed 15 April 2008.

———. *Preparations for the London 2012 Olympic and Paralympic Games – Risk Assessment and Management*, Report of the Comptroller and Auditor General, HC252, Session 2006–07, 2 Feb. 2007, available at www.nao.org.uk, accessed 15 April 2008.

Newham Council. *Regeneration Projects: Stratford City*, available at http://newham.gov.uk/services/regeneration/, accessed 20 April 2008.

Offer, A. 'Between the Gift and Market: The Economy of Regard', *Economic History Review*, L(3): 450–76.

Parkinson, M. and M. Boddy (Eds). *City Matters, Competitiveness, Cohesion and Urban Governance.* Bristol: The Policy Press, 2004.

Philostratus. 'On Athletics'. In *Sport and Recreation in Ancient Greece: A Sourcebook with Translations*, edited by W. Sweet. Oxford: Oxford University Press, 1987.

Polanyi, Karl. *The Great Transformation.* Boston: Beacon Press, 1944.

Polanyi, K., M. Arensberg and H.W. Pearson. *Trade and Markets in the Early Empires.* Glencoe, IL: Free Press, 1957.

Poynter, G. 'Manufacturing in East London'. In *Rising in the East, the Regeneration of East London*, edited by T. Butler and M. Rustin. London: Lawrence and Wishart, 1995.

———. *From Beijing to Bow Creek.* London: LERI Working Paper no. 1, 2006.

Putnam, Robert. *Bowling Alone: The Collapse and Revival of American Community*, 1995.

Roche, M. *Mega-events and Modernity.* London: Routledge, 2000.

Sahlins, M. *Stone Age Economics.* Chicago: Aldine and Atherton, 1972.

Sennett, R. 'Capitalism and the City'. In *Cities of Europe*, edited by Y. Kazepov. Oxford: Blackwell, 2005.

Toohey, K. and A. Veal. *The Olympic Games: A Social Science Perspective.* Wallingford: CABI, 2007.

Young, Kevin and K. Wamsley, eds. *Global Olympics: Historical and Sociological Studies of the Modern Games.* London: Elsevier, 2005.

A Sustainable Sports Legacy: Creating a Link between the London Olympics and Sports Participation

Vassil Girginov and Laura Hills

Introduction

Modern Olympic Games have always attracted significant public attention, but the level of social, political and economic mobilization generated by the 2012 London Olympics, even before the games in Beijing in 2008 had taken place, has been truly unprecedented. There are a number of reasons for this, and two of those will be the subject of the present study. First, in 2002, the International Olympic Committee

(IOC) began framing the concept of 'legacy', which, together with the concept of 'sustainable sports development', has become an essential part of the IOC and the Organizing Committee of the Olympic Games (OCOG) vocabulary. As a result, the IOC, among other things, amended the Olympic Charter to include a particular reference to the creation of positive legacies from the games and the promotion of sports for all in the host country. [1] In addition, the IOC developed the Olympic Games Impact (OGI) project, which requires host cities to undertake a comprehensive longitudinal study designed to measure the economic, social and environmental impact of the games. [2] Second, a central plank of the London 2012 bid was that the games will be used to promote sports participation across the country and for all groups. Both the bid committee and the UK government, as a major stakeholder in this project, promised to use the games to inspire the country's people to become more physically active. [3–4] This is the most ambitious project in the history of the Olympic Games in terms of both its scope and level of change, as, in order to be implemented successfully, it has to address not only people's behaviour but also deeply rooted social structures and relations. The conceptual, political, economic and logistical challenges which this undertaking presents are enormous and have already created a number of tensions.

This paper addresses the little explored issue of the link between hosting the Olympic Games and sports participation in the host country. In particular, it takes a process-oriented approach to the Olympic legacy that suggests that legacies are constructed and not given. Most studies so far have concentrated on measuring legacy effects after the games had finished and, with some limited exceptions [5], there has been a dearth of information on the actual processes involved in envisioning, framing and implementing Olympic legacies. The paper has three interrelated sections. The first looks at the nature of the Olympic legacy enterprise both as a conceptual issue and a set of institutional practices. The second examines the delivery of the sports participation vision (i.e., creating sustainable sports development) by using two original case studies. One focuses on the English Volleyball Association (EVA), which oversees an Olympic sport, and the other involves a community initiative, StreetGames. Finally, the key processes involved in constructing a sustainable Olympic sports development legacy are discussed.

The Olympic Legacy Enterprise

Although games-impact analyses were carried out as early as the 1988 Calgary games, [6] the first concerted attempt to 'interrogate' Olympic legacies was made in 2001 under IOC stewardship. [7] In addition, a sociology of mega-sports events and their legacy also started to emerge. [8] Increasingly, Olympic legacy discourse and practical policies have been framed within the notion of sustainable development and its corollary of sustainable sports development. The former places the legacy of an Olympic Games within the wider social and economic context of the host city and country, while the latter looks at the effect of this mega-event on sports participation and the overall development of the national sports system. This paper considers the process of Olympic sports development legacy construction. It involves an open and flexible design amenable to learning derived from implementation, a relationship between legacy actors critical for constructing and implementing of visions and issues dealing with the political, economic and social uncertainties of legacy delivery. [9] Before concentrating on Olympic legacy, the analysis will first examine the concepts of sustainability and sports development.

Understanding Sustainable (Sports) Development

It is impossible to pinpoint the origins of the phrase 'sustainable development', but undoubtedly it was the Brundtland Report of the World Commission on Environment and Development (WCED) in 1987 that put it on the social and political agenda. The WCED defined sustainable development as 'development that meets the needs of the present without compromising the ability of future generations to meet their own needs'. [10] Since then, sustainable development has been a much contested concept for two main reasons. First, there is a lack of agreement on the meaning of the principal constructs of the concept – needs and development, and the resultant difficulties in operationalizing them. Second, achieving sustainability requires a substantial capacity to predict the future and to handle uncertainty.

The concept of human development has evolved in response to the disillusionment with mainstream, neo-liberal models of economic growth and their unfulfilled promises of social progress and equality. As the champion of human development, Mabub ul Haq, has commented, 'There is a missing moral core in our technological advance. In rich nations and poor, the moral foundations of economic growth are often lacking. And we are too embarrassed even to mention morality any more.' [11] In contrast to the Human Development Index (HDI), which was devised explicitly as a rival to the gross domestic product (GDP), the principal measure of economic growth, [12] sustainable development serves a different purpose. In the words of the economist Desmond McNeill, 'the idea of "sustainable development" … sought to extend and supplement – rather than directly confront – the established wisdom.' [13] Similarly, Simon Dresner has argued that the very idea of sustainability has arisen out of increasing pessimism about the capacity of human institutions to handle problems that are far less challenging than dealing with an uncertain future. [14] Therefore, sustainability is not a radically new idea designed to curb growth, but rather an attempt to redirect it. It has been suggested that it is an oxymoron, and, as Tomi Kallio, Piia Nordgerg and Ari Ahonen recently noted, 'while obviously a powerful and important concept, due to its ambiguousness, sustainable development lacks the real power of change.' [15] Sustainable Olympic legacy is also an ambiguous concept, as it tries to satisfy the games' insatiable drive for faster, higher, stronger (growth) while delivering equality, solidarity and accountability across all sports and groups around the world.

From the insights of several contemporary scholars on sustainability designs, it is proposed that sustainable sports development is neither a state of the sports system to be increased or decreased, nor a static goal or target to be achieved. [16] Sports development concerns a process of construction, destruction and maintenance of opportunities for people to participate and excel in sports and life. [17] Sustainable sports development is an ideal and a moving target. Sports participation patterns around the world illustrate this point and reflect an evolution of ideas, changing organizational forms, delivery systems and performances. [18] Sports development visions, therefore, represent ideals that come from ethics and values we hold that are indeed non-quantifiable. Improvements in our understanding of the social and economic environment in which sports development occurs affect the goal-setting approaches and interventions we choose. Thus, sports development visions inevitably involve a process of social learning. This renders sustainable sports development into a construction process aimed at creating value but with an unknown end point. It also places local actors centre stage, as any meaningful vision of change in individuals, communities and organizations produced by sports has to be derived from local symbols, knowledge and behaviours.

The Olympic Games Legacy as Intended Development

Development, as the sociologists Michael Cowen and Robert Shenton eloquently put it, 'emerged to ameliorate the perceived chaos caused by progress'. [19] They have contended that it was in the European context that development was first conceived as a state practice and as 'one means to construct the positive alternative to the disorder and underdevelopment of capitalism'. [20] Intentional development is concerned with the deliberate policy and actions of the state and other agencies, which are expressed in various developmental doctrines. The visions promoted by these doctrines are rooted in the normalizing practices of the modern state and its efforts to produce disciplined citizens, solders, leaders and governable subjects. Sports have always been used as a main means for that.

Many of the current visions of sports development have actually been designed to compensate for the negative propensities of capitalism through the reconstruction of social order by tackling class, poverty, gender and age inequalities. [21] What originally emerged as inherent sports development in the form of private sports practices was gradually transformed by the state and its institutions into intentional development. The modern Olympic Games can be seen as the first major international sports development project. It emerged as a reaction to the dissatisfaction with the process of capitalist accumulation and the poor fitness of youth experienced by the founders of the modern Olympic movement, in particular Baron Pierre de Coubertin. Coubertin was disillusioned with the growing internationalization of life, with its emphasis on material culture, and proposed an educational doctrine to counter this negative trend. [22] Olympism, however, was based on a logic of exclusion with regard to gender, culture, social background and practices that still exists today. [23] It was also a model of downward diffusion manifested through the Olympic Games, and is a prime example of intentional development at international level in which the newly established IOC (1894) entrusted itself and its constituencies, the National Olympic Committees (NOCs), with the educational role of spreading sports for the betterment of the world. [24]

Writing in 1911, Coubertin lamented: 'It would be very unfortunate, if the often exaggerated expenses incurred for the most recent Olympiads, a sizeable part of which represented the construction of permanent buildings, which were moreover unnecessary – temporary structures would fully suffice, and the only consequence is to then encourage use of these permanent buildings by increasing the number of occasions to draw in the crowds – it would be very unfortunate if these expenses were to deter (small) countries from putting themselves forward to host the Olympic Games in the future.' [25] Coubertin's statement was made only three years after the first London games in 1908, which were a modest operation with 23 participating nations, 2,035 athletes and a budget of £136,000. Their scale pales in comparison with the 2012 Olympics, which are expected to attract 11,000 athletes, 6,000 coaches and officials, 5,000 members of the 'Olympic family', 7,000 sponsors, 20,000 media representatives, and an army of 63,000 operational personnel responsible for an operating budget of £1.53 billion. [26] As in the case of other economic development models, over the past century, the Olympic Games have grown immensely in size and complexity. This has threatened their sustainability. The issue, therefore, becomes how to reconcile the apparent concentration created by a 16-day festival, held in a city or, in the case of London, merely in one part of it, involving huge infrastructure and operating costs, with the tenets of sustainable development advocating the sharing and dispersion of social, economic and environmental impacts across time and space for the benefit of all. Contradictions surrounding sustainable Olympic sports develop-ment are not limited to time, space and investment. They concern fundamental ethical issues as well. Two of the IOC's TOP sponsors, Coca-Cola and McDonald's, are among the main contributors to a modern Western epidemic, which Geoff Dickson and Grant Schofield have called 'globesity'. [27] The Olympic Games provide those companies with exclusive access to the markets of 202 countries around the world to promote calorie-dense food and beverages, but this is the antithesis of the healthy eating and sports participation that games organizers are trying to encourage. It is worth noting that obesity costs the UK economy £2 billion a year, [28] and each McDonald's restaurant sends 100 tonnes of waste to landfill each year. [29] Paradoxically, one of the key principles of the UK government's sustainable development strategy is to ensure 'a strong, healthy and just society by meeting the diverse needs of all people in existing and future communities, promoting personal well-being, social cohesion and inclusion, and creating equal opportunity for all'. [30]

Two recent studies identified apparent contradictions in the concept of a sustainable Olympic legacy. Drawing on the 2006 Turin Olympics, they both argue that, if carefully planned, it is possible for the games to offset some of the negative developments and to deliver a range of positive legacies for the host city and region. The 2006 winter games, they point out, set an instructive example for public consultation and sustainability reporting. Ironically, both studies failed to highlight that the Olympic growth model is based on the logic of exclusion, serving only to perpetuate the contradictions regardless of any legacy planning. [31] This is because it undermines the two main tenets of sustainability – sharing and dispersing Olympic development benefits across communities and sports. The inequalities that this model of sports development reinforces are glaring. At the 2004 Athens games, 101 (50%) NOCs had 10 or fewer athletes, and five (2.5%) NOCs have won 38% of the medals. More worrying, however, is the undetected impact that failing to win Olympic medals has on sports development nationally. When the British swimming team came back from the 2000 Sydney games without medals, its funding was cut by £1.3m. The funding of UK athletics was similarly cut after the 2004 Athens games for 'failure' to achieve the target of five to seven medals; 'only' three gold medals were won. The punishment of UK athletics was twofold – a reduction in funding of £1,100,000 for elite athletes for the period 2005–09, and a cut by Sport England in developmental programmes in 2005–06 – from £2m to £1.35m. [32] The key point is that not only hosting and participating in the games, but also winning Olympic competitions has become critical for sustaining sports development nationally. Constant winning, however, is not sustainable across all sports and nations, but only in the case of some; thus, the problem is accentuated.

Since the 1990s, the IOC has been trying to address the 'Olympic growth' problem, mainly through a revision of the Olympic programme, a diversification strategy that led to the introduction of a two-year cycle between the summer and winter Olympic Games in 1992, and, more recently, to the idea of sustainable sports development. In 2002, the new IOC president, Jacques Rogge, established the Olympic Games Study Commission with a mandate to devise strategies to manage the inherent size, complexity and cost of staging the Olympic Games. The commission's report proposed a range of size-capping and cost-saving measures but concluded:

> The Commission firmly believes that the principle of unity in space and time, or 'One Games – One City', should be maintained in order to ensure that the Games remain the world's greatest sporting event and to guarantee that the athletes' experience remains intact. In that regard, the Commission did not want to damage precisely the essential elements that have made the Games such a universal success. [33]

There is no denying the positive energy, creativity and long-term infrastructural improvements that hosting the Olympic Games can bring to the host city and country. However, it has to be recognized that, at the same time, the games serve as a source of negative development, and the role of the Olympic legacy is to compensate for these propensities of Olympic growth. This is particularly true for promoting sports participation. At the national level, the lottery funding was raided to help pay rising games costs to the tune of £65m, reducing funds for sports development. The diversion represented an 8% cut of Sport England's budget, but because Sport England levers in £3 for every £1, 'what that really means is that £1.6 billion is not going to community sports; that would buy the same number of coaches that there are in the whole of France, or 186,000 fewer participants from his [UK government's] target of two million.' [34] Regionally, the reduction in lottery funding means that projects in former mining areas in Wales lose £107m. Locally, as a result of lottery cuts, Waltham Forest, one of the five Olympic boroughs, is closing its best swimming pool, which is used by 11 local schools and is regularly used by club swimmers, because Waltham Forest College, where it is housed, cannot afford the £74,833 it now loses every year, or the £159,000 one-off maintenance payment that will be required in 2007–08. [35] No amount of future planning and investment can compensate for what is being lost by present sports participants. The above examples illustrate the negative impact of staging the games on sports participation in the UK in terms of funds diversion, lost opportunities and benefits distribution, as the present needs of some groups are sacrificed with promises to meet the needs of future generations. This contradicts the main premise of sustainable development. These negative impacts are far-reaching, as they not only concern the present capabilities of communities, organizations and individuals to participate in sports but also create a whole new structural, demographic and opportunity environment that significantly transforms their future development potential.

The Sports Participation Puzzle

The value of participation in sports for individuals and society has long been established. Notwithstanding decades of concerted effort by governmental, voluntary and private agencies, the general physical inactivity of the population remains a major concern for politicians and sports developers. Nick Rowe, Ryan Adams and Neil Beasley have commented that

> sports participation rates in England remained broadly unchanged over the last two decades or so and that sport in England has continued to be characterized by considerable social inequalities. The 1980s and 1990s saw the development of the recreation management profession, an increase in sports development officers, an expansion of local authority leisure departments, a number of national campaigns, a national junior sport development programme, improved support and training for volunteers and a number of coaching initiatives. And still participation rates did not go up or inequalities become narrowed. [36]

Two recent authoritative international studies on leisure and sports participation have largely confirmed this trend for many Western societies. [37] Is it reasonable, then, to expect that staging the Olympic Games can reverse this trend and produce the desired participation rates? The UK government's position is clear: 'hosting events is not an effective, value for money, method of achieving a sustained increase in mass participation.' [38] The sports management expert Fred Coalter's examination of the sustainable sporting legacy of London 2012 also concluded that 'most of the evidence suggests that major sporting events have no inevitably positive impact on levels of sports participation.' [39]

The concept of Olympic legacy consistently presents sports participation as a macrolevel target. Table 1 demonstrates this in relation to global (IOC), national

Table 1 London 2012 Olympic sports development legacy landscape[i]

Agency	Report and author	Vision of sports development	Delivery system
IOC	*Olympic Games Impact* (2003) International Sports Science and Technology Academy (AISTS)	Increased sports participation rates, promoting school sports	OGOCs with public and sports authorities
LOCOG	*Towards a One-Planet 2012* (2007) LOCOG, WWF and BioRegional	The games will be used to inspire people across the country to take up sports and develop active, healthy and sustainable lifestyles	Partnerships, stakeholders and procurement; sustainability management system
HM Government	*PSA Delivery Agreement 22* (2007) HM Treasury	Sports participation for all	Olympic Board; GOE; ODA; LOCOG (154 measurement indicators)
House of Commons	*London 2012 Olympic Games and Paralympic Games: Funding and Legacy* (2007) The Stationery Office Ltd	Maximum increase in UK participation at community and grass-roots level in all sports and across all groups	UK government and Sport England
DCMS	*Our Promise for 2012* (2007) DCMS	Inspire a new generation of young people to take part in local physical activity	Legacy Trust – competition
DCMS	*Olympic Games Impact Study* (2005) PriceWaterhouse Cooper	Sporting facilities; increased participation and 'feel good factor'	The London Olympic Institute – programmes

(*continued overleaf*)

Table 1 (*Continued*)

Agency	Report and author	Vision of sports development	Delivery system
London Assembly	*A Lasting Legacy for London?* (2007) London East Research Institute	Turning hard (facilities) into soft legacy (social networks and participation)	A stakeholder's approach
Commission for a Sustainable London	*On Track for a Sustainable Legacy?* (2007) Commission for a Sustainable London	Use the games as a springboard to inspire young people to take up sports	Multi-agency Public Service Agreement
The London Health Commission and the London Development Agency	*Rapid Health Impact Assessment of the Proposed London Olympic Games and Their Legacy* (2004) E R Management	Improved health benefits; create a 'showcase natural environment'	DCMS and multiple agencies – programmes and projects
London Five Olympic Boroughs Sports Development Framework	*Sports Development Framework* (2007) Ploszajski Lynch	Community engagement; improved health and capacity building	Access 2012, Fit 4 2012 Club 2012, Talent 2012, Skills 2012
Mayor of London	*Your 2012* (2007) Mayor of London	By 2012 many more Londoners will be part of a new active generation	A network of multi-sports community centres; 'ActiveWork-places' NHS, Sport England
Sport England	2012 Olympic and Paralympic Programme Objectives (4.5) (2006) Sport England	Maximize the increase in participation at grass-roots level in all sports across all groups	Access Club, Skills, Talent and Fit 4

[i]All legacy documents referred to in this table are available on agencies' websites.

(Department of Culture, Media and Sport, DCMS) and local (five London Olympic boroughs) strategic legacy plans. It should be stressed, however, that sustainable sports participation is more about microtargets and concerns specific groups, communities and activities. Making and delivering macroprojections for Olympic-inspired participation becomes even more problematic when the background and histories of different groups and communities are considered. The average participation level of the five Olympic host boroughs is alarmingly low at 18.5%. [40] The problem is further compounded by a high level of deprivation and obesity levels of 20% for boys and 22% for girls aged 7–11. [41] Subsequently, sustainable sports participation will have particular meanings and delivery implications for the people of East London that may differ from other communities in the UK. The same applies to other sports and activities, as the two case studies show.

If existing evidence reveals the lack of positive effects of the Olympic Games on sports participation, and the UK government acknowledges it, one might ask, what is the point of insisting on developing plans to prove otherwise? While we will probably never know for certain how the games affect sports participation, the real issue is to understand how the concept of Olympic legacy is being constructed and whether this construction can deliver sustainable sports development.

Constructing an Olympic Sports Development Legacy: Conceptual Considerations

In the course of the past 20 years, five principal interrelated events were responsible for the evolution of the legacy concept within the Olympic movement: the development of the concept of sustainable development by the United Nations in 1987 and the related Human Development Index; the Rio Earth Summit in 1992, which adopted the Agenda 21 sustainable policy and the resultant Olympic Movement *Agenda 21* in 1992; the environmental disaster produced by the 1992 Albertville Winter Olympic Games; the moral crisis of the IOC in 1999, which led to developing a code of ethics and a drastic revision of the games bidding process; and, in the global context, the redefinition of the role of the local welfare state with its emphasis on place marketing and a move from collective or social consumption to urban growth and urban regimes, which become the main driving force behind cities vying to host the games. [42]

The IOC framed the legacy as a three-stage process: a framework developed by the IOC, a vision produced by the candidate city, and implementation secured by the OCOG. The framework has been supported politically (new rules in the Olympic Charter and the IOC *Manual for Candidate Cities*, 2001), legally (through the Host City Contract between the IOC, the host city and the OCOG), and scientifically (through the OGI). The legacy framework has been rationalized and operationalized through the OGI, which measures the economic, environmental and social impact of the games through a set of indicators over a period of 12 years and four reports. [43] However, those indicators rather vaguely capture only quantitative developments in general participation and school sports.

The vision produced by the candidate city represents the second stage of the legacy process. As the London bid file claims, it is 'the first time that games and legacy planning has worked hand in hand'. [44] Table 2 shows the evolution of thinking in the sports development legacy in the UK Olympic bids from 1992 to 2005 and indicates that the three previous unsuccessful bids mainly addressed local or regional affairs and were not concerned with sports legacy issues. The London 2012 bid was

Table 2 Evolution of Olympic legacy thinking in the UK bids

Olympic bid	Birmingham 1992	Manchester 1996	Manchester 2000	London 2012 2005
Image of city	UK principal sports city	Powerhouse of British industry	Powerhouse of British industry	A diverse, creative and vibrant city devoted to sport
Main theme	Games back to athletes	Driving the dream	Commitment, capability, continuity	Games that make a difference
Vision of legacy	Local/regional development; no reference to sports participation	Local/regional development; no reference to sports participation	Local/regional development; post-games use of sports facilities	UK-wide, leaving a legacy for sport in Britain
Projected cost	£700m	£620m	£1.3bn	£3.3bn

Source: Compiled by authors.

markedly different in terms of scope, legacy projections and cost. However, in the space of under three years, the London 2012 vision has undergone a considerable transformation with a threefold increase in the contribution of public funds to pay for the games, from £3,298bn (2004) to £9,325bn (2007). [45] We can only speculate what the final figure might be in 2013. Thus, the games legacy model has been effectively seeking to encourage public spending in order to deliver the promised sustainable development. As Fred Coalter rather sceptically observed about the main conditions that must be met by public and voluntary bodies in order for the games to deliver sports legacies, 'If this is done in terms of sports development, there is little need for the Olympics!' [46]

As a result, the legacy concept has become highly politicized and charged with the promise to deliver tangible benefits that can be measured. Talking about what the Olympics mean for Britain, Tessa Jowell, Culture, Media and Sport Secretary and Olympic Minister, stated, 'I believe Olympic values are Labour values.' [47] She added, 'There is nothing inevitable or God-given about the legacy of the 2012 Games, it was up to those involved to "make it and create it".' [48] Similarly, the House of Commons Sport, Media and Culture Committee recommended that '"the 'legacy" of the Olympics should not start after 2012, but rather right now.' [49] These comments amply illustrate the socially constructed nature of the Olympic legacy concept. As J.R.B. Ritchie noted, 'Regardless of the actual form that a legacy may take, the idea underlying legacy creation is that it represents something of substance.' [50] The Labour government in 2007 even turned the Olympic legacy vision into 'Our Promise for 2012', containing five election-type substantive pledges. [51] Labour's substantive interpretation of the Olympic legacy challenges the most elaborate attempts to refine the concept so far, suggesting that 'irrespective of the time of production and space, legacy is all planned and unplanned, positive and negative, tangible and intangible structures created for and by a sport event that remain longer that the event itself.' [52]

The third stage of the IOC framework, implementation of the legacy delivered by LOCOG, also serves to complete the institutionalization of the Olympic legacy. 'Institutionalization.' as Tomi Kallio and his colleagues explain, 'refers to collective habitualization, as a result of which a certain rule or habit becomes established as a relatively unquestioned part of the minds of a mass of people.' [53] A rather pretentious RAND report entitled *Setting the Agenda for an Evidence-Based Olympics* (2007) illustrates this habitualization. The report celebrates the power of human rationality and both highlights the illusive character of legacy and endorses the need for turning the Olympics into an evidence-based enterprise: 'London's bid to host the 2012 Olympic Games, like those of all its competitors, relied on a great deal of (sincere) guesswork, promises and hopes. Now that the London bid has been accepted, everything that it promised has to be turned into real commitments, plans, budgets, and operational workstreams.' [54]

The Olympic legacy framework transforms the idea into an enterprise rationalizing and legitimizing its major stakeholders and organizations concerned with monitoring the legacy and producing reports about promised benefits and a myriad of delivery partners. As Table 1 shows, there has been a burgeoning number of Olympic legacy producers and enforcers, and this number does not include a range of other legacy-inspired agencies such as Podium (higher education), Skills Active (employment), Legacy Trust (culture, arts and community), Soil Association (catering/food industry) and Proactive (West London regional partnership with the Olympic legacy appointed officer). While this multiplicity of institutions may be indicative of the catalytic effect of the London Olympic bid, it should not prevent us from seeing the dangers it poses to delivering actual sustainable legacies. Desmond McNeil has documented the diffusion of the idea of human development and has warned of the risk of distortion, as it gets taken up, interpreted and quantified by various agencies. [55] There is a danger that the organizations in the enterprise may lose sight of the actual content of the legacy, and concentrate only on enforcing legacy rules and indicators that provide them with a rationale for existence. There is a danger also that organizations are likely to look for new forms of legacy to be delivered. However, it is important to recognize that with every legacy rule and indicator created by the Olympic enterprise new forms of 'underdevelopment' and 'unsustainability' emerge. For example, the legacy enterprise, among other things, is a labelling game. Every time a claim is made that a target for physically active young people has been achieved, it automatically classes the rest of youngsters into the category of 'inactive' or 'unfit'. The implications for sustainability are considerable.

In summary, as with other economic development models, the idea of Olympic legacy emerged as a means to redirect and expand the growth of the Olympic Games. Despite its controversial and ambiguous nature, the concept of a sustainable Olympic sports development legacy is very appealing because of its seeming ability to combine the practical and policy-relevant with the scientifically respectable. However, it cannot be fully evaluated if interpreted only as an 'input–output system' monitored by large-scale surveys (OGI). Equal attention needs to be paid to the process of legacy construction as a moral, political and sports delivery enterprise.

Constructing an Olympic Sports Development Legacy: Empirical Evidence

Following the conceptualization of legacy construction and sustainable sports development established earlier, five conceptual elements were employed to explore the data generated in each of the two case studies below. These were the sports participation discourse created by the main legacy promoters and the EVA and StreetGames; the process of social learning and knowledge development; engagement with participating members and groups; organizational structures and management models; and the capacity to create, test and maintain opportunities for sports participation. The EVA and StreetGames were used to explore the discourses, practices and processes involved in the delivery of the sports participation vision. In particular, the selection of these case studies was designed to help understand how particular types of organizations perceive the dynamic relationship between the material and symbolic qualities of the Olympic legacy and their own organizational development and aims. Volleyball was chosen, as it offers a rare opportunity for investigating the link between the London 2012 Games and a UK 'developing' sport. Volleyball does not have traditions in the UK and has never enjoyed the level of publicity, and commercial and public funding available to other sports. The Olympic Games rules allow the host country to enter a team in the competition without having to go through tough qualifications for a quota, and the EVA will take advantage of that. Volleyball presents an ideal case, as it permits direct study of the effect of the games on this sport's development, and on participation in particular.

StreetGames is a recent national community initiative geared explicitly towards increasing sports participation in areas of deprivation. Although StreetGames has no formal link to LOCOG, their work has been acknowledged by key players involved in the delivery of London 2012 as consistent with their widening participation aims. StreetGames, therefore, provided an opportunity to explore the impact of the games on sports development in deprived communities throughout the country. Interviews with key individuals from each sports organization, as well as relevant documentary evidence, were used to gain understanding of the relationship between each organization, the London Olympic Games, and sports participation and sustainability. An overview of each case study is provided below prior to a more detailed analysis of the findings.

The case of the English Volleyball Association (EVA)

The EVA is one of the newest sports-governing bodies in the UK. It emerged as a result of the disbanding in 1968 of its predecessor, the Amateur Volleyball

Association of Great Britain and Northern Ireland (AVA), formed in 1955, to make way for separate English, Scottish, Welsh and Northern Ireland Volleyball Associations. The EVA was essentially a one-man, top-down creation and did not result from a club-driven, bottom-up drive for unification. In the words of EVA's founder and Honorary Life President, volleyball is a case of 'a 3rd world sport' in a '1st world country'. [56] Volleyball is not among Sport England's 20 priority funded sports; it is in the 10 development sports category, which has a number of promotional implications for sports participation. [57]

The EVA is a semi-professional body, as all key leadership positions are performed by volunteers. The only senior full-time manager is the chief executive officer. The EVA operates in all nine regions of the country, but its club network geography is very unevenly developed and ranges from 2% of the clubs in the North-East to 25% in the South-East. The club base is mainly grounded in specialized sports schools, which account for 74% of all 1,336 affiliated clubs. Local clubs make up only 17% of the club base. The association has 21,463 members with an average club size of 17 members compared to a UK average of 45. Despite its school grounding, volleyball is played in only 30% of all schools in England in a six-week block, but the school–club play conversion rate is very low. There are 399 registered coaches and 16 community development officers, of whom three work in the five Olympic boroughs. EVA is funded mainly by Sport England grants amounting to £350,000 a year for the period 2005–09 on the basis of a 'Whole Sport Plan'. EVA was also successful in obtaining further £350,000 from Community Investment Funding for three years (2006–09) for work with juniors in regional clubs. The positions of key sports development officers are funded separately from various sources and usually for only 3–4 years. There are no Olympic standard volleyball facilities in Britain and only one suitable indoor beach court. There are some 283 referees, but none is internationally qualified, and as the number of retirements increases, there are few new referees coming forward. The volunteer base is very limited, as is the level of public awareness about volleyball. EVA's officials complain that they still have to explain to people what this sport is about, as many would confuse it with netball. [58] According to EVA, the number of people regularly playing volleyball in the UK is about 17,000 although the authoritative Active People survey (2006) claims 68,000. [59] This is a significant discrepancy with potential implications for sustainable legacy.

Developmentally, EVA is governed by a 'Whole Sport Plan', which has three main priorities: to *start*, increasing participation in order to improve health; to *stay*, retaining people in sports through an effective network of opportunities and services; and to *succeed*, achieving sporting success at every level. With regard to 'start', EVA works through a school–club links approach, using the 'Let's Play Volleyball' national youth volleyball initiative, which involves 36 such partnerships between schools and accredited clubs. A significant development of particular value to EVA in 2006/07 was the inclusion of volleyball in the UK school games as the first team sport. [60] Owing to the host nation's right, Great Britain's team will be one of only 12 teams competing at the Olympic Games (out of 201 member national federations around the world, of which 47 are in Europe). The 2012 games present a rare chance to put the sport on the map. While developing grass-roots volleyball is an ongoing task, entering a competitive national team in the Olympic tournament must be done in five years. The relatively low level of elite volleyball in the UK stimulated EVA to experiment in order to prepare for the 2012 Olympic Games by placing the men's squad in the Dutch first division under the name 'Club Nautilus'.

The Case of StreetGames

StreetGames is a relatively new national charity that was developed with the explicit aim of promoting sports for young people living in the most disadvantaged communities. StreetGames began in 2006 after a successful football tournament that was organized in April 2003 by the Football Association, the Government Office for the North-West, and the regional New Deal for Communities. The tournament successfully combined sports and renewal issues and provided a basis for establishing the organization more formally as a way of increasing participation in deprived areas. [61] StreetGames defines its approach to sports delivery as 'doorstep sports' that bring sports to communities 'where they want it, at times when they want it and in a style they want'. [62] This reflects a desire to circumvent traditional barriers to young people's involvement such as concerns about safety, expense, travel, activity choice, experience, adult support, familiarity with the environment, and knowledge of activities.

StreetGames operates as a network throughout the country to assist local agencies in developing the capacity to deliver doorstep sports. StreetGames has a relatively small number of 'core' staff, including the chief executive, financial manager, and regional and subregional managers. Most of the staff are on contract for one or two days per week. The core members are quite experienced and have worked with Sport England or related organizations in the past. Sport England is the primary funding agency; however, a number of agencies and sponsors contribute funding, including the DCMS (£350,000 for 3 years); V, the charity responsible for taking forward the recommendations of the Russell Commission on youth volunteering; the Co-operative; SHOKK; and the Football Foundation. At the moment, the funding extends through a maximum of three years, and finding funding remains central to ensuring StreetGames' continued growth and ability to meet its aims. The staff of StreetGames use their expertise to assist organizations wishing to develop programmes within target areas. In addition, StreetGames uses its financial and experiential resources to lobby for greater investment in disadvantaged communities; to develop the skills and knowledge of sports workers; to promote selected organizations linking sports and citizenship, including anti-discrimination training and activism; and to consider ways to improve the quality of sports delivery in renewal areas.

While StreetGames operates throughout the country, the activities offered under the StreetGames banner differ with respect to the needs of specific communities. These range from day events, where young people can try a range of activities;

tournaments; opportunities to participate in cheerleading, dance, handball, football, cricket and other sports; and support for a small group of girls who wish to plan and deliver a sports day to girls who live on their estates. At present, organizations contact StreetGames if they wish to initiate a project, and primarily the contact is made through word of mouth or the influence of the regional and subregional managers, who work to develop networks among those who deliver sports to deprived areas. Initial StreetGames projects were in London and the North-East, but it has spread rapidly and there are projects in regions throughout the country. Each agency that is affiliated with StreetGames is encouraged to apply for a Sportmark award as part of establishing a formal partnership and gaining access to the expertise and resources of StreetGames. Programmes are monitored through a monthly Streetmark survey that focuses on participation figures relating to the number and characteristics of participants and leaders. Although StreetGames is currently engaged in limited marketing activities, it does have a website giving information about the background of the programme, events, contacts, some resources, and a mailing list for members. It also runs an annual conference for sports providers.

StreetGames has few official ties to the London Olympics; however, such ties have been discussed by sports and government officials in relation to the aim of widening participation. As the StreetGames website states, 'Lord Coe described StreetGames as an "excellent organization" and stated that their input will be valuable in engaging deprived communities in sports. They were achieving many of the things he hoped the Olympics would be able to do.' [63] The focus of StreetGames is clearly on issues of widening participation and equality with a remit to provide sports in the most deprived areas. Its aims, however, do incorporate the development of talent and national sporting achievements with respect to increasing the opportunities for talented young people in under-represented groups. Subsequently, its stated target populations include young people, coaches and leaders, and talented athletes. [64]

Creating a Link between the London Olympics and Sustainable Sports Participation

Several key processes constitute crucial links between the London 2012 Olympics and sports participation. As previously discussed, five such processes pertinent to the main legacy promoters and the two organizations have been identified (Table 3).

Sports Participation Legacy Discourse

The EVA and StreetGames have become involved in the construction of the London 2012 bid vision only indirectly and in very different ways. Volleyball has been connected through the collective voice of Sport England, which demanded that no investment, including lottery funding, be diverted from grass-root sports and that the games deliver a substantial and sustainable sporting legacy. [65] StreetGames became involved as an example of the kind of initiatives the bid committee was going to

Table 3 Constructing sustainable Olympic sports development legacy

Organization	Understanding of legacy	Main target group	Key legacy construction processes	Delivery implications	Olympic Games contribution
EVA	To get people to think in a different way; new facilities; what will the young people be doing in 2013 and 2023?	12–27 years old	(i) sports participation discourse creation; (ii) social learning and knowledge development; (iii) engagement with participants; (iv) establishing organizational structures and management models; (v) developing capacity to create, test and maintain opportunities for participation	Translating the elite image of the game to individual level; building spectator public; building community club network	Training facilities; test events publicity; funding through FIVB (International Volleyball Federation)
StreetGames	To provide all individuals with access to sports; making sure that people in the most deprived communities share in the legacy	Individuals and agencies involved in the delivery of sports in socially deprived areas – young people and leaders in particular		Developing networks and resources throughout the country, lobbying and advocacy, capacity building at local and regional levels	Involved with the Legacy Trust in a bid to participate in pre-Olympic festivals Informal link in facilitating widening participation

promote through the Olympics. A group of children from deprived East London boroughs were even flown to Singapore to support London's presentation to the IOC Session. [66]

Both EVA and StreetGames interpret the sports participation discourse in different ways. Whereas 'volleyball experienced a "now what?" moment in 2005 when London was awarded the Games and lost twelve months to figure out what needs to be done', StreetGames, seized the opportunity to strengthen its political lobbying. The difference comes from the role of those organizations as a deliverer and a facilitator/network, respectively. Although EVA's mission is to put 'volleyball at the heart of your community', its sports developmental objectives are not really supported by the London 2012 egalitarian legacy vision for an inclusive sport. This vision, as expressed in the current UK government target of everybody doing at least 30 minutes of physical activity five times a week, does not accord with what volleyball development is about. It is concerned with a specific target group, ranging from the typical starting age of 12 to the peak performance at 27 years. This is why the EVA's discourse and related activities are designed to 'translate the elite image of the game to individual level'. [67]

StreetGames' discourse is fundamentally about 'doorstep' sports or bringing sports to deprived communities. It uses a politically sensitive language aiming to develop partnerships through networks facilitated by a core group of administrators and managers. A programme development manager (PDM) who is currently delivering a StreetGames project reinforced this message: 'All the sporting landscape wants to know is what is this legacy going to look like, what kind of money are you talking about, what kind of projects are you talking about … you've got world class athletes, world class facilities but is that really a legacy, because your world class athletes are at the moment the top 20% of the population? To me a world class facility … is in the middle of a housing estate where 90% of the kids are going to use it. That's the legacy to me, not a velodrome.' [68] The London Olympics vision provides the StreetGames staff with a rationale for lobbying with the aim of 'enhancing the capacity of doorstep sports workers to access funding through beating on doors of officialdom in politics', [69] but one PDM insists that the legacy should have no political colour: 'I think all political parties need to sign up to that legacy. Labour one day, Conservatives the other, it chops and changes and everyone uses it for their own political agenda.' [70] Clearly, the London Olympic sports participation legacy discourse as a macrolevel target finds very different interpretations at microlevel due to specific organizational roles and objectives. Sustainable sports participation implies the involvement of local communities as well as a global policy. This renders constructing and delivering sustainable Olympic sports participation very problematic.

Social Learning

Legacy construction implies different learning curves for the two organizations in terms of time, pace and form. Whereas volleyball has only five years to learn how to develop capacities for elite performance at the games, there has been a long tradition of political lobbying in sports in the UK for StreetGames' experienced staff to build on. Owing to their different roles, learning within EVA is taking more formal and organizational forms, as opposed to StreetGames, where it is mainly individual. As both organizations grow, however, changes are anticipated. For example, Street-Games' new and less experienced staff will need access to training. Training programmes are 'becoming necessary as we're starting to recruit younger, less experienced workers in those regional or subregional management roles.' [71] In addition, a financial director has been employed. [72] Marketing is an issue that StreetGames will need to develop further, as it appears that while many sports workers are aware of the project, potential participants are not. Different learning curves will produce different learning outcomes, making the transfer of knowledge across organizations and fields and the capacity to predict future scenarios very difficult.

Public Engagement

The process of public engagement also follows different patterns for both organizations. The EVA is involved in three main forms of engagement: partnerships with schools, clubs and local authorities; spectator augmentation with the help of the media and commercial organizations to ensure both loyal participants and a paying public; and negotiations with LOCOG to establish testing events and training facilities. In contrast, StreetGames works with sports workers rather than sports participants. It provides resources in terms of experience, funding and networking for individuals who wish to initiate programmes targeting socially deprived areas and demonstrating attention to equity issues. Projects are typically developed through informal connections. 'StreetGames has a little mantra which is that we do sports at a time and a place and a style and at a price that people can afford. To get involved in StreetGames children do not need adult support. You don't need much money in your pocket, you don't need to buy into a challenging new culture or environment by and large, although it's extremely structured it appears to be laissez faire.' [73] Therefore, for EVA and StreetGames, ensuring sports participation has different forms: volleyball relies on a market-oriented approach to project the game as a form of entertainment, and access to participation is based on participants' ability to pay and partnerships with public bodies, whereas StreetGames is issue driven and essentially publicly funded.

Capacity Building

This process involves developing the social networks, knowledge and skills needed for participation. Under the slogan 'putting volleyball at the heart of your community', EVA concentrates mainly on expanding its club network, school sports partnerships, and staff and volunteer training. [74] Although StreetGames also tends to institutionalize the delivery process, its focus remains on the participants. As the StreetGames chief executive explained, 'In terms of project sustainability, I'm in favour of trying to find the resources to institutionalize doorstep sport into doorstep multi-sport projects'. [75] They are both, however, striving to develop local leadership and empowering communities to design and deliver their own sports. At present, neither organization has the capacity to conduct the independent or in-house research (apart from collecting background figures on participation) required by the evidence-based Olympic legacy framework, and there are no plans to address this issue. It would appear that capacity building can be undertaken in the name of developing sports (volleyball) and developing individuals and communities through sports (StreetGames). As Vassil Girginov has argued elsewhere, a sameness of approach to sustainable sports development reinforces the dichotomy between development *of* sports and development *through* sports and neglects the cultural, change and delivery potential of the enterprise. It also creates internal and external competition between legacy actors for limited resources. [76] Both EVA and StreetGames in their different approaches avoid these problems.

Capacity to Create, Test and Maintain Opportunities

Sustainable sports participation is contingent on agencies' capacity to create and maintain opportunities. This capacity largely results from the four processes above but also has to accommodate the uncertainties presented by changing funding and sports priorities and mechanisms, as well as participants' interpretation of legacy and behaviours. Volleyball is facing the double task of expanding its club network and supplying regular elite tournaments to maintain the public interest in it. In this regard, the Olympic Games are not going to contribute a great deal. In the words of EVA's chief executive, 'For us there is not going to be any tangible legacy from the Games except from 400 tonnes of sand at the back of the Horse Guards left after the beach volley tournament and a few nice balls, poles and nets.' [77] The contradiction of legacy ambitions and delivery has already become evident in other ways. The EVA was not consulted in the production of the five Olympic boroughs' sports development strategy, which makes no provision for sustainable volleyball development in East London after the games. [78]

　StreetGames, too, has reservations about the Olympic strategy. StreetGames has been trying to create and maintain opportunities for participation within the framework of the Streetmark Award. Signing up for this award establishes a formal partnership and provides agencies with a press pack, reduced rates to events and other opportunities. As part of the Streetmark programme, agencies submit monthly monitoring forms that require quantitative data on participants' characteristics. The criterion for success is numbers of participants from the target groups. StreetGames' primary formal link to the Olympics is through the Legacy Trust, which has the remit of 'supporting a wide range of innovative cultural and sporting activities for all, which celebrate the London 2012 Olympic and Paralympic Games and which will leave a lasting legacy in communities throughout the United Kingdom'. [79] The chief executive states that 'our name is mentioned in the Olympic legacy document in the bid'; however, the trust has not been approached by LOCOG despite claims to 'make sure the most disadvantaged communities in the country share in the Olympic Legacy'. [80]

Maintaining opportunities for participation entails a commitment by all agencies concerned, but uncertainties persist about when the legacy begins and ends. In addition, as is clear from above, taking advantage of local expertise leaves something to be secured. There is concern on the part of the StreetGames chief executive that 2012 is perceived as an end point: 'I think we need to be quite clever about what a legacy is going to look like. If it's a legacy programme to give us more athletes at 2016 then fine and I don't think we'll see an impact of this Olympic Games until 2016 … all the programmes that are in place now, talent identification, etc. you're looking to 2016, 2020 … and if that's the legacy then how are you going to involve the 80% of the population that you're not selecting from at the moment … that's where the legacy should look.' [81] This view is shared by EVA. If the opportunities presented by the games are to be realized, the real legacy will become evident in 2023. [82] But motivating young people to strive for success has not been easy and will not be useful, and, as a PDM observed, 'Everyone is on burnout already.' [83] There is also concern that getting people involved in sports requires local solutions and input. 'A legacy project that says we're looking at each local area what do you need, what do you want, what does the legacy mean to you, I think we'd get 400 different answers but if it gets that population actively engaged in sport then that's the legacy, it's not just one size fits all.' [84]

The five legacy construction processes highlighted the importance of the meaning of legacy to various stakeholders, revealed a number of relations, and exposed the variable quality of transactions taking place. The sustainable development target groups range from 'new generation' to 'all groups', and the management approaches to participation include interventions based on programme, facility, community and partnership, and require different sets of skills and time frames. Thus, developing a capacity for creating and maintaining opportunities for participation requires a national policy and long-term investment strategy. At present, most funding opportunities and posts available to both organizations are short-term and are run as projects. This is not enough. Project management entails a clear, short-term vision, well-defined organizational boundaries, and methods of delivery that are very different from delivering sustained participation. The Olympic Games are a prime example of project management with a deadline, outputs which are not negotiable, and an organizing committee with a fixed lifespan. Sustainable sports participation demands a longer perspective.

The concept of sustainable Olympic sports development legacy is a controversial and contested one. However, its appeal is that it offers grounds for agreement between Olympic aspirations for social progress and equality and the striving for growth by staging faster, higher, stronger and ever better games. It is difficult to imagine, however, how sustainable sports participation can be achieved without addressing the issues of the rights of different communities and sports and Olympic versus non-Olympic sports development. As the House of Commons Report warned:

> We conclude that the substantial financial contribution by Sport England to the 2012 Games need not necessarily have a major effect on programmes to enhance participation in sport at community level. However, there is a clear risk, if we are not careful, that programmes outside the capital may suffer because of the focus on London and in particular in sports which are either not part of the Olympics or which are not recognised as mainstream Olympic sports. [85]

Achieving sustainable sports participation remains attainable, but the IOC and the UK government are the two powerful organizations that can exercise considerable influence over the framing of sustainable Olympic sports development legacy by placing it on the agenda and by channelling collective efforts and resources effectively. This has not been the case to date.

Notes

[1] International Olympic Committee (IOC), *Olympic Charter*, New rules 2.13 and 2.14.
[2] IOC, *The Olympic Games Global Impact*.
[3] For the London 2012 bid promises, see British Olympic Association.
[4] For the UK government promises, see DCMS, *Our Promise for 2012*.
[5] See, for example, K. Owen, 'The Local Impacts of the Sydney 2000 Olympic Games: Processes and Politics of Venue Preparation', and F. Coalter, 'London 2012: A Sustainable Legacy?'
[6] Ritchie, 'Promoting Calgary Through the Olympics'.
[7] Moragas *et al.*, *The Legacy of the Olympic Games: 1984–2000*.
[8] Horne and Manzenreiter, 'An Introduction to the Sociology of Sports Mega-events'.
[9] Mosse, 'Process-Oriented Approaches to Development Practice and Social Research'.
[10] World Commission on Environment and Development (WCED).
[11] Haq, *Reflections on Human Development*, 202.
[12] Sen, 'The Human Development Index'.
[13] McNeill, '"Human Development": The Power of the Idea', 13.
[14] Dresner, *The Principles of Sustainability*.
[15] Kallio *et al.*, 'Rationalizing Sustainable Development', 49.
[16] See, for example, Voss and Kemp, 'Reflective Governance for Sustainable Development' and Bagheri and Hjorth, 'Planning for Sustainable Development'.
[17] Girginov, *Management of Sports Development*.
[18] Da Costa and Miragaya, *Worldwide Experiences and Trends in Sport for All*.
[19] Cowen and Shenton, 'The Invention of Development', 29.
[20] Cowen and Shenton, *Doctrines of Development*, 57.
[21] Girginov, *Management of Sports Development*, 17
[22] See MacAloon, *This Great Symbol*.
[23] For an extended discussion on the topic, see Girginov (2004) and Segrave (2000).
[24] See Girginov, 'Eastern European Sport: Nomen'.
[25] Coubertin, *Olympic Review*.
[26] British Olympic Association, *London Olympic Bid*.
[27] Dickson and Schofield, 'Globalisation and Globesity', 170.

[28] Vlad, 'Obesity Costs UK Economy £2 billion a Year'.

[29] Paul Eccleston, 'McDonalds to Use Waste to Generate Power', available at http://www.telegraph. co.uk/earth/main.jhtml?xml=/earth/2007/09/18/eamac118.xml, accessed 19 September 2007.

[30] UK Government. *Securing the Future*, 16.

[31] See Frey *et al.*, 'The Impact of Wide-Scale Sport Events on Local Development' and Furrer, 'Sustainable Olympic Games'.

[32] Cited in Green, 'Olympic Glory or Grassroots Development?'

[33] Olympic Games Study Commission, *Report to the 115th IOC Session*, 21.

[34] Quoted by A. Culf, *Guardian*, 22 March 2007.

[35] Available at http://www.gamesmonitor.org.uk, accessed 1 Jan. 2008.

[36] Rowe *et al.*, 'Driving up Participation in Sport', 12.

[37] See G. Cushman *et al.*, *Free Time and Leisure Participation* and Van Bottenburg *et al.*, *Sports Participation in the European Union*.

[38] DCMS (Department of Culture, Media and Sport), *Game Plan*.

[39] Coalter, note 5 above, 11.

[40] Sport England, *Active People*.

[41] Queen Mary University, 'Research with East London Adolescents: Community Health Survey (2003)', available at http://www.qmul.ac.uk/research/newsrelease.php?news_id=23, accessed 3 March 2008.

[42] See Cochrane *et al.*, 'Manchester Plays Games' and Shoval, 'A New Phase in the Competition for the Olympic Gold'.

[43] For an overview of OGI (formerly OGGI), see Christopher Dubi and Gilbert Felli, 'What Is the Olympic Games Global Impact Study?', *Olympic Review*, June (2006), Lausanne: IOC; for the IOC requirements to the candidate cities, see *Manual for Candidate Cities*, Lausanne: IOC, available at http://multimedia.olympic.org/pdf/en_report_298.pdf, accessed 3 March 2008.

[44] British Olympic Association (note 3 above), 3.

[45] House of Commons, Culture, Media and Sport Committee, *London 2012 Olympic Games and Paralympic Games*.

[46] Coalter (note 5 above), 11.

[47] Tessa Jowell, 'What Social Legacy of 2012?', Speech at the Fabian Fringe in Manchester, 27 Sept. 2006.

[48] Tessa Jowell speech to a Labour conference on 15 Sept. 2005, quotation, available at www.labour.org.uk, retrieved 4 Dec. 2007.

[49] House of Commons (note 44 above), 4.

[50] Ritchie, 'Turning 16 Days into 16 Years Through Olympic Legacies', 156.

[51] DCMS, *Our Promise for 2012*.

[52] Preuss, 'The Conceptualisation and Measurement of Mega Sport Event Legacies', 211.

[53] Kallio *et al.*, 'Rationalizing Sustainable Development', 43.

[54] RAND Europe, *Setting the Agenda for Evidence-Based Olympics*, 1.

[55] McNeill, '"Human Development": The Power of the Idea', 10.

[56] Personal communication from EVA's Honorary Life President, 22 Dec. 2007.

[57] Ibid.

[58] Personal communication from EVA's chief executive officer, 3 Jan. 2008.

[59] Sport England, 'Active People Survey' (2006), available at http://www.sportengland.org/index/ get_resources/research/active_people/active_people_survey_headline_results.htm, accessed 9 Jan. 2008.

[60] See 'English Volleyball', available at http://www.volleyballengland.org/About_Us/index.php, accessed 28 Dec. 2007.

[61] StreetGames, 'Who We Are', available at http://www.streetgames.org/drupal-5.0/?q=node/ 182, accessed 7 Jan. 2008.

[62] Ibid.

[63] StreetGames, 'StreetGames "Excellent" Says Lord Coe', available at http://www.streetgame-s.org/drupal-5.0/?q=node/182, accessed 7 Jan. 2008.

[64] Personal observations and communications from StreetGames chief executive officer, 27 Nov. 2008.

[65] Sport England, *Sport England Written Statement to the Culture, Media and Sport Select Committee.*

[66] See http://www.london2012.com/news/archive/bid-phase/beckham-joins-london-youngsters-in-singapore.php [5959] English Volleyball, accessed 28 Dec. 2007.

[67] Personal communication from EVA (note 57 above).

[68] Personal communication from a StreetGames PDM, 11 Jan. 2008.

[69] Personal communication from StreetGames chief executive officer, 27 Nov. 2008.

[70] Personal communication from a StreetGames PDM, (note 67 above).

[71] Personal communication from StreetGames chief executive officer (note 68).

[72] Ibid.

[73] Ibid.

[74] See EVA website, available at http://www.volleyballengland.org/index.php, accessed 15 Jan. 2008.

[75] Personal communication from StreetGames chief executive officer (note 68 above).

[76] Girginov, *Management of Sports Development.*

[77] Personal communication from EVA's chief executive officer (note 57 above).

[78] Ibid.

[79] Legacy Trust UK, available at http://www.legacytrustuk.org/, accessed 15 Jan. 2008.

[80] Personal communication from StreetGames chief executive officer, 27 Nov. 2008.

[81] Ibid.

[82] Personal communication from EVA's chief executive officer (note 57 above).

[83] Personal communication from a StreetGames PDM (note 67 above).

[84] Personal communication from StreetGames chief executive officer (note 79 above).

[85] House of Commons (note 44 above), 26.

References

Bagheri, A. and P. Hjorth. 'Planning for Sustainable Development: A Paradigm Shift Towards a Process-Based Approach'. *Sustainable Development* 15 (2007): 83–96.

British Olympic Association. *London Olympic Bid: Candidature File.* London: BOA, 2004.

Coalter, F. 'London 2012: A Sustainable Legacy?' In *After the Gold Rush: A Sustainable Olympics for London*, edited by A. Vigor and M. Mean. London: ippr and Demos, 2004.

Cochrane, A., J. Peck and A. Tickell. 'Manchester Plays Games: Exploring the Local Politics of Globalisation'. *Urban Studies* 33, no. 8, (1996): 1319–36.

Coubertin, P. *Olympic Review* April (1911): 59–62.

Cowen, M. and R. Shenton. 'The Invention of Development'. In *Power of Development*, edited by J. Crush. London: Routledge, 1995:

—— and ——. *Doctrines of Development.* New York: Routledge, 1996.

Cushman, G., A. Veal and J. Zuzanek, eds. *Free Time and Leisure Participation: International Perspectives.* Wallingford: CABI Publishing, 2005.

Da Costa, L. and A. Miragaya, eds. *Worldwide Experiences and Trends in Sport for All.* Oxford: Meyer and Mayer, 2002.

DCMS (Department for Culture, Media and Sport). *Game Plan.* London: DCMS, 2002.

——. *Our Promise for 2012: How the UK Will Benefit from the Olympic and Paralympic Games*. London: DCMS, 2007.

Dickson, G. and G. Schofield. 'Globalisation and globesity: the impact of the 2008 Beijing Olympics on China'. *International Journal of Sport Management and Marketing* 1, nos. 1/2, (2005): 169–79.

Dresner, S. *The Principles of Sustainability*. London: Earthscan, 2003.

Frey, M., F. Iraldo and M. Melis. 'The Impact of Wide-Scale Sport Events on Local Development: An Assessment of the XXth Torino Olympics Through the Sustainability Report'. Paper presented at RSA, Region in Focus? International Conference, Lisbon, 2–5 April 2007.

Furrer, P. 'Sustainable Olympic Games'. *Bollettino della Societa Geografica Italiana* Series XII, 7, no. 4, (2002).

Girginov, V. 'Eastern European Sport: Nomen'. *International Journal of the History of Sport* 21, no. 5, (2004): 690–710.

——. *Management of Sports Development*. Oxford: Butterworth–Heinemann, 2008.

Green, M. 'Olympic Glory or Grassroots Development?: Sport Policy Priorities in Australia, Canada and the United Kingdom, 1960–2006'. *International Journal of the History of Sport* 24, no. 7, (2007): 921–53.

Haq, M. ul. *Reflections on Human Development*. Oxford: Oxford University Press, 1995.

Horne, J. and W. Manzenreiter. 'An Introduction to the Sociology of Sports Mega-events'. *Sociological Review* Suppl. 2, Oct. (2006): 1–24.

House of Commons, Culture, Media and Sport Committee. *London 2012 Olympic Games and Paralympic Games: Funding and Legacy*, Second Report, vol. I (HC 69-1). London: Stationery Office, 2007.

International Olympic Committee (IOC). *The Olympic Games Global Impact*. Lausanne: IOC, 2003.

——. *Olympic Charter*, Lausanne: IOC, 2007.

Kallio, T., P. Nordgerg and A. Ahonen. 'Rationalizing Sustainable Development' – A Critical Treatise'. *Sustainable Development* 15 (July 2007): 41–51.

MacAloon, J. *This Great Symbol: Pierre de Coubertin and the Origins of the Modern Olympic Games*. Chicago: University of Chicago Press, 1981.

McNeill, D. '"Human Development": The Power of the Idea'. *Journal of Human Development* 8, no. 1, (2007): 5–22.

Moragas, M., C. Kennett and N. Puig, eds. The Legacy of the Olympic Games: 1984–2000. *Proceedings of the International Symposium*. 14–16 Nov. 2002. Lausanne: IOC, 2003.

Mosse, D. 'Process-Oriented Approaches to Development Practice and Social Research'. In *The Local Impacts of the Sydney 2000 Olympic Games: Processes and Politics of Venue Preparation*, edited by D. Mosse, J. Farrington and A. Rew. London: Routledge, 2001.

Olympic Games Study Commission. *Report to the 115th IOC Session*, Lausanne: IOC, 2005.

Owen, K. *The Local Impact of the Sydney 2000 Olympic Games: Processes and Politics of Venue Preparation*. Sydney: Centre for Olympic Studies and the School of Geography, The University of New South Wales, 2001.

Preuss, H. 'The Conceptualisation and Measurement of Mega Sport Event Legacies'. *Journal of Sport and Tourism* 12, nos. 3/4, (2007): 207–28.

RAND Europe. *Setting the Agenda for an Evidence-Based Olympics*. TR-516. Cambridge: RAND Europe, 2007.

Ritchie, J.R.B. 'Promoting Calgary Through the Olympics: The Mega Event as a Strategy for Community Development'. In *Social Marketing* (Chap. 20). Boston: Allyn and Bacon, 1989.

——. 'Turning 16 Days into 16 Years Through Olympic Legacies'. *Event Management* 6 (2000): 149–66.

Rowe, N., R. Adams and N. Beasley. 'Driving up Participation in Sport: The Social Context, the Trends, the Prospects and the Challenges'. Cited in Sport England, *Driving up Participation: The Challenge for Sport*. London: Sport England, 2004.

Segrave, J. 'The (Neo)Modern Olympic Games'. *International Review for the Sociology of Sport* 35, no. 3, (2008): 268–81.

Sen, A. 'The Human Development Index'. In *The Elgar Companion to Development Studies*, edited by D.A. Clark. Cheltenham: Edward Elgar, 2006:

Shoval, N. 'A New Phase in the Competition for the Olympic Gold: The London and New York Bids for the 2012 Games'. *Journal of Urban Affairs* 24, no. 5, (2002): 583–99.

Sport England. *Sport England Written Statement to the Culture, Media and Sport Select Committee London Olympic Inquiry*. London: House of Commons, 2003.

——. *Active People*. London: Sport England, 2007.

UK Government. *Securing the Future*. London: HM Government, 2005.

Van Bottenburg, M., B. Rijnen and J. van Sterkenburg. *Sports Participation in the European Union: Trends and Differences*. Nieuwegein: W.J.H. Mulier Institute and Arko Sports Media, 2005.

Vlad, I. 'Obesity Costs UK Economy £2 billion a Year'. *British Medical Journal* 327, 6 Dec. (2003): 1308.

Voss, J.P. and R. Kemp. 'Reflective Governance for Sustainable Development. Incorporating Feedback in Social Problem-Solving'. Paper for ESEE Conference, Lisbon, 2005.

World Commission on Environment and Development (WCED). *Our Common Future*. Oxford: Oxford University Press, 1987.

Epilogue: Athletic Clashes of Civilizations or Bridges Over Cultural Divisions? The Olympic Games as Legacies and the Legacies of the Olympic Games

Mark Dyreson

The legacies of the modern Olympics litter the landscape of the twentieth century, and have begun to crop-up in the new terrain of the twenty-first century. The Olympics gave birth to their great rival in the quest to garner the enthusiasm of the world's fans, the World Cup football tournament. [1] Beginning during the 1930s in Los Angeles and Berlin, the Olympics sparked the merger of the global sports and entertainment industries, producing a powerful new conglomerate that now consumes the attention of billions of people and creates the world's most popular stars, a diverse group that ranges from Michael Phelps to Maria Sharapova, from David Beckham to Usian Bolt, from Liu Xiang to Tiger Woods, and from the 'Flying Tomato' to Ronaldo. This global conglomerate generates enormous profits, consumes entire television networks for weeks a time, [2] and has spawned a *lingua franca* that simultaneously reinforces and transcends national and cultural borders. [3]

Olympic legacies include less successful monuments as well–the multitude of Olympian 'white elephants' J.A. Mangan spots lurking about the modern world. [4] Over-priced and under-utilized venues rust away in some former host cities – Montreal comes immediately to mind. Lingering resentments toward money spent on sport rather than urban renewal plague other Olympic cities and roil the political waters of future hosts, particularly London. [5] Winter Olympic sites that leave ski-run scars on alpine slopes irritate environmentalists around the world. The IOC promises a commitment to 'green' practices, sustainable development, and the extinction of 'white elephants'. [6] Critics, and even some fans, remain to be convinced.

Olympic legacies include more than a century of memories of stellar athletic performances, grand gestures that illuminate the nobility of humanity, and great concern to include all of the world's cultures and peoples in Olympian pageants. In fact, the International Olympic Committee (IOC) recognizes more nations that any other international agency, including the United Nations. [7] Dark clouds dot other vistas in collective memories of Olympic legacies. Olympic platitudes about the impact of the games on world peace confront the gruesome world wars of the twentieth century that cancelled three Olympic celebrations. Allusions to the Olympic harmony of nations sometimes remind the world of the tragedy and terror of the Munich, Mexico City, and Kwangju massacres, of the cynical Cold War politics of the Moscow and Los Angeles boycotts. The gigantic profits corporate interests derive from the Olympics, the chummy scandals that have plagued the IOC, and the long histories of involvement by some members of the IOC's exclusive club in authoritarian or totalitarian political regimes also taint Olympic legacies. [8] Some condemn the Olympic mantra, *Citius, Altius, Fortius*, for promoting an epidemic of doping in elite sport. A few voices even blame Olympic doping for expanding the global drug plague that is the scourge of contemporary societies. [9]

The Olympic movement has recently become more conscious of its own legacies, of finessing criticism and focusing global attention on the athletic festivals that they claim celebrate the unity of the 'human family'. Indeed, the IOC has begun to sponsor legacy conferences. [10] Corporate consultants, as Olympic ethnographer John MacAloon observes, increasingly promise host cities and the IOC that they can package, promote and polish Olympic sites as gleaming beacons of consumer-friendly heritage, drawing tourist dollars long after their brief Olympian fortnights fade to the realm of collective memory. [11]

To grasp the power of legacies in the contemporary Olympic universe requires a retreat to the past, since the Olympics are themselves the legacies of other historical movements and moments. The modern Olympics are a heritage of the complex currents of modernity. Identifying the movements and ideas that shaped and propelled the Olympics is a daunting task, but any list of Olympian progenitors would have to include many of the intellectual and ideological currents that have flowed through modern Western civilization. The Olympics represent the heritage of the Enlightenment, particularly its moderate variants that promoted the concept of progress as history's central engine. [12] An Enlightened, abiding faith that ever-growing material abundance, increasing political liberty, evolving scientific knowledge, improving social conditions and a host of other incremental progressive developments that day-by-day and decade-by-decade made the modern world better than the past animated the founders of the modern Olympic movement and undergirded the construction of Olympic spectacles. [13]

The Olympics themselves are, in part, legacies of one of the great Occidental monuments to modern ideologies of progress, the world's fair movement. The world's fair movement began nearly a half-century before the modern Olympic movement, emerging in Victorian Great Britain, the nation most committed to moderately enlightened visions of progress. The original world's fair, London's 1851 Crystal Palace Exposition, set the foundation for world's fairs to serve for the next century as the most important sanctuaries for singing the evangel of Western progress. In the second half of the nineteenth century and the first half of the twentieth century, world's fairs drew millions and millions of people to see technological marvels, to worship the abundance of the industrial revolution, to witness contrasts between the world's so-called primitive or traditional cultures and its allegedly superior modern cultures, to revel in all the many blessings of progress. From London these global exhibitions moved around the 'core' capitals at the Occidental centre of the world-system, replicating the archetypal thanksgiving to progress first celebrated in London. [14]

Under the beneficent canopy of world's fairs, the modern Olympic movement first drew sustenance. The founding generation of the modern Olympics gathered at the 1889 *Exposition Universelle* in Paris to proselytize the linkages of sport and education to modern progress. [15] The early staging of the Olympics frequently occurred under the sheltering eaves of fairs, including the 1900 Olympics in Paris that were subsumed in another *Exposition Universelle*, the 1904 Olympics in St. Louis that served as a sideshow within the Louisiana Purchase Exposition, and the 1908 Olympics in London that were connected to the Franco-British Exhibition. [16] The 1920 Olympics in Antwerp were initially slated as the centrepiece of a summer-long world's fair. [17] The Japanese planned both a 1940 Olympics and a 1940 world's fair for Tokyo. The outbreak of the Second World War scuttled Japanese designs to reconnect the two forms of modern spectacle. [18]

Since the war global exhibitions have nearly become extinct while the Olympics have escaped the shadow of the fairs and have sprouted into colossal spectacles that have stolen much of the 'mega-event' light from their old hosts. Though the international expositions have been eclipsed and forgotten since the mid-twentieth century, a number of rituals and patterns reveal the ancestry of the Olympic sporting spectacles in the world's fairs. The practice of circulating the Olympics through the world's great metropolises evolved from the traditions of the expositions and not the model of antiquity with its singular stage at Olympia. The Olympic competitions in art and literature as well as sports, though little noticed on the modern programme, are sometimes seen as a homage to the ancient Greeks but should more properly be seen as vestige of the material pantheism of the fairs' enormous catalogues. The exhibition of peoples and cultures from every corner of the globe, a hallmark of contemporary Olympic 'human family' rhetoric, grew from the 'human zoos' of the ethnology divisions that were a common feature of many expositions. In one infamous case in St. Louis, the fair's management and staff scientists put their 'exhibits' into what the local press labelled a 'savage Olympics', forging a link between the exhibition of so-called 'primitives' for the amusement of modern audiences and later efforts to expand the field of Olympians to include what the Occidental gaze characterized as 'exotic' athletes. [19]

World's fairs provided platforms for advertising cities, regions, and nations, functions the Olympics quickly adopted to ensure similar legacies. World's fairs sparked fervent bidding wars between cities and countries for hosting rights. The Olympics have followed suit. World's fairs promoted international exchanges and touted transnational development while simultaneously reinforcing national chauvinism by structuring participation through the nation-state and fostering comparison and competition between nation-states. The Olympic movement clearly reveals this heritage of world's fairs in the paradoxical Olympic conjunction of transnational visions that are firmly bounded by the role of nation-states as the fundamental units of Olympic organization. Indeed, the international exhibitions claimed to be global events but were invented and dominated by Occidental industrial powers, just as have been the modern Olympics. [20]

Clearly the programme of sports contested reveals the nearly universal hegemony of Western cultural forms in modern sport. [21] Though the International Olympic Committee (IOC) does not formally sanction such counts, the 'complete all-time medal standings' tabulated by the news media who eagerly cover these national comparisons reveal the Occidental domination of the games. The US has raked in the grandest haul of this particular component of Olympic legacies, garnering 2197 medals since 1896. The second-place nation, the old Soviet Union, claimed 1122 medals before it dissolved. While some might dispute whether the USSR belongs entirely to the Occident, it was clearly more Western than anything else during its nearly eight-decade history. The rest of the top of the list reads reveals complete domination by the West, with Great Britain, Germany, France, Italy, Sweden, Hungary, the old East Germany, and Australia following the Soviets. Japan, the most Occidental of non-Occidental nations, makes an appearance in eleventh position, with 335 medals. China is thirteenth with 286–a total likely to rise in the near future but still far behind the US and the rest of the Western leaders atop the standings over the *longue durée*. Among other non-Western nations, South Korea ranks twenty-first. Turkey, perhaps the most Occidental of Islamic nations, ranks thirty-fourth. South Africa, the top African nation, ranks thirty-sixth, though Western colonists have won the preponderance of its Olympic medals. Kenya ranks thirty-seventh, and though it seems too win a score of medals in every games in distance running events it has actually won a grand total of only 61 in modern Olympic history. [22]

China won 100 of its 286-medal total at one Olympic Games–the recent 2008 Olympics held in Beijing. [23] China not only performed well on the fields of 'friendly strife' but also marketed itself to the world through the Beijing Olympics as a thoroughly modern colossus that will in the twenty-first century compete with the West for global dominion. [24] In this process, China borrowed and adapted Westernized notions of nationalism and internationalism. 'Chinese participation and interest in modern sports are largely motivated by nationalism, but by importing sports from the West and taking part in world competitions, China has also engaged the world community', observes the Sinologist Xu Guoqi in a recent history of the influence of Chinese 'Olympic dreams' on the world's most populous nation. [25]

Guoqi follows the arguments developed by historian Barbara Keys in her compelling contentions that in the volatile international climate of the 1930s, the Olympics and other international sporting events provided a common space for rule-bound exchanges between nations of vastly different ideologies and markedly different histories. [26] Non-Western nations submitted to the thoroughly Western codes and conventions embedded in modern sport in order to participate in the Olympics and other global sporting contests. In the very act of adopting the belief that sport serves as a primary agent of national self-identification, however, the non-Western world has accepted a fundamentally Western definition of nationhood. The spread of that idea has been as important in the history of globalization as the spread of the Western sports. [27]

The Olympics have played a central role in this process. Indeed, one of the most powerful Olympic legacies has been the incorporation of non-Western nations into a transnational movement that channels the international relations generated by sport into a very Westernized framework. When China in 2008, or South Korea in 1988, or Mexico in 1968, or Japan in 1964, hosts an Olympics to announce their entry or re-entry, as the case may be, onto the world stage, they accept an Occidental framework for their Olympic 'coming out part[ies]', as the historian of modern Korea, Brian Bridges labelled Seoul's 1988 Olympic production. [28]

Even this use of the Olympics to stage 'coming out parties' for developing nations to showcase their 'progress,' and to create a relatively pacific structure for comparisons and competitions between nations represents an additional inheritance from the older world's fair movement. 'The major expositions were also playing fields on which the leading states of the Western world tussled for symbolic power and prestige', contends the historian Wilbur Zelinsky. [29] The anthropologist Burton Benedict has indicted the Olympic movement as the culprit that stole this crucial component from the world's fair movement and thus consigned the expositions to decay and extinction while their Olympic offspring flourished and expanded. Benedict asserts that 'the national competition element in world's fairs was siphoned off by the Olympic Games', dooming the former to destruction. [30]

It was not, however, solely the theft of 'national competition' that killed the expositions. More than any factor, the adaptation of the Olympics to modern mass media technologies, especially television, explains why the global sporting spectacles thrived while the global exposition movement has died. Ironically, while world's fairs were an expression of modern Western faith in technology, new technologies shifted the fairs' functions too other, more accessible sites. At the same time, the rapid development of new media technologies during the twentieth century–especially television–vastly expanded the Olympic stage. [31]

Television and other media killed the world's fair movement by providing a more accessible and less expensive venue for depicting the staples of the expositions' appeal, images of progress and development, demonstrations of technological marvels and achievements, displays of exotic peoples and odd curiosities. The international expositions could not compete with the stunning cinematography of

National Geographic or British Broadcasting Corporation television documentaries. Television broadcast the globe's many marvels to the globe's curious consumers, rendering the world's fairs obsolete. Viewers could sit in the comfort of their homes and see everything they once could only view after journeying to a fair city and pushing their way through great crowds of sharp-elbowed fellow gawkers. Television offered a far less painless and far less expensive alternative. [32]

At the same time television killed world's fairs it transformed the Olympics into lucrative commodities. During the twentieth century sport became, as C.L.R. James, the sagacious West Indian historian, has posited, the most popular dramatic attraction of the world's masses, a grand narrative that reveals the wishes and frailties of nations and peoples. As James points out, the unscripted character of sporting events represents one the great attractions of the genre. [33] The unscripted structure of sport makes it difficult for television to manufacture sporting events by replacing the older venues that staged them. Television did not need world's fairs to film dramas about exotic cultures or fascinating animals, indeed, 'natural' and 'native' locations work better. Television does, however, need the IOC to stage the Olympics in order to broadcast athletic dramas to the world. Sporting events cannot be scripted nor simulated in studios–though broadcasters have made a few efforts to do so in the guise of professional wrestling and 'American Gladiator'-style broadcasts, programs that have gained small market niches but hardly rival 'live' (or not so 'live' in the case of Olympic broadcasts to many markets) telecasts of unscripted sporting dramas. [34]

Instead of replacing the Olympics, television has partnered with the IOC to produce increasingly grand entertainment spectacles for the world. The alliance has proved wildly successful. As the historians Robert Barney, Stephen Wenn, and Scott Martyn have observed about this symbiotic partnership, at the beginning of the twenty-first century the Olympics Games provide transnational corporations with 'the opportunity to advertise products to a global audience unmatched in size by any other sport audience in the world'. [35]

The IOC's embrace of television beginning in the second half of the twentieth century has sustained and enlarged the Olympic movement's global reach, transforming the games into a worldwide entertainment phenomenon. With no place on television, the world's fair movement has during the same era withered into insignificance. Television has certainly impacted on Olympic legacies, as even the most acerbic critics of the Olympics admit. 'Admirers of the Olympic "movement" can point to the success of a show business internationalism that has survived a tumultuous history', insists sport studies scholar John Hoberman in one of his few 'compliments' on the games as a global force in a recent muckraking exposé in *Foreign Policy*, an important U.S. journal of international relations. 'An institution this hardy, one might argue, must offer something of value', Hoberman sardonically observes, expressing his doubts that granting Beijing the 2008 Olympics will forward the cause of human rights while conceding that it might highlight China's 'astonishing economic success story'. [36]

Hoberman has a point about the power and nature of Olympic legacies. One cannot grapple with the contemporary role of the Olympics without confronting its location in the modern global entertainment industry, a phenomenon that predates television and was certainly evident by the 1930s when the Olympics were first staged in the entertainment capital of Los Angeles and then staged from cleverly designed sets in Berlin built to broadcast Nazi propaganda. In forecasting future Olympic legacies, it seems certain that 'show business internationalism' will remain a powerful component in the equation. The legion of managerial 'magicians' that John MacAloon has spotted currying favour with the IOC and potential host cities betray the fact that Olympic-legacy formation will continue to develop its 'Disney-esque' qualities. [37]

Other, more authentic legacies remain possible. The IOC's newfound convictions about 'green' games and sustainable venue-productions offer, as Jean-Loup Chappelet notes, some hope for the future. The environmentally progressive promises of such plans should be tempered by similar 'green' conversions among many other members of the global corporate order and the memory that 'Disneyfication' and environmentalism are not necessarily incompatible, a reality Disney projects from the design for the 1960 Squaw Valley Winter Olympics to the 'eco-friendly' themes of Epcot Center at Disney World reveal.

Any Olympic legacies for the next century will continue to manifest the tensions between nationalism and internationalism that have historically been at the dramatic heart of these spectacles. 'The Olympic Games were founded to bridge cultural divides and promote peace', observes John Hoberman in his *Foreign Policy* essay. Hoberman then scores the Olympic movement for failing to live up its founding 'legacy', indicting the Olympics as events that 'mask human rights abuses, do little to spur political change, and lend legitimacy to unsavory governments'. [38] Hoberman's argument, in my estimation, is not entirely without merit but it is incomplete. The Olympics were also founded by Pierre de Coubertin to energize French patriotism and promote French national vigour. Other nations quickly joined the 'Olympic family' motivated by the same desire to revitalize their national heritages. The Olympics have always been about national identities as well as about bridging cultural divides or nurturing pacific relations.

I also concur with Hoberman's contentions that the Olympics are essentially political and his assessment that they have generally failed to serves as catalysts for changing totalitarian regimes such as Nazi Germany. [39] I dissent, however, from his implication that they have not under any circumstances functioned as catalysts for political and social reform. Indeed, to draw an example from U.S. history, African-American athletes from Jesse Owens to John Carlos have served as catalysts in the process of changing American race relations. They represent imperfect, incomplete catalysts to be sure and they certainly were not the always the sufficient and never the sole causes for change but catalysts they were nonetheless. [40]

In the U.S. at least, the contemporary clash of American athletes and Chinese Olympians such as Yao Ming and Liu Xiang represent the 'profound threat', to follow the arguments of literary scholar Grant Farred, posed by contemporary China to the 'American empire.' Farred reads in American conversations created by these skirmishes opportunities to change and alter U.S. views of China and the world– though he certainly is not blindly optimistic that such changes will necessarily be progressive, cultural bridge-building alterations. [41]

In the US and other nations, the Olympics will continue to develop a legacy that casts them as a televised, athletic version of the political theorist Samuel Huntington's infamous 'clash of civilizations', provoking debates about the meanings of modernity, globalization, and the conflicts between Western and other cultures. [42] That insight came to me during August of 2008, as the Beijing Olympics opened. Through bad planning and a series of accidents, I managed to end up on a visit to my parents home in a small town in Montana over the first week of China's Olympic fortnight. My father, who long ago turned his back on commercial network television, had promised to secure a cable-television installation–for which I promised to pay the bill–in order for us to watch the Olympic spectacle since the town in which my parents live is remote enough that tuning in over-the-air telecasts is a difficult proposition. My father unfortunately waited too late to make cable arrangements and we were reduced to trying to find webcasts or other internet viewing opportunities. Though as a retired computer scientist my father possesses a small fleet of personal computers, we soon discovered that his affinity for arcane and obscure software made seeing the Olympics through the web impossible. I relied on newspaper coverage for a few days, an unsatisfactory adaptation for a committed Olympic voyeur such as myself.

In desperation, I finally repaired to a local sports bar, an establishment decorated in typical Montana fashion with the severed, stuffed heads of more Rocky Mountain fauna than the average tourist could see in a month spent at Yellowstone National Park. There, among the cowboy-hatted natives, I watched with great fascination Olympic men's diving and women's gymnastics, sports not normally fixtures on televisions in small-town Montana pubs. The experience convinced me of the integral role of television in making the Olympics a global phenomenon. My conversations with fellow patrons about their 'readings' of China's challenge to U.S. global hegemony based on their televised observations from Beijing confirmed my convictions that the core appeal of the Olympics remains the paradoxical collisions of national and international patterns that the spectacle creates. Through images beamed around across the globe, bridges across cultural divides and athletic clashes of civilizations inhabited the bar simultaneously, a rough approximation of the near and perhaps distant future of Olympic legacies.

Notes

[1] Murray, *The World's Game*.
[2] On the rise of the Olympic branch of this conglomerate see Barney, Wenn, and Martyn. *The International Olympic Committee and the Rise of Olympic Commercialism*. On the influence of

the US in shaping the Olympic 'brand' see Dyreson 'Crafting Patriotism–Meditations on "Californication" and other Trends', 307–11; Dyreson, 'Johnny Weissmuller and the Old Global Capitalism', Dyreson, 'Marketing Weissmuller to the World: Hollywood's Olympics and Federal Schemes for Americanization through Sport', 284–306.

[3] Dyreson, 'Globalizing the Nation-Making Process', 91–106.

[4] Mangan, Prologue, Guarantees of Global Goodwill: Post-Olympic Legacies – Too Many Limping White Elephants?

[5] Girginov and Hills, 'A Sustainable Sports Legacy', 1945–70; Macrury and Poynter, 'The Regeneration Games' 2060–78.

[6] Olympic scholar and bid expert Jean-Loup Chappelet predicts that the IOC, very much aware of the power of legacy, will increasingly move toward progressive environmental and economic programs in order to garner broad public support for their Olympic designs. Chappelet, 'Olympic Environmental Concerns as a Legacy of the Winter Games', 1898–916; Chappelet, *The International Olympic Committee and the Olympic System*.

[7] The IOC currently includes 205 'nations'. http://www.olympic.org/uk/organisation/noc/, accessed 12 September 2008. The United Nations currently recognizes 192 member 'states'. http://www.un.org/members/list.shtml, accessed 12 September 2008.

[8] For controversial, muckraking exposés of the Olympics see Simson and Jennings, *The Lords of the Rings*; Jennings and Sambrook, *The Great Olympic Swindle*. On linkages between the IOC and the right-wing political ideologies see Hoberman, 'Toward a Theory of Olympic Internationalism', 1–37; and Hoberman, 'The Olympics', 22–8.

[9] Beamish and Ritchie. *Fastest, Highest, Strongest*; Pound, *Inside Dope*; Wilson and Derse, *Doping in Elite Sport*; Hoberman, *Mortal Engines*; Hoberman, *Testosterone Dreams*.

[10] De Moragas, Kennett, and Puig, eds. *The Legacy of the Olympic Games*.

[11] MacAloon, 'Legacy' as Managerial/Magical Discourse in Contemporary Olympic Affairs', 2029–40.

[12] Brinton, *The Shaping of Modern Thought*; Louden, *The World We Want*.

[13] MacAloon, 'Special Issue: This Great Symbol', 331–686. Young, *The Modern Olympics*.

[14] Allwood, *The Great Exhibitions*; Greenhalgh, *Ephemeral Vistas*; Rydell, Findling, and Pelle, *Fair America*; Rydell, *All the World's a Fair*; Rydell, *World of Fairs*. On the linkages between fairs and the Olympics see Roche, *Mega-Events and Modernity* and Gold, *Cities of Culture*.

[15] MacAloon, *This Great Symbol*.

[16] Dyreson, *Making the American Team*, 53–153; Roche, *Mega-Events and Modernity*, 88–90.

[17] Belgian Olympic Committee to U.S. State Department, Memorandum on the Program for the VIIth Olympiad, State Department Records Division, Record Group 59, Foreign Relations Microfilm Files, National Archives and Records Administration II, College Park, Maryland, USA. The similarity of the festivals to the organizational scheme for a world's fair owed in part to the fact that the same group of civic leaders who staged the fetes had before the war been planning to stage a world's fair in Antwerp. War damage prevented their larger scheme from becoming a reality but they used some of the fair design for the Olympic project. Renson, *The Games Reborn*, 81.

[18] Collins, 'Special Issue: The Missing Olympics', 955–1148; Constable, *The XI, XII, and XIII Olympiads*, 108–11.

[19] Dyreson, 'The "Physical Value" of Races', 114–40; Rydell, *All the World's a Fair*.

[20] Rydell, Findling, and Pelle, *Fair America*; Rydell, *All the World's a Fair*.

[21] Guttmann, *Games and Empires*, 120–40; Guttmann, *Sports*.

[22] The US-based NBC television network provides an online listing of this 'historic' medal count. Their tabulations begin in 1896, assigning gold, silver, and bronze to the first, second, and third place finishers in events even though the actual assigning of medals did not begin until the 1904 Olympics. <http://www.nbcolympics.com/medals/alltime/index.html>, accessed 10 September 2008.

[23] < http://www.nbcolympics.com/medals/2008standings/index.html >, accessed 10 September 2008.

[24] Mangan and Jinxia, 'Special Issue: Preparing for Glory', 751–951.

[25] Guoqui, *Olympic Dreams*, 3.

[26] Keys, *Globalizing Sport*.

[27] Dyreson, 'Globalizing the Nation-Making Process', 91–106. For a very interesting contemporary critique of the proposition that adopting Western sports requires the adoption of Western standards of nationhood see Susan Brownell's fascinating *Beijing's Games*. For an equally interesting critique rooted in the more distant past, see Andrew Morris, *Marrow of the Nation*. Brownell, 'Challenged America', 1173–93.

[28] Bridges, 'The Seoul Olympics: Economic Miracle Meets the World'. See also, Ok, *The Transformation of Modern Korean Sport*.

[29] Zelinsky, *Nation Into State*, 85–9.

[30] Benedict, *The Anthropology of World's Fairs*, 60.

[31] Dyreson, '"To Construct a Better and More Peaceful World" or "War Minus the Shooting"?', 337–51.

[32] Rydell, *World of Fairs*, 213–6; Rydell, Findling, and Pelle, *Fair America*, 131–40; Roche, *Mega-Events and Modernity*, 159–61.

[33] James, *Beyond a Boundary*, 195–211.

[34] Dyreson, '"To Construct a Better and More Peaceful World" or "War Minus the Shooting"?', 337–51.

[35] Barney, Wenn, and Martyn, *Selling the Five Rings*, xii.

[36] Hoberman, 'The Olympics', 28.

[37] On the influence of Disney in American culture see Watts, *The Magic Kingdom*.

[38] Hoberman, 'The Olympics', 22.

[39] Ibid., 22–8.

[40] Dyreson, 'Prolegomena to Jesse Owens', 224–46; Dyreson, 'American Ideas About Race and Olympic Races in the Era of Jesse Owens': 247–67; Bass, *Not the Triumph But the Struggle*; Hartmann, *Race, Culture and the Revolt of the Black Athlete*.

[41] Farred, *Phantom Calls*, 87–8.

[42] Huntington, *The Clash of Civilizations and the Remaking of World Order*. For a history of American readings of this clash through the Olympics see Dyreson, *Crafting Patriotism for Global Domination*.

References

Allwood, John. *The Great Exhibitions*. London: Studio Vista, 1977.

Barney, Robert K., Stephen R. Wenn, and Scott G. Martyn. *The International Olympic Committee and the Rise of Olympic Commercialism*. Salt Lake City: University of Utah Press, 2002.

Bass, Amy. *Not the Triumph But the Struggle: The 1968 Olympics and the Making of the Black Athlete*. Minneapolis: University of Minnesota Press, 2002.

Beamish, Rob and Ian Ritchie. *Fastest, Highest, Strongest: A Critique of High-Performance Sport*. London: Routledge, 2006.

Benedict, Burton. *The Anthropology of World's Fairs: San Francisco's Panama Pacific International Exposition of 1915*. Berkeley, Cal.: Lowie Museum of Anthropology and Scolar Press, 1983.

Brinton, Crane. *The Shaping of Modern Thought*. Englewood Cliffs, N.J.: Prentice-Hall, 1963.

Bridges, Brian. 'The Seoul Olympics: Economic Miracle Meets the World'. *International Journal of the History of Sport* 25 (December 2008): 1884–97.

Brownell, Susan. *Beijing's Games: What the Olympics Mean to China*. Lanham, Md.: Rowman & Littlefield, 2008.

——. 'Challenged America: China and America–Women and Sport, Past, Present, and Future'. *International Journal of the History of Sport* 22 (November 2005): 1173–193.

Chappelet, Jean-Loup. *The International Olympic Committee and the Olympic System: The Governance of World Sport*, trans. Brenda Kübler-Mabbott. London: Routledge, 2008.

——. 'Olympic Environmental Concerns as a Legacy of the Winter Games'. *International Journal of the History of Sport* 25 (December 2008): 1898–916.

Collins, Sandra. 'Special Issue: The Missing Olympics: The 1940 Tokyo Games, Japan, Asia and the Olympic Movement'. *International Journal of the History of Sport* 24 (August 2007): 955–1148.

Constable, George. *The XI, XII, and XIII Olympiads*. Los Angeles: World Sports Research, 1996.

De Moragas, Miguel, and Christopher Kennett, and Noria Puig, eds. *The Legacy of the Olympic Games, 1984–2002*. Documents of the Olympic Museum. Lausanne: International Olympic Committee, 2003.

Dyreson, Mark. "American Ideas About Race and Olympic Races in the Era of Jesse Owens: Shattering Myths or Reinforcing Scientific Racism?" *International Journal of the History of Sport* 25 (February 2008): 247–67.

——. *Crafting Patriotism for Global Domination: America at the Olympics*. London: Routledge, 2008.

——. "Crafting Patriotism–Meditations on 'Californication' and other Trends." *International Journal of the History of Sport* 25 (February 2008): 307–11.

——. 'Globalizing the Nation-Making Process: Modern Sport in World History'. *International Journal of the History of Sport* 20 (March 2003): 91–106.

——. "Johnny Weissmuller and the Old Global Capitalism: The Origins of the Federal Blueprint for Selling American Culture to the World." *International Journal of the History of Sport* 25 (February 2008): 268–83.

——. *Making the American Team: Sport, Culture and the Olympic Experience*. Urbana: University of Illinois Press, 1998.

——. "Marketing Weissmuller to the World: Hollywood's Olympics and Federal Schemes for Americanization through Sport." *International Journal of the History of Sport* 25 (February 2008): 284–306.

——. 'The "Physical Value" of Races: Anthropology and Athletics at the Louisiana Purchase Exposition'. In *Bodies Before Boas: The 1904 St. Louis Olympic Games and Anthropology Days*, edited by Susan Brownell. Lincoln: University of Nebraska Press, 2008: 114–40.

——. "Prolegomena to Jesse Owens: American Ideas About Race and Olympic Races from the 1890s to the 1920s." *International Journal of the History of Sport* 25 (February 2008): 224–46.

——. '"To Construct a Better and More Peaceful World" or "War Minus the Shooting"?: The Olympic Movement's Second Century'. In *Onward to the Olympics: Historical Perspectives on the Olympic Games*, edited by Stephen Wenn. Waterloo, Ontario: Wilfrid Laurier University Press, 2007: 337–51.

Farred, Grant. *Phantom Calls: Race and the Globalization of NBA*. Chicago: Prickly Paradigm Press, 2006.

Gold, John Robert. *Cities of Culture: Staging International Festivals and the Urban Agenda, 1851–2000*. Aldershot, UK: Ashgate, 2005.

Greenhalgh, Paul. *Ephemeral Vistas: The Expositions Universelles, Great Exhibitions and World's Fairs, 1851–1939*. Manchester, U.K.: Manchester University Press, 1988.

Girginov, Vassil and Laura Hills. 'A Sustainable Sports Legacy: Creating a Link between the London Olympics and Sports Participation'. *International Journal of the History of Sport* 25 (December 2008): 1945–70.

Guoqui, Xu. *Olympic Dreams: China and Sports, 1895–2008*. Cambridge, Mass: Harvard University Press, 2008.

Guttmann, Allen. *Games and Empires: Modern Sports and Cultural Imperialism*. New York: Columbia University Press, 1994.

——. *Sports: The First Five Millennia*. Amherst: University of Massachusetts Press, 2004.

Hartmann, Douglas. *Race, Culture and the Revolt of the Black Athlete: The 1968 Olympic Protests and Their Aftermath*. Chicago: University of Chicago Press, 2003.

Hoberman, John. *Mortal Engines: The Science of Performance and the Dehumanization of Sport*. New York: Free Press, 1992.

——. 'Toward a Theory of Olympic Internationalism'. *Journal of Sport. History* 22 (Spring 1995): 1–37.

——. *Testosterone Dreams: Rejuvenation, Aphrodisia, Doping*. Berkeley: University of California Press, 2005.

——. 'The Olympics'. *Foreign Policy* 167 (1 July 2008): 22–8.

Huntington, Samuel P. *The Clash of Civilizations and the Remaking of World Order*. New York, Simon & Schuster, 1996.

James, C.L.R. *Beyond a Boundary*. Durham, N.C.: Duke University Press, 1993; orig. 1963.

Jennings, Andrew and Clare Sambrook. *The Great Olympic Swindle: When the World Wanted Its Games Back*. London: Simon & Schuster, 2000.

Keys, Barbara. *Globalizing Sport: National Rivalry and International Community in the 1930s*. Cambridge: Harvard University Press, 2006.

Louden, Robert B. *The World We Want: How and Why the Ideals of the Enlightenment Still Elude Us*. New York: Oxford University Press, 2007.

MacAloon, John J. 'Legacy' as Managerial/Magical Discourse in Contemporary Olympic Affairs'. *International Journal of the History of Sport* 25 (December 2008): 2029–40.

——. 'Special Issue: This Great Symbol: Pierre de Coubertin and the Origins of the Modern Olympic Games'. *International Journal of the History of Sport* (May-June 2006): 331–686.

——. *This Great Symbol: Pierre de Coubertin and the Origins of the Modern Olympics*. Chicago: University of Chicago Press, 1981.

Macrury, Iain and Gavin Poynter. 'The Regeneration Games: Commodities, Gifts and the Economics of London 2012'. *International Journal of the History of Sport* 25 (December 2008): 2060–78.

Mangan, J.A. and Dong Jinxia. 'Special Issue: Preparing for Glory: Beijing 2008–Chinese Challenge in the "Chinese Century"'. *International Journal of the History of Sport* 25 (June 2008): 751–951.

——. Prologue: Guarantees Of Global Goodwill: Post-Olympic Legacies – Too Many Limping White Elephants?. *International Journal of the History of Sport* 25 (December 2008): 1869–83.

Morris, Andrew D. *Marrow of the Nation: A History of Sport and Physical Culture in Republican China*. Berkeley: University of California Press, 2004.

Murray, Bill. *The World's Game: A History of Soccer*. Urbana: University of Illinois Press, 1996.

Ok, Gwang. *The Transformation of Modern Korean Sport: Imperialism, Nationalism, Globalization*. Seoul: Hollym, 2007.

Pound, Richard W. *Inside Dope: How Drugs Are the Biggest Threat to Sports, Why You Should Care, and What Can Be Done About Them*. Mississauga, Ont.: J. Wiley & Sons Canada, 2006.

Renson, Roland. *The Games Reborn: The VIIth Olympiad, Antwerp 1920*. Antwerp: Pandora, 1996.

Roche, Maurice. *Mega-Events and Modernity: Olympics and Expos in the Growth of Global Culture*. London: Routledge, 2000.

Rydell, Robert. *All the World's a Fair: Visions of Empire at American International Exhibitions*. Chicago: University of Chicago Press, 1984.

——. *World of Fairs: The Century-of-Progress Expositions*. Chicago: University of Chicago Press, 1993.

Rydell, Robert W., John E. Findling, and Kimberly D. Pelle. *Fair America: World's Fairs in the United States*. Washington: Smithsonian Institution, 2000.

Simson, Vyv, and Andrew Jennings. *The Lords of the Rings: Power, Money and Drugs in the Modern Olympics*. London: Simon & Schuster, 1992.

Watts, Steven. *The Magic Kingdom: Walt Disney and the American Way of Life*. New York: Houghton Mifflin, 1997.

Wilson, Wayne, and Ed Derse. *Doping in Elite Sport: The Politics of Drugs in the Olympic Movement*. Champaign, Ill.: Human Kinetics, 2001.

Young, David C. *The Modern Olympics: A Struggle for Revival*. Baltimore: Johns Hopkins University Press, 1996.

Zelinsky, Wilbur. *Nation Into State: The Shifting Symbolic Foundations of American Nationalism*. Chapel Hill: University of North Carolina Press, 1988.

Index

Active Australia 76-7
Agenda 21: Olympic Movement
    1, 11-12, 217
Aizicovici, F. 24
Albertville Winter Olympics (1992):
    budgetary criticism 25-8; and Chirac
    23; decentralization laws 22; deficit
    27, 34; economy and tourism legacy
    28-32; environmental issues 8-9, 14,
    33-4, 217; facility legacy 28-9; French
    mountain holiday legacy 30;
    infrastructure costs 23-4, 28, 34-5;
    local sports equipment production
    stimulation 24-5, 30-1; media image
    and recognition 31-4; and Olympic
    spirit 33; organizing committee 21-2,
    24, 25, 27, 30, 33; political
    enthusiasm 21-5; press reaction 26;
    primary expectations 23;
    self-satisfaction 25-8; socio-economic
    impact 24-5; television 32, 34; ticket
    sales 32; tourism and access
    difficulties 23-4, 28; unexpected
    legacies 20-38
Alevras, N. 96
Amateur Athletic Foundation of Los
    Angeles (AAFLA) 120
Amsterdam Olympic Games
    (1928) 110, 111
Andreff, W. 24-5
Antwerp Olympic Games (1920) 110, 236
Appadurai, A. 200
Arrighi, G. 145

ARUP: and London Olympic bid report
    192-3
Asian Games (2006): and image 45
Athens Olympic Games (2004) 89-107;
    Agios Kosmas Sailing Centre 99,
    101-2, 103; Ano Liossia Olympic
    Centre 100; Attica Road construction
    90; badminton facility renovation 98,
    103; beach volleyball facilities 100;
    canoe kayak slalom utilization 97,
    99, 103; cost 93-6; exploiting
    Olympic assets 97-104; Galatsi
    Olympic Centre renovation 98, 103;
    Helleniko Olympic Complex 100;
    international broadcast centre
    renovation 98, 103; legacy 2; legacy
    utilization planning and political
    dispute 93-6; main press centre
    (MPC) 99, 103; Markopoulo
    Equestrian Centre 100, 103; metro
    system 90; new sports facilities 89-92;
    Nikea Olympic Centre 101, 103;
    Olympic Sports Centre 91; Olympic
    Village 90-1, 98; Pagkretio Stadium
    99, 102; post-Olympic infrastructure
    use *xx-xxii* 93-104; railway system 90;
    Schinas Olympic Rowing Centre 99,
    100-1, 103; Tae-Kwon-Do Hall 100,
    103; urban infrastructure 89-92
Atlanta Olympic Games (1996): legacy 2
Auge, M. 199, 202
Australia: and Olympic achievement
    70-1; Sydney Olympics legacy 70-88